D1594377

lives
through
time

lives through time

Jack Block

Psychology Department
University of California, Berkeley

In collaboration with

Norma Haan

Institute of Human Development
University of California, Berkeley

Bancroft Books
Berkeley

Library of Congress Card Number: 70-156597
ISBN: 0-9600332-0-3

Printed in the United States of America

DEDICATION

For the men and women, subjects in the longitudinal studies of the Institute of Human Development, who have permitted—with courage and with grace—the study of their lives.

De te fabula narratur (this is a story, told about you).

PREFACE

For the reader, a preface is an anticipation of a book; for the author, it is the end of his journey and a time for remembering those who have helped him along the way. The effort that has culminated in the following pages is predicated upon the work, diligence, good sense, vision, and support of many individuals over a period that now passes forty years. Many of these people I have never met and they, in turn, could not have known of me. This is the way of science and of life; we are sustained by a sense of continuity and of contribution. So, to all the research staff of the Institute of Human Development who over the long and thankless years kept alive the longitudinal venture, I extend thanks and salutation.

And, from among all of these contributors, special homage is due to Harold and Mary Jones, to Jean Macfarlane and Marjorie Honzik, and to Herbert Stolz, for their selflessness and generativity in moving the longitudinal idea toward a realization. It was Harold Jones who first encouraged my interest in longitudinal study. Mary Jones has been, in numerous and cumulative ways, warmly supportive of the effort to reap the harvest she and her late husband had sown years before in the Oakland Growth Study. When the research sought to include as well the Guidance Study subject sample, Jean Macfarlane and Marjorie Honzik were open and generous to the intentions of the research plan. And, although I did not know him, it was Herbert Stolz, the very first Director of the Institute who started the venture underway and moving well. I would like them all to be proud of this book.

The course of progress of this enterprise is conveniently divided into two phases. From 1961 to 1966, the study was supported by National Institute of Mental Health Research Grant MH 05300, given to the Institute of Human Development and for which I was co-principal investigator, together with John Clausen. From 1966 through 1969, the present study received its support from NIMH Research Grants MH 13724 and MH 13761, granted to the Psychology Department, University of California at Berkeley and for which I was principal investigator. Further important support at this time came from the Committee On Research and from the Computer Center, both at the University of California at Berkeley. This diverse but substantial support is herewith gratefully acknowledged.

During the first phase of the research project, the research plan involved many kinds of work and complications in order to generate data from the available material, to identify and evaluate and systematize information in the archives, and to co-ordinate and monitor the team of psychologist-judges that were crucial to the study. I was fortunate in being able to collaborate with Norma Haan in this effort and to share with her many of the important responsibilities of this time. Her dedication to the research during these years greatly facilitated its progress. Our collaboration of necessity ended in August, 1966, when I left the Institute.

In this day and age, and with masses of data, very little can happen without a computer. And very little can happen *with* a computer, unless there is a programmer who can enslave it. Every single one of the many analyses upon which this study is based has depended upon the system of computer programs designed and coded by Elinor Krasnow. The abundant and easy analytical possibilities that she made available permitted concentrations on the meaning of the data rather than a miring in the mechanics of data processing. She was creative, dedicated, and necessary in her help. And her great acerbic wit lightened days of tedium. I prize her contribution.

During the second phase of this study, when most of this book was written, more data generation and judging were required as well as data analysis. Judith Casaroli responded superbly to the many kinds of tasks I placed with her. Her quiet, casual competence made the difficult seem so simple that I was tempted, time and again, to impose upon her good temper. She never failed me and I think she knows by now that I appreciate her.

But many more individuals helped implement this study. At one time or another, Janice Stroud, Darla Foley Grubman, Noel Torkelson Galbraith, and Fiona De Groot served well as assistants. While the study was still within the Institute, Ann Volmer and Ann Brixner facilitated the enterprise in ways that only Administrative Assistants at Berkeley can. Margaret Heick was consistently responsive to the many requests made of her, as gatekeeper for the Guidance Study data. And Ella Barney, Florence Cho, and Nancy Polin contributed their secretarial and manuscript skills on numerous occasions.

The list of clinical psychologists who applied their judging skills to the archival material, thus generating much of the data on which this book is based, is a long and important one. For their talent and seriousness in formulating their personality descriptions, thanks are due to Bernard

Apfelbaum, Jeanne Block, Betty Borenstein, Hilda Burton, Grace Cox, Mervin Freedman, Sarahlee Futterman, Marion Handlon, Shirley Hecht, Christoph Heinicke, Ann Miller, Mary Rauch, Stephen Rauch, Harold Renaud, Francis Sampson, Albert Shapiro, Elaine Simpson, Arlene Skolnick, Robert Suczek, Hobart Thomas, and Erica Weingarten.

Added gratitude is due to Jeanne Block, Shirley Hecht, and Elaine Simpson for the judgments of family environmental context they contributed in the later portion of the study.

Although, as already indicated, the contributors to this study have been legion, individually discernible for the quality and duration of their contribution are the following: From the Oakland Growth Study, Judith Chaffey and Caroline Tryon; from the Guidance Study, Lucille Allen and Doris Elliott, both with thirty year tenures, George Sheviakov, Pearl Bretnall, Helen Campbell, Loretta Smith Maxwell, Read Tuddenham, Anne Stout, William Smelser, and Louis Stewart.

Various of the chapters were read in draft form by various people. The readings by Marjorie Honzik, Mary C. Jones, and Jean Macfarlane caught certain errors of historical fact or understanding that only they could have detected. Harrison Gough suggested a number of ways in which the presentation, particularly in regard to the CPI, could be improved. Hilde Himmelweit, Paul Mussen, and Ellen Siegelman all made valuable editorial suggestions. I am grateful for all of this help and must absolve them all for such errors and lack of clarity as may still remain.

The typing of the final manuscript, from inelegant copy, was resourcefully accomplished by Joan Clampitt. The several figures in the text were prepared, with care, by Katherine Eardley.

This has been a difficult and lonely book to write and I often wondered whether the game was worth the candle. In her wifely role, Jeanne Block heartened me.

Jack Block
Berkeley, June 1969

TABLE OF CONTENTS

xi

Chapter IX: (cont'd) COURSES OF PERSONALITY
                DEVELOPMENT—THE FEMALE SAMPLE

        Character Changes from Senior High
        School to Adulthood   214
        Further Findings from the Adult Years   215
        Adjustment and Continuity Over the
        Years   216
        Familial and Environmental Antecedents   217
        Interpretive Resume   218

    Personality Type X (the Dominating
    Narcissists)   220

        Their Character During Junior High
        School   220
        Their Character During Senior High
        School   221
        Character Changes from JHS to SHS   222
        Further Findings from the Adolescent
        Years   222
        Their Character as Adults   223
        Character Changes from Senior High
        School to Adulthood   223
        Further Findings from the Adult Years   224
        Adjustment and Continuity over the Years   225
        Familial and Environmental Antecedents   226
        Interpretive Resume   227

    Personality Type Y (the Vulnerable Under-
    controllers)   228

        Their Character During Junior High
        School   228
        Their Character During Senior High
        School   229
        Character Changes from JHS to SHS   230
        Further Findings from the Adolescent
        Years   230
        Their Character as Adults   231

Chapter I

INTENTIONS AND ORIENTATION

This book is oriented around a theme, a time, and a method. The theme is the importance of studying personality development and personality change in a differentiated way, of identifying and understanding the alternative paths along which people evolve over time. The time is adolescence, with its implications for the life that is later led. And the method is longitudinal, an approach that can respond to questions regarding psychological development not otherwise scientifically accessible.

THE THEME OF DIFFERENT COURSES OF PERSONALITY DEVELOPMENT

It is an instructive, somewhat wry experience to attend a high school reunion twenty years after one's graduation. In the passage of almost a generation, the capriciousness of adolescence has been left and lives have taken their essential form and direction. There are the usual indicators of the passage and action of time—the formerly lissome and lithe may now be pudgy and stiff; the great adolescent dreams of glamour and omnipotence largely have been deflated by reality; for most, money, comfort, and status have become the order of the day. But such observations taken alone are too simple, too gross, and too established to be sufficiently true.

Although many friends from adolescence have become the kind of person implicitly anticipated long before, others have not. The class literary esthete went into public relations work. Why? The tense, big-boned, not really attractive girl at seventeen is now, two decades later, a sophisticated, intellectual, sex-radiating woman, while the classically pert and pretty cheerleader of yesteryear is several times divorced and older, yet less changed than she should be. Why?

1

There are psychological mysteries that will remain mysteries, but there are others—such as the different ways in which personality can evolve over time or the conditions and consequences of personality change—into which we can delve more than we yet have. Developmental psychology has been slow to move toward an understanding of these complexities, and later in this chapter some reasons why this is so will be proposed. For the present, the reader need simply note the explicit and programmatic concern of the present study to trace, more closely than before, the ways of personality development and change from adolescence to adulthood.

THE TIME OF ADOLESCENCE

Adolescence is a poignant time, celebrated by poets and returned to often in memory by the rest of us. No longer a child and not yet an adult, the adolescent must confront a surge of, for him, unique emotions, while responding to the increasing responsibilities imposed by his culture. Although the child enters adolescence with a personality already appreciably formed, he enters a time of maturational turbulence, of multiple conflicting and compelling role demands, of a world widening beckoningly and frighteningly before his eyes. Contrary to the view still largely held within psychoanalysis, with its emphasis on the irreversible and determinative significance for character formation of the first few years, adolescence is a time of considerable change and considerable consequence. Contrary to the cumulative, continuous view of personality evolvement held within reinforcement theory, which heavily influences the field of developmental psychology, adolescence is a time often of dramatic personality flux, consolidation, and redirection.

Erikson (1956; 1963) and Blos (1962), in their perceptive essays on the adolescent experience, have helped redress the over-emphasis on continuity in personality development. In their reflections on identity achievement, adolescent experimentation, and the ways in which adolescents come to recognize the limitations on life's possibilities, these writers have introduced a humane wisdom that has informed and helped many adolescents and their elders.

But the way of psychological science requires more than clinical insights developed in unusual circumstances with perhaps atypical teenagers. Rather, a cumbersome, simplistic, distancing research design and methodology must be invoked to guard against the persuasiveness of clinical perceptions *per se* and to establish the scope and the limits, the generalizations and the exceptions to what is known about adolescence and its consequences. One's existential sense of adolescence is diminished by this approach, but another kind of confidence is gained.

The study before you was undertaken in order to investigate adolescence, personality change and later adjustment in a large number of boys and girls followed longitudinally from their junior high school years to the time they were well established in career and in family. We know reasonably well how these individuals turned out and what kind of people they are. Are there clues in the nature of their adolescent years and in their origins that can tell us why these men and women developed as they did?

THE METHOD OF LONGITUDINAL STUDY

The investigator who would embark upon a longitudinal study of human development must be imbued with a rare sense of dedication and selflessness. The motivations for *not* initiating a longitudinal research program are many. The inertial problems of locating and maintaining a proper subject sample are oppressive; the would-be longitudinal researcher must make fundamental procedural decisions in the Now that are only gambles into the future; he knows that, despite his contemporary sophistication, retrospective wisdom a generation later will make him appear outdated; quick, neat research possibilities that are *not* longitudinal seductively compete for his attention and promise more immediate professional rewards; and finally, inescapably, there is a recognition that much of the harvest of one's efforts may be realized in another's lifetime—these are some of the reasons why longitudinal studies are few, rarely prolonged, and of fluctuating quality over time.

And yet, magnetically, psychologists are now increasingly drawn toward longitudinal studies for the ineluctable reason that there simply is no other way by which certain questions regarding development, cause and effect may be approached. Correlational, cross-sectional, or experimental methods have great and suggestive contributions to make toward an understanding of the bases of behavior. But these approaches do not encompass time and the trajectory of individual lives. It would be pleasant if the world were differently arranged; it is not, and so the burdens of longitudinal study must, albeit perhaps reluctantly, be accepted and endured by psychology. When the long season of waiting has been survived and the data are in, then the excitement of the longitudinal approach begins. Time is surmounted; in a richly-detailed longitudinal study, belated or unanticipated questions can be asked and their answer found quickly in data collected many years before. The payment, in patience and barrenness during the beginning or middle of the longitudinal study, can be justified at its end when a flood of questions finds answers not otherwise providable.

The present book is a major, integrative report of the findings developed to date in the course of two still on-going longitudinal studies conducted at the Institute of Human Development (IHD). The one study was initiated and monitored, until his retirement, by the late Professor Harold Jones; the second study was begun and directed, until her retirement, by Professor Jean Macfarlane and thereafter by Dr. Marjorie Honzik. In late 1960, I was invited to assume the responsibility for organizing a comprehensive and systematic study of the early and contemporaneous archival material relating to the personalities of the longitudinally-studied IHD subjects.

Longitudinal studies will always be hard to come by. Few have been reported before this one, and the foreseeable future will not add many to this small number. Because longitudinal studies are so rare, they invariably attract interest and have significant impact upon the field of human development. Any research, however, is importantly influenced by the preconceptions and premises of the investigator. In view of the influence the results of longitudinal studies can have, it is well to indicate the several kinds of orientation—conceptual and methodological—which have conditioned the analyses and the way in which the findings are reported. But first, it will be useful to describe briefly some earlier longitudinal studies and their circumstances so that a frame of reference is provided within which the present research may be evaluated.

PREVIOUS LONGITUDINAL STUDIES OF PERSONALITY DEVELOPMENT

To date, there are three reports from longitudinal studies that have followed, with some effort toward comprehensiveness, the personality development of a sample of subjects from childhood or adolescence into adulthood. These are: (1) the volume of Kagan and Moss (1962) reporting the findings developed at the Fels Research Institute; (2) the account by Symonds and Jensen (1961) of their Columbia study; and (3) the monograph by Tuddenham (1959) describing some personality continuities observed within the IHD study directed by H. E. Jones. Other longitudinal studies have focussed on intelligence rather than personality (e.g., Terman and Oden, 1959) or shorter time spans (e.g., Witkin, Goodenough, and Karp, 1967) or different stages of life (e.g., Neugarten and associates, 1964). A useful summary of the extant longitudinal investigations is provided by Kagan (1964).

The Kagan and Moss Fels Study is by far the most ambitious and extensive of these studies, and it well illustrates both the contributions and the complications attending the longitudinal enterprise.

The Fels subject sample consisted originally of 89 children from 63 different families. Forty-five of the subjects were supplied by only 19 families, the consanguinity within the sample being further enhanced by the inclusion of a set of triplet boys of unstated zygosity. Subjects were closely studied from birth to the age of 14 years. The media employed included intelligence tests, projective tests, and interviews and narrative accounts of the child at school, in the Fels Institute context and at home. These longitudinal data were divided into four sections for the age periods—birth to three years, three to six years, six to ten years, and ten to fourteen years. One psychologist—the same for all cases—then studied the longitudinal material for each subject and, for each time period, rated the subject with respect to four broad classes of personality variables: motive-related behaviors, sources of anxiety, defensive responses, and modes of social interaction.

In a follow-up study, conducted when the Fels subjects were at an average age of 24 years (range from 19 to 29 years), 36 of the males and 35 of the females were interviewed by a different, but still solitary, psychologist. This interviewer expressed his assessments of each subject in the form of ratings on 39 variables. These 39 variables, after being screened for reliability, were reduced to the set of 27 dimensions used in subsequent analyses. Additional data—projective, tachistoscopic, cognitive, autonomic, and inventory—were collected after the interview sessions from varying numbers of subjects. However, the primary focus of the Kagan and Moss analyses and report is on the several sets of personality ratings and on the correlations between broadly similar or related rating variables characterizing subjects in their mid-twenties and in their childhood or adolescence.

The positive findings reported by Kagan and Moss are many and provocative. Some of their results will be cited in apposite places later, but the interested reader will have to consult their work for a full account of their substantive results. The review of the Fels study by Honzik (1965) is especially useful, for it evaluates the Kagan and Moss methodology and data interpretations and summarizes many of the findings, placing them in the larger longitudinal perspective. In the comments now to follow, Honzik's remarks have been heavily leaned upon.

The limitations of the Fels study are several, some unavoidable and others, perhaps, reflecting simply differences in the aesthetics of, or orientations towards, data analysis. Although the ratings of personality are central to the Kagan and Moss design, yet each set of ratings was made by only one rater. While partial checks on the consensual validity of these individual judges were made by other raters, it is not at all clear that these tests of inter-rater agreement were extensive or independent enough to warrant the total reliance ultimately placed on the single rater, with all the systematic idiosyncracies in personality assessment he may introduce. Particularly unfortunate was the use of the same rater for all of the four time periods defining childhood and early adolescence. Despite intervening ratings of other subjects, the judge, in returning to the new material describing a previously evaluated subject would still carry to an unknown extent memories of the essential way the subject had been characterized earlier. The independence between the childhood-adolescence ratings by the one rater and the early adulthood ratings by the other rater is clear and is the strength of the Fels study; the dependence, to an unknown extent, among the several sets of ratings for the four childhood and adolescent periods must leave uncertainty in regard to the relations among these developmental intervals.

Consanguinity within the Fels subject sample is, as Honzik has noted, especially troublesome because it operates to inflate correlation coefficients. Its extent among the subjects studied as adults is not indicated, but the consanguinity effect may have been further increased since the participation of siblings, as adults, is likely to be strongly linked. If one sibling participates, the other is likely to as well. Honzik has suggested a re-analysis of these data, restricting the sample to include only one child from a family; however, carrying out this suggestion would reduce the Fels sample of 71 adult subjects (including both sexes) by something like one-third, and the remaining sample would be frustratingly small.

The Kagan and Moss variables rated during childhood-adolescence and during early adulthood are not clearly spelled out. They are further grouped or clustered into classes of variables that sometimes seem amorphous or counter-intuitive and, most importantly, the variables describing the subjects as adults are different from the variables used to describe the subjects at earlier periods. Although broad equivalences exist between the variables from the earlier and later periods, these are by no means entirely clear and necessarily introduce another uncertainty.

The age and life stage of the Fels subjects at the time of the Kagan and Moss study pose another problem. At an average age of 24, with an age range from 19 to 29, the subjects probably have not yet settled down and may not have attained the style of adaptation that will characterize their later lives. In contemporary America, a quarter of a century is spent before an individual is expected or expects himself to fix his life's course. The early and middle twenties are, more than ever, times of personal experimentation with a moratorium being benignly or indifferently permitted the seekers for identity. The relationships found by the Fels investigators to characterize the early adulthood of their subjects, although of great interest, may well change radically as these subjects are assessed again a half-generation later. Subsequent assessments, if carried through, will bear upon this strong possibility.

Finally, the small samples of men and women available in the Fels study prevent the attempt to identify patterns of personality development, i.e., the finding of homogeneous subgroups within the larger undifferentiated sample. Instead, the Fels investigators were restricted to straightforward correlational analysis employing the full samples available. Although correlations employing the full sample are usually interesting, and are often sufficiently useful or descriptive, such correlations can be misleading when fundamentally different subtypes exist within the larger sample. The Fels sample sizes at early adulthood (36 men and 35 women) precluded an evaluation of this more differentiated view of personality and its lines of development.

Having summarized the several qualifications that must surround the Kagan and Moss findings, the uniqueness and great psychological interest of their study must again be emphasized. The methodological concerns noted may introduce certain interpretive uncertainties, but they are by no means vitiating of the Fels enterprise. The spirit and intention of the Kagan and Moss inquiry is well conveyed by their remarks: "We view this research report primarily as a source of new hypotheses and not as an almanac of facts. It is an invitation to our colleagues to select ideas according to their taste and to submit to more rigorous testing the provocative hunches uncovered by this investigation."* Psychologists informed of this aspiration and knowing too of the unreported complications, frustrations, and tedium that inevitably accompany longitudinal research can clearly recognize the great and signal contribution of the Kagan and Moss study.

The Symonds-Jensen study is a report essentially on the test-retest correspondence of projective test protocols separated by an interval of 13 years. Twenty-eight adolescents (12 boys and 16 girls) who had taken the Symonds Picture Story Test in 1940 were again given this procedure and the Rorschach in 1953, at an average age of about 28 (range from 26 to 31 years). The subjects were also interviewed in 1953, the interviews and the projective protocol serving separately as bases for rankings of "general adjustment." Similar rankings had been developed in 1940.

The stories contributed by the subjects were thematically coded, classified, and compared for the two times. Analyses were largely non-statistical, but were judged to indicate theme persistence over the thirteen-year interval. Symonds and Jensen report consistency over this time in general personality characteristics, including aggressiveness, symptoms of nervousness, and attitudes. Some diminishing of aggressivity was noted. Interpersonal relationships as adults could not be anticipated from adolescent attitudes. The Rorschach interpretation showed low agreement with the thematic analyses of the Picture Story Test. The most striking finding reported is the correlation of .54 between a ranking of "general adjustment" during adulthood and the "general adjustment" ranking developed thirteen years earlier.

The Symonds and Jensen study does not require much in the way of evaluation. It was not designed initially as a longitudinal study, and it is

---

*Kagan, J. & Moss, H. A. *Birth to maturity: A study in psychological development.* New York: Wiley, 1962, p. 19.

explicitly circumscribed in its intentions and analyses. Its findings cannot be given great weight because of the small sample, the almost exclusive reliance on projective measures, and the absence of checks on the construct validity of the interpretations it adduces.

The Tuddenham monograph (1959) reports on the constancy of ratings of 53 personality variables over periods ranging from thirteen years for some variables to nineteen years for others. The sample consisted of 32 males and 40 females from the OGS sample. Some of these subjects are included in the study to be reported in this book. The subjects were about 33 years old when they were interviewed on two separate ninety-minute occasions by two different psychologists. The interviewers independently rated the subjects and the averages of these judgments became the ratings used as the follow-up data.

The earlier data used for comparison were developed in two different ways. One subset of ratings consisted of the average evaluation contributed by two psychologists who had observed the subjects in a noon-hour free play situation some nineteen years previously (Newman, 1946). The second group of ratings was developed thirteen years before the follow-up interviews, and represented the cumulative impressions—sometimes independently contributed and sometimes issuing from a conference—of several OGS staff members (Frenkel-Brunswik, 1942). Reliability of the average ratings, although variable, was usually quite good; the mean reliabilities for the two time periods and the two sexes ranging from .58 to .71. The correlations between corresponding variables over time were for both sexes predominantly positive (only 8 of 106 correlations were not positive, but the average correlation was only .27 for men and .24 for women). There was, however, substantial and informative range in the continuity coefficients (from $-.11$ to .68). All things considered, this is an impressive summary result, achieved despite appreciable differences in the rating context and despite a comparative unfamiliarity of the follow-up interviewers with the OGS subjects and the OGS rating scheme.

The specific findings of Tuddenham that relate to the present work will be cited in the appropriate place (cf. Chapter V); for a complete account of his findings, the reader must turn to the Tuddenham monograph. It is distinguished by the use of consensual rather than solitary ratings, complete independence of the adolescent and adult ratings, identical rating variables for the two compared time periods, and the use of subjects further along in life who could be presumed to be more definitely fixed in their adaptational patterns.

The limitations of the Tuddenham study derive primarily from necessary adaptations of research design to what was feasible at the time. The 53 variables evaluated had been predetermined by earlier investigators; these variables were sometimes not truly rated as a continuum; they were often excessively redundant, and on occasion they were concep-

tually discomforting. Despite their large number, many aspects of personality were not encompassed by the variables to which Tuddenham necessarily was committed. The adult follow-up interviews were perhaps too
brief to permit a full manifestation of the character of the subjects being
assessed, and, most importantly, only correlational analysis, which
emphasizes personality continuities, was tried. Although unstable personality variables were recognized by Tuddenham as being of great psychological significance as indicators of personality change, the analytical
possibilities for identifying the nature of these character discontinuities
over time were limited, and he could do little more than point to the problem. In the present study, it was possible to go beyond the Tuddenham
investigation, using later resources to enlarge and enrich the scope of
inquiry and to deepen the analytical approach.

CONCEPTUAL BACKGROUND

The concern of this book is with personality and with personality development. The state of personality theory is, as ever, chaotic and there is no
single theoretical viewpoint that can be followed rigorously. However,
from the nature of the variables that have been employed for the description and understanding of personality, it will be clear to the reader that
the conceptual position being applied has been heavily influenced by
psychoanalysis and, in particular, by "the new look" in psychoanalytic
theory—ego psychology (Rapaport, 1960; Hartmann, 1958), and by the
stages of ego development as formulated by Erikson (1959) and Loevinger (1966).

Some previous writings (e.g., Block, 1950, 1965) indicate some of the
special emphases and distinctions with which we conceptualize ego
within the domain of personality theory. In general, personality may be
viewed in terms of motivations operating through ego structures which
respect and react to both the drives energizing the person and the environmental context in which that individual necessarily must function.
These ego structures or apparatuses can be multi-faceted and function-
ally resourceful in the way they mediate inner and outer constraints, or
they may be undifferentiated and perseverating before the pressures that
impinge.

In this theoretical framework, personality development is understood
as the history of how certain motivations develop, change, and become
enduring; how ego structures form and function so that all of an individual's behavior expresses his personal stamp; and how the individual comes
to shun or gravitate toward certain environmental niches or classes of
opportunity.

Within the present study, begun by earlier psychologists of other persuasions, theory in a rigorous sense cannot have an important place. The relationships that will be reported describe individuals and describe developmental periods. Interpretation of these relationships can be informed by a personality theory but, as descriptive findings, the results obtained stand in their own right and doubtless can be interpreted from diverse viewpoints. Personally persuasive theoretical notions have been applied in interpretation of the relationships obtained; the reader is invited to try his own understandings of the results as they unfold.

There are ways, however, in which certain broad features of conceptual orientation do determine the results to be reported. Thus, where it has been conventional in earlier longitudinal studies to emphasize normative trends and continuities in personality development, the emphasis in the present work, to achieve more complete understanding, is upon consideration of *different life trends* and the significance of *personality changes* for later behavior and adjustment. Where it has been conventional to focus on variables *per se* (e.g., the correlation of measures of *dominance* over the years), the study here is of *the interplay of personality variables* within the people these dimensions characterize and to examine the significance of different patterns of interplay. Some elaboration of both of these switches (or balances) in emphasis is in order.

Uniformity Versus Differentiation in the Study of Personality Development

Developmental psychology has been hampered in its progress to date because, in its preferred world, it has staked much on and clung too long to the potent assumption of uniformity of relationships. The massive influence of this expectation on the strategy of empirical research in developmental psychology may be seen in two ways: across people and across time. Across people, the presumption in its pure form asserts that *all* people develop in essentially the same way. There may be differences in initial or terminal status and in the rate or timing of development, but these differences pose no conceptual problem so long as the sequence or direction of development remains constant. Across time, the hypothesis of uniformity suggests that relationships or qualities observed at one time may be expected to apply later as well. There may be changes over time in the specification of an individual or group but, in the main, temporal correspondence or stability is to be expected if measurement has been adequate and important, central variables are considered.

Across people, it is often recognized that the sexes may mature differently. Within like-sexed groups, however, there usually is reluctance to abandon the paradigm of relationship uniformity for a Pandora's box of so many different lawfulnesses that their aggregation appears conceptually unmanageable. The idea of different developmental paths—different in kind and in direction, rather than simply different in rate of traversal—is anathema to the nomothetic view that seeks universal laws applicable to one and all. When a differentiated view of personality development is applied, theories must proliferate, and there must be a theory of theories to explain the choice among different developmental paths. For heuristic reasons, then, there is a compelling convenience in psychological laws or descriptive relationships viewed as applying, in effect, to all individuals.

But universal applicability and lawfulness need not go together, and the meagre accomplishments of contemporary psychology suggest that the seeking of the one may preclude finding the second—a greater lawfulness may be discerned as what is general and undifferentiated is partitioned into smaller but more homogeneous classes for study. In the field of personality development, this conceptual recognition demands a respect for the possibility of different courses of character evolution without a denial of what indeed may be universal for all persons.

Across time, the preference for uniformity of relationships has infused developmental psychology in perhaps less obvious ways. The way things are at one time is most readily viewed, if not explained, as due to the way they were at an earlier time; temporal stability, when found, tends to be magnified in size and importance. Change over time disappoints the investigator, for he is prevented from the visible accomplishment of predicting the future. Given this pre-focus, inconstancy over time is viewed as indicative of poor psychological measurement or as due to an unanalyzable, irreducible random component in human behavior or as evidence of the unimportance of the variable involved (by definition, since only an unimportant variable would provide such whimsical discrimination).

There are additional, related reasons to be mentioned for the conventional emphasis on continuities rather than on changes in personality development.

Historically, the dominant conceptualizations of the basis and laws of development—psychoanalysis, reinforcement theory, and the constitutional-genetic viewpoint—concur in construing later personality as the result primarily of an orderly unfolding of capacities and qualities intrinsic to an individual or laid down earlier.

Metrically, if changes in personality as well as continuities are to be studied longitudinally, there must first be a way of measuring qualities of character in an absolute sense, so that indices of change may be derived. Achieving absolute measurement poses some significant psychometric problems. On the other hand, relative measurement at different time intervals is readily feasible, since only orderings are involved. Whereupon the modest question of whether individuals maintain their relative order over time can be easily asked—and this is a question oriented toward continuity or stability of personality. So measurement considerations have also fostered the investigation emphases on stability.

The orientation toward personality continuity rather than personality change in developmental psychology also may have been influenced, at least in part, by an extrapolation from developmental inquiries in other domains where the idea of continuity has proved itself in the past, e.g., the predictability of adult height from early bone measurements or the essential stability of the intelligence quotient.

And, lastly, there may be a linguistic reason as well for the research emphasis on continuity instead of change. The connotations of words indicating absence of change are generally positive, viz., *consistency, stability, constancy, continuity, congruence.* The connotations of change are often pejorative, viz., *inconsistency, instability, inconstancy, discontinuity, incongruence.* The Puritan value of solidity appears to have affected our language so that an unchanging character carries the aura of moral and mental soundness, while a transmogrified person is suspect. Connotatively neutral labels to identify continuity and change are most difficult to find, suggesting that an implicit value orientation may have influenced the cast of prior developmental research.

The intent of these several remarks on assumptions and values in the study of personality continuity and change has not been to depreciate the significance of the continuities in the stream of behavior. Rather, it has been to show the need for seeking out and using both temporal stability and change.

The idea of differentiation over time (and over people) has been a prime guiding principle of the present enterprise. If the study of personality as homogeneous and continuous has properly been the first order of business for a psychology of personality development, it may now be the time to widen our view of the possibilities of personality evolvement and change.

Variable-Centered Versus Person-Centered Approaches in the Study of Personality Development.

A second analysis-shaping consideration affecting the procedures and results in the present study relates to a centering on people as well as on variables as the entities for understanding. Some years ago, Klein and Schlesinger (1949) wrote an article wistfully entitled, "Where is the perceiver in perceptual theory?" They complained that psychology had identified a host of stimulus and response variables which clearly underlay the realm of perceptual behavior, but had not been concerned with the necessary interrelation or interpretation of these separate variables required so that a person could come to *see.*

In the realm of personality psychology, a preoccupation with variables *per se* also seems to be dominant. Psychologists of personality often write of the correlation between variables, somehow without explicit recognition that these variables are represented and system-organized within persons. Variable-centered analyses are useful for understanding the differences between people and what characteristics go with what characteristics in a group of individuals. But as well, and ultimately, psychology will need to seek understanding of the configuration and systematic connection of personality variables as these dynamically operate within a particular person. This is the way lay people in their implicit theories of personality tend to conceptualize. The approach is not less fruitful by virtue of its ubiquity.

In the field of psychology, thinking along subject-oriented lines seems easy and natural for the intra-psychically-minded, such as clinical psychologists; thinking oriented around the behavior of variables seems more appropriate and intrinsically correct for the differential psychologist with his heritage in the study of inter-individual differences. Both approaches are useful, of course. Accordingly, the longitudinal data have been analyzed from both the variable-centered and the person-centered points of view, seeking to respond to both the *between* and the *within* questions of psychology. The particular analytic tactics employed will be detailed later, in appropriate chapters.

A PHILOSOPHY OF RESEARCH ANALYSIS

This is a complicated book, with many kinds and shapings of findings. It is a book of the computer age, when data analyses are free and easy, but also inundate the investigator and data integrator. Much more has been done than shall be reported; the basis for selection must be explained.

Of necessity, I will be introducing, here and throughout, discussion—general and particular—of research methodology. My intentions are psychological and I shall be speaking psychology. But psychological findings of substance depend upon specifiable and appropriate methodological decisions. Without such knowledge and assurance, the scientific reader is in no position to evaluate the credibility of the relationships and interpretations presented to him.

Specific methodological or statistical decisions and their rationales will be discussed in the chapters of this book where they have an immediate relevance. In this section, I indicate certain general considerations orienting and controlling the ways chosen to explore, analyze, and report the data. The very uniqueness of the IHD archives was highly influential; it was necessary to live with unreliability on occasion; statistics sometimes have been employed only as descriptive aids; there has been redundancy by choice in certain of the analyses; and convergent, discriminating and elaborating findings have been sought to bolster the several modes of subject classification.

The Uniqueness of the IHD Archives.

To begin, note that there are costly, irreplaceable data and there are inexpensive, easily replicable data; there is one research strategy for an undeveloped science where exploration must be the prime emphasis and quite another for a relatively far-advanced field where the essential variables are agreed upon and theory-testing is at the core of scientific industry. In these terms, the unique nature of the archives of IHD must be recognized together with the undeveloped state of developmental psychology.

The IHD longitudinal studies are unprecented for their size and duration. Developing, maintaining, accumulating, and now mining and refining the archival material has cost, in the aggregate, the time of perhaps a score of professional careers and the resources of a large fortune. The archives are priceless, for it would require more than four decades to replace them. Given the product of so much cooperation, labor, money (and love), it behooves would-be integrators to approach these archival resources constructively rather than hypercritically, to make them respond as fully as possible to as many questions as may be generated.

In the larger context set by the dearth of longitudinal findings in the still largely uncharted realm of personality development, an analytical approach was adopted that risks one kind of error to avoid another. Early in the research progression, it is strategic to scan widely and tolerantly in the search for incisive variables and important relationships. Some—perhaps many—of such permissively-identified variables and relationships will prove, on subsequent study, to be unimportant or ephemeral. But the investigator willing to incur false leads early in the game stands a better chance of discerning the outlines of what later will prove significant for his still hazily perceived domain of inquiry. Rigorous standards for accepting findings are premature when applied to necessarily inefficient investigations into unexplored fields; they can prevent the recognition of conceptual leads which would be fundamentally clarifying in subsequent, more informed, and more attuned research designs. It is the strength of the scientific method that continued and replicating research will separate the early wheat from the early chaff. An omnidirectional inquiry will not for long remain so directionless; rather, this strategy of research focus can have a good likelihood of being fruitful.

In other—and simpler—words, it was the intention of the present study to make the most of the IHD longitudinal archives, to be venturesome in the analyses and interpretations, to sketch a broad picture that in many respects might later require revision or erasure. To do otherwise, to narrowly use these unprecedented data resources, would be a failure of faith in the possibilities of psychology.

Living with Unreliability.

The effects of unreliability always plague the efforts of psychologists to discern the orderliness they seek. In many research situations, the achievement of reliable measurement is viewed, properly, as the necessary first condition to be met before pursuing further relationships. "If you can't measure it, how can you study it?" If the reliability of a measure is inadequate, energy must first be expended to remedy this deficiency.

In a longitudinal study, however, the attitude toward unreliability and its ills must accommodate to the facts of the past but not be defeated by them. Measures found upon later evaluation to be unreliable cannot be repeated and improved; subjects found to have been unreliably evaluated cannot be replaced or restudied with a view toward better specification. Of necessity, if certain measures are not to be abandoned, or if a precious subject is not to be deleted from the sample, lower standards of reliability must on occasion be accepted.

This lowering of standards is not so difficult to live with as may be supposed. The effects of unreliability generally may be expected to operate randomly and to introduce no bias into the relationships later and independently observed. By continuing with measures that have at least a modicum of reliable discrimination, relationships may still be observed despite the attenuating drain of error. In the present analytical context, given the ambitious aspirations for the IHD longitudinal data, it was decided to stay with and use some psychometrically poor measures and uncertainly evaluated subjects, as long as the error thus introduced could be anticipated to be non-biassing in its consequences. In so doing, it may well be that, on occasion, certain subsequently observed relationships have been reified which are, in fact, attributable to chance fluctuations. But the expectation has been that the full set of findings surrounding the several analytical classifications has prevented fundamental misreadings of the data.

The Descriptive Use of Statistics.

As will be seen, many variables were employed to describe many subjects and the data have been analyzed in many different ways. Concern has been more with distinctions among individuals and groups of individuals than with high statistical sophistication in the analytical inquiries. Thus, except for the use of factor analysis as a means of simplifying and reducing data or as a basis for grouping subjects, the statistics relied upon are little more complicated than correlation coefficients, t tests, the hypergeometric distribution, and the analysis of fourfold tables in the search for relationships.

In part, the more complicated multivariate statistical techniques (e.g., multiple regression, discriminant functions, canonical correlation) have been avoided because of their unrealistic assumptions, their reification of error, and the non-psychological nature of the results they issue. These procedures are calculated to optimally serve known criteria in a simply-construed world. But we do not yet know the criteria we wish to respect and it still seems likely that the world that psychology must encompass is interactively rather than additively arranged. Beyond the insufficiencies of present-day statistical procedures for many of the analyses, it is my belief that the psychology of personality development is better advanced for the present and a long time to come by heuristic efforts to cleave the anatomy of personality at its joints than it is by elegant, but psychologically quite unreal, statistical and mathematical models.

For these reasons, the use of statistical procedures in the present study is sometimes deliberately casual and descriptive rather than formal and rigorous in specifying probability levels. This characteristic of the analyses will be visible most readily when a group of subjects is compared against each of several other groups, using a host of variables as the basis of comparison. The multiple comparisons are not independent nor are the variables being evaluated. This conjunction of interdependencies defies satisfactory and succinct statistical analysis.

Often, as will be observed, these inferential problems could be partially confronted by resorting to empirically-developed sampling distributions which appropriately reflected the data realities (Block, 1960). But this method responds only to the problem of interdependence among variables and does not yet respond to the conjoined and sticky problem of multiple comparisons among different groups.

The procedure invoked in such complicated data situations was to use statistical thresholds of significance as arbitrarily convenient cutting points to find the sets of variables or relationships characterizing a particular group. This approach simplifies greatly the job of communicating the findings, and since reasonably stringent statistical acceptance-rejection criteria were used, the departures from precise interpretations of significance levels are small in import. Further, as a rule, several quite diverse lines of evidence are brought to bear upon an interpretation.

There is no magic in the significance levels psychologists conventionally employ; rigid adherence to such standards for declaring the "existence" or "non-existence" of a relationship is evidence more of dichotomous thinking and of prostration before an imperfectly understood statistics than of an understanding of science and its tools of inference. For further and specific aspects of the descriptive use of statistical indices as employed in the present study and for a better basis to evaluate this usage, the reader is delayed until later data-presenting chapters.

The Uses of Redundancy.

The several ways in which the longitudinal data were analyzed overlap to varying degrees. For this reason, certain kinds of results and interpretive refrains will be repetitively heard. This redundancy, I find and suggest, is comforting and clarifying rather than evidence of uneconomy. Too often in psychology, apparently substantive results prove to be conditional upon a particular, perhaps fortuitously employed method of analysis, so that it is reassuring to come across results constant across methods of analysis.

The redundancy has the larger purpose, however, of exchanging one kind of efficiency for another. Although it is often possible to logically derive certain analytical results from other analytical approaches, these deductions are complicated and are not readily comprehended by the investigator or by his subsequent readers. For example, given two groups of subjects that, combined, constitute the total available sample, it is possible to derive analytically but laboriously the full characteristics of the total sample from knowledge of the characteristics of each of the two part samples. This feat, however, fails to convey concisely and compellingly the nature of the sample *in toto*. Direct analysis of the entire sample, although redundant, provides full and psychologically comprehensible results in a form comparable to the results developed from the part samples. This economy of comparison and understanding far outweighs, in my judgment, the computer costs of the redundant analyses or the presumed economies implicitly justifying elegant demonstrations of redundancies. In the present effort, overlapping analyses were tolerated and even sought if relationships were more cleanly discerned or more surely confirmed by so doing. The various modes of classification are brought into interrelation for the reader at a number of junctures, but the different facets or vantage points provided by alternative analyses are not thereby abandoned.

Bolstering the Findings Obtained.

The central data to be reported are of a special kind, and the analyses are largely within and between various independent sections of these special data. Further, there is frustratingly little information available concerning the nature and impact of environmental events on the subjects or in regard to the role of intervening experience in accounting for personality change over time. Of necessity, then, the focus of the research has been compelled toward what may be called an "internal" study of personality, a study of personality trends, and personality changes as defined by and within a constant set of personality measures sequentially applied.

Internal studies, as such, can be extremely powerful if the measures employed are valid because the usual problem of finding or positing comparable variables across time or context does not arise. But the larger significance of internally derived relationships must be sought as well, not only to validate externally what was observed within, but also to elaborate upon the implications of initial findings. The tactic applied here has been to hold separate certain forms of data, thus maintaining their independence from the core data, upon which the analyses build. Subsequent analyses of these withheld data then provide an opportunity for bolstering and ramifying the relationships discerned in the internal analysis. Something akin to convergent and discriminant validation (Campbell & Fiske, 1959), but in a looser sense, is the intent of these subsequently focussed analyses of independent data. The network of associated relationships thus adduced which surrounds many of the internal analyses lends appreciable weight to the interpretative themes to be proposed.

THE PLAN OF THIS BOOK

The reader, before he plunges ahead, may wish a better guide than is provided by the table of contents to the organization and purpose of the chapters beyond this one. Moreover, many readers may wish to approach this book with an eye toward the conclusions asserted rather than toward the methods and specific data which underlie them; for this class of readers, too, some further remarks here may be helpful.

Chapter II (The People Studied) and Chapter III (The Archival Material and the Consequent Research Approach) should be read in their entirety because they describe the basic context and conditions of the research. The committed reader will wish to tour through Chapter IV (The Judging Process), but the necessarily selective reader can omit this section, which is devoted to technicalities and complications that had to be hurdled before the data could be confronted for their significance.

The following four chapters are data-presenting. Chapter V (Personality Attributes Studied Over Time) reports the behavioral trends characterizing the full or undifferentiated samples of male and female subjects. Chapter VI (Personality Consistency and Change Over Time as a Moderator Variable of Longitudinal Trends) employs a first, rough basis for differentiation—the fact of personality change—to partition the samples into groups of *changers* and *nonchangers* and explores the differential characteristics and trends consequent upon this differentiation. Chapters VII, VIII, and IX introduce a still finer categorical scheme—developmental typologies as issued by the method of inverse factor analysis—and examine the characteristics, concomitants, antecedents and consequences of the men and women in these different homogeneous subgroups. The skimming reader may wish, for each of these data-presenting chapters, to peruse the first orienting or structuring sections and then consult the clearly-identified interpretive summaries for the various chapter subsections.

Finally, Chapter X (Taking Stock) summarizes in a highly condensed and declarative form what I think has been found or can be said from these analyses regarding personality development, personality change, and personality continuity. Having come this far, it becomes possible to have a better idea of the directions the study of personality development might fruitfully take, and accordingly some proposals are offered for subsequent and better longitudinal programs.

We have been at this introduction for some pages now. Let us get on to the reason for it all.

Chapter II

THE PEOPLE STUDIED

THEIR SELECTION

The men and women whose personality development is the focus of this book are members of two initially separated but here conjoined longitudinal studies initiated a generation and a half ago within the Institute of Child Welfare, later renamed the Institute of Human Development (IHD).

The one study was started in 1929 by Jean Macfarlane and her colleagues, when the families of every third baby born in Berkeley over an 18-month period were provided the opportunity of participating in what was announced as a study of normal children over a number of years. Some 248 infants and their families were selected for study. Within this group of infant subjects, there was a further allocation to either a "guidance" condition or a "control" condition on the basis of pairs matched socio-economically. The infants—later children and adolescents—within the Guidance Group experienced frequent and involving contacts with Dr. Macfarlane and her collegues as they grew up. The subjects within the Control Group were seen much less frequently, essentially only for routine testing, during the years of the study. Richly variegated data exist for the intensively studied "guidance" subjects, and it is only these subjects from the Macfarlane project who were included in the present analyses. A full description of the Guidance Study (GdS) and its sampling and data collection procedures is contained in the monograph by Macfarlane (1938).

Dr. Harold Jones and his colleagues began their own enterprise in 1932 by contacting 212 fifth-grade children from five elementary schools in Oakland, California. Initially, this longitudinal effort was called the "Adolescent Study"; since 1955, however, it has been designated the "Oakland Growth Study" (OGS). The basis for including fifth-graders in the OGS was two-fold: (1) the student had indicated an intention to attend a particular junior high school which operated as part of the Education Department of the University of California, and whose staff was willing to facilitate systematic behavioral observation by the OGS staff; (2) both the child and his family were willing to cooperate with the research, and expected to remain in the locale for the next seven years. The basic design and orientation of the Oakland Growth Study, as initially conceived, is presented by Jones (1938, 1939a, 1939b).

The intellectual levels of the OGS and GdS samples are shown in Table 2-1. In order to provide a comparison of the OGS and GdS subjects on the same intelligence test—the Stanford-Binet 1937 revision—it was necessary to contrast the two samples at slightly different ages; the OGS subjects were 17 years of age and the GdS subjects were 14 or 15 years of age at the time of testing.

Table 2-1
Frequency Distribution of IQ Scores for the Subjects Studied

IQ Level	OGS Sample	GdS Sample
80–90	2	2
91–100	9	4
101–110	19	10*
111–120	34	14*
121–130	21	19
131–140	12	17*
141–150	0	6
151–160	0	2
Mean IQ	116	123
S. D.	11.81	15.99

NOTE:—The OGS subjects were tested at 17 years of age while the IQ score reported here for the GdS subjects is based on a testing administered when these subjects were 14 or 15 years of age. For all cases, the Stanford-Binet, Form L or M, 1937 revision was used.

*Indicates several subjects in category did not have an intelligence quotient for the 14–15 year-old testing, so the quotient from the nearest time of testing was used.

It will be observed that the GdS sample has a higher mean IQ than does the OGS sample (123 versus 115). However, according to Honzik (personal communication, 1965), successive re-testing, over the years, of the GdS children with the Stanford-Binet probably accounts for an average increase of about 10 IQ points. The OGS subjects, on the other hand, had only one previous testing with the Stanford-Binet, when they were 12 or 13 years of age. Thus, an argument can be made that there is not an important difference between the OGS and GdS samples in their general level of intelligence. However, the distribution of IQ scores in Table 2-1 reveals a number of GdS individuals reached unusually high intellectual levels, levels unapproached by any of the OGS subjects. It is sensible, then, to remain undecided as to the intellectual comparability of the two samples studied. It seems likely that the GdS sample indeed has a somewhat higher verbal facility, and consequently higher IQ, if only because, as will be reported shortly, their parents stem more from the professional class than do the parents of OGS subjects.

At the outset of each study both samples, of course, were much larger than the sample that has now been followed through to adulthood. The investigation here being reported includes all persons, from both the GdS and the OGS, who participated in an interviewing and testing program in their middle, adult years and for whom, in addition, there existed reasonably full information for either the period of junior high school (JHS), or the period of senior high school (SHS), or both. Of 171 individuals who returned to IHD as adults, there was judged to be sufficient data during the JHS period for 170; for the SHS interval, the data were judged adequate for 160 cases. The sexes are represented about equally at the several time periods (e.g., for the adult period, 84 males and 87 females).

Initially, the GdS contained 248 subjects, while the OGS began with 212 participants. Obviously, the dropping away of subjects from the ongoing studies poses significant questions regarding changes in subsequent characteristics of the reduced samples. Accordingly, there have been continuing studies within IHD of the implications of subject attrition.

Careful analyses by Haan (1962) for the OGS, and by Honzik (personal communication, 1966) for the GdS, provide encouraging evidence that sample evaporation has not introduced important biases over time in regard to demographic, intellectual, or personality characteristics of the present sample. The slight changes that have been observed suggest that OGS male subjects who continued to participate in the study had a larger discrepancy between their self and ideal; OGS women subjects who continued were more likely to be from smaller families.

In any event, the design underlying the present analyses contrasts the *same* subjects at three different life periods and so the usually troublesome problem of sample modification over time does not arise.

The question, to what universe may we generalize the relationships observed within the subject sample studied? leads to an intricate, epistemological thicket that I cheerfully refuse to enter. No one knows how a proper universe of subjects for a longitudinal study should be defined nor, for significant considerations in regard to the systematics of research design, is random selection from a definable universe necessarily the most efficient strategy for developing understanding. Randomness, unaided, cannot be depended upon to represent sufficiently often certain types of individuals who, although not numerically frequent, are nevertheless of great conceptual significance.

The information shortly to be offered testifies to the diversity of the subjects with respect to all the usual variables of stratification. They come from many origins, with many qualities, and have traveled along many paths. Although typicality cannot be claimed for the subjects, they nevertheless have led recognizable American lives—lives of interest that warrant understanding.

It will be useful and will provide a better understanding of the subjects under longitudinal study if a sense is conveyed of the environment and historical time in which these children became adolescents and these adolescents became adults. It will also provide perspective for the differentiated analyses which are the primary emphasis of this book if the subjects are characterized broadly as a group, at the different time intervals focused upon and with regard to their life direction and accomplishments. Much of what follows in later chapters is aseptically statistical and the reader may be better motivated to pursue the analytical complications if he carries with him a recognition that the data spewed at him deal with lives that have been formed in dramatic times under many influences.

THE DEVELOPMENTAL SETTING FOR THE SUBJECTS

The San Francisco Bay Area is considered to be one of the choicest living areas in America and, within the Bay Area, Berkeley and that portion of Oakland immediately bordering Berkeley—the adolescent environment of the OGS and GdS subjects—are especially blessed.*

Berkeley is a long-established community across San Francisco Bay from the City of San Francisco. Although many of its residents now commute to San Francisco or to Oakland, or are involved locally in business or industry, the nature of Berkeley is, nevertheless, greatly shaped by the central presence of the campus of the University of California. In 1940, the city had a population of 86,000. A quarter of a century later its population was about 125,000.

The Berkeley-Oakland locale consists of flat lowlands beginning at the Bay and, two miles or so inland, the beginnings of the rise known as the Berkeley-Oakland hills. On the "flats," during the times we write of, were pastel-colored stucco houses built in rows along squared-off streets. Up on the "hill," spacious, gracious, costly homes along winding roads were

---

*That portion of Oakland under consideration, which is adjacent to South Berkeley, is in many respects—in its topography, residential areas, cultural values, and the like—equivalent to Berkeley proper. However, the larger City of Oakland is importantly different in character from Berkeley or the particular Oakland border area with which we are here concerned. For convenience, only Berkeley is mentioned in characterizing the community setting in which the subjects developed. The reader should understand that the border area of Oakland is included as well in this description.

The People Studied

the rule, architecturally individualized and with splendid views of the Bay and city lights below.

On the far side of these hills lies Tilden Park, formally established in 1936, a natural preserve of great beauty and great expanse, easily available for picnics, sports, nature study, hiking, and for achieving isolation. San Francisco Bay itself was a place for a ferry ride, or to fish, or even, on occasion, to swim. The climate is predictable and benign so that the outdoors and space for free movement was immediately and insistently present for all—even those low on the socio-economic scale. And, of course, the automobile in California was sought and retained even by those economically under strain because of the autonomy of mobility it afforded.

With the opening of the San Francisco-Oakland Bay Bridge in 1936, cosmopolitan San Francisco—"The City"—became readily available to the adolescent who would anonymously roam from home or who sought the opulence and derivative prestige that only San Francisco could provide. Youngsters of lesser means, particularly the girls, could acceptably seek the pleasure of interpersonal adventure at several public ballrooms, such as the Ali Baba and Sweets in Oakland.

By the fact of its presence, the University of California has catalyzed in Berkeley an unusual degree of civic liveliness. Cultural heterogeneity abounds, there is community introspectiveness, there is educational experimentation. The aura of Berkeley surely influenced the subjects, orienting them to the multiple values of a college education and generating, also, an expectation that it would be possible to attend the University.

A study by Haan (1964) of the socio-economic mobility of the OGS subjects perhaps demonstrates the contribution of atmosphere and of possibility made by the Berkeley environment. Although upward mobility was a trend of American life for all people at this time, the upward mobility of the OGS sample is greater than is usually reported, and it seems clear, all sampling considerations recognized, that the subjects have been characterized by unusual improvement in their socio-economic lot.

In sum, the subjects studied grew up in essentially benign, encouraging circumstances insofar as community and ecological offerings are concerned. But the vicissitudes of history enforced upon them two major socio-political crises during their developmental years—the Great Depression and World War II.

The OGS subjects were in secondary school from about 1933 to 1939; the GdS subjects were in junior and senior high school from about 1940 to 1946. Hence, the OGS subjects were of an age during the Depression when the economic strains on the familial fabric could be deeply apprehended; the GdS subjects were younger and may have registered the impact of parental joblessness or the indignities of seeking charitable help in a different way. About one-third of the OGS families were in extreme straits during the Depression, reporting public or private welfare contacts. For the OGS sample, the median family income was reduced in 1933 by 39 percent from its pre-Depression figure. Within the GdS sample, one-third of the fathers of the subjects reported unemployment at some point during the Depression years. Clearly, then, the economic consequences of the Depression were experienced in substantial ways by the participants in the study.

The OGS subjects were about 20 years old when World War II began, while the GdS subjects were about 13 years of age. Again, it may be presumed that World War II had far greater and more direct impact upon the OGS subjects, men and women, than it did upon the personal lives of the GdS subjects. Ninety-four percent of the OGS men served in the armed forces. For the OGS sample, the years of World War II were the years also of personal unencumbrance, adventure-seeking, and courtship, all intensified by the context of war. The military participation of the OGS men earned for them the right to free or subsidized higher education after the war and doubtless influenced a number of the subjects toward goals they might otherwise have set aside.

Although the GdS subjects were too young to participate directly in World War II, their adolescence was conditioned by the wartime setting and by wartime values. For some of them, there was sibling participation in the war and, in various small but significant ways, the nature of war and its waste must have been impressed upon them. (Several GdS male subjects participated in the Korean conflict.)

While the period from the end of World War II to the late 1950s cannot be said to be uneventful in America, this was a time of relative continuity of trends established earlier. There was prosperity, with some fluctuations now and then, but nevertheless, prosperity and a general predictability of the society. For the subjects, it was a time essentially of marriage, of family, and of career. In short, the pattern of each individual life had been more or less formed by the time of renewed study by the Institute of Human Development.

THE FAMILIAL ORIGINS OF THE SUBJECTS

Of all the subjects, 89 percent were natives of California and only one was not born in the United States (but in Canada). Those subjects who were not native Californians reached the state at an early age and hence experienced the acculturating effects only of California.

The parents of the subjects, however, were considerably more migratory and culturally diverse. Only 42 percent of the parents had been born in California while another 41 percent were from other areas of the

United States. The remainder of the parents were immigrants from such countries as Canada, Mexico, England, Italy, Germany, Scandinavia, Russia, Switzerland, Australia, Greece, Turkey, and Armenia.

Although 83 percent of the parents of the subjects were born in America, the national or ethnic origins claimed by these parents in turn is of interest for indicating, if only broadly, certain likely contexts of value inculcation that may have filtered down to their children. Noting the national origins of the maternal grandparents and of the paternal grandparents, only two nationalities or groupings of nations account for appreciable percentages of the grandparents of the subjects—the English at 20 percent, and Germany, Switzerland, and Austria (combined) at 15 percent.

Most of the subjects (81 percent) experienced intact families, both the mother and father being present through adolescence. Sixteen percent lost a parent by reason of divorce or separation by the time of their adolescence and, of the five cases remaining, three subjects lost parents by death and in two instances the Institute records are not clear. The rate of divorce or separation for the sample is in line with the national divorce and separation rates for 1930 and 1940 reported by Kephart (1961).

The size of the families of the subjects generally was not large: fifteen percent were only-children; 36 percent were from two-child families; 29 percent were from three-child families; 13 percent were from four-children families; and seven percent were from families with five or more siblings. Within these variously-sized families, the subjects occupied the

Table 2–2
Adolescent and Adult Social-economic Status, as Indexed
by the Edwards (1933) Scale

		OGS Sample Adolescent[a]	Adult[b]	GdS Sample Adolescent[a]	Adult[b]
I	Professional, semi-professional	10%	22%	18%	26%
II	Promoters, managers, officials	18	33	12	28
III	Clerks, small proprietors	29	28	44	23
IV	Skilled workers and foremen	31	12	13	16
V	Semi-skilled workers	8	4	7	4
VI	Unskilled workers	4	1	7	3

[a]Classified on the basis of the family's status during the subject's adolescence. For OGS subjects, who were adolescent during the depression, family status was determined on the basis of the father's usual occupation.
[b]Husband's occupation is the basis for status classification of the married women.

following ordinal or family positions: oldest, 27 percent; youngest, 42 percent; a middle position, 16 percent; and only-children, 15 percent.

The Edwards Scale (1933) of social status, computed for the families of the subjects at the time of their adolescence, shows a wide range with, however, a greater representation than is usual of families of comfortable means in both OGS and GdS samples. Table 2–2 shows proportionately more OGS fathers were businessmen than professionals, and more GdS fathers were professionals than businessmen. Furthermore, more GdS fathers tended to have clerical-white-collar jobs, whereas more OGS fathers tended to be skilled workers and foremen. The two samples, although somewhat different, both impress as representative of the stable, on-the-whole prosperous Berkeley community of the time.

THE SOCIAL ACHIEVEMENTS OF THE SUBJECTS AS ADULTS

At the time the subjects of both samples were approached as adults to evaluate their status in maturity and to begin the inquiry as to how and why they had developed along their now essentially-determined life paths, the OGS subjects were about 37 years old and the GdS subjects about 30 years of age. Although career and personality lines may change after the age of 30, by this age one is pretty much the kind of person he will continue to be. The subjects by this time had finished their education and had made most of their occupational, marital, and parental commitments. What were they like, what had they done, and what were they directed toward doing?

Of the entire sample, two percent (three subjects), members of the GdS sample, had not graduated from high school. Thirty percent of the entire sample were high school graduates only, and another 31 percent had experienced college work without, however, achieving graduation. Sixteen percent were college graduates and another 21 percent had gone on to graduate work of various kinds, so that there are three Doctors of Philosophy, two physicians, a lawyer, nine Masters of Art, three certified public accountants, and one dentist in the group. One important difference in educational level between the OGS and GdS samples is evident: none of the OGS women went on to graduate work although 21 percent of the GdS women have attended graduate school. Note, however, that each of the two samples has an equal proportion (15 percent) of female college graduates.

The heterogeneity in occupations of the male subjects is suggested by the following partial list: Doctor, dentist, pharmacist, architect, lawyer, professor, teacher, high school principal, engineering test analyst, designer, civil engineer, electrical engineer, commercial artist, food market manager, salesmen of various kinds, cabinet shop owner, manager of lumber company, night club owner, band leader, private detective, policeman, draftsman, machinist, linotype operator, garbage collector, construction foreman, carpet layer, delivery truck driver, janitor, butcher, bartender, and shoe repairman. No Indian chiefs are listed.

It is a sign of our era and of the range of the sample to note that one of the male subjects, since the time of the adult follow-up study, received a heart transplant but, nevertheless, died.

A majority of the women (60 percent) in the sample describe themselves as full-time housewives. But among the women working part- or full-time may be found: a doctor, accountant, landscape architect, professor, deputy superintendent of schools, teacher, department store buyer, nursery school director, shop owner, nurse, convalescent home owner, secretary, IBM operator, beautician, dental assistant, sales clerk, and teletype operator.

The classification of socio-economic status for the subjects as adults can be seen in Table 2–2. The subjects from the OGS and GdS samples have achieved quite similar levels of socio-economic status and the group as a whole has few representatives of occupations of low status.

All but five percent of the subjects have been married and 19 percent had been divorced by the time of the adult assessment. The divorce rate for the OGS sample is slightly higher than the rate for the GdS sample—22 percent versus 15 percent—but this difference may very well disappear as the GdS subjects become older and are subjected longer to the conjugal strains that eventuate for some in separation. Although the GdS adults have had a shorter time to produce children than the OGS subjects, the average number of offspring produced is the same for both studies (2.5 children). Altogether, the subjects had had about 450 children at the time they were assessed as adults. Seven percent of the married subjects had no children; nine percent had one child; 33 percent had two children; 27 percent had three children; 16 percent had four children, and eight percent had five or more children.

With respect to religion, 59 percent of the subjects are Protestant, but of these only a third attend church regularly. Catholicism has 16 percent of the subjects as adherents, two-thirds of these being regular churchgoers; there are three Jews in the sample, three followers of the Greek Orthodox Church, and two Mormons. Seventeen percent of the subjects as adults indicate they have no religious affiliation.

In sum, the surface characteristics of the subjects as adults offer no special surprises. The group appears prosperous and conventional enough in regard to vocation, family orientation, and religious profession and practice. Although the subjects were perhaps affected in important ways by the fact of their participation in a longitudinal study, they nevertheless manifest both a diversity and a typicality in their individual lives. Despite any influence introduced by study over the years, there is still enough variegation and relevance in their lives to seek for the order that must be there. The fact of their participation permits the effort to understand why these people turned out as they have.

Chapter III

THE ARCHIVAL MATERIAL AND THE CONSEQUENT RESEARCH APPROACH

THE RESEARCH COMPLICATIONS

Like Harold E. Jones, Jean Macfarlane, and other IHD psychologists, it was the potential in the archival material at IHD that first drew my interest to the longitudinal studies. As the present integrative effort was mounted, the nature and limitations of this already secured information necessarily influenced the research approach that was employed.

The OGS and the GdS had accumulated over thirty years an impressively large quantity of diverse information about their chosen subjects. The files bulk large and are filled with folder after folder of material: interest and attitude check lists, anthropometric measurements, X-rays, intelligence test records, teachers' ratings, Rorschach responses, tracings of psycho-physiological reactions, ratings of the home and mother, silhouettes of body builds, sociometric records, muscular coordination indices, interview protocols from subjects, parents, teachers, and spouses, news clippings involving the subjects, and more, much more. The sheer volume and breadth of the archival material gathered during the course of these two longitudinal studies is inundating, and beyond any effort at entire mastery.

Yet, for many purposes—and for the central intention of the present study—the information collected during the longitudinal studies and deposited in the archival files was insufficient or otherwise inadequate. Given a focal concern with personality and its development, much of what is filed can confidently be ignored as irrelevant. The archival material remaining, while still widely ranging, was usually not in the form of *data*, i.e., quantified or otherwise comparable and contextualized information permitting analysis and evaluation. The task of regularizing and transforming the IHD informational material into usable data was a formi-

31

dable one, onerous sometimes beyond a simple or polite description. Not everything that was done to collect or code the available information or to check on the usefulness or sufficiency of methodological decisions needs to be explicated. Rather, the concern here is with larger matters of research design and how the research plan ultimately evolved was shaped by adaptations and compromises necessitated by various pre-existing complications.

The Problem of Incomplete Information

The first problem was that, from procedure to procedure, or test to test, a great number of subjects have at least some missing data. The circumstance is perhaps inevitable. Over many years and many periods of study, subjects can miss an experiment or a planned measurement because of sickness or vacation or boredom or other bases for absenteeism. The effect of these missing data, however, especially when such departures from completeness are extensive, is to prevent neat, systematic and fully powerful comparisons and analyses of subjects and their developmental trends.

An indication of the pervasiveness of this problem is provided by the fate of an early and blithe decision to settle on a group of five different procedures applied solely to the OGS sample as a nuclear set of adolescent data to be evaluated. It was discovered that no one subject had scores on all five of these informational sources. Although for any subject reported on in this study, there are many scores and extensive information, if the requirement had been imposed that only the subjects to whom the same set of archival procedures was applied could be evaluated, there would be no one left to study. So the desire for tidiness, at this level, reluctantly but realistically was abandoned.

The Problem of Procedural Changes

The second problem was that, over time, procedures and testing tended to change. There are both fortunate and regrettable reasons for these changes in data collection through the years. And the consequences of procedural changes likewise can be either attractive or annoying. As new devices or tests or experimental situations are developed, it is certainly warranted to include them in the continuing assessment of the subjects being studied, so that the special contribution of these later procedures can be realized. As these new procedures aggregate and are added to the longitudinal program, however, the burden being imposed on subjects and on staff increases substantially, perhaps beyond the point of endurance.

On the other hand, the essence of the longitudinal approach is *continuity of evaluation,* in order that trends can be charted and juncture points identified. Procedures administered early should be administered as well at later stages, so that a firm comparative base is afforded. Of course, a poor procedure administered early is a poor procedure when administered late. Early decisions which prove wrong or ineffectual should not be permitted to control later options. Clearly, there is a properly inevitable tension in a longitudinal study—between continuity for continuity's sake on the one hand, and possible improvement of the study via change, on the other.

In the actual context of the ongoing longitudinal studies at IHD over the years, there were changes in the staff and changes in the sophistication of the subjects, with consequent changes of procedural emphasis. New techniques sometimes replaced older ones. Despite these changes, there is direct comparability of performance or scores at ages separated in time on a reasonable number of procedures or test forms. But those procedures for which there was a continuity of usage are not extensive or rich enough to serve as the base for a longitudinal study of personality development. This deficiency should not be cause for surprise or criticism. With the developmental increase in an individual's complexity with age, many assessment procedures that tapped personality early become inadequate or change in their meaning over the longer time span. Other assessment techniques that are extremely informative at later ages would have been inappropriate if applied earlier.

A priori, and now in retrospect, it is difficult to claim that the departures from procedural continuity on balance increased or diminished the sum of "knowledge" caught by the longitudinal assessments. What can be asserted is that there are insufficient personality-relevant data directly comparable over different time periods in the IHD projects. Therefore, there is little to investigate within the longitudinal approach given an insistence on procedural uniformity over the years. The research design had to accommodate to this reality but not be defeated by it.

The Problem of New Conceptual Foci

A third problem complicating ready use of the IHD archival material derives from the difference in conceptual language and professional concerns between contemporary psychologists and the psychologists of a generation ago. Psychological variables around which interest centers today are different from those preoccupying professionals when the longitudinal studies were initiated. Thus, we are concerned today with such notions as "identity formation" and "ego mechanisms," where the orientation of the 1920s and 1930s was generally less theoretical and was directed more toward practical matters such as "behavior problems" and "leadership." Also, in the earlier days, "premature theorizing" was eschewed with a consequent commitment to the usage of descriptive, empirical continua. The implicit expectation was that, in time, theoretical and organizing concepts would be drawn from this base of naturalistic description.

It may well be, as the French have it, that the more things change, the more they remain the same. I would not insist that contemporary conceptualizations necessarily represent an advance over earlier ways of viewing behavior. I happen to hope, and to think, this is the case but for the purposes of this particular study, it need simply be noted that we are all creatures of our time and that the present intention was to approach and to organize the archival information of an earlier era using contemporary concepts. This orientation has the consequence of permitting use, but not dependence upon, such archival information as is already transmorgrified or rationalized by concepts we would now avoid. In particular, where available, informational items recorded in the archives as raw, unmodified responses were used. By so doing, and given archival resources of sufficient intrinsic richness, the opportunity is developed of letting information collected in another time, for another purpose, speak to the conceptual questions of today.

The Problem of Differentiated Analysis

A fourth factor influencing the research approach devolved from the desire to merge into one larger sample the subjects from both the OGS and the GdS. An influential *a priori* conceptual interest in these longitudinal studies, from the outset, was to examine issues regarding the continuity-discontinuity, convergence-divergence, multipotentiality-equifinality of personality. The anticipated strategy of analysis was to differentiate subgroups of subjects or patterns of adaptation and to examine the lines of development of these alternative modes of being.

A troublesome aspect of this analytical orientation is that, in advance, one cannot be sure how subjects will distribute themselves among the several person-categories to be established. It might well be found that the subjects meeting the specified criteria for inclusion in a subgroup—a most fascinating subgroup—are too few to permit the objectification afforded by statistical description and analysis. If a person-category is defined by only two subjects, there is little security in characterizing the subgroup or in seeking to understand the antecedents or consequence of subgroup membership. However, that same subgroup, if defined perhaps by ten members, can be investigated for its homogeneities and its connections to other things and times. Thus there was worry, in anticipation and with no clear idea of what the situation ultimately would be, for the sample size of the smallest subgroups. Clearly, the intention of this orientation is best served by employing the largest possible sample, in this instance, by merging the OGS and the GdS samples.

Combining the OGS and the GdS samples could not be done casually. The merger entailed certain large consequences for the overall research design, and it was clear that various kinds of empirical support would have to be found to affirm this decision. Chapter IV reports on the way the study proceeded and the several checks employed to test the appropriateness of merging samples. For the present, simply note that the noncomparability of archives of the two studies does not pose a problem especially larger than the problem posed by noncomparability of the files for subjects *within* each study.

The Problem of Abundant Naturalistic Data

A fifth consideration which strongly influenced the research approach ultimately employed is uniquely related to the nature of these longitudinal studies (and perhaps all longitudinal studies). The longitudinal approach is basically an approach to individuals and to individual lines of development. Yet, as one looks solely at the quantitative tests and measures that accrue over the years with respect to the subject samples, one feels an insufficiency of knowledge about any one subject. In part, this insufficiency derives from the problems of missing data and measurement inadequacy or anachronism previously mentioned. But perhaps the larger reason for this sense of data meagreness is that, in general, the most crucial and expressive aspects of an individual may not be catchable by standardized tests or pre-planned experimental situations. Unpredictable events happen, and people react complexly. The psychologist simply cannot be prepared *a priori* for the dimensionality and objectification of the complex behaviors he may observe in uncontrolled life situations—where patterns of adaptation are actually formed.

At the same time that the tests and measures surrounding an individual subject in the longitudinal studies fail to provide a conviction that, by these indices, this particular individual can be well understood, other sources of information are most extensive and compelling. For each OGS subject, over the many years of the study, there had developed a file and record of anecdotes about his behavior in school, or social settings, of news clippings about his various doings, of remarks he had made that an observing psychologist had thought it relevant to jot down, of his private aspirations and fears as conveyed during interviews or the many informal encounters with staff members, and so on. The GdS subjects, in particular, had been directly confronted by interviews with staff members who

became increasingly familiar as the years went by. This kind of information, although haphazard and not strictly comparable, was most abundant. The data so obtained are opportune and alive, and sample incisively,
albeit unsystematically, from the lives of the subjects. In a most fundamental way, the richness of these longitudinal studies lies in the close
observation and recording of subject behaviors in their natural world,
rather than merely in the tests and situations to which the subject samples were exposed. The present effort to integrate the IHD longitudinal
studies and to study developmental processes would not have seemed
worthwhile given the small available set of immediately comparable data,
e.g., intelligence tests, physical measurements, and several short objective tests. It is the dossiers on the subjects, each containing a wealth of
information uniquely pertinent to a particular life, that persuaded us to
attempt the task and that give possibility to eventual understanding.

But how are these motley archival records, different for each subject,
to be employed so that comparative analyses become feasible? This consideration, like the others already noted, helped shape the design formulation ultimately settled upon.

THE RESEARCH ACCOMMODATIONS

The Time Periods Studied

It will be recalled that the Oakland Growth Study, as initially conceived
by Harold E. Jones and his colleagues, was to employ the genetic method
in an explanation of personality development in late childhood and adolescence (Jones, 1938), whereas the purpose of the Guidance Study was
to study "the course of development of numerous aspects of personality
and to investigate relationships between behavior patterns and other
variables" (Macfarlane, 1938a, p. 529) from the age of 21 months. Given
concern with merging these two studies so that the increased sample size
could permit more differentiated analyses, it is immediately apparent that
the personality information regarding the Guidance Study subjects, collected when these subjects were in their first decade, could not be
employed because there were simply no similar data available within the
OGS files.

Therefore, the research was constrained to three specified and clearly
partitioned time periods. Early adolescence (the Junior High School
years) and middle adolescence (the Senior High School years) were evaluated and the significance of these intervals for a third time of life—the
fourth decade, when career lines and patterns of adjustment have largely
stabilized (Adulthood)—was studied.

In developing the data and the sample to be described, a reverse sequence actually was employed. During the years 1957–58, and prior to the initiation of this particular analytical approach to these materials, all the available subjects from the two longitudinal studies had been invited to the Institute by Doctors Jones and Macfarlane for a follow-up study, so that their life status as adults could be evaluated. All subjects from both the OGS and GdS from whom information had been collected regarding their personalities and situation during their fourth decade and for whom there existed abundant data from the adolescent years are included in the present sample. The nature of the material and data regarding each subject collected during the follow-up study and taken from the files is described later in this chapter.

The Choice of a Rating Approach

The second fundamental research commitment, after the restriction to the designated time periods, was to the use of personality ratings contributed by multiple judges via the Q-sort procedure as a means of responding to the several methodological problems described earlier.

The enterprise of psychology is not yet ready to escape its reliance upon considered opinion as a basic kind of datum about people. Observations and impressions of an individual as coded in the form of a rating by a personality assessor are widely employed in psychology for a variety of reasons—they are simple to use, applicable in diverse and experimentally untrammelled circumstances, and can be directed toward the indexing of unusual and most complex psychological dimensions. Not least, personality ratings are impressively valid with regard to criteria concepts presently not measurable by alternate means within psychology.

A gnawing deficiency of personality ratings, as they have often been employed, is that they have been predicated on the impressions or formulations of a single observer whose idiosyncratic judgmental vagaries were unknown. Such data may not be reproducible and hence not fall within the scientific domain. But judgments derived independently from each of several raters rise above this limitation because their consensus has the reproducibility required without importantly losing the individual perception of the contributing observers.

The Q-sort procedure is simply a set of mildly technical rules for the scaling of a group of personality-descriptive variables (Q items) vis-à-vis a particular individual, so that the ultimate ordering of the Q items expresses well the judge's formulation of the personality of the individual being evaluated. The method, as applied in the present study, was intended to permit the comprehensive description, in contemporary psychodynamic terms, of an individual's personality in a form suitable for quantitative comparison and analysis.

In actual application, and for compelling reasons, the Q procedure imposes certain methodological constraints in that the judge must order the Q items into a designated number of categories and, most important, with an assigned number of items placed in each category. At one end of the judgmental continuum are placed those items most characteristic of the person being described or most "salient" in describing him. At the other end of the continuum are placed the items most uncharacteristic or most "salient" in a negative sense in formulating the personality description of the designated subject.

Conventionally, the Q items are printed separately on cards, a convenience which permits easy arrangement and rearrangement until the desired ordering is obtained. After the sorting, the placement of each of the items is recorded. The categories into which the judge has placed the Q statements are themselves numbered, from 9 through 1, with 9 by convention referring to the most characteristic end of the continuum and the number 1 to the least characteristic end. For each item, the number of the category in which it was placed is recorded as that item's value in the personality description. With the data entered in this fashion ready for subsequent analysis, the procedure is completed.

The description of the Q-sort procedure in the preceding several paragraphs is paraphrased from Block, 1961, pp. 3, 11–12. This earlier work discusses in greater detail and generality the necessity of ratings in personality research, the logic of combining raters and the rationale and rules for Q sorting. Within the present volume, remarks or exemplifications regarding this broad-gauge procedure are directed toward the particular research problems encountered in this longitudinal study and the ways in which the chosen methodology responded to the previously described shortcomings of the archival material.

Regarding *the problem of missing data,* the use of a rating scheme permits specification of an individual's placement on a dimension if the judge believes he has *sufficient* information, *from whatever source,* to make a sensible decision. In particular, the judge is permitted to place items about which he has uncertain evidence in middle, essentially nondiscriminating categories. There is no requirement, under this approach, that for all subjects the information be of the same particular kind; rather, some general sense of sufficiency of information (admittedly vaguely defined and employed) must infuse the personality assessor and permit him a confidence in his evaluations. If he is wrong in having confidence or extrapolates unwisely in constructing his character evaluation, then he is contributing error to the study. But although errors of this kind can obscure relationships, with the design controls employed (see Chapter

IV), judges' extrapolations could not erect artifacts that would be mistaken as realities.

Regarding *the problem of procedural changes over time,* the use of a rating scheme can again rise above the changes and particulars of method and of scores, provided that the information available for each subject, whatever its source, continues to have relevance for the dimensions to be rated.

Regarding *the problem of new conceptual foci,* the use of a rating scheme offers the opportunity of introducing contemporaneous variables not specifically of interest at earlier times. The information required for ratings on these new dimensions must, of course, reside somewhere in the archival file of each subject, even if not earlier recognized as present.

Regarding *the problem of differentiated analysis,* the use of a rating scheme develops a way of making commensurate the OGS and GdS subject samples so that more venturesome analyses become feasible. The application of a common set of rating variables to the subjects from the two different studies brings them into the same conceptual and metrical framework so that the study may proceed to the kinds of questions which motivated the merging. Of course, there must be confidence that the two initially separate and different studies each contain sufficiently comprehensive information for each subject so that when comparable data are created by the Q procedure, the resulting scores are commensurate in a valid as well as a Procrustean sense. The next chapter will report on this matter.

Regarding *the problem of abundant naturalistic data,* the use of a rating scheme offers perhaps the only way of registering the compelling behavioral information recorded in the file of each subject. This "free response" material is richly descriptive when aggregated for a subject, and brings him "alive" in a way that no objective test score by itself can. Too often, data of this kind are set aside as interesting but unusable. For the present research, it was felt to be vital to incorporate this kind of information. The natural record more than test scores was to influence the summary description of each subject and only through a rating procedure could this intention be realized.

Fixing on a Set of Personality Variables

A commitment to the use of ratings required the further commitment to a set of personality variables—in the present instance, Q items—to be rated. Here, the choice was determined—or rather, over-determined—by the fact that, prior to the formal inception of the present integrative effort, a small number of the IHD subjects had been described as adults by means of a slightly modified version of the California Q set (CQ set) (Block, 1961).

The Q items constituting the CQ set were carefully evolved over a number of years with the intention of permitting, by their arrangement, the characterization of any kind of personality. The developmental history and rationale of the CQ set is provided elsewhere (Block, 1961).

The modification of the CQ set employed throughout the present study is presented in Appendix A. The changes it incorporates are for the most part minor and to some extent regressive since these changes were not based upon a rationale and a consensus. The usage by IHD of a slightly revised version of the CQ set rather than the standard form came about somewhat fortuitously and occurred prior to the initiation of the present integrative study. In order to get this particular research effort underway, it was necessary at the time to plunge into a welter of negotiations within IHD and to make a number of compromises. Thus, on the understanding that IHD had already developed an appreciable backlog of personality formulations using the changed version of the CQ set, it seemed wise for intra-institutional reasons to continue with the IHD modification of the CQ set to describe the subjects as adults despite concerns regarding the modifications, data comparablity, and subsequent analytic complications that were thus introduced. It was only later discovered that the early Q descriptions that had prompted the compromise decision in fact were quite few in number and further, had been developed under circumstances that made them methodologically unacceptable.

In order to describe the IHD subjects as adolescents, two additional Q sets were employed. The first, containing 104 items, was a further modified version of the adult CQ set, adapted in the hope of more aptly characterizing adolescent personality structure and dynamics. Ninety items in this Q set are parallel to those in the CQ set used to describe adults. This Q set is presented in Appendix B, and is designated as the Adolescent CQ set.

The second Q set designed for adolescents emphasized the interpersonal behaviors of the subjects during this period. It contains 63 items, presented in Appendix C. Differential behavior with peers and with adults, attitudes toward parents, roles in peer groups and the like are the concerns of this set of descriptive variables. It is designated as the Interpersonal Q set.

The Data Available from the Adult Period

In 1957–58, the Ford Foundation provided funds to bring to IHD all the available subjects from the OGS and GdS samples. Many Institute subjects still reside in the San Francisco Bay Area. A special enlistment effort and the provision of some travel funds encouraged a number of subjects who had moved away to return for several days required.

The follow-up study employed, as its primary tool, an intensive interview with each subject. The OGS and GdS interview intentions were fairly comparable. Interview topics included: close and extensive stocktaking of self and of marriage; a bringing up to date of the records with regard to life, career, and experiences during the interval since adolescence; a retrospective account of the subject's developmental years (through adolescence); reflections on family interaction in the subject's present role as a parent, contrasted with family interaction in his former role as a child; his ambitions, defeats, pleasures, and despairs and so on, and on. For some of the subjects in the follow-up study, the interview proved to be a particularly important personal experience because it represented a confrontation of self with usually unacknowledged aspirations toward purpose and meaningfulness.

The interviews had an average length of twelve hours—the length of time with each subject being a function of his personal schedule, talkativeness, motivation, and psychological accessibility. The material developed during the interview was integrated and summarized in the form of a written report and evaluation of the subject by the interviewer. Interviewers included verbatim remarks where these seemed cogent or illustrative. The reports on the interviews of each adult subject were most carefully prepared, for it was early recognized that these protocols would contain the primary information collected by the follow-up study. It should be kept in mind that the characterizations of adult personality on which this investigation depends for many of its analyses derived fundamentally from the interviews as conducted and reported by interviewers who did not know how their reports subsequently would be utilized in this, then unanticipated, study.

Some differences in interview procedures between the OGS and GdS warrant mention. Each OGS subject was interviewed by only one psychologist. Six experienced clinical psychologists and one psychiatric social worker served as the team of interviewers. The GdS subjects were interviewed by five different staff members, each interviewing in regard to his assigned set of topics. Presumably, "the several pairs of eyes" judging each GdS subject might provide a consensually more valid evaluation of that subject than does the solitary perception provided by the single OGS interviewer. But, in compensation, it may be countered that the OGS interviewer enjoyed fuller knowledge of the subject he was to evaluate. The specific methodological issue of comparative validity here cannot be responded to properly, given the data available. Later analyses and relationships to other entirely separate data affirm a useful validity in both interview procedures and the personality formulations derived therefrom.

Beyond the extensive interview procedures, the comparability of the OGS and GdS follow-up studies is to be found in the administration of the Rorschach and TAT projective techniques, and the California Psychological Inventory (CPI), a 480-item personality inventory. The CPI will be used in analyses later in this book; the projective procedures have not been employed in the present study, partly by preference and partly by prior agreement. The OGS follow-up program included various experimental measures, the Minnesota Multiphasic Personality Inventory and repetition of certain attitude scales administered during adolescence; the GdS follow-up program included interviews with the spouses of subjects and a checklist. None of these follow-up data, unique to the separate longitudinal studies, was used in developing the adult CQ formulations. Because of a desire for an approximate comparability of the data-basis from which the adult personality characterizations were to be derived, these latter, nonmatchable data were excluded from the consideration of the judges.

The Data Available from the Adolescent Period

For each of the longitudinally studied subjects, a voluminous file of information and test data exists from his adolescent years. From this material, for each subject, "case assemblies" were developed for the junior high school, and separately, the senior high school periods. A subject's adolescent case assembly, from either the OGS or the GdS studies, included, when available, such information as school grades, comments and ratings on sundry variables by teachers, ratings of social or interview behavior by IHD staff members, intelligence test performance (on the Stanford-Binet and the Wechsler tests), Rorschach protocols, TAT protocols, peer sociometric ratings, the subject's reports of areas of agreement or disagreement with his parents, his wishes for possessions, news clippings in which he figured, his attitudes toward various issues, his likes and dislikes, and so on. The general principle for data inclusion was that information reflecting the subject as presented by himself or by Institute staff members or by teachers was included; excluded from the case assemblies were data derived from parent interviews which were abundant in the GdS but rare in the OGS.

The case assemblies derived from the OGS data differed in marked ways from those derived from the GdS data. The OGS adolescents presented themselves through a series of objective tests that were supplemented by reports, entered in their dossiers, recounting conversations between the subject and staff members or between the subject and his adolescent peers regarding various personal, school, or familial concerns.

In addition, a great number of observation-based accounts and ratings of social behavior was available for OGS subjects. Clubhouses, staffed by OGS personnel, had been established at both junior and senior high schools for these youngsters, providing the opportunity of observing our adolescents interacting among themselves and with adults in a naturalistic setting. Further, OGS adolescent subjects had filled out a number of interest, opinion, social attitude, and activity records, and, because most of the OGS subjects had attended the same schools, it had been simple for the schools to provide the Institute with attendance records, health forms, changes of programs, and other indicants of the adolescence of our subjects. But direct interviews with subjects are infrequent in the OGS adolescent case assemblies.

The GdS adolescent case assemblies contained essentially the accounts of biennial interviews held directly with the subjects. These tended to be long, scrupulously recorded meetings of the adolescent with a GdS staff member with whom he had often developed a personal relationship. The interview notes are sufficiently extensive and rich so that a picture of the adolescent emerges. An important limitation of the interviews is that only one interviewer is involved. There are few objective non-interview-based measures or procedures in the GdS adolescent case assemblies. Thus, by way of contrast, the OGS adolescent data are heavily weighted by self-reports and staff observations that are multiple in origin but not especially psychodynamic; the GdS adolescent data are interviewer-dependent but are more directly transformable into personality formulations.

To each case assembly was added an informational sheet containing a limited number of life context facts about the subject. The information provided consisted of the subject's birth place and birth date, the years of education of his parents, the religion and marital status of his parents, the occupation of his parents, the number, age, and sex of his siblings, and the presence of other adults in the household. Certain indications of physical characteristics which would be apparent to the casual observer early in junior high school or late in senior high school were also entered into appropriate case assemblies: the subject's height, weight, and androgyny rating, relative strength and coordination, his hearing and visual defects (if any), complexion, illness frequency, and any additional physical features or capacities deemed to have psychological relevance.

Certain test or rating data or antecedant family data available from the adolescent and adult periods were withheld from the judges in order to provide later independent or extended bases of validation for inferences drawn from the assemblies or follow-up interviews. These separate data resources will be described in Chapter VII, before they are brought into play.

The Research Design Summarized

It is crucial to recognize that the two case assemblies—JHS and SHS—carefully compiled for each subject, were strictly independent of each other; there were no data except for certain of the life context facts which appeared in both assemblies for a given subject. And, of course, the follow-up information available for each subject as an adult was developed with no reference or pre-formulation based upon adolescent data available regarding him. These three time-separated sets of data, different in important respects for each subject, were the primary material of the study, around which most of the analyses are organized. By selecting and partitioning the data available for a subject, extensive material for each of the three time periods—JHS, SHS, and adulthood—was aggregated. These non-overlapping sets of information provide the informational grist for the analytical mill.

A second feature of the research design, beyond the independence of the data for the different time periods, was the use of non-overlapping sets of independently judging psychologists to draw inferences from the several case assemblies. The Q-sort procedure was employed so that the personality formulations issuing from a variety of psychologist-judges readily could be made comparable and usable. Judgments and their use are complicated matters, and the next chapter spells out, in some detail, the judging process employed.

Further significant features of the research design, the analytical approach, and the data employed for validity supports will be encountered and discussed in later chapters, where appropriate.

Chapter IV

THE JUDGING PROCESS

The research reported in this volume is highly dependent on the use of clinically trained judges as a means of codifying information and incidents that otherwise would not be comparable among subjects. Because the commitment to the use of judges as instruments for the reduction and metricizing of data was so heavy, it is necessary to present (and for the reader to understand) the general logic and the specific details surrounding this portion of the study.

The Judges

In all, a total of twenty-six clinical psychologists and one psychiatric social worker were involved in the present study, which took formal shape in 1960–61. All but two of these judges at the time had 10 or more years of clinical experience; twenty-one had doctorates, primarily from the University of California, although Yale, Harvard, and Minnesota were also represented among the judges' backgrounds. As further indications of the nature of the judges employed, a number of them had clinical and research publications of their own, many had had a personal analysis, and many were engaged in the part-time private practice of psychotherapy and psychodiagnostics. Eleven of the judges were male and sixteen were female.

Orienting and Calibrating the Judges

The judges, in two separate groups, underwent a preliminary orientation and calibration period. All of the judges had had prior experience, of course, in developing clinical formulations of the patients they saw in their professional work, but an introduction was required to the logic and formalities of the judging process to be used in the study. Accordingly, the case assembly for an actual subject was duplicated and given to each of the participating judges (a different subject was used as a specimen case for each group of judges). After reading the materials, each judge formulated a *CQ* description and an Interpersonal *Q* description of the common subject and wrote a short clinical evaluation. The comparable *Q* descriptions of the judges were then correlated with each other, and an individual report was prepared for each judge identifying the particular *Q* items he had placed at values which were highly discrepant from those in the group's consensus.

At a subsequent meeting, the judges and the researchers discussed the case, clarified the meanings of particular *Q* items, and suggested a number of improvements in the wording of the items which were accepted. The judges were given the orientation of developing general agreement and understanding among themselves as to the meaning of each *Q* item so that discrepancies in item placement would not be due to diverse interpretations of language or item phrasing. But, it was additionally emphasized that high agreement *per se* among judges was *not* a criterion; the truly different understanding of a subject by a judge was an entirely acceptable source of disagreement.

The materials of a second case assembly then were distributed, and the sequence of sorting and discussing of item placement discrepancies was repeated. The first group of judges was introduced to the judging process via a junior high boy's case assembly and then the data describing a senior high girl; the second group of judges was calibrated using first a junior high girl's assembly and then the information describing a senior high boy. After two trial cases, and the consequent group discussions, it was felt that the judges understood the task and the medium of communication they were required to employ. Thereafter, the judges no longer met together and each embarked upon his particular portion of the judging task.

A number of problems surrounded the judging process, some anticipated and some soon generated, on which a conceptual decision was required. Thus, the judges were instructed as follows:

1. The *Q* descriptions were to be formulated from an *ipsative* frame of reference, i.e., the saliency or decisiveness of the variable in shaping or characterizing the subject's behavior was to be the criterion for item placement.

2. When a subject provided clear evidence of disjunctive behavior, e.g., being both extremely overcontrolled and extremely undercontrolled, or being both extremely dependent and extremely independent, judges were asked to indicate both of these extreme qualities as characteristically salient for the subject. Although superficially contradictory, the

conjoining of opposites within an individual is a well-recognized psychological phenomenon. Judges were explicitly enjoined against averaging such disjunctive behaviors.

3. When the behavior of a subject varied in a more graded or continuous way (e.g., showing social presence in one situation but less poise in another), judges were to place the relevant Q item so as to express some kind of average for the subject's behavior. The likely reason for such behavioral variability is the effect of context. Within the Interpersonal Q set, an effort had been made to specify some context-dependent behaviors. But this kind of specification could not be made extensively because the data were insufficiently detailed or systematic to keep up with the complications thus introduced. Therefore, the decision to take an implicit average seemed warranted for such behaviors. If the averaging procedure provided a lesser truth than in principle might be achieved, it nevertheless provided a substantial and useful one. Under the circumstances, there was hardly an alternative.

4. The level of interpretation of Q items was to be the behavioral or manifest level, unless the item specifically indicated otherwise and called for a clinical judgment of the subject's intrapsychic structure and the inferred pushes and pulls characterizing him.

5. Besides the Q descriptions, each judge was asked to provide a clinical summary in his own words, characterizing the subject in ways or with qualifications he could not convey using the Q items. By so doing, the judge could escape the occasional constraints imposed by the Q language and could offer a more vivid picture of the subject.

6. For each subject, the judge rated on a 5-point scale his confidence in the formulation he had offered.

During the 27 months required for the judging phase of this research, each judge was provided periodically with an index of his level of agreement with the other judges who had evaluated the same subset of cases and, as a frame of reference, the average level of agreement attained by judges vis-à-vis their peers. When the judging process was about one-third completed for each individual judge, the items he had employed thus far in a non-differentiating way were identified. By this stage, most of the judges had evaluated an appreciable number of cases and, presuming a diversity among the subjects assigned to a judge, it was expected that each Q item would manifest a reasonable amount of variance within a judge's set of formulations. Since the focus of the study was on subjects and not judges, a persistent tendency on the part of a judge to place a particular item uniformly at a high or intermediate or low position did not contribute to the item-variance sought. Only six judges showed a tendency toward non-differentiation, with only three or four items for each judge being involved. Upon being informed of these findings, these judges subsequently manifested increased variability in their use of these few items, presumably or hopefully introducing discrimination. However, in some instances discrepant judges felt their item placements were warranted by the cases they had encountered thus far.

The Assignment of Cases to Judges

The clinical psychologists serving as judges contributed their efforts on a part-time basis, superimposing the research requirements upon already crowded schedules. Not all of the 27 judges were able to participate during the entire course of the project. Of the 27, 17 judges read and evaluated OGS adult material, 21 the OGS adolescent material, 17 the GdS adult material, and 18 the GdS adolescent material.

For each case assembly of the JHS and SHS material, at least three judges were employed; the evaluations of the adult material were contributed by two judges for 47 percent of the adult subjects and by at least three judges for the remaining 53 percent. The plan to employ three judges to evaluate every adult subject regrettably had to be abandoned because of insufficient access to funds. With respect to certain subjects, the assigned judges manifested insufficient agreement and for these subjects, as will be described below, additional judge-evaluations were employed in order that a consensus might emerge.

Judges were assigned to cases in a manner which systematically varied the judge combinations. A crucial feature of judge assignment was that no judge evaluated a subject at more than one time period. Insofar as possible, an attempt was made to allocate cases so that each judge evaluated comparable numbers of males and females and equivalent numbers of JHS, SHS, and adult cases. This goal could not be achieved completely, given the necessary vagaries of the judges' schedules, and the reduced degrees of freedom of combination encountered near the end of the subject-judging period. Nevertheless, the general intention of diversifying and balancing the judge-subject assignments was realized reasonably well. For the 170 JHS case assemblies, there were 125 unique judge trios, 21 twice-repeated judge trios, and one thrice-repeated judge trio. For the 160 SHS case assemblies, there were 139 unique judge trios, nine twice-repeated judge trios, and one thrice-repeated judge trio. For the ninety adult cases evaluated by three judges, there were 59 unique judge trios, 11 twice-repeated judge trios, and three thrice-repeated judge trios; for the 81 adult cases evaluated by two judges, there were 20 unique judge pairs, 10 twice-repeated judge pairs, 3 thrice-repeated judge pairs, two four-times repeated judge pairs, two judge pairs repeated five times, one judge pair used six times, and another judge pair employed eight times. The higher incidence of reiteration of particular judge combinations in evaluating the adult material was undesirable, but also unavoidable since it was a consequence of earlier Institute administrative decisions. The subsequent constraints of funds prevented further judge-evaluations to escape the possible bias introduced into the adult Q formulations by repeated judge pairings.

The design presumption underlying the emphasis on a reasonably large sample of judges, permutation of judge assignments, and the use of multiple, independently evaluating judges for each subject was that by so doing, the ensuing consensual personality formulation established to represent each subject at each of the time periods would achieve substantial validity. Too often, when ratings are employed in psychological research, they are the expression of a private set of assumptions held by a solitary judge or perhaps a pair of symbiotically-linked (and bias-sharing) raters. The use of several, independently formulating judges largely escapes the limitations of other studies, wherein a single, perhaps idiosyncratic judge is used. Further, the use of several Q descriptions for a given subject fosters reliability in the composite or consensual evaluation that is then derivable. Reliable composite evaluations based upon diversified judge combinations selected from a relatively large and heterogeneous pool of judges cannot be understood as due to the *folie à trois* of a rather special and unrepresentative group of judges. Thus, the judging procedures were designed to develop Q characterizations of the subjects which were reliable, relatively independent of the judging proclivities of any particular judge, and representative of the implicit principles of personality evaluation held by contemporary clinical psychologists.*

The Use of Additional Judges to Evaluate Certain Cases

The paucity of subjects available in most longitudinal investigations has constituted a major barrier to close, differentiated analyses. In the present study, therefore, there was great reluctance to discard cases when the initially assigned three judges (or two judges for many adult cases) were unable to arrive at a consensual picture of the subject. Failure of consensus could be due to deficient performance by one or more of the judges, or it could arise from an intrinsic psychological elusiveness of the particular subject. To clarify matters, and to salvage as many of the irreplaceable subjects as possible, the cases for which the reliability of the composite Q formulation was low were assigned to additional, re-sort judges if they met the following criteria of unreliability:

1. Those adolescent cases for which the reliability of the initial composite of *either* the CQ or the Interpersonal formulations was less than .60 were evaluated by an additional judge.

*Various analyses, which will not be reported here, indicate that the subgroup of subjects who required additional sorts were not homogeneous in nature.

2. Those adolescent cases for which the reliabilities of the initial composite of *both* the CQ and the Interpersonal formulations were less than .65 were evaulated by an additional judge.

3. Those adolescent cases for which *either* the reliability of the initial composite of the CQ or of the Interpersonal formulations was between .60 and .65 where the other Q composite enjoyed a reliability of greater than .65 were evaluated by an additional judge, provided one or both of the following conditions obtained: two of the three initial judges agreed reasonably well (the agreeing pair correlating more than .50 with each other and/or two of the three judges in the initial judge trio placed in the bottom quartile of judges in regard to average degree of consensuality.

4. Those adult cases for which the reliability of the initial composite CQ formulation was less than .65 were evaluated by an additional judge.

These rules were framed so that reliability in general would be raised, with particular emphasis on raising the reliability of the Q formulations derived from the adolescent material. The re-sort effort, limited as it was, was directed toward cases most likely to be benefited. More than one additional judge was employed when the pattern of judge intercorrelations suggested a consensus could yet emerge. Decisions as to cutting points and pattern designations were arbitrary in reasonable ways.

With respect to the adolescent material, the initially assigned set of three judges provided sufficient reliability in 65 percent of the cases. Of the remaining 35 percent, four judges were employed for 26 percent of the adolescent case assemblies. With respect to the adult material, two judges provided sufficient reliability for 47 percent of the cases and three judges were sufficient for another 31 percent. The supplementary evaluations involved four judges for 15 percent of the cases, five judges for 6 percent, and six judges for 1 percent of the adult subjects.

It may be of interest to note that the OGS adolescent case assemblies required somewhat more additional evaluation than the GdS case assemblies. On the other hand, the OGS adult interviews required fewer additional judgments than did the GdS adult interview material.

It can be argued that all the Q evaluations available for a particular subject should be employed in developing the composite personality formulation to be employed subsequently, on the democratic principle of one judge—one vote. Instead, however, it was decided to select the three most consensual judges and base the composite evaluation only on these three. This decision is by no means an ideal one since certain similarities in evaluation that may have been based on chance or stereotypy were treated as true agreements. But this decision, if wrong, does not prejudice the results issuing from later, independent analyses; these subsequent analyses can only have their power attenuated by this methodological choice. The alternative choice, of weighting equally all the available Q formulations for a subject, seemed unwise, for it gives credence to judges who, characteristically or in regard to certain subjects, were comparatively idiosyncratic in their personality assessments.* Furthermore, when judge agreement is low, the resulting composite for a subject contains little or no variance and therefore might as well be dropped from subsequent analyses.

The Reliabilities of the Composite Q Formulations

The reliability of the composite Q formulations was calculated by averaging the z transformations of inter-judge correlations, then applying the Spearman-Brown reliability formula for three (or where appropriate, two) sets of observations. The reliabilities were generally satisfactory, the mean reliabilities for formulations derived from the several data sections ranging between .72 and .78. The reliabilities of the Interpersonal formulations tended to be a little higher than those for the CQ formulations, but the difference was slight and perhaps expectable since the Interpersonal Q set emphasized items with a specified behavioral reference, while the CQ set more often required inference. Appendix D reports these results in greater detail.

The selection of consensual judges for the re-sorted cases did not especially influence the reliabilities of the composite formulations that were derived. For all re-sorted cases, the reliability of the composite based upon the three most consensual judges and the reliability of the composite based upon all judges was compared and only slight differences were found. The explanation here is due to the operation of two counterbalancing factors: the use of only three judges as compared to more than three judges works toward lowering the reliability of the three-judge composite; on the other hand, the greater agreement among the smaller set of judges heightens the reliability of their composite evaluation. Overall, these factors balanced out, the mean differences in the reliability of these two kinds of composites rarely exceeding $\pm.05$.

It will be remembered that the research design called for setting a floor underneath the reliability of the Q formulations being laboriously developed. Thus, no subject was studied further for whom these minimal reliabilities in evaluation could not be developed.

It should also be noted before continuing that these reliabilities are the reliabilities of a total personality characterization, i.e., these are reliabilities of *ipsatively*-ordered data. The reliabilities of individual Q items, when these items are treated as normative variables (cf., Chapter V) is another, albeit related matter, and will be reported later.

---

*The consensus achieved by the judges conceivably could be due largely to routinized or stereotypic Q descriptions. A later section of this chapter evaluates this possibility.

The Interagreement of Individual Judges

Although the reliabilities of the composite evaluations reflect the antecedent inter-judge agreements which underlie them, it is informative to report directly on the level and variability of this agreement for individual judges. In general, the level of interjudge agreement was consistent, ranging around an overall mean of .511, with an overall standard deviation of .155. This mean includes the contribution of several judges whose interjudge agreements tended to be low in regard to the OGS material and who were among those who discontinued their participation.

The Influence Upon the Judges of Stereotypes Regarding Adolescence

This study not only depended heavily upon judges as personality assessment instruments, but also required the judges in dealing with the adolescent data to assess individuals distant in time and often not described in contemporaneous terms. Adults often have nostalgic projective fantasies about the nature of adolescence and the judges were no exception. They certainly held personally or culturally or professionally influenced conceptions regarding adolescence. Were they letting these conceptions or "stereotypes" importantly influence their Q descriptions? Acknowledging this possible stereotype effect, however, it should also be noted that stereotypes about adolescence are not to be confused with the very real homogeneities one might expect to find more readily among adolescents than among adults. These homogeneities occur because, inevitably, common societal and maturational experiences during the adolescent years limit the opportunities for individual divergence. Thus, in evaluating the possibilities of stereotyped, nonindividuated personality assessments by our judges, it is also necessary to respect the ways in which a stereotype of adolescence might well be veridical. Some positive relationships between a stereotype of adolescence and actual adolescents should exist, but these should not be so powerful as to suggest that adolescents cannot be individuated. Further, it may be expected that certain adolescents may exemplify the adolescent stereotype more than others.

To evaluate these matters, before a judge formally began any case evaluations, he was asked to describe, via the CQ and Interpersonal Q sets, his personal conception of a modal JHS boy, a modal JHS girl, a modal SHS boy, and a modal SHS girl. When a judge finished his schedule of evaluation of actual adolescents, he was asked again to Q-sort his understanding of these four adolescent stereotypes. The second, terminal, set of modal Q descriptions was sought in order to ascertain the effect on a judge of the experience of reading and evaluating a great deal of adolescent material. There proved to be almost no change in the composite stereotypes the judges advanced at the outset and at the completion of their evaluations of adolescence. Their correlations were never less than .92 and so this report limits itself to the initially contributed modal descriptions or "stereotypes."

As a first, descriptive approach to the stereotype problem, each judge's stereotype was correlated with his Q formulations of actual cases. Only the age-and sex-appropriate stereotypes were applied, i.e., a judge's Q description of a JHS girl was correlated only with that judge's stereotype of a JHS girl.

In general, low positive correlations on the order of .2 (or four percent of the variance) were found, suggesting perhaps a small influence from stereotypes, but also and alternatively a certain modality to adolescent personality. Comparison of group means indicates that girls are judged in a less individuated fashion than boys (.24 vs. .17). This result perhaps finds its explanation in the greater emphasis placed by our culture on the conformity of girls than on the conformity of boys. The Interpersonal formulations relate more to the stereotypes than do the Core descriptions (.22 vs. .19), a result understandable in terms of the concerns of adolescents with behavioral uniformity even when their underlying personalities may be quite different.

Several judges have relatively high means and sizable variances, suggesting that their personal means are elevated by an occasional high correlation of their stereotype with an adolescent subject. Almost without exception, closer analysis of the subjects evaluated by these judges reveals that the trios of judges describing these cases all tended to characterize these individuals as conforming with their adolescent stereotypes. Thus, there are indications that certain adolescents glaringly exemplify the commonly held and not invalid stereotype of adolescence. In later chapters (Chapters VIII and IX), the personality characteristics and developmental fate of these prototypical adolescents is examined.

In order to establish that judges were responding to the adolescent data in an individuated, more-than-stereotypic way, two related analyses were undertaken. In the first analysis, for every judge and for every adolescent case, the levels of agreement (i.e., correlations) were computed between that judge's stereotype of adolescence and the two Q formulations contributed separately by the two other judges who had evaluated the particular adolescent case. The mean of these two correlations was taken. Correlations then were computed between that judge's individualized Q description of the designated adolescent and the two Q descriptions contributed by the two remaining judges of the same adolescent. Again, the mean of the two correlations was taken. Thus, two comparable indices were available for each judge-case combination—an index of the predictive effectiveness of the judge's stereotype for that case and an index of the predictive effectiveness of that judge's individualized Q description. The question may now be asked: *Is a judge's individualized evaluation of an adolescent case more predictive of other evaluations of the same case than is his monolithic modal description or stereotype of adolescence?* The answer to this question is overwhelmingly affirmative—when each of the adolescent cases are examined for each judge (combining JSH and SHS, a total of 330 cases $\times$ 3 judges), the judge's individualized Q sort is superior to the stereotype Q description in 929 of 990 instances for the CQ formulations and 905 of 990 instances for the Interpersonal formulations.

The second analysis, not entirely independent of the first, involves computations for each judge-subject combination of the correlation between the judge's stereotype and his individualized Q description. Again there was available, and paired with this index, the mean correlation between that judge's individualized Q description of the adolescent and the Q description provided by the two other judges of that adolescent. Thus, two comparable indices were available—an index of the predictive effectiveness of a judge's individualized Q description (his sort of the actual adolescent compared with the other two sorts of that adolescent) and an index of the possible influence of his stereotypic description (his sort of the actual adolescent compared with his own stereotype of adolescence). The query now becomes: *Is the judge responding more to the individual adolescent as separately proclaimed by the other two judges than he is to his own stereotype of adolescence?* Again, the answer is strikingly affirmative—for the CQ set, the individualized Q description agrees better with the other judges than with the judge's own stereotype in 933 of 990 instances; for the Interpersonal Q set, the comparison is positive in 943 of 990 instances.

There are a number of other analytical possibilities worthy of exploration with the stereotypes that bear upon the judging behavior of psychologists, but these will be left for other times and other investigators. The focus of the present study is upon *using* judges as instruments of personality assessment, not upon the multifarious components underlying the interpersonal perception of sophisticated clinicians. This latter problem is of great interest but not for these pages. The demonstration that stereotypes do not nullify the contributions of the judges is, for the present purposes, necessary, and also quite sufficient.

Additional Quality Controls and Checks on the Q Formulations

Beyond evaluating the possibility of an important stereotype effect in the Q formulations, a number of other checks on potential artifacts within these judge-developed data were applied.

Thus, the amount of material available for each subject was found to have no relation to the personality description formed by judges. The presence or absence of certain test protocols, e.g., adolescent Rorschachs, did not have influence on the assessments of subjects. There was a slight tendency for cases that the judges expressed confidence in judging to enjoy a higher reliability. No simple relationships between the confidence of the judge in the description he offered and the nature of that description was found. Over time of judging, the judge's Q evaluations showed no trends toward non-individuated assessments or toward some modal personality types. Q formulations developed late in the prolonged judging process were not different in respect to reliability or character portrayal than Q formulations developed early.

The justifiability of merging the OGS and GdS samples in the light of the different data bases underlying the two studies was a special concern. Thus, judges were asked, after finishing their OGS evaluations and, separately, their GdS evaluations, to arrange the Q items so as to express their sense of the adequacy with which these items could be evaluated, given the information available within the OGS (or GdS) material. The correlation between the composite assessment of OGS information adequacy and of GdS information adequacy was .83 for the CQ set and .62 for the Interpersonal Q set. The magnitude of the correlations suggests, particularly with respect to the CQ set, that there was little difference in the judged informational adequacy of the two studies and that the judges' formulations reflected primarily the difficulty inherent in the level of inference required. Nevertheless, a few items are distinguishable as differentially specifiable within the two data sources. The OGS material was judged to be more adequate primarily with respect to interpersonal variables, e.g., "attention-getting behavior with peers," "tends to arouse liking and acceptance in peers." The GdS material was deemed more helpful in rating attitudes toward family, e.g., "perceives parents as fair, equitable, and reasonable," "feels his father is a respected man as judged by societal standards."

The differences between the two studies with respect to the judged relevance of their data for certain interpersonal variables reflect their different initial orientations but were not considered especially damaging to the aspiration of merging the samples. The great majority of Q variables did not manifest this effect. Moreover, the different degrees of "judging comfort" for a few variables does not, of course, imply different degrees of validity for these several variables. The lesser certainty with which a variable is judged does not in any way predestine its relationships with other independent antecedent or consequent measures. A second, more persuasive argument for letting the two samples remain merged is that later analyses (cf. Chapters VI through IX) were systematically checked to see whether a subject's placement on a dimension or within a category could be understood as due to the study from whence he came. Without exception, subjects from *both* studies were found to be intermixed on any classifying basis that was later employed.

Nevertheless, the OGS sample and the GdS sample differ during their adult period in regard to, for example, their responses on personality inventories, achieved social status, educational attainment, and vocational directions. Paralleling these objective differences between the samples are certain differences between the samples with respect to the psychological content of their Q evaluations. Conceivably, these differences in the personality assessments issuing from the two studies are due to the different data available within each of these two programs. The interpretation preferred here, however, bolstered by the nature of the objective differences between the two samples as adults, is to consider these differences in personality ratings as valid indicators of the ways in which these samples, in fact, were importantly different in their initial sampling basis. Further separation of the psychological characteristics of the OGS and GdS samples might also be expected as a consequence of the different kinds of motivation employed by each study to encourage continued participation of their subjects. The reader can form his own judgment regarding this matter; the bias here, *a priori* and *post hoc,* is that the overlaps between the two samples are far more impressive than their differences and that the analytical methods employed were unlikely to be misled by the relatively few differences that were discernible.

More than in other longitudinal studies or in most other studies that employ ratings, this study was preoccupied with specifying and maintaining the judging conditions necessary to achieve reliability and an essential validity of consensus personality evaluations. Many of the inescapable labors as this goal was pursued were tedious, delaying, and, despite the ultimate substantive concerns, intrinsically uninteresting. The satisfaction during and after this long period was that, through the use of numerous, sophisticated, independent judges permutated across the cases, through the assessment and rejection of the stereotype interpretation, and through other quality controls, the personality portrayals that eventuated were ones in which greater confidence than is usual can be placed. It was clear also, before embarking upon the judging process, that the systematic personality codifications generated for the purposes of this integrative study would prove a unique and fundamental data resource of the Institute of Human Development and would be central to the otherwise unfeasible analyses by a host of other IHD investigators for many years to come. For this reason, too, the complicated, protracted, and closely surveyed judging process seemed worth the effort.

Chapter V

PERSONALITY ATTRIBUTES STUDIED OVER TIME

The analytical approach characterizing previously reported longitudinal studies has been largely restricted to the correlation of variables over time. Using the entire available sample, perhaps segregated as to sex, measures developed early have been correlated with measures developed late. Personality ratings have provided the primary data related across time.

The correlations thus far observed have been of interest, if only because they came into existence in a prior vacuum. Although the conceptual emphasis motivating this study is different (see Chapter I), this chapter is used to report the results of correlating measures over time, using the full, undifferentiated samples of men and women. These analyses are largely equivalent to those studies which have gone before and will be related to them. Even here, however, because of dissatisfaction with the correlation coefficient, taken alone, as an index of continuity or of change, an effort has been made to define a more refined classification of time-affected behavior.

METHODOLOGICAL CONSIDERATIONS

Deficiencies of the Correlation Coefficient as a Longitudinal Measure

The simple correlation coefficient, calculated between ratings developed at Time 1 and at Time 2, has usually been the statistic chosen for longitudinal studies, but it is an incomplete descriptive index. The correlation coefficient responds primarily to the degree of correspondence between two orderings; with respect to the dispersion characterizing a sample at a given time, the correlation coefficient is a weak and often

confusing indicator; with respect to the salience or primacy of characteristics in the longitudinal sample being evaluated at different points in
time, the correlation coefficient tells nothing at all.

However, the notions of consistency or change imply more than a correspondence in ordering or a failure of such correspondence over time. Is
it consistency or is it change if subjects are ordered equivalently during
JHS and during SHS with respect to heterosexual interest, but the mean
level of interest is low during JHS and high during SHS? Two variables
may manifest equivalent across-time correlations, but the one variable
may have moderate standard deviations during each of the two time
periods being compared, while the other variable may have a very large
standard deviation at one time and a very small standard deviation the
second time. Are these two variables of comparable stability? The salience of a variable and its convergence-divergence over time must be
attended to as well as the simple correspondence of subject-orderings if
personality continuity and change are to be investigated more deeply.

In order to evaluate change by attending to continuities or changes in
mean levels and the dispersions of variables, as well as their correlations
across time, it is necessary to have measures or scores that warrant interpretation in these "absolute" terms. However, very many score distributions in psychology are arbitrary in their form and metric, containing only
ordering information. If a distribution of ratings contains information that
is comparative only within a sample of subjects, it is useless for comparisons other than correlational with ratings developed for the same subjects at another time. Previous longitudinal studies have been restricted
to correlational analysis in large part because there was no basis for
assuring the comparability of scores developed at different times. However, within the present study, by virtue of the logic and procedures of the Q
method, a case can be made for respecting changes in Q ratings over
time as indicative of changes in the salience and range of personality
attributes in the sample being longitudinally surveyed. Because this position is of great consequence for the present, and perhaps later studies,
the rationale underlying it merits elaboration.

On the Comparability Across Time of Q Ratings

Judges, in Q-sorting a subject, employ an *ipsative* frame of reference.
That is, the set of Q items is ordered by the judge with respect to the
comparative *salience* of these variables within the particular subject
being evaluated.

In ipsative ratings, the decision between qualitatively different variables as to "salience" is made with reference to a very large apperceptive body of information and

evaluation as to the psychology of human beings. This "adaptation level" is based upon some sum of integration of the rater's lifetime experience with the conceptualization of various personalities. (Block, 1957, p. 52–53).

Aggressivity or *dominance* or *deceitfulness* or *introspectiveness,* as qualities or traits, are evaluated in their interconnections within the subject under scrutiny and arranged along a complex continuum. The extremes of this continuum convey the personality characteristics evaluated as principally determining of the behavior of the subject or crucially important with respect to his perceptual and reactive tendencies. Intermediately positioned *Q* items are not so decisive; they take on their significance only in the context set by the apical qualities or themes characterizing the subject.

Two features of the *Q* method permit a usage of the *Q* scores for across-time comparisons involving more than simple ordering correspondence. First, be it noted that the *Q*-sort formulations of the subject are independent of the *Q* descriptions of other subjects. The composite formulation arrived at with respect to one subject does not (or should not) affect the composite formulation constructed for another subject by a different combination of judges.* That is, the adaptation level or frame of reference of each judge "is a very stable one, accumulated over many years and not subject to radical change when a short run of disproportionate personalities is encountered. Something like an absolute scaling of the rater's impressions is obtained" (Block, 1957, p. 53).

As ratings have more frequently been employed (ordering a group of individuals with respect to a particular variable rather than a group of variables with respect to a particular individual),

> the reference frame is usually a specifically delimited population; e.g., military offices, applicants to medical school and so on. Because in an absolute sense populations may reliably differ with respect to their mean and range on various personality variables, relationships among these variables are likely to shift appreciably as a function of the particular samples studied. A "masculine" graduate student may not be a "masculine" military officer when rated *vis-à-vis* this second population. But in the (intra-individual) frame in which the ipsative rating is made, his rating for "masculinity" is likely to remain the same, regardless of the particular sample (of subjects) of which he is a member (Block, 1957, p. 53).

Although each *Q* rating was developed ipsatively, within the context of other variables describing a subject, one can—and this is the second crucial property of the procedure and the data it generates—treat these ratings in the more conventional, *normative* way. That is, one can abstract out of the ipsative context the scores of *all* subjects with respect

---

*The analyses of judges' stereotypes, reported in Chapter IV, affirm the individuation and independence of the separately developed *Q* formulations.

to a particular Q variable. A convenient way to visualize this treatment of
Q data is to consider a Q-sort data matrix wherein each row represents a
subject and each column represents a Q item. The data—Q
composites—are developed one row at a time, the cells along each row
containing the salience values assigned to each of the Q variables. The
score entries along each row or Q composite relate to an individual subject and are developed independently of the score entries along all other
rows. If one looks at a *column* in this Q-data matrix, one sees the salience
values earned by a given Q item in the particular *subject sample*. Most
importantly, although the means of the saliency values calculated along
rows are identical for all rows, and the row standard deviation of these
values are very similar (because of the relatively narrow range of Q-
composite reliabilities), the saliency means and standard deviations when
computed for each column (i.e., the subject sample) differ widely and in
ways to which meaning can be ascribed. The mean salience values of Q
items when computed across a subject sample identify the typical configuration of personality within that sample of individuals; the standard
deviations of these Q items computed over the subject sample identify
the areas of homogeneity and of heterogeneity in that sample of persons.
The ipsative method of developing the saliency values and their independence between subjects implies that the subject sample *per se* did not
provide anchor points for the values assigned. Therefore, the means and
standard deviations of the Q items *vis-à-vis* the particular subject sample
reflect intrinsic characteristics and homogeneities of that sample rather
than being arbitrary consequences of forced normative discriminations,
the more usual case. An earlier article (Block, 1957) describes this orthogonal usage of Q data in a non-longitudinal context and adduces empirical support for the utility of this application.

In the longitudinal setting, the additional normative slicing of ipsatively
collected Q data is of especial significance. Correlation between normatively treated Q variables at different time intervals is feasible, as in other
studies. But, in addition, the means and dispersions of these normatively
employed Q variables convey important information. Consider the saliency values attributed to the Q item, *interested in opposite sex*, during
the junior high school interval and during the senior high school interval.
We can expect, as a function of psycho-sexual maturation, that the typical importance of this variable in an individual's psychological economy
will be less during JHS than it is during SHS. When, over all subjects, the
mean saliency value of this item is computed during JHS and again during SHS, the means are found to differ in the direction anticipated.

As another instance, consider the Q item, *questing for meaning*. We
may presume, from knowledge of ego development, that this variable will
almost uniformly lack salience for early adolescents. By later adolescence, there has been a widening of experience and introspective con-

frontation and this variable consequently should take on a central significance for some individuals and perhaps be vehemently denied salience by
others. In fact, it is found that the normatively treated salience values for
this item during JHS are characterized by a small standard deviation; at
SHS, a significantly larger standard deviation is found to exist for this
variable. Thus, in this instance too, the Q scores when treated normatively permit evaluation of group changes over time in regard to the psychological salience of various qualities and themes of personality. The
results to be presented shortly will permit the reader to judge for himself
the fruitfulness of this approach to "absolute" measurement within the
domain of personality psychology. In any event, he should note that the
rationale being employed is non-biasing and does not determine the
nature or content of the resulting findings.

Recognizing the Effects of Unreliability in Evaluating Continuity and Change

Before proceeding to an account of the analyses, another frequently
unacknowledged aspect of the study of continuity and change must be
considered. It is a psychometric truism that the conceptual relationship
between two variables is attenuated or blurred by the unreliability present
in the measures being related. In comparing early and late measures, the
manifest correspondence over time may give too pessimistic a view of
personality continuities if the measures being correlated are of low reliability.

The present uncertainties in personality and developmental theory are
great. The contribution of longitudinal research to theory-building will be
enhanced if the nature and extent of personality continuity or equivalence
over time are assessed with due regard to the unreliability effects that are
present. Failure to do so will prevent important across-time relationships,
which happen to be largely obscured by inadequate but improvable measurement procedures, from being discerned or given the significance they
conceptually warrant. A more extensive discussion of the rationale and
strategic implications of recognizing attenuation effects in research evaluation is to be found in Block (1963; 1964).

In longitudinal studies where the reliability of measures collected
some years before is not or cannot be ascertained, the influence of
unreliability on subsequent results cannot be taken into account. In the
present study, the use of multiple and independent judges permits assessment of the reliabilities of each ipsative Q formulation, and also
assessment of the reliability, computed via intra-class correlations, of
each Q item when treated normatively. In studying variables over time,
correspondence has been evaluated, for conceptual and heuristic rea-

Table 5–1
Mean Reliabilities of *CQ* Items for the Various Time Periods

	Men		*Women*	
	Mean*	S.D.	Mean	S.D.
JHS	.63	.24	.63	.22
SHS	.69	.23	.67	.24
ADULT	.70	.20	.67	.20

*Means were calculated using the z transformation and were based on 104 items for the JHS and SHS intervals and 100 items for the adult period.

sons, in terms of the across-time correlation, adjusted for attenuation by the usual formula. However, for the convenience of the reader, Appendices E and F report, for men and women respectively, both the uncorrected and the corrected correlations of all Q items over time. Appendix G contains the reliabilities of the Q items. Table 5–1 summarizes the means and standard deviations of the Q-item reliabilities for the several sections of data.

A Formal Classification of Variable Trends Over Time

If the usefulness of treating Q-salience values in something akin to absolute terms is accepted, a number of different categories of continuity or of change suggest themselves. Table 5–2 lists the criteria employed to define seven categories of continuity and change, together with diagrammatic representations of these various across-time trends. The seven categories are intended to cover, in reasonably inclusive fashion, continuities or changes in our group of subjects over time with respect to three developmental facets—*correspondence* (i.e., correlation), *salience level* (i.e., mean level), and *salience heterogeneity* (i.e., dispersion). The particular cutting points used to classify variables are, of course, arbitrary, but reasonably so.

1. *Sameness.* This category is defined to include those personality variables in regard to which there is evidence of strong across-time correspondence together with no indication of changes in salience level or salience heterogeneity. It is required in this category that the mean salience value of the variable not change importantly over the years, that there be insignificant change in the heterogeneity of the group with respect to the variable, and that the Q ratings correlate quite highly (corrected for attenuation) for the two time periods being compared. The label, *sameness,* for this category is not a felicitous one, but it avoids the

undesirably positive and presumptuous connotations of such terms as "consistency" or "stability."

2. *Increasing salience values, order-maintained.* This category includes those Q variables manifesting a reasonably strong correspondence of salience values over the years, *conjoined with* evidence for the increasing psychological primacy of the variable in the later period. Although the relative ordering of subjects remains much the same, the group as a whole shows an increased salience of the variable at the later time.

3. *Decreasing salience values, order-maintained.* This category complements the preceding one, identifying those variables correlating well

Table 5-2 The Criteria Employed To Define Categories of Continuity and Change

1. SAMENESS
   a. r ≥ .70 (corrected for attenuation)
   b. t-ratio of differences between the means ≤ 1.00
   c. t-ratio of differences between the standard deviations ≤ 1.99

2. INCREASING SALIENCE VALUES, ORDER-MAINTAINED
   a. t-ratio of differences between the means ≥ 1.99
   b. r ≥ .60 (corrected for attenuation)

3. DECREASING SALIENCE VALUES, ORDER-MAINTAINED
   a. t-ratio of differences between the means ≤ -1.99
   b. r ≥ .60 (corrected for attenuation)

4. INCREASING SALIENCE VALUES
   a. t-ratio of differences between the means ≥ 1.99
   b. r ≤ .60 (corrected for attenuation)

5. DECREASING SALIENCE VALUES
   a. t-ratio of differences between the means ≤ -1.99
   b. r ≤ .60 (corrected for attenuation)

6. CONVERGENCE OF SALIENCE VALUES
   a. t-ratio of differences between the standard deviations ≥ 1.99

7. DIVERGENCE OF SALIENCE VALUES
   a. t-ratio of differences between the standard deviations ≤ -1.99

over time, but indicating also that the psychological salience of the variable has decreased by the later interval. The relative positionings of subjects are strongly similar, but the group as a whole manifests a *decrease*
in the salience of the variable at the later time. This category, together
with the preceding two categories (i.e., Categories 1, 2, and 3) are, in the
aggregate, equivalent to the previous undifferentiated approach to personality continuity by means of correlational analysis alone. *

4. *Increasing salience values, order not well maintained.* There can be
change over time, in the typical psychological salience of personality variables even though the ordering of individuals with respect to the variables
is not strongly maintained. This category includes variables which, for the
group as a whole, show significant movement toward increased psychological relevance without, however, the strong ordering correspondence
characterizing the order-maintained categories. For the individual subject,
the relative extent of increased salience is not especially predictable.

5. *Decreasing salience values, order not well maintained.* This category mirrors the preceding one and contains variables significantly diminishing in psychological salience over time for the group as a whole. For
each subject within the sample, however, the extent of this change cannot be predicted so well as in the order-maintained categories. This category, together with the preceding three categories (i.e., Categories 2, 3,
4, and 5), identify those personality variables typically changing in their
salience within the psychic economy through adolescence and into adulthood. As such, these variables portray the age or stage changes characteristic of the periods being studied.

6. *Convergence of salience values.* This category includes those personality variables that manifest reduced individual differences with the
passage of time in regard to their psychological salience. At one period,
subjects may vary markedly in regard to the personal importance of a
characterological quality; at a later time, for whatever the reason, subjects may have moved or been shaped toward a uniformity in regard to
the intrapsychic relevance of the personality variable. This reduction in
salience heterogeneity characterizing the group in its entirety may, as
will be noted when appropriate, be linked occasionally with changes in
the mean salience value of the variable.

7. *Divergence of salience values.* This category identifies those personality variables that manifest an increased heterogeneity of salience
values over time, and hence marks an increasing individuation or differentiation of subjects during the later period. At an earlier time, the intrapsychic significance of a personality variable might have been similar for

---

* The criterion for continuity is lower (.6) in Categories 2 and 3 than it is in Category 1 (.7).
When there are changes in the mean salience of a Q item with respect to the fixed 9-point rating
continuum, a ceiling is placed on correlations over time. The slight change in criteria for Categories 2 and 3 represents an effort to allow for this lowering effect.

the subjects within the sample; at a later time for whatever the reason, the personality characteristic manifests great variability, from subject to subject, in its psychological salience.

The Number of Q Items Classified According to The Criteria

When the criteria defined in Table 5–2 are applied to all the Q items, the resulting pattern of category frequencies is of interest. Table 5–3 reports the number of items that were classifiable according to the various criteria. It is recognized that on occasion the Q items may be incorrectly classified since the categorizing scheme employs criterial indices that are subject to chance effects. However, a reasonable expectation is

Table 5–3
Frequency of CQ Items in Various Trend Categories

	JHS to SHS		SHS to Adult	
	Men	Women	Men	Women
Sameness	15	15	2	0
Increasing salience values, order-maintained	4	4	2	6
Decreasing salience values, order-maintained	6	7	4	2
Increasing salience values	5	3	13	18
Decreasing salience values	7	1	12	22
Convergence	0	0	4	13
Divergence	4	7	6	9

N.B. These figures are based on 104 CQ items for the JHS to SHS comparison and on 90 CQ items for SHS to Adulthood comparison.
There were 76 men and 83 women available for study in the JHS to SHS comparison; 76 men and 84 women were available for the SHS to Adulthood analyses.

that such random effects will balance out with respect to numerosity and that the contentual coherence of the classified items will in general suggest an appropriate interpretation of the changes being indexed.

It is not surprising to note that, for both male and female subjects, the sameness and order-maintained categories hold more Q items for the JHS–SHS comparison (a matter of three years) than they do for the SHS–Adult comparison (a matter of 20 years). More noteworthy, although no trend toward convergence is identifiable during adolescence, women particularly become more alike after SHS. Women, furthermore, appear to be subject to more developmental change than men in the period after SHS (31 Q items show increase or decrease for men after SHS as compared to 48 for women).

Organization of the Data Presentation

In the next, data-presenting sections of this chapter, the particular Q-items meeting the category criteria are reported through the medium of "text tables" and are then interpretively evaluated. Several aspects of this mode of presentation require comment.

With so many relationships to communicate, "text tables" were employed with the intention of easing the task of the reader. Otherwise, page after page of numerical presentation would be required at this juncture, which would then have to be perceptually organized by the reader. For the majority of the anticipated readership, the usage of "text tables" seemed preferable. The reader who would have preferred a more conventional data display will find all the necessary information in Appendices E, F, and G. These appendices will repay much study, from a variety of points of view.

Although the abundant relationships conveyed through the "text tables" are presented descriptively, the reader should understand that statistical significance underlies these textually expressed relationships. The criteria for the category quality, "order-maintained," were set so that the correlations over time, uncorrected for attenuation, would reach handily the .05 level of significance or beyond.* The criteria for the category qualities, "increasing salience values" or "decreasing salience values," likewise were set to net mean differences over time that reached the .05 level or beyond. And the category qualities, "convergence" and "divergence," were defined so as to include only those dispersion changes over time significant at or beyond the .05 level. So, although flags indicating probability levels do not accompany the findings about to be reported, their statistical significance should be understood.

Finally, and again for the convenience of the reader, the tactic has been adopted of abbreviating Q-items to a key word or phrase adding italicization for emphasis. For stylistic simplicity, on occasion different grammatical forms of the key word are used, but the same root is always maintained. The reader should encounter no difficulty in keying the summary words or phrases to the full items from which they are derived.

PERSONALITY CONTINUITIES AND CHANGES WITHIN THE MALE SAMPLE

From Junior High School to Senior High School:

Sameness: *arouses liking, turned to for advice, warm, socially perceptive, undercontrolled, skilled in imaginative play, views self as causative,*

* In the two instances where an across-time correlation qualified an item for a category but that correlation uncorrected for attenuation fell short of the .05 level of significance, the item was deleted from the category.

feelings satisfied with self, satisfied with physical appearance, physically attractive, uncomfortable with uncertainty, reluctant to act, feels victimized, self-dramatizing, irritable.

Increasing salience values, order-maintained: *high intellectual capacity, philosophically concerned, high aspiration level, questing for meaning.*

Decreasing salience values, order-maintained: *dependable, fantasizes, extrapunitive, thin-skinned, somatizes, bodily concerned.*

Increasing salience values: *calm, interesting, affected, eroticizing, interested in opposite sex.*

Decreasing salience values: *self-defensive, projective, favoring of status quo, fearful, gregarious, arousing of nurturance, accepting of self-dependency.*

Convergence: No items converged.

Divergence: *affected, favors status quo, calm, philosophically concerned.*

Evaluative Summary. What are the continuities in the adolescent boys over the three or four years from JHS to SHS? A variety of qualities show correspondence; in grouping them, a factor analysis of the *Q* items in the males' SHS *Q* composites has been helpful. Thus, there is continuity with respect to an expressiveness dimension (*skilled in imaginative play, undercontrolled, self-dramatizing,* and—reversed—*reluctant to act*). There is continuity also of concern for interpersonal relatedness and compassion (*dependable, warm, arouses liking* and—reversed—*extrapunitive*). A personal resiliency or self-instrumental dimension shows continuity over this period (*satisfaction with self, views self as causative, dependable,* and—reversed—*feels victimized and is thin-skinned*). The cognitive orientation of the adolescent boys shows continuity over this short time period (*intellectual capacity, questing for meaning, philosophically concerned, high aspiration level,* and—reversed—*discomfort with uncertainty*). Finally, the degree of somatic concern manifests a strong correspondence over this short interval.

What are the changes from early adolescence to late adolescence for the boys? The changes over the years are also patterned. There is an intensification of cognitive concerns (*increased intellectual capacity, increased questioning for meaning, increased philosophical concern,* and *higher aspiration level*). A surge of sexual interest becomes apparent (*eroticizes, interested in opposite sex*). The adolescent boys from JHS to SHS tend toward becoming, in contemporary parlance, increasingly "cool" (*increased calmness* conjoined with *increased affectedness*). They move away from dependence and dependability and are increasingly confident in evaluating self and society (*less extrapunitive, less self defensive, less projective, less fearful, less thin-skinned, less gregarious, less favoring of the status quo, less bodily concern*).

There are no indications of convergence of attributes, but several personality qualities show divergence during this time and hence may signal a pivotal importance of these variables in the psychology of the adolescent. By SHS, the adolescent boys vary markedly in regard to their philosophical concern, their respect for the status quo, their calmness and the extent to which they have developed affectations. Although the group as a whole has changed significantly with respect to the intrapsychic salience of these attributes, for many subjects there has been little or no change and the salience heterogeneity of these personality variables accordingly increases appreciably.

What broadly characterizes these continuities and changes in the adolescent boys from JHS to SHS? The basic character structure of the boys remains much the same in regard to expressive style, cognitive orientation, interpersonal emphasis, and adaptive resourcefulness. But there is an opening to experience and an enhanced reality commitment in the context of an increased coping competence. In the interpersonal realm, at least for the time being, there is movement toward less effectiveness. The complexities of life have begun to be realized, by some if not all of the subjects, and the future is pondered and approached with both eagerness and concern. The sexual motivation has become important, but the development of and accommodation to this drive lie ahead.

From Senior High School to Adulthood:

Sameness: *Values intellectual matters, verbally fluent.*

Increasing salience values, order-maintained: *dependable, prides self on objectivity.*

Decreasing salience values, order-maintained: *intellectual capacity, esthetically reactive, undercontrolled, fantasizing.*

Increasing salience values: *feels satisfied with self, philosophically concerned, fastidious, overcontrolled, productive, talkative, giving, turned to for advice, proffers advice, ruminative, complicates simple situations, has a clearcut consistent personality, interested in opposite sex.*

Decreasing salience values: *responds to humor, interesting, sensuous, lacks personal meaning, self-defeating, has bodily concern, withdraws when frustrated, rebellious, pushes limits, seeks reassurance, compares self to others.*

Convergence: *productive, eroticizes, interested in opposite sex, physically attractive.*

Divergence: *Self-defensive, somatizes, brittle, expresses hostile feelings directly, evaluates situation in motivational terms, insightful.*

Evaluative Summary. What are the continuities in the male subjects from SHS to their mid-thirties? Using the results of a factor analysis of the Q items in the Adult Q composite as a structuring aid, it appears that the cognitive orientation discernible during SHS also characterizes our subjects as adults (*intellectual capacity, values intellectual matters, esthetically reactive, verbal fluency, prides self on objectivity*). There is a great stability into the adult years with respect to such central character traits as dependability and impulsivity (*dependable, undercontrolled*). The use of fantasy also appears consistent over this 20-year period.

What are the changes from late adolescence to adulthood? Our male subjects have, in general, become more integrated and more assured in their personal lives and in relation to their achievement goals (*more dependable, more productive, more satisfied with self, more clearcut and consistent in their personalities; less undercontrolled, less rebellious, less pushing of limits, less seeking of reassurance, less self-defeating, less withdrawing when frustrated*). Interpersonally, our male subjects have moved toward greater and somewhat more aggressive interaction, perhaps because age has brought them experience in the several roles of masculinity (*more talkative, more giving, more turned-to-for-advice, more proffering of advice, more interested in opposite sex*). The movement toward greater self-control and self-confidence has an obsessive tinge (*more rumination, more complication of simple situations, more fastidiousness, more priding of self on objectivity*) and appears to have been achieved at the cost of personal flair (*less responsive to humor, less sensuous, less fantasizing, less interesting, less esthetically reactive*). Over the years, there is a diminishing of competitiveness (*less comparison of self with others, less seeking of reassurance*), and a further increase in the centrality of philosophical concerns. Preoccupation with somatic problems for the group at large has lessened, at least for the time of adult life we are considering. Finally, our subjects are judged as adults to have decreased in intellectual level as compared to their SHS status. This finding is an anomalous one and may find its explanation in a tendency of the judges to evaluate more positively the potential of youths facing their careers where the judges of the same subjects as adults had prior accomplishment to inform them.

The sample, *en masse*, converges with regard to productivity—in order for self- and societally-imposed standards of adulthood to be met, a minimal level of capability must be developed when in adolescence no requirements for responsible work were applied. Heterosexual focus converges as our subjects, widely discrepant in this regard during adolescence, grow into or down to a sufficient sexuality. The convergence of salience values of physical attractiveness is especially interesting—where external characteristics were so important in adolescence, by adulthood these formerly distinctive qualities have been rounded off by time and in their stead other facets of personality assume primacy.

The personality attributes that diverge with time show a differential development of ego-resources, with at least some of our adult subjects living toward the end of their tethers (*brittle, self-defensive*). Our adult subjects diverge greatly with respect to the interpersonal wisdom (*insightful, evaluates situations in motivational terms*) they have absorbed since the self-centeredness of adolescence. And, they differ too as adults in the freedom with which they are angry (*expresses hostile feelings directly*) when in adolescence they were almost uniformly constrained in the overtness of their hostility.

Taken altogether, the data suggest that the experience of becoming an adult is not entirely beneficent, but is more a matter of driving a bargain between the self and the world. To meet widening responsibility, our subjects became more effectively controlled and this imposition upon self was evidently rewarded by reduced intrapsychic agitation. However, to an extent, these gains of comfort and competence were at the expense of giving up important qualities of personal expressiveness; accordingly, the reality orientation of our adult man has a mildly obsessive flavor. Within the sample, there is impressive correspondence over the years with respect to cognitive orientation, degree of impulse control and interpersonal responsibility, but these continuities must be viewed as further pulled or compressed by the exigencies of adulthood.

PERSONALITY CONTINUITIES AND CHANGES WITHIN THE FEMALE SAMPLE

From Junior High School to Senior High School:

Sameness: *values intellectual matters, esthetically reactive, overcontrolled, undercontrolled, talkative, thinks unconventionally, socially perceptive, complicates simple situations, does not vary roles, self-defensive, submissive, other-directed, eroticizes, emotionally bland.*

Increasing salience values, order-maintained: *philosophically concerned, questing for meaning, deceitful, basic hostility.*

Decreasing salience values, order-maintained: *dependable, productive, arouses liking, warm, cheerful, straightforward, has clearcut, consistent personality.*

Increasing salience values: *distrustful, affected, interested in opposite sex.*

Decreasing salience values: *expresses hostile feelings directly.*

Convergence: No items converged.

Divergence: *prides self on objectivity, interesting, questing for meaning, deceitful, affected, extrapunitive, self-dramatizing.*

Evaluative Summary. What are the continuities characterizing these adolescent girls in the interval from JHS to SHS? The results of a factor analysis of the Q items in the girls' SHS Q composites have been used to help order the many facets of personality being evaluated. There are strong similarities, but, as will be seen, important differences too between the personality continuities of our adolescent girls and those of the adolescent boys reported earlier. There is continuity with respect to an expressiveness dimension (*talkative, undercontrolled,* and—reversed—*overcontrolled, complicates simple situations*). There is correspondence also with respect to concern for interpersonal relatedness and compassion (*dependable, arouses liking, warm, straightforward,* and—reversed—*self defensive, deceitful, basically hostile*). The cognitive orientation of our adolescent girls shows continuity over this time period (*values intellectual matters, thinks unconventionally, esthetically reactive, philosophically concerned, questing for meaning*). The cognitive orientation of the girls, however, appears intuitively responsive (*esthetically reactive, thinks unconventionally*) where the cognitive orientation of the boys is more hard-headed and reality-oriented (*high aspiration level, less discomfort with uncertainty*). Something akin to a personal adjustment cluster shows an essential continuity over these three or four years (*clearcut personality, cheerful, emotionally bland, does not vary roles*), but the personality attributes involved suggest that the adolescent girls exemplifying this quality are adapted rather than adaptable. They are continuing with psychologically differentiated behavioral modes that have worked before and are continuing to work, but are not evidencing growth into new coping capacities. Degree of sexual interest, as identified even in JHS, continues to order adolescent girls similarly in SHS—those eroticizing their social contexts in JHS continue to sexualize their situations in SHS. Interpersonal sensitivity or insensitivity (*socially perceptive*) as discerned in JHS, continues to characterize girls in SHS. Finally, a sense of social insecurity (*other-directed*), if established by JHS, also dominates the lives of our adolescent girls in SHS.

What are the changes in adolescent girls from JHS to SHS? Our subjects show an intensification of life-orientation reflections (*questing for meaning, philosophically concerned*). They become more frankly heterosexual in their interests. But the most striking phenomenon is a multifaceted move toward greater interpersonal deviousness (*more deceitful, more distrustful, more basic hostility, more affected; less dependable, less warm, less cheerful, less arousing of liking, less direct in expressing hostility*)!

No personality attributes show convergence, but a number diverge during this interval and their nature largely explains the group trends in salience changes. Thus, the trend toward interpersonal deviousness just mentioned is clearly due to the assumption of this tactic by a number—but not all—of our adolescent girls, creating divergence. There is also increasing separation among our female subjects during this time with respect to preoccupation with the meaning of life, the complexity of their self-differentiation and their tendencies toward affectation and histrionics.

Viewed broadly, our adolescent girls from JHS to SHS show a general continuity with respect to expressive style, cognitive-esthetic orientation, interpersonal relatedness and personal adjustment. But they appear also to be seeking more or redefined experience in terms of self-meaning and heterosexuality. Our findings indicate that this accessibility to the new and different is accompanied often by a turning away from a previously achieved warmth and honesty. The invocation of such simulating techniques as deceitfulness, distrustfulness, affectation, undependability, and so on provides, for that portion of our female sample involved, a screen behind which the adolescent girl can privately work over and assimilate or reject the consequences of her experience.

There are important similarities and differences between the ways our male and female subjects negotiated their adolescent periods. Both sexes moved toward a concern with the nature of life, toward sexual interest, and toward affectations of various kinds in their efforts to achieve personal and interpersonal identities. But the boys generally decreased their affective vulnerabilities and their dependence and have clearly become composed and better able to cope with the world for which they are beginning to plan.

Our adolescent boys, in the interval from JHS to SHS move significantly more than our adolescent girls toward *greater intellectuality, greater assertiveness, greater calmness*, and *greater awareness of their social stimulus value*. They also become *less self-defensive, less thinskinned, less hostile, less fantasizing, less self-indulgent*, and *less projective*.

The girls, on the other hand, manifest change not so recognizable as progressive. More than the boys, it is the adolescent girls who fit the culturally held expectation that adolescence is the time of interpersonal dysynchrony, when the turbulent teenager is hostile, affected, no longer frank, and altogether less likeable. Thus, the adolescent girls in the period from JHS to SHS significantly diverge from the boys in moving toward becoming *much less straightforward, less warm, less calm, less aware of their social stimulus value, less assertive*, and *more hostile, more self-indulgent*, and *more projective*.

From Senior High School to Adulthood:
Sameness: No items met the requirements for sameness.
Increasing salience values, order-maintained: *wide interests, values intellectual matters, philosophically concerned, submissive*.

Decreasing salience values, order-maintained: *rebellious, intellectual capacity.*

Increasing salience values: *introspective, straightforward, cheerful, feels guilty, prides self on objectivity, insightful, dependable, overcontrolled, productive, high aspiration level, giving, protective, sympathetic, arouses nurturance, turned-to-for-advice, warm, rapid tempo.*

Decreasing salience values: *fantasizing, sensuous, undercontrolled, power oriented, gregarious, interested in opposite sex, feminine, thin-skinned, self-indulgent, uncomfortable with uncertainty, does not vary roles, self-defensive, extrapunitive, withdraws when frustrated, conventional, pushes limits, projective, negativistic, distrustful, bothered by demands, eroticizes, compares self to others.*

Convergence: *expressive, responds to humor, intellectual capacity, dependable, overcontrolled, talkative, self-dramatizing, does not vary roles, pushes limits, deceitful, eroticizes, interested in opposite sex, physically attractive.*

Divergence: *introspective, satisfied with self, evaluates situation in motivational terms, arouses nurturance, brittle, bodily concerned, lacks personal meaning, conventional.*

Evaluative Summary. What are the continuities discernible within the female sample for the period from SHS to the middle thirties? Again, a factor analysis of the Q items in the adult Q composites is employed to assist in organizing the findings. There is persistence over the years with respect to a dimension indicative of a passive-conforming femininity at one end and an expressive-aggressive autonomy at the other (*submissive,* and—reversed—*wide interests, rebellious, intellectual capacity*). The ordering of the subjects does not change appreciably in regard to their cognitive-intuitive orientation (*values intellectual matters, philosophically concerned, wide interests, intellectual capacity*).

What are the changes from SHS to adulthood for our female subjects? The sample, as a group, has moved toward a culturally conventional deferent femininity (*more arousing of nurturance, more sympathetic, more giving, more protective, more submissive, more warm, more cheerful; less intellectual capacity, less negativistic, less power oriented*). There is evidence of growth toward an interpersonal differentiation or "psychological-mindedness" (*more introspective, more evaluating of situations in motivational terms, more insightful, more warm, more valuing of intellectual matters; less discomfort with uncertainty, less conventional*). There are trends for the group as a whole, or perhaps only for an average-affecting subgroup, toward increased coping with the world via control and the abnegation of impulsive selfishness (*more dependable, more overcontrolled, more productive, higher aspiration level, more pride in self-objectivity; less withdrawing when frustrated, less negativistic, less undercontrolled, less self-indulgent, less rebellious, less fantasizing).* There is greater social comfort and security by the mid-thirties for our women as they settle into the pattern of their lives (*more turned-to-for-advice, more straightforward; less thin-skinned, less extrapunitive, less projective, less comparing of self with others, less bothered by demands, less distrustful, less self-defensive*). As women, they are busier and more integrated now (*more rapid tempo, more productive*), perhaps because of family responsibilities. The place of sex in everyday life is not so exquisitely central (*less eroticizing, less feminine, less sensuous, less interested in opposite sex*) if only because married life has brought accommodation and routinization even to this domain of experience. There is a further deepening, for the group in its entirety, in interest in self and the world (*philosophically concerned, wider interests*).

Our female subjects as adults manifest convergence with respect to a number of qualities. They come together at moderately high levels of responsibility and self-control (*dependable, overcontrolled, feels guilty*) and moderately low levels of duplicity and insinuation (*deceitful, pushes limits, eroticizes, self-dramatizing*). The salience of intellect has dropped, but also converged as these women established their lives. They are more homogeneous as adults than in late adolescence on a spontaneity or responsiveness continuum (*expressive, responds to humor, talkative, does not vary roles, self-dramatizing*). And individual differences have reduced significantly in the sexual realm (*eroticizes, interested in opposite sex, physically attractive*).

The significant divergences by this time probably are of central importance for the way in which our subjects will confront that portion of their lives still to be led. There has been great separation with respect to self-resiliency (*lack of personal meaning, arouses nurturance, brittle,* and conditionally, *satisfaction with self*). The greater differences now discernible with respect to conventionality can be seen as deriving from these divergencies in self-resilience and intraception. And finally, the extent of bodily concern has begun to be a pivotal variable for our female subjects.

Taken altogether, our women subjects appeared to be essentially continuing in their ways of conformance and cognition identifiable during senior high school. But the group changes are of larger moment and indicate, on balance, a great step toward increased coping capacity. Our women in their mid-thirties have increased the extensiveness and appropriateness of their impulse control *vis-à-vis* society, they have consolidated and apparently clarified their sense of intrapersonal integration, and they have decreased their interpersonal vulnerability and moved toward relatedness and commitment. There are some contrary indications as well—the active experiencing of the mind and of the senses is no longer so relished and for enough of the subjects to influence group trends, there is increased potential for psychopathology.

Our women subjects traversed the period from SHS to their mid-thirties in ways both similar to and different from our male subjects. In both sexes, there was the assumption of responsibility for self and for others, with a concomitant or consequent constraint on narcissistic impulsivity. But in both sexes, the increase in coping capacity is accompanied by a disuse of fantasy and of sensuality. The clarity and consistency of personality structure have increased in our men and women, and there is a common tendency toward inquiry about the meaning of life. As adults, both our men and women are now in the roles of givers rather than takers.

The differences between the sexes at this stage reflect differential cultural pressures and cultural permissiveness perhaps as much as the innate psychological differences of men and women. Men are more goal-oriented and more satisfied with themselves while the women more vaguely define their sense of purpose. But the men are also more detached and cognitively obsessive and are less responsive to the unpredictables involved in art and in humor.

When statistically compared to our female subjects, our male subjects have in the time since SHS, changed significantly toward a *narrowing of interests, less esthetic reactivity, less responsiveness to humor, less straightforwardness, greater fastidiousness, greater condescension* and *more proffering of advice*. Further, they are perceived in adulthood as having become relatively *less interesting* and *less intelligent* over the years.

Women more than men are now psychologically-minded and tender in their interpersonal attachments. More than men, women worry and they direct their actions so as to avoid or minimize anticipated guilt. And, more than men, our women subjects have de-emphasized or turned away from sexuality and its derivative preoccupations.

Our women, more than the men, have since SHS moved significantly away from *gregariousness* (formerly so emphasized, *conventionality, self-indulgence, being bothered by demands, thin-skinnedness,* and, to an extent, *fastidiousness*. They have changed, more than the men, in becoming relatively *wider in their interests, more valuing of the intellect, more esthetically oriented, more ambitious, more protective, more sympathetic,* and, especially, these adult women have, since their SHS days, learned to *feel guilty*.

Thus, for the group as a whole, the price paid for the significant coping attainments posted by adulthood by the IHD men appears to be an increased obsessiveness and a diminished self; for the IHD women, the price of their feminine competence is a greater affective vulnerability and reduced assertiveness of a self that is still there.

RELATING THE PRESENT RESULTS TO PREVIOUS FINDINGS

The task now is to relate the present findings to those already reported in the literature, in particular the results of Kagan and Moss (1962), and of Tuddenham (1959). In order to do so, the analytical ground must be shifted somewhat so as to establish a proper basis for comparison.

Thus, where a number of categorical distinctions have been maintained until now, certain of these categories must now be abandoned and others collapsed so as to focus solely on continuity as indexed by correlation coefficients. Further, where for conceptual purposes until now, correlation coefficients have been evaluated *after* correction for attenuation, the coefficients to be reported in this section will not be so corrected in order to facilitate comparison with previously reported figures. The Kagan & Moss study and the Tuddenham study did not employ variables strictly equivalent to the ones here employed but, inspectionally, a good bit of comparability in emphasis is to be seen. A matching has been attempted between certain variables in these studies and those in the present one for the purpose of evaluating the congruence of the relationships observed in these separate investigations.

Comparison with the Findings of Kagan and Moss

In relating the IHD results to the Kagan & Moss study, it is possible to reference only their time interval from age 10 to age 14 (approximately our JHS period) and their adult evaluation (their subjects at the time had an average age of 24 years where the IHD adults were in their thirties). These time periods correspond, if only roughly, to the time periods in the present study, so a comparison is relevant. A further comparison with the Kagan & Moss findings in regard to ages prior to ten years cannot be justified.

In Table 5–4 are presented nine pairings of variables. It is suggested these paired variables are sufficiently equivalent in their psychological meaning in the two longitudinal studies to warrant comparison of the continuities they manifest. These variables are taken from the set of variables employed in each study to characterize adults. At the 10–14 year interval, in the Kagan & Moss study, somewhat different versions of these variables were employed and so a further matching or selection was required; in the present study, for the three time periods, the variables being related are coordinate.

Table 5-4
Matched Variables in the Kagan-Moss and Present Studies

Kagan-Moss Study	Present Study
Dependency	
46. Withdrawal from potential failure situations	30. Gives up and withdraws where possible in the face of frustration and adversity
Aggression	
14. Competitive behavior	89. Compares self to others; is alert to real or fancied differences between self and other people
16. Anger arousal	34. Over-reactive to minor frustrations; irritable
38. Repression of aggressive thoughts	14. Expresses hostile feelings directly (reversed)*
Achievement	
19. Achievement behavior	71. Has high aspiration level for self
Sexuality	
21. Heterosexual interaction	80. Interest in opposite sex
Social Interaction	
29. Anxiety in social situations	92. Has social poise and presence. Appears socially at ease (reversed)*
Miscellaneous	
31. Impulsivity	53. Tends toward under-control of needs and impulses; unable to delay gratification
32. Introspectiveness	16. Is introspective (N.B. introspectiveness *per se* does not imply insight)

*Two variables in the present study, *CQ* items 14 and 92, required reflection in order to be oriented comparably.

Table 5-5 reports the across-time correlations for these nine variables common to the two studies for both male and female samples separately.

With respect to *withdrawal from potential failure situations,* Kagan and Moss report significant continuity from the ages 10–14 to the age of about 24 years for women, with male subjects evidencing a similar, but not quite significant trend. In the IHD study, from the age of about 15–17 to the age of about 31–37 years, very little correspondence is to be found, although moderate continuity is present between the proximate JHS–SHS periods.

Extent of competitive behavior appears unstable over appreciable time periods in both studies, although perhaps over shorter time intervals,

Table 5–5
Across-Time Correlations for Variables Common
to Kagan-Moss and Present Studies

Kagan-Moss Labels	Kagan-Moss Study		Present Study			
			JHS to SHS		SHS to Adulthood	
	Men	Women	Men	Women	Men	Women
Withdrawal from failure Childhood variable: withdrawal task	40	49*	41***	34**	05	17
Competitive behavior	39	08	27*	19	–06	10
Anger arousal			45***	32**	29*	10
Childhood variable: aggression to mother	77***	24				
Childhood variable: indirect aggression to peers	16	24				
Repression of aggressive thoughts			16	34**	26*	29**
Childhood variable: aggression to mother	–56**	–02				
Childhood variable: indirect aggression to peers	–11	–04				
Achievement behavior	40*	42*	64***	42***	36**	36***
Heterosexual interaction	–32	–05	46***	32**	09	19
Social interaction anxiety			51***	47***	31*	39***
Childhood variable: withdrawal from social interaction	65**	54				
Impulsivity Childhood variable: compulsivity (reversed)	(–)05	(–)16	57***	57***	59***	24*
Introspective	35	27	25*	22*	28*	41***

N.B.   *means significance beyond the .05 level, two-tailed;
    **means significance beyond the .01 level, two-tailed;
    ***means significance beyond the .001 level, two-tailed.
    All decimals omitted.

ranging from adolescence into the early twenties, there is some persistency in competitiveness for males.

Anger arousal enjoys a spectacular relationship (.77) with *aggression to mother* for the male sample of Kagan and Moss, but has a low correlation with *indirect aggression to peers*. For the IHD male subjects, aggressive reactivity shows a moderate consistency over time. The women from both studies show little consistency with respect to this dimension.

Expression of aggressive thoughts, a variable that to some extent would be expected to mask anger reactions, also relates well but reversed (−.56), with *aggression to mother* in the Fels male sample, but manifests no persistence in the female sample. For both men and women in the IHD study, there is significant durability of placement on this dimension over the years.

Achievement behavior is moderately or even appreciably consistent for both sexes and in both studies, a uniformity of relationship that is rare.

With regard to extent of *heterosexual interaction,* the Fels male subjects show no continuity from their early adolescence to their early adulthood while the female subjects manifest, surprisingly, a *negative* relationship over time that almost reaches statistical significance. The IHD samples, male and female, show a fair degree of continuity of heterosexual interest during the adolescent period itself—a thoroughly expectable finding. But over an appreciable period of time, from Senior High School to Adulthood, the IHD samples show little or no across-time correspondence in degree of heterosexual interest. This motley set of relationships, ranging from negative through zero to positive, can only be discouraging to the would-be seeker for trends and lawfulness.

Anxiety over social interaction is evidently a stable trait, since for both sexes and for both studies, the continuities are significant.

Impulsivity does not show consistency in the Kagan and Moss sample, in terms of the variables as matched, but is persistent in the IHD study, impressively so for the male sample. Since this variable, or variables closely related to it, often have been viewed as having long-term persistence, the absence of correlation over time with respect to this variable in the Kagan & Moss study is puzzling. Perhaps the matching of variables as proposed here for evaluating the Fels results is incorrect. But the related, converse variable, *compulsivity,* which is similarly identified by Kagan and Moss at adulthood and at the interval 10–14 also manifests no continuity in their study (r of −.13 for males and .18 for females). The seemingly most relevant relationship, between *impulsivity* as an adult and *hyperkinesis* as an adolescent, does not appear to be reported in the Fels volume.

Finally, *introspectiveness* displays moderate correlational continuity in both studies and for both sexes over time.

Comparison with the Findings of Tuddenham

The IHD study by Tuddenham employed subjects largely included within our present samples. Of the 72 subjects used by Tuddenham, 52 are included in the present sample. Thus, Tuddenham used 20 subjects

Lives Through Time

Table 5–6
Matched Variables in the Tuddenham and Present Studies

Tuddenham Study	Present Study
Self-expressiveness	Is facially and/or gesturally expressive.
Eager v. Listless	Has a rapid personal tempo.
Attractive v. Unattractive physique	Is physically attractive; good-looking (N.B. The cultural criterion is to be applied here).
Well-groomed v. Unkempt	Is fastidious.
Masculine v. Feminine behavior	(a) Behaves in a masculine style and manner.
	(b) Behaves in a feminine style and manner. (N.B. If subject is male, 93a applies; if subject is female, 93b is to be evaluated.) (N.B. again. The cultural or subcultural conception is to be applied as a criterion.)
Enjoys social activities v. Indifferent	Emphasizes being with others; gregarious.
Submissive v. Self-assertive	Basically submissive.
Uninhibited v. Inhibited	Tends toward over-control of needs and impulses; binds tensions excessively; delays gratification unnecessarily.
Assured v. Self-conscious	Has social poise and presence; appears socially at ease.
Matter-of-fact v. Shows off	Is self-dramatizing; histrionic.
Cheerful v. Glum	Is cheerful. (N.B. Extreme placement toward uncharacteristic end of continuum implies gloominess.)
Autonomy	Values own independence and autonomy.
Achievement	Has high aspiration level for self.
Succorance	Seeks reassurance from others.
Introspection v. Absence of introspection	Is introspective. (N.B. Introspectiveness *per se* does not imply insight.)

unavailable to the present study which was able to include 118 subjects not studied by Tuddenham. Tuddenham's analysis was based on data collected five or six years prior to, and entirely independent of, the follow-up study upon which the present adult evaluations are based. Tuddenham's data were ratings of social behavior and personality attributes developed from specific situations or procedures during the adolescent period. These ratings were later repeated, based upon interview impressions developed when the subjects were at about the age of 32 years; the present data are Q ratings based upon a broad variety of data sources for a longer time interval and a largely augmented, but somewhat over-lapping sample of subjects. Thus, the two studies, although partially redundant, are largely independent.

In Table 5-6 are presented 15 variables selected from the Tuddenham report as sufficiently matchable with Q items in the present study. Table 5-7 reports the across-time correlations of these variables for both samples.

There are a number of corroborations of expectancy in comparing the results of the two studies, but the discrepancies are more compelling. Thus, both studies find masculinity and femininity, degree of inhibition, cheerfulness, and introspectiveness to be moderately continuous over-time and for both sexes. But Tuddenham finds degree of fastidiousness

Table 5-7
Across-Time Correlations for Variables Common to the
Tuddenham and Present Studies

Tuddenham Labels for Variables	Tuddenham Study		Present Study			
			JHS to SHS		SHS to Adult	
	Men	Women	Men	Women	Men	Women
Self-expressive	36	25	39***	40***	17	19
Eager v. Listless	49***	19	50***	51***	20	32***
Attractive v. Unattractive Physique	-11	06	62***	51***	43***	45***
Well-groomed v. Unkempt	49***	-06	57***	57***	30**	35**
Masculine v. Feminine behavior	32	32*	37**	52***	39***	38***
Enjoys social activities v. Indifferent	28	00	40***	39***	36**	43***
Submissive v. Self-assertive	14	33	27*	50***	11	46***
Uninhibited v. Inhibited	38*	34*	56***	54***	43***	25*
Assured v. Self-Conscious	13	43**	51***	47***	31**	39***
Matter-of-fact v. Shows off	20	36*	49***	61***	43***	46***
Cheerful v. Glum	26	20	57***	50***	26*	36***
Autonomy	38	02	38***	39***	18	48***
Achievement	21	15	64***	42***	36**	36***
Succorance	12	03	34**	20	00	33**
Introspection v. Absence of introspection	62**	44	25*	22*	28*	41***

N.B.   *means significance beyond the .05 level, two-tailed;
         **means significance beyond the .01 level, two-tailed;
        ***means significance beyond the .001 level, two-tailed.
         All decimals omitted.

(grooming) to be continuous for males only, where the present study finds it persistent in both men and women; Tuddenham finds social activity to be of low or no persistence, where in the present study, it is found to be continuous for both sexes; Tuddenham finds degree of assuredness to be continuous for women but not for men, where we find it enduring for men as well as women; Tuddenham finds autonomy persistent for men, but not women, where the present analyses find it more for women than for men. Need for achievement shows persistence in this study but not in Tuddenham's. Succorance shows continuity for our women, but not for our men, and not at all in Tuddenham's study.

Whether these differences relate to differences in method or sample or in time period studied is obscure. The present study enjoyed richer resources than were available to Tuddenham. More and perhaps population-different subjects were employed, more judges were used, a wider array of data sources and a different methodology were available. It may be significant that, for the potpourri of 15 variables that can be compared between the two studies, the correlations over time generated in the present study from SHS to adulthood (the primarily relevant period) have a much higher average for women than the correlations reported by Tuddenham (.38 vs. .21). However, these averages are the same in the two studies for the male samples involved (.29 vs. .29). Overall, the presently reported evidence for personality continuity over time seems somewhat stronger.

VARIABLES MANIFESTING UNUSUALLY LOW ACROSS-TIME CORRELATIONS

The usual emphasis in a longitudinal study is on correlational continuity. The "order-maintained" Q-items, earlier presented, are the variables that have shown unusually high across-time correlations. But of special psychological interest, in their own right and for important conceptual reasons, are personality variables that over time show little continuity. Certain of these variables will be unstable simply because of their low reliabilities at each of the periods being evaluated. However, other personality attributes may show no correspondence over time although they are reliably specifiable at each time period. What are these variables in the present study and does any pattern emerge from contemplating these temporally disjunctive measures?

Since it was not intended to delve into these analytical possibilities in any depth, some simple, arbitrary but reasonable scanning criteria were applied to identify "reliably unreliable predictors." For the short period from JHS to SHS, there tends to be appreciable correspondence of subject orderings for both sexes and so the criterion of a JHS–SHS correlation (corrected for attenuation) of less than .40 was employed as the definition of an "unstable" item. For the longer SHS-to-adulthood period, a criterion of less than .10 was applied to the across-time correlations (corrected for attenuation) to identify volatile attributes. Because the attenuation corrections of the across-time correlations are crucially dependent upon the reliabilities involved, a further criterion was applied to select only those personality variables unpredictable over time even though reliably specified, and to exclude those variables not predictive over time, perhaps because of their low reliabilities. For screening purposes, a rough convention was employed of calling an item reliable if it enjoyed an average reliability of .60 or better, and labeling an item as unreliable if its average reliability was .45 or less. Attributes with intermediate reliabilities earned intermediate labels.

From the period from JHS to SHS, the adolescent males manifested little continuity with respect to *expresses hostile feeling* directly. Although of slightly lower reliability, the personality variable, *insightful,* also displays poor consistency over this interval. The adolescent girls, from JHS to SHS, re-order themselves markedly with respect to *feeling victimized* and *negativism,* and the slightly less reliable variable, *seeking reassurance.*

For the period from SHS to adulthood, the male subjects show no ordering correspondence with respect to the personality attributes: *withdraws when frustrated, moralistic, socially perceptive, projective,* and *straightforward.* The variables, *power oriented,* and *complicates simple situations,* also did not correlate over time and have intermediate reliabilities. The female sample from SHS to adulthood is markedly re-ordered with respect to *straightforward, ruminative,* and *protective.* Barely missing our reliability criterion are the attributes *fantasizing* and *moralistic,* which also correlate poorly over this time period. For both sexes over this span, the qualities *moralistic* and *straightforward* are not constant.

The several findings do not constellate in any unambiguous way—the attributes involved are neither obviously phenotypical or obviously genotypical in nature. Certain of the variables displaying inconstancy are perhaps surprising because of the usually-held expectancy that these attributes are especially central and likely to be enduring (e.g., *withdraws when frustrated, socially perceptive, ruminative*). A likely explanation of these somewhat anomalous findings, to be substantiated in suceeding chapters, is that the existence of reliably unenduring personality attributes is an accident of this chapter's mode of analysis—correlation over time for a sample in its entirety. An orderliness and configuration of across-time consistencies not now apparent will be evident later, when the data are approached in a more differentiated way.

A MEASURE OF PSYCHOLOGICAL ADJUSTMENT AND ITS USES

As a final complication of an already complicated chapter, a measure of psychological adjustment is introduced which will be employed frequently in the remainder of this book. Although interest here lies primarily in identifying various patterns of personality development and personality change, it is important as well to assess the over-all psychological or adaptational balance characterizing a subject or a subgroup of individuals. This kind of inquiry asks a summary or averaging question—i.e., abstracting from the nature or style or motivational content of an individual's personality system, where does the individual place on the complex continuum defined at one end by mature, resourceful, self-fulfilling adaptational patterns and at the other end by defensive, perseverating, self-impoverishing adaptational patterns? It makes sense to view people in this simplifying way. Despite the many patterns in which personality can be enduringly organized and lives can be shaped and directed, it is useful for certain conceptual purposes to be able, at least roughly, to order individuals along such a continuum.

When professional psychologists or, for that matter, laymen, wish to characterize someone broadly, they talk of "adjustment." What is meant by this term, and how shall we employ and measure this concept? The notion of "adjustment" is value laden and properly so. The shades of meaning the term "adjustment" may have are many, but we may distinguish a basic and traditional dichotomy in usage—between adjustment in the social sense and adjustment as viewed psychologically.

Social adjustment and measures derived from this concept tend to emphasize the ability of an individual to fit into a social structure in an applauded way, or at least not in a deviant, society-threatening fashion. The individual naturally or by personal accommodation conforms to a set of societal rules and, by so doing, is termed to be "adjusted." The unusual person, with unusual perceptions or values or aspirations, cannot—almost by definition—be viewed as "socially adjusted," because this concept proclaims the virtues of the static and the predictable. The phrase, "getting along in the world as it is" conveys the usual sense of social adjustment. Be it noted that "getting along" carries no implication regarding adaptability in a world that is on the move, nor does it suggest that the heights of happiness have been scaled or that individuals have developed toward their personal potentials. We shall not be employing the term "adjustment" in this social sense.

The psychological view of adjustment—the one we shall be using—is less concerned with social achievement than it is with the resourcefulness, versatility, and resilience of individuals in creating and responding to their life encounters. The emphasis is on the ability to manage problems rather than on the absence of personal difficulties, on the psychological genotypes that underlie behavior rather than culture-defined phenotypes that can be activated by many quite different instigators.

The easiest way to convey and elaborate upon the concept of adjustment as used by psychologists is to report a consensus definition established several years ago and reported in Block (1961). Nine clinical psychologists, all holding the doctorate and with extensive clinical experience, separately sorted the CQ set so as to embody their concept of the optimally adjusted or psychologically healthy personality. Their average intercorrelation was .78, and so the reliability of the *composite* description of optimal adjustment based upon these nine psychologists may be estimated as .97—a very high figure indeed. This formulation of psychological adjustment may be taken as a criterion definition because of the impressive consensuality among psychologists in characterizing the concept.

What does psychological adjustment look like, as viewed by psychologists? The salience values for each Q item in this conceptual definition are reported in Block (1961, p. 146). To convey the sense of "psychological adjustment," the thirteen most positively salient Q items (categories 9 and 8) and the thirteen most negatively salient items (categories 1 and 2) delineating the construct are reported here.

CQ items most positively defining of optimal adjustment: warm, dependable, insightful, productive, socially perceptive, ethically consistent, valuing of independence, straightforward, incisive, valuing of intellectual matters, calm, sympathetic, has wide interests.

CQ items most negatively defining of optimal adjustment: brittle, feels victimized, repressive, lacks personal meaning, self-defeating, fearful, aloof, basically anxious, deceitful, negativistic, basically hostile, projective, emotionally bland.

Clearly, the psychologically adjusted person looks pretty good, as he should. The primary advantage of this psychological definition of adjustment stems from its emphasis on personal capabilities and characteristics, rather than social accomplishment. Psychological adjustment usually has positive implications for social adjustment, of course. But social adjustment *per se* can characterize an individual who is not psychologically adjusted; the definition of social adjustment may vary over time or differ in different societies; and, in some societies at certain times, it seems fair to assert a psychologically adjusted person cannot be socially adjusted. A psychological conception of adjustment, therefore, has a constancy of definition not readily achieved by a social conception.

Now, the reason for a definition of psychological adjustment is to reference individuals against this concept, to order them along a continuum of adjustment. If we can do so, then we can start to compare apples and oranges, judging both in terms of their desirability as fruit. Two very different life patterns, incommensurate and even diametrical, as usually viewed, can be evaluated and compared in regard to the happiness, zest, productivity, and personal realization they each provide. Changes over time, which imply approaching or departing from psychological adjustment take on a clearer significance. Thus, a measure of psychological adjustment taken at different times provides a convenient way of assessing the psychological status of an individual, his absolute and relative position on a maturity-psychopathology dimension, together with his developmental trend toward resilience or brittleness. We shall not rely overly much on an index of psychological adjustment—the alternative routes to equivalent levels of psychological health or psychological illness will remain the central focus. But a "score" on psychological adjustment will provide a useful summary way of making comparisons among groups or in charting the progression or regression of individuals over time.

The way chosen here to construct a psychological adjustment score for the longitudinally-followed subjects issues directly and easily from the criterion definition (Block, 1961, pp. 100–107). The *CQ* composites characterizing each subject at each of the time periods were each correlated against the criterion definition of psychological adjustment.* A high correlation in this context signifies that a subject's personality is highly similar to the prototypically adjusted personality; a low or negative correlation indicates the subject is distant in character from our conception of psychological health. These correlations or psychological adjustment scores thus can be used to operationalize the overall psychological status of an individual at any time *vis-à-vis* a psychologist's definition of psychological health. This score shall be referred to hereafter as the *PA* Index. As computed by the split-half technique, the reliabilities of this index for the two sexes and the three time periods range from .95 to .98.

It can be argued that a definition of psychological health appropriate for the adolescent period should be different from a definition of psychological health appropriate at adulthood. Similarly, a conception of psychological adjustment for men can be different from psychological adjustment as it is defined for women. With regard to specially selected personality attributes, it is clear that life phase and sexual role should affect the definition of optimal adjustment. With respect to a comprehensive array of personality traits, however, it is no longer obvious or required that age and sex should affect a definition of psychological health. The reader is invited to inspect again the *Q* items reported above which are most influ-

* Only 90 of the 100 *CQ* items used to define psychological adjustment were included in the *Q* set used to describe our subjects during JHS and SHS. Accordingly, correlations involving JHS and SHS *Q* composites can be based only upon the 90 comparable items. The 100-item *Q* set employed to characterize our subjects as adults is not subject to this restriction, but, to insure comparability at each time interval, the correlations of the adult *Q* composites also were based on these 90 items.

ential in defining psychological adjustment. There he will note that the picture of adjustment developed by psychologists is not age- or sex-specific and therefore the use of a constant criterion is appropriate, or, at worst, not importantly wrong.

After this lengthy prologue, required because the *PA* Index for individuals or for subgroups will be reported often in subsequent chapters, we can turn to some general and normative characteristics of the *PA* Index as it applies to our subject samples at different times.

In Table 5–8 are presented the means, standard deviation, and ranges of the *PA* Index for each sample at each time period. The intercorrelations of the *PA* Index for the different periods is also reported. It will be

Table 5–8
Properties of the *PA* Index as Calculated for the Full Samples at Each Time Interval

	Mean	S.D.	*Males* Range	Across-Time Average Correlation
JHS interval	.001	.367	–.652 to .686	
SHS interval	.058	.385	–.671 to .830	JHS – SHS = .623
				JHS – Adulthood = .230
				SHS – Adulthood = .325
Adulthood	.134	.407	–.741 to .806	
JHS interval	.087	.327	*Females* –.635 to .691	
SHS interval	.018	.348	–.662 to .735	JHS – SHS = .498
				JHS – Adulthood = .202
				SHS – Adulthood = .234
Adulthood	.150	.369	–.785 to .717	

observed that the ranges and dispersions are extraordinarily great at each interval, indicating that for the individual case the group mean is quite uninformative.

The *changes* in the group means over time are of interest, for they express via this summary index the psychological trends already noted in more specific detail. The boys from JHS to SHS moved toward psychological health and continued to make significant progress toward this criterion in their adult years. The girls, on the other hand, look comparatively well in JHS but regress appreciably by SHS when, as described earlier, they adopted experimental roles of deviousness, selfishness, and affection. By adulthood, however, the women have more than recouped their earlier losses in coping ability and now look out on life with an adaptational resourcefulness at least as effective as that characterizing the male sample.

The intercorrelations among the *PA* Indices for the several time periods point up a couple of morals. Psychological health is moderately continuous from JHS to SHS for both sexes, but, and again for both sexes, the psychological adjustment of adults is very poorly predicted from knowledge of psychological adjustment during JHS or SHS. This poor correspondence over time is not due to unreliability of the measures involved, since the measures being related are highly reliable.

The second recognition to be taken away from inspection of the *PA* intercorrelations is the generally poorer predictability of adult status from JHS or SHS that characterizes the female sample. The female subjects appear to fluctuate more than the males with respect to the dimension of psychological health. This finding is in keeping with our earlier observation of the inchoate, contradictorily experimental nature of the SHS period for the female subjects. For the groups taken in the large, there is a more orderly progression of personality development in boys as they become men than is evidenced in girls as they become women. The reader should keep in mind, however, that this trend is not a striking one; when more differentiated analytical approaches are applied, this conclusion becomes more complicated.

THE ACCOMPLISHMENTS AND THE DEFICIENCIES OF THIS CHAPTER

In this chapter, the focus has been upon variables *per se,* and the various continuities and trends they display within the IHD sample of males and within the IHD sample of females. The methodology used has permitted the charting of maturational trends in adolescence and into adulthood. The findings have been related to the two earlier longitudinal studies most comparable to the present investigation in regard to span of time and the particular period being evaluated. It has been shown that correlational continuity, as judged by the number of personality variables reaching the threshold of statistical significance, is impressive—for men and women, respectively, 96 percent and 89 percent of the JHS–SHS Q-item correlations are significant beyond the .05 level; 59 percent and 60 percent of the SHS-Adult Q-item correlations achieve the .05 level of significance. Some personality variables that are unusually inconstant over time have been identified. And, the course of psychological adjustment over the years has been studied.

But the plethora of slight to moderate across-time relationships supports only the by-now banal recognition that human beings do indeed remain somewhat true to themselves over considerable lengths of time.

The sheer numerosity of the significant across-time correlations is testimony to the reliability achieved through the use of multiple judges and to the relatively large sample sizes being studied. The generally significant, but low, correlations which have been reported in longitudinal studies probably can be repeated whenever sufficient and sustained funding and competence are available to insure the adequacy of measures. But low correlations are as frustrating as they are informative. Why are the correlations not higher? Why are certain reliable variables not predictive?

A fundamental fault of correlations based upon an undifferentiated aggregation of individuals is that importantly different subgroups may exist in the larger aggregation and not be discerned. The correlation, as computed using all subjects, may reveal only an arbitrarily weighted or slight relationship where a differentiated approach that seeks homogeneous types or patterns of personality could identify more impressive within-subgroup relationships. A greater lawfulness of behavior will be evident within the realm of personality as psychology moves from the nomothetic approach toward the recognition of different, but each orderly, ways of development. The next chapter reports the first of several efforts to apply this view.

Chapter VI

PERSONALITY CONSISTENCY AND CHANGE OVER TIME AS A MODERATOR VARIABLE OF LONGITUDINAL TRENDS

In a study which independently evaluates an individual's character at several widely separated intervals, it is a natural and intrinsically engaging question to inquire as to the degree of personality consistency or change which has been manifested by the individuals who have been followed over time. In the everyday world, this kind of interest looms large. We reflect upon the changes time and experience have wrought upon an old friend now re-encountered. We ponder—or should—upon how it will be to live a life with someone else. Is a current infatuation a mate "for all seasons?" In career projections, we ask—Is this student worth special backing because he is likely to become a productive and creative member of his society? Irretrievable decisions are predicated upon the answers, usually formulated viscerally, to such questions. Considerations of personality consistency and personality change are important here and the present study brings some data to bear on these matters.

The question of consistency and change over time, as it is usually put by the layman, is framed in an overall, somewhat naive, but nevertheless telling way, and this is the way we shall be attempting to answer it. The initial impulse of psychologists when asked "Is the character of people consistent or does personality change over time?" is to reply primly, "Consistent with respect to what? Change with respect to what?" If pressed to an empirical response, the psychologist usually will correlate subject positionings on a single variable over time and report consistency or change only in these variable-qualified terms.

This approach is not wrong; indeed, its usefulness has been evidenced in the preceding chapter. But it does not speak to the overall question with an overall answer. Do people change a lot or a little over time? The

91

question makes sense and this chapter marshalls data to answer it. Further, because some individuals stabilize their character early and others are markedly transformed over the years, an attempt has been made to trace the developmental implications of such personality consistency and personality change.

PERSON CONSISTENCY OVER TIME

In Figures 6–1 and 6–2 are presented the distributions, for the male and female samples respectively, of across-time correlations between each subject's Q composites. The correlations between these personality portrayals, taken *in toto*, of each subject at different time periods provides a good index of the extent to which the individual has shown personality change or consistency. These correlations are reported both in their original form and after correction for attenuation.

Inspection of Figures 6–1 and 6–2 reveals some most compelling and intriguing findings, whether one focuses on the directly-computed, or, as preferred here, attenuation-adjusted figures.

1. The average across-time correlations, based upon separate sets of judges, and non-overlapping data bases seem impressively high (means of .77 and .75 for the JHS–SHS interval; .56 and .54 for the SHS–Adult interval for men and women respectively, corrected for attenuation). On the average, there appears to be appreciable, statistically significant personality consistency over time.

2. There is extraordinary variation in the extent of personality consistency shown. For the male sample, from JHS to SHS, the across-time correlations after attenuation adjustment range from −.01 to 1.00; for the period from SHS to Adulthood, the range is from −.40 to .99.

For the female sample, from JHS to SHS, the range of across-time correlations is from −.02 to 1.00; for the period from SHS to Adulthood, the range is from −.30 to .97. The figures prior to adjustment for attenuation, which are less satisfactory conceptually, also manifest astonishing range.

The reader is reminded that an average is useful descriptively insofar as the distribution of scores on which it is based has a small range. Accordingly, the extremely wide dispersion of Q correlations over time indicates that the seemingly impressive mean Q correlation characterizing the sample as a whole is in fact rather uninformative about any particular subject. Although for some subjects the adolescent personality descriptions are almost totally predictive of the way they are independently evaluated a generation later, for other subjects there is no, or even a reversed, relationship between their character organization at the two widely separated assessment periods. We shall be returning shortly and at

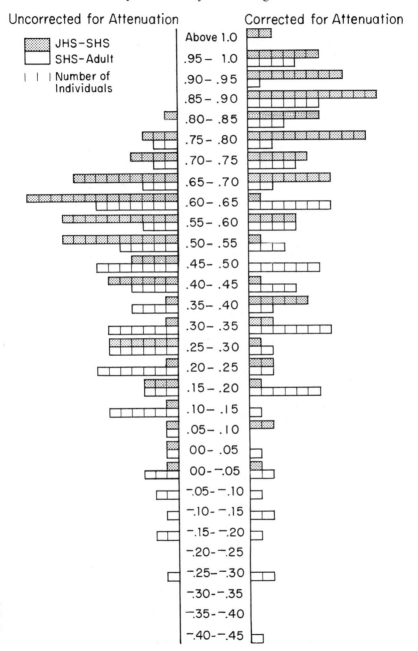

Figure 6–1 Distribution of Across-Time CQ-correlations—Male Sample

Data missing on 8 subjects for JHS–SHS and 8 subjects for SHS–Adult (uncorrected and corrected).

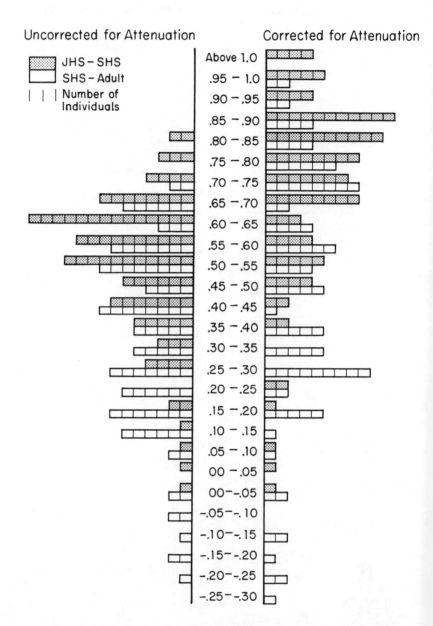

Figure 6-2 Distribution of Across-Time CQ-correlations—Female Sample

Data missing on 4 subjects for JHS–SHS and 3 subjects for SHS–Adult (uncorrected and corrected).

length to this finding of great individual differences in across-time consistency of personality.

3. It is a reasonable presumption that personality consistency will be greater over shorter periods of time than over longer intervals. This expectation is borne out for the JHS–SHS comparison *vis-à-vis* comparisons into the far more distant adult years—the mean JHS–SHS Q correlations are appreciably higher than the Q correlations linking either JHS or SHS to Adulthood. For the male sample, the corollary expectation also holds—that the JHS–Adulthood correlations will average lower than the SHS–Adulthood Q correlations because a longer time interval is involved (.47 vs. .56). But for the female sample, the relationship is reversed. The average JHS–Adulthood Q correlation for our women subjects is *higher* than the average SHS–Adulthood Q correlation (.55 vs. .54). Thus, an expectable difference does not exist—the personality characterization of a girl during JHS is no worse, or perhaps even better, as a predictor of her adult personality status than is the formulation of her personality developed during SHS. The evidence on this point is by no means firm, but there are indications, to be developed later, that especially for girls, the maelstrom of the SHS years proves to be threatening because of the uncertain but decision-demanding situations into which they are plunged. Their tolerance for change and for experience is exceeded, with the result that they revert back in their later years to former characterological positions which do not discomfort them. This sequence, if correct, can explain the relatively enhanced relevance of JHS characterizations for an understanding of the adult personalities of the women subjects.

PERSONALITY CHANGE AS A MODERATOR VARIABLE

We have seen that some of the IHD subjects changed over time and some did not. Is there an order or lawfulness or patterning that can account for this range of developmental consistency, or are these individual differences not especially reliable or worthy of closer attention? One way of responding to this question is to compare straightforwardly individuals who change with individuals who do not change in order to ascertain what, if anything, characterizes changers and non-changers.* This we have done, although with some conceptual and methodological reservations. Personality change *per se* is a gross concept since the particular *direction* of change is not ordained by the fact of inconstancy. There are much more incisive bases for grouping individuals and the next chapters report efforts along these lines. The conceptual reservation having been stated, the interest in the comparison remains.

* The idea for this analysis is due to Norma Haan.

The subjects were divided into groups of "changers" and "non-changers" by the following arbitrary but reasonable and non-biassing procedure. Using the mean of the attenuation-corrected distribution of JHS–SHS Q correlations as a simple and sole dividing point, all subjects *below* the mean were categorized as JHS–SHS Changers and all subjects *above* the mean were categorized as JHS–SHS Nonchangers. Using the mean of the analagous distribution of SHS–Adult Q correlations, the subjects *below* the mean were labeled SHS–Adult Changers, and those *above* the mean were labeled SHS–Adult Nonchangers. These categorizations were developed separately for the male and female samples.

Particularly in regard to the JHS–SHS comparison, for which period the across-time correlations are usually rather high, the categorization of subjects as Changers or Nonchangers to some extent capitalizes on chance. To the extent this effect may be operating, substantive differences between the groups will be diminished or cannot become evident. So much for the methodological reservation.

The implicit reason underlying our interest in Changers and Nonchangers is that, across-time, the variables characterizing a group of subjects is a (usually accidental) function of the constituency of the group being studied. The results developed in the preceding chapter, using the entire sample, group Changers and Nonchangers together with the unstated expectation that the overall trends then manifest are general and apply to any subgroup within the full sample. But low or moderate correlations over time may result simply from the fact that some individuals change and others do not. When such diverse subjects are aggregated, systematic relationships existing within any one group are diluted, if not lost. The focus on Changers and Nonchangers, then, in men and in women, is a first, acknowledgedly gross effort to identify orderly patterns of personality organization that may have been masked by the essentially traditional analytical approach of the last chapter.

THE CHARACTERISTICS OF MALE CHANGERS AND MALE NONCHANGERS

From Junior High School to Senior High School

When the male subjects changing appreciably from JHS to SHS are contrasted with those changing comparatively little, at each of the three time periods JHS, SHS, and Adulthood, there are appreciable personality differences to be observed. The differences are consistent throughout but are few in adolescence and are striking at adulthood.*

Comparing the JHS Adolescent *CQ* (*ACQ*) and Interpersonal *Q* composites of the JHS–SHS Changers with the JHS *ACQ* and Interpersonal *Q* composites of the JHS–SHS Nonchangers, the following variables are statistically differentiating:

Relatively characteristic of male J/S Changers * *—accepting of self-dependency, reluctant to act, fantasizing, self-defensive, favors status quo, initiates humor with his peers.

Relatively characteristic of the male J/S Nonchangers—socially perceptive, verbally fluent.

Comparing the SHS *ACQ* and Interpersonal *Q* composites for these groups, the following variables are significant:

Relatively characteristic of male J/S Changers—seeks reassurance, esthetically reactive, sensuous, insightful; is able to have appropriate relationships with adults, predominant orientation is toward adults as opposed to peers.

Relatively characteristic of male J/S Nonchangers—no *ACQ* items were positively associated with Nonchangers in this analysis; the differ-

---

* It should be remembered that the *content* or *nature* of the personality differences between Changers and Nonchangers is not implicit in the fact of change. In identifying the *quality* of the differences between Changers and Nonchangers, the findings are of substantive import and are not artifactual consequents of the separately measured *quantity* of personality change used to partition our sample.

** Very many of the analyses to be recorded in this book involve the comparison of two groups, usually by means of the *t* test. In reporting the results of these analyses, the convention has been to report variables positively associated with one group, and separately, the variables positively associated with the second group. Generally, the results are most readily apprehended when conveyed in this fashion, but two interpretive cautions need to be kept in mind by the reader. First, comparisons are *relative*. Although one group may be (relatively) higher than another group with respect to a variable, this finding carries no information regarding the *absolute* level of the groups on the dimension nor does it necessarily imply the results of comparisons with a third or other groups. Thus, Group A may be relatively higher than Group B on a variable, but both may be absolutely high (or low) and both may be higher (or lower) in turn than Group C. The reader should be prepared to recognize these complications on the occasions they develop.

The second small sophistication required of the reader stems from our practice of reporting the positively associated variables for each of the two groups in a comparison. It is of course the case that a variable or *Q* item relatively characteristic of one group may be viewed as well as relatively *un*characteristic of the other group. The numerical preponderance of variables or attributes characterizing one of the two groups being compared has no special significance *taken by itself*, but rather represents accidents or biases in the original selection of variables and in their labeling. Thus, when in a comparison 10 *Q* items are relatively characteristic of Changers, and no items are relatively characteristic of Nonchangers, it should be understood that 10 *Q* items distinguish these two groups and the sense of their difference may be viewed in one group by direct interpretation of the variables named, and in the second group by interpreting the same variables *after reflection* of their meanings.

entiating Interpersonal item was: involved in fantasy level with opposite sex.

The comparison of Changers and Nonchangers as defined in the JHS–SHS period with respect to their personality evaluations as judged twenty years later provides differences both more numerous and of clearer import. Comparing the Adult *CQ* composites of the JHS–SHS defined Changers and Nonchangers, the following *Q* items prove significant:

Relatively characteristic of male J/S Changers—thin-skinned, fearful, brittle, self-defensive, overconcerned with own adequacy, compares self with others, uncomfortable with uncertainty; complicating of simple situations, reluctant to act, aloof, condescending, deceitful.

Relatively characteristic of male J/S Nonchangers—intellectual capacity, values intellectual matters, rapid tempo, insightful, introspective, arouses liking, socially poised, straightforward, gregarious, giving, physically attractive, interested in opposite sex.

As incidental findings, in adulthood J/S Nonchangers significantly more often described themselves as resembling their fathers more than their mothers in personality. Also, male J/S Nonchangers fathered more children than did Changers.

Considering that in each of the first two analyses, 167 item comparisons were made (104 items in the Adolescent *CQ* set, 63 items in the Interpersonal *Q* set), rather few and small differences appear to exist between the Changers and Nonchangers as defined during the JHS–SHS period. But these differences consolidate into a pattern prefiguring the later adult character of the Changers and Nonchangers.

Finally, we note that the *PA* Index, our measure of overall psychological adjustment, indicates little or no difference between the male JHS–SHS Changers and Nonchangers during either of two adolescent periods; however, the male Nonchangers appear appreciably and reliably more adjusted than the Changers, as adults. For the J/S Changers, the *PA* Index averages for the JHS, SHS, and adult periods are—.04, .07, and .04 respectively—little evidence for psychological growth. For the J/S Nonchangers, the *PA* Index averages for these periods are .06, .04 and .23—displaying appreciable maturation within the adult years.

Evaluative Summary. During early adolescence, male J/S Changers appear avoidant of new experiences and the development of their self-capacities. Later in adolescence they are dependent individuals, adult oriented, and receptive (or vulnerable) to the complexities in their external and internal experience.

The male J/S Nonchangers seem relatively uncomplicated individuals who are on top of their adolescent worlds, radiating confidence and capability at this time. They are quick and eager, but are not as psychologically differentiated as the Changers, as witnessed by the greater tendency of the Nonchangers to employ fantasy in the sexual realm.

In adulthood, the implications of adolescent personality change in males appears most striking and consequential. Adolescent changers in the fourth decade of life appear extraordinarily unsure of themselves. They are tense, vulnerable, guarded, and still working on the problems of identity that should have been settled years before.

Nonchangers, those fortunate males whose adolescent course was so uneventful, continue to be blessed as adults. They appear to be individuals of appreciable ego resourcefulness. They are vigorous producers, at ease with their world, they are not preoccupied with questions as to who they are although they do not lack in inner life, they have been able to take on and to welcome the new roles the years have brought them.

In sum, our data suggest that, in American middle-class boys in the middle of the 20th century, discontinuities from JHS to SHS will be predictive in adulthood of a marked tendency toward a defensively organized character; boys manifesting comparatively little or continuously progressive personality change during adolescence will tend in their adulthood to have impressive ego resources.

From Senior High School to Adulthood

It is worthwhile to describe separately the implications of personality change and continuity from SHS to Adulthood because the groupings of Changers and Nonchangers defined over these time intervals are almost completely unrelated to the Change and Nonchange groupings established from JHS to SHS (the phi coefficient of relationship is only .03). Although some overall similarities will be observed between the results just reported and the findings now about to be presented, there are important differences as well which would be lost by neglecting the time interval during which personality change was observed.

When the male subjects changing appreciably from SHS to Adulthood are contrasted with those who manifested little personality change, at each of the three time periods, there are appreciable differences to be seen. Again the differences are consistent but more abundant at one time period than another.

Comparing the JHS *ACQ* and Interpersonal *Q* composites of the SHS–Adulthood Changers with those of the SHS–Adulthood Nonchangers, the following items prove differentiating:

Relatively characteristic of male S/A Changers—uncomfortable with uncertainty, extrapunitive, withdraws when frustrated, negativistic, deceitful, gregarious, self-defeating, other-directed, self-indulgent, eroticizing, projecting, masculine, conforming, communicates through non-

100   Lives Through Time

verbal behavior; claims the privileges and excuses afforded the adolescent in this culture, emphasizes being with peers, dependent on peers, accepts and appreciates sex-typing as it affects self, spends time with opposite sex.

Relatively characteristic of male S/A Nonchangers—wide interests, intellectual capacity, introspective, prides self on objectivity, productive, aware of social stimulus value, unconventional thought processes, values intellectual matters, interesting, insightful, has high aspiration level, philosophically concerned, fluent; views his family as an interesting one, feels mother is a respected woman, has genuine and appropriate relationships with adults, views mother as an attractive woman, adult oriented.

Comparing the SHS *ACQ* and Interpersonal *Q* composites for these groups, 53 *ACQ* and 21 Interpersonal *Q* variables are significant. For convenience, and because they are sufficient, only the 29 *ACQ* items and 7 Interpersonal items significant beyond the .01 level are reported.

Relatively characteristic of the male S/A Changers—brittle, uncomfortable with uncertainty, self-defensive, extrapunitive, withdraws when frustrated, self-defeating, self-pitying, other-directed, rebellious, pushes limits, negativistic, bothered by demands, expresses hostile feelings directly, communicates through non-verbal behavior; claims the privileges and excuses afforded the adolescent, covertly hostile to adults, rebellious with adults.

Relatively characteristic of male S/A Nonchangers—wide interests, prides self on objectivity, values intellectual matters, philosophically concerned, has high aspiration level, views self as causative, insightful, esthetically reactive, interesting, verbally fluent, productive, dependable, protective, satisfied with self, comfortable with past decisions; views his family as interested, perceives parents as equitable, protective of friends, selective in choice of friends.

As further distinguishing marks, we note that the male S/A Nonchangers from SHS to Adulthood earned significantly higher IQs on the Stanford-Binet during adolescence than did the S/A changers (means of 126 and 111, respectively). With respect to some factor dimensions developed from Free Play Ratings* of our subjects during senior high school, S/A Changers more than S/A Nonchangers are high on Heterosexual Orientation and Buoyant Self-confidence. With respect to some factor dimensions developed from the Things to Talk About questionnaires, also administered during senior high school and also withheld from the later

*The Free Play Ratings were contributed at the time by observers of the subjects who watched them systematically at various phases of the schooling. For the present research, these ratings were withheld from the judges who contributed the *Q* formulations so that the Free Play Ratings could provide a totally independent source of information. After the Free Play Ratings were partitioned and composited appropriately, they were factor analyzed with the result that several dimensions of interest emerged. The procedure and the factors are more fully described in Chapter VII.

judges who provided the Q formulations, the Changers scored higher than Nonchangers on the Heterosexual Socializing and the Orientation toward Movies-Song Hits-Girls factors.

At adulthood the differences between our S/A Changers and Nonchangers continue to be marked. The following CQ items discriminate:

Relatively characteristic of the male S/A Changers—self-defensive, extrapunitive, projective, undercontrolled, self-indulgent, irritable, bothered by demands, deceitful, fluctuating moods.

Relatively characteristic of the male S/A Nonchangers—wide interests, verbally fluent, values intellectual matters, socially perceptive, incisive, ethically consistent, philosophically concerned, introspective, warm, calm, overcontrolled.

By adulthood, male S/A Nonchangers have obtained significantly more education than the S/A Changers (15.9 years of education versus 14.5 years), probably as a function of the earlier noted IQ differences between the groups.

Finally, the PA Index objectifies in an overall way the greater psychological adjustment of the male S/A Nonchangers throughout the three time periods. For the SHS–Adulthood Changers, the PA Index averages for the JHS, SHS, and Adulthood periods are $-.07, -.07$, and $.06$, respectively—only a slight trend to maturity being evidenced. For the SHS–Adulthood Nonchangers, the PA Index averages for these periods are $.13, .23$, and $.23$—all significantly higher than the corresponding PA Indices of the Changers. Of special interest as suggested by these indices is the sizable leap into maturity the S/A Nonchangers manifest from JHS to SHS where the S/A Changers show no progress whatsoever during this interval, and little later on as well.

Evaluative Summary. During their JHS years, clearly prior to the late personality change noted in the interval between SHS and Adulthood, our male S/A Changers show themselves to be prototypical adolescents wallowing in the culturally given and culturally indulged role of the "adolescent." The S/A Changers, as adolescents, are intensely peer-oriented, they are interpersonally fitful, they are sly, they are hedonistic. Adrift without the rudder of character to give them direction, their pleasures are immediate and easily knowable; their fears distant and unrecognized. At adulthood, these male changers still appear comparatively adolescent —unsettled, brittle, insistently preoccupied with enhancing or protecting the self, ill-prepared for the second half of life that has begun. They have matured to some degree since their teen years, but they had a long way to go and still do.

The male S/A Nonchangers, on the other hand, are impressive for their compassionate, informed maturity even during adolescence. They are reaching out for experience also but where the Changers seek gratification and self-reinforcement, the Nonchangers seek growth into competence and a self-differentiation. The male Nonchangers are alert, diligent, and parent-respecting without, by these societally-responsive attributes, losing the self-responsive qualities of intraceptiveness and concern for fulfilling relationships. At adulthood, the Nonchangers continue with their maturity. On balance, as conveyed by the PA Index, they have shown no further development toward a standard of psychological health but this observation perhaps speaks more for their early character accomplishment than of a personality stasis.

The carefully comparative reader will have discerned a number of differences between the characteristics of J/S Changers and those of S/A Changers. Similarly, the significance of an unchanging character from JHS to SHS is not to be equated with the significance of not changing from SHS to the time of evaluation as adults.

Thus, the male S/A Changers *vis-à-vis* the male J/S Changers appear to be comparatively more uncomfortable with uncertainty, more extrapunitive, more withdrawing and in general more self-defeating. The male S/A Nonchangers *vis-à-vis* the J/S Nonchangers are relatively dependable, introspective, productive, valuing of intellect, insightful, ambitious, esthetically inclined, and philosophically concerned. As already indicated, there is no association (phi equals .03) between personality change in the JHS–SHS interval and change in the SHS–Adulthood period. Clearly, the *time* of personality change (and of personality stabilization) is an important parameter of understanding.

THE CHARACTERISTICS OF FEMALE CHANGERS AND FEMALE NONCHANGERS

From Junior High School to Senior High School

Contrasting the female subjects changing greatly from JHS to SHS with those changing little during this interval, an interesting number of personality differences become manifest. The differences are perhaps not so numerous as those to be observed within the male sample, but they are clearly reliable and coherent. As will be seen, the character implications of personality change or continuity within the female sample are quite different from those noted for the male sample.

Comparing the JHS *ACQ* and Interpersonal *Q* composites of the JHS–SHS Changers with the JHS *ACQ* and Interpersonal *Q* composites of the JHS–SHS Nonchangers, the following variables are statistically differentiating:

Relatively characteristic of female J/S Changers—No *ACQ* items were positively associated with Changers (but see immediately below for *ACQ* items that when reflected are indicative of Changer qualities); the differentiating Interpersonal items were: feels her parents are old-fashioned, assertive with peers, directly hostile with peers.

Relatively characteristic of female J/S Nonchangers—dependent, introspective, perceives family as affectionate, perceives family as egalitarian, perceives father as an attractive man, accepts and appreciates sex-typing as it affects self.

For the SHS period, the comparison of the *ACQ* composites reveals somewhat more, but still rather few, distinguishing personality characteristics:

Relatively characteristic of female J/S Changers—values independence, physically attractive, satisfied with physical appearance, fastidious, withdraws when frustrated; covertly hostile to adults.

Relatively characteristic of female J/S Nonchangers—somatizes, has bodily concern, submissive, accepting of self-dependency, clearcut and consistent personality; perceives parents as fair, perceives parents as consistent.

Some additional relationships of the JHS–SHS Changer-Nonchanger distinction emerge from data not available within the case assemblies upon which the Q formulations are based: Adolescent girls who change are rated higher on Heterosexual Orientation during the Free Play Observations in SHS. They are also higher than Nonchangers on occupational interest dimensions relating to becoming a Youth Leader and occupations ordinarily involving Aggressive Masculinity. The *mothers* of Changers were rated as significantly higher on the characteristics, Dissatisfied, Worried.

Later, as adults, girls who changed from JHS to SHS continued to show moderate differences from girls who did not manifest appreciable adolescent change. The following *CQ* items discriminate:

Relatively characteristic of female J/S Changers—productive, turned-to-for-advice, ethically consistent, physically attractive.

Relatively characteristic of female J/S Nonchangers—moody, self-pitying, self-deceiving.

As adults, female Changers more than Nonchangers are politically conservative, are more involved in politics, have more family income, and felt their parents had urged them on to high standards of conduct. Female Changers currently write their parents more frequently than do Nonchangers. Changers did not feel that financial security would be a decisive consideration in their evaluation of a job possibility.

Finally, the *PA* Index can be used to trace the psychological progression of the female J/S Changers and Nonchangers over time. For the J/S Changers, the *PA* Index averages for the JHS, SHS, and Adulthood periods are, respectively, .09, .02, and .20. For the J/S Nonchangers, the corresponding figures are .09, .02, and .11. Both groups manifest a regressive, maladaptive phase during SHS and both take a positive turn subsequently. But the rebound toward maturity appears greater for those girls who experienced appreciable character change during adolescence.

Evaluative Summary. During their adolescent years, the female J/S Changers appear to be bursting out of themselves almost as if they *want* to change. They are in a hurry, dissatisfied with their archaic parents, impatient with their peers, intensely focused upon achieving an independent and attractive self. They have embarked upon a long travel and their mothers are worried.

The female J/S Nonchangers, on the other hand, manifest a passive, somewhat musing but never confronting acceptance of what their lives have brought them. In these girls the blandness of the *persona* intimates a fearfulness underneath. They are not so troublesome as the Changers but neither are they exceptionally appealing; they do not make ripples but instead float in the stream.

As adults, the implications of the different adolescent orientations is more clearly to be seen. The Changers now seem competent and comfortable, with a clear sense of who and what they are. There is a curious but by no means incomprehensible turnabout in the remembrances of the Changers regarding their parents. The Changers resented their parents during adolescence, but in adulthood the Changers communicate more frequently with their parents and recollect fondly the insistence of their parents on standards and achievement.

By way of contrast, the Nonchangers are disappointed in the way their lives have gone. They are moody, still vulnerable, and verge on the hyperfeminine. Their niche had been established early and now they are wistful wishers that they had been jarred from the securities they required then and still emphasize. The Nonchangers are not badly off but there is a sense, in them and in the observer, of adolescent possibilities not reached for and a recognition that the possibilities no longer exist.

From Senior High School to Adulthood

The differences between the female S/A Changers and Nonchangers are, on the whole, more impressive than those characterizing the J/S groupings. The relation between the J/S and S/A categorizations is small (phi of .23). Comparing their JHS *ACQ* and Interpersonal *Q* composites, the following items emerge as differentiating:

Relatively characteristic of female S/A Changers—seeks reassurance, withdrawing, brittle, distrustful, body-concerned, bland; passive with adults, feels parents are old-fashioned, seeks reassurance from peers, tends to be butt of group.

Relatively characteristic of female S/A Nonchangers—prides self on objectivity, productive, emotionally involved with members of same sex; able to have appropriate relationships with adults, views mother as attractive, perceives parents as accepting her steps toward maturity.

Comparing the SHS *ACQ* and Interpersonal *Q* composites, the following items prove distinguishing:

Relatively characteristic of female S/A Changers—brittle, self-defensive, withdraws when frustrated, undercontrolled, unpredictable, rebellious, pushes limits, self-indulgent, affected, communicates through nonverbal behavior, negativistic, basic hostility, deceitful, distrustful, feels a lack of meaning in life, extrapunitive, self-dramatizing; covertly hostile to adults, attention-getting behavior with peers, assertive with peers, condescending with peers.

Relatively characteristic of female S/A Nonchangers—dependable, straightforward, clearcut and consistent personality, overcontrolled, productive, high aspiration level, giving, sympathetic, arouses liking, aware of impression created, insightful, submissive, arouses nurturant feeling, wide interests, protective, prides self on objectivity, warm, values intellectual matters, esthetically reactive, satisfied with self, favors status quo; closer to mother than father, respecting of parents, perceives parents as fair and consistent, sees parents as singling her out for special evaluation, able to have appropriate relationships with adults, protected by peers.

The factor scores based on Free Play Observations during senior high school show the S/A Changers to be less oriented than the S/A Nonchangers toward heterosexual socializing. In responding to various interest inventories administered at that time, the Changers express a greater interest in being a Concert Singer and claim greater conversational concern during SHS in regard to Problems of Racial Minorities. The Nonchangers at this time indicate a greater frequency of discussion of boys when within groups of girls.

At adulthood, the number of differences between female S/A Changers and Nonchangers becomes smaller, and there is no longer so clearly a self-discordancy dimension separating the two groups. The differences that remain, however, still cohere and may be viewed as personality qualities implicit in and evolved from the earlier characteristics we have noted. The following *CQ* items discriminate the two groups in their middle thirties:

Relatively characteristic of the female S/A Changers—fantasizing, thinks unconventionally, initiates humor, sensuous, rebellious.

Relatively characteristic of female S/A Nonchangers—conservative, moralistic, conventional, self-defensive, high aspiration level.

As adults, the female Changers have married more frequently and they are in contact with their parents more often.

As evaluated by the Psychological Adjustment Index, Changers and Nonchangers are quite equivalent as adults. For the three time periods, JHS, SHS, and Adulthood, the mean *PA* Indices of the S/A Changers are, in order, .05, −.08, and .15. For the Nonchangers, these averages are .14, .13, and .16. Thus, the Changers appear less adjusted during the adolescent years and particularly during the SHS period displayed a marked neuroticism. However, they then manifested appreciable maturation and by the adult years, the earlier differences *vis-à-vis* an overall criterion of psychological health appear to have vanished. There are certain strengths and certain weaknesses in the Changers as adults and there are different strengths and different weaknesses in the Nonchangers in the most recent interval during which they were assessed. In the average, they cannot now be distinguished, but the qualities underlying these averages are still clearly visible.

Evaluative Summary. During their SHS years, prior to the change and redefinition they experienced later, our female S/A Changers *vis-à-vis* the Nonchangers appear to have been other-directed, tensely bland, and despairing individuals. They sought attention and acceptance, sometimes by the strategem of becoming the fool or foil of their peers.

By SHS, this pliability before others and generalized capitulation of self was exchanged for more active, if not yet effective, efforts toward a personal definition. During these years, the Changers are stridently bitchy, histrionic, manipulative girls. They are relatively narcissistic, irresponsible, and nasty—all adjectives denoting how unlikable as individuals they are at this time. Withal, however, these girls remain brittle and unhappy, communicating only fitfully with themselves and with others.

The signs of their later adult lives are in evidence during these years, despite the significant inner disturbance and social unacceptability they manifest as adolescents. During SHS, the optimism inherent in activity has replaced the core of passivity that earlier predominated and this more vigorous orientation toward self and surround, although evidenced during SHS in criticizable behaviors, has the potential for growth and realization that the earlier passivity could not generate. As adults, then, the Changers appear to be cognitively more interesting people, still somewhat rebellious but now more relaxed with themselves and with their place in life.

The Nonchangers during JHS appear rather well off—they are capable, self-respecting kids in tune with their parents rather than caught up by resentment or the pleasures of superciliousness. There are indications in them at this time of the ability to relate meaningfully to other people. In SHS the Nonchangers continue to be psychologically impressive—they are reliable, self-congruent individuals with a clement attitude towards others. The indications of overcontrol and submissiveness are comparative only and derive from our method of analysis. Relative to the Changers, the S/A Nonchangers are indeed more constrained and yielding, but when evaluated more absolutely, they are not to be characterized especially in these terms.

Or so it would appear. Except that at adulthood, the Nonchangers have not shown psychological maturation beyond what was to be observed in their adolescent years and the facets of their character that are highlighted by contrasts with the S/A Changers as adults reveal an essential and now hardened conservatism and conventionality in the Nonchangers. They are ambitious still and in societal terms would still be judged more advanced than the Changers. But in a more psychological context, as objectified by the *PA* Index, the Nonchangers although reasonably adaptable may not be evaluated as more suitable than the Changers for the rigors and flux of life.

Chapter VII

COURSES OF PERSONALITY DEVELOPMENT
—RATIONALE, METHODOLOGY,
AND BACKGROUND

Preceding chapters have focussed upon personality variables abstracted from their context or have sought the implications of personality change and continuity defined in a statistical, content-free way. In this and the next two chapters, the concern is with *kinds* of personality development and the different organization and implications of variables *within* these several character formations. The changes over time of alternative personality paths will be tracked. The available information will be mustered so as to picture the familial and environmental context linked with each of these several routes of character development. And the way the individuals representing these different life styles are faring as they begin the second half of their lives will be reported. This chapter presents rationale, methodology, and necessary background information; Chapter VIII reports the substantive findings surrounding the male sample; Chapter IX conveys the results for the female sample.

ORIENTATION

The Typological Approach

The study of personality patterns is a continually attractive, yet ever untidy and discouraging personological approach. The dismaying aspects of the patterning orientation are left until a bit later in this chapter. For now, the allure of typologies is our concern.

For a developmental context, a type may be defined as a subset of individuals characterized by a reliably unique or discontinuously different pattern of covariation across time with respect to a specifiable (and non-

109

trivial) set of variables. This definition is not new—it derives from earlier formulations of the idea of type (cf., e.g., Block, 1955; Cattell, 1952; Cronbach, 1953; Stephenson, 1953).

In the last few years, the patterning approach has become increasingly inviting because it asserts an argument many psychologists have become ready to accept—that the nomothetic, monolithic view of personality functioning is gross, misguided, and outworn. To illustrate the argument, consider the moderating influence of the masculinity-femininity variable. Thus, it is widely recognized that the relations among psychological variables are frequently importantly different in men and in women. Generalizations that apply to the one sex often do not apply to the other.

However, the larger implication of the recognition that sex differentially links a host of variables is not so clearly held and has not been thoroughly applied. Within each sex as well, there can be fundamental bases for partitioning samples into relatively homogeneous subgroups, e.g., over-controllers and under-controllers, dissonance-reducers and dissonance-enhancers, field-dependent and field-independent individuals. Highly lawful relationships characterizing one subsample may not characterize another subsample which is equally but differently determinate. If only because personality study within the nomothetic tradition has to date issued empirical results slight in power and bland in substance, psychologists have come to direct more attention to the possibility (I believe likelihood) of homogeneous subgroups that are lawful in different ways.

In opposing the nomothetic position, it is not necessary to advocate the converse idiographic position. The nomothetic-idiographic controversy in psychology has been argued in binary terms when it is more reasonable and more productive of understanding to conceptualize a continuum between these allegedly disjunctive opposites. Thus, although there apparently is not one model of personality functioning that can be employed across the board, this is not to say there are an infinite number of ways in which personality can be organized. All "organizations" of personality are directed toward achieving a temporally tenable system of perception and response in a complex and fluxional world. But some arrangements of personality submit the self to such extremes of anguish as to be not viable; they exist, if at all, only transiently before being replaced by other "system designs" with more enduring properties. These more durable modes of personality organization are probably reasonably few in overall number—there are not endlessly unique ways of achieving the psycho-economic requirements of the personality. Although we are all unique at the level of historical incident and in the content of our experience, although uniqueness is a satisfying phenomenological belief, when individuals are looked at in terms of modes of adaptation, we are none of us so exquisitely different as to defy a rather useful categorization.

The categorization may often employ blurred boundaries so that borderline individuals cannot fairly be located in any one category. The defining properties for category membership may be gross and imprecise so that it seems inappropriate to consider all members of a category *a priori* as interchangeable or equivalent. But these concerns are simply (sic!) matters of practice and implementation. They do not deny the principle and the usefulness of the pigeon hole.

Prospective, Retrospective and Conjoint Orientations Toward Understanding

If one is going to apply the typological approach in a longitudinal context, what is the conceptually most fruitful way to proceed? There is a conceptual issue or choice to be pondered here before going on because the psychology of adolescence is not the psychology of adulthood. The problems, orientations, and fixities of these different times are different and consequently, personality patternings will reflect their eras.

Is a personality typology established at adolescence more useful or more interesting than a personality typology established at adulthood? Certainly, one can argue that "the adolescent is father to the man." During adolescence, the developing individual is establishing personal ways of dealing with the central adaptational problems that beset us all. Confronting the teenager is the emergence of interest in and opportunities for heterosexuality; he must begin to find a satisfying (or tolerable) life work commitment; he must learn to maintain an integrity-preserving stance before authority figures; he must respond to insistent, pervading ramifications of the need for a sense of self in a society that is only temporarily permissive. He is leaving safe harbor and setting out into the ocean of experience for a destination he cannot know.

By the onset of the teen years, the adolescent has a character structure already substantially formed. The patternings of behavior that are discernible at this time are coherent, integral manifestations of the personality organization each adolescent carries over from childhood. Subsequent adolescent behaviors, however, will take on a fuller meaning and predictive significance when they are viewed within the ongoing *and changing* matrix of each individual's style and hierarchy of responses. A typology established at the beginning of the adolescent years, no matter how trenchant it may be for the period of adolescence from which it immediately derives, necessarily will lose relevance with the passage of only a few years.

The close student of our adolescent subjects, cognizant of their different patternings of personality, must be intrigued by the theoretical problem of anticipating what these young people will become twenty-five

years later. Prediction is our aspiration; yet how dare we assert outcomes when our adolescent subjects are undergoing change and the con-
tingencies and reinforcements in their subsequent environments involve
so many imponderables and unknowns. Broad extrapolations may be
feasible; excitingly specific predictions will fail.

By the time in adulthood when we encounter our subjects, the bloom is
off the peach tree and the fruits of the years are in evidence. In your middle thirties, you are pretty much the kind of person you are going to be.
Character strengths and weaknesses have been developed and stabilized;
career lines are largely set; men have become husbands and fathers, and
women have become wives and mothers. Selfhood has been won by this
time or, almost without exception, it will not be.

For the observer, there is less curiosity now about what will happen to
our longitudinally followed subjects. Instead, the curiosity is retrospective, concerned more with how and why these people turned out to be
the way they are.

Somewhere, Freud remarks that, prospectively, it is most difficult to
anticipate or know what will happen to someone whereas, retrospec-
tively, the patterns of a life seem inexorable and most lawful. "The trouble
with life is that it must be lived forward but can be understood only
backward" (a remark, cited here in approximate form, by Freud. I have
been unable to locate the precise source).

We know what happened to our subjects. What had been the future is
now largely past and the determination (and over-determination) of an
individual's life is clearly to be seen. For this reason, a typology at adulthood offers conceptual advantages over one established, say, at adolescence or in childhood. Uniformities in experience can be sought and
responsible post-diction can be attempted because personality is being
studied in its environmental context. Predictions forward in time from
adolescence are offered in the abstract, with a fundamental variable in
the equation—the environmental context—being absent. Post-dictions
backward in time from adulthood—as noteworthy an accomplishment if
responsibly executed as is prediction—can be offered *in vivo,* with recognition of the contextual variables that were operative.

Yet, an adult typology taken alone is not sufficient for our longitudinal
purposes. A personality typology established at any one time period is a
cross-sectional, essentially static way of conceptualizing. For our purposes and interests, the preferred typology should reflect in some *con-
joint* way the personality types manifested during adolescence as well as
those discernible during adulthood. It should also provide information on
the personality changes that have accrued with time. Personality types
change and evolve in lawful ways over time and we are interested in the
developmental trends manifested by these various modes of personality

organization. A personality type early is a personality type later, albeit a different one perhaps. We need to be able to plot the various separate trend-lines of our personality types, attending both to the cross-sectional comparisons available at each slice of time and to the directions and the significance of the changes observed over the years. It is *types of personality development*, not *types of personality* that serve the conceptual purposes of the longitudinal inquiry.

The orientation and recognitions of the past several pages are more a beginning than an end. The task now becomes a messy and arbitrary one—to identify *the* set (or an incisive or interesting set) of psychologically coherent ways of personality development.

PROCEDURAL RATIONALE

The essential logic that must underlie efforts at discerning types of patterns of personality organization involves, first, specification of the similarities or resemblances between each pair of subjects being studied and, second, locating groups or clusters of like individuals within the similarity matrix that has been developed. A third, more particular problem to be faced arises from our concern with studying the courses of personality development. That is, the data set within which the types of personality organization are to be discerned should be of proper form, nature, and arrangement so that the historical changes characterizing each type are also expressed.

The Similarity Question

In the specification of similarity of a pair of individuals we must ask, *similarity with respect to what set of variables,* since similarity in an abstract sense is not intellectually graspable. Further, the particular index or coefficient in terms of which similarity is objectified is often important because of the ways in which the index selected may influence subsequent analyses.

The typological analyses to be reported in the next two chapters all involved the *CQ* formulations available for each subject. The items or variables constituting these *Q* sets are, as indicated in earlier chapters, broad in their coverage and extensively pre-tested. It is fair to say they represent reasonably well contemporary conceptualizations of the dimensions with which it is fruitful to view personality. Because of the comprehensiveness of the *Q* sets employed as the data bases, there is ample opportunity for individuals to be different as well as similar and further, to be different in diverse, orthogonal ways as well as different in diametrical ways. More constraining sets of variables might have determined the finding of marked similarity of all subjects or a simple bipolar dimension along which individuals are bimodally distributed. The multifaceted psychological possibilities afforded by the Q sets used did not dictate such findings. Although the results are inevitably a function of the variable set employed, this variable set appears to have sufficient degrees of freedom so that personality diversities can be manifested. Thus, the dependency of the relationships found upon the particular Q items employed is not methodologically bothersome. The limitation, to the extent it exists, is the limit on current ways of viewing personality rather than a deficiency of a particular method.

The choice of a similarity coefficient, a problem worried in other contexts (cf., e.g., Cronbach & Gleser, 1953; Cattell, Counter & Tsujioka, 1966), appears of small consequence in our own application. Conventionally, it has been argued that the profiles characterizing individuals can differ with respect to (a) the average *level* or mean of the set of variables expressing the pattern, (b) the *scatter* or variance manifested over the set of variables for that individual, and (c) the *ordering* of the variables as they describe the subject.

Unfortunately, it has been a further convention for the coefficients that have been advocated to recognize these three sources of variance to conglomerate them so that a given coefficient (such as D^2) is ambiguous as to its implications for level or scatter or ordering. These similarity scores, if less than maximal, do not convey whether the remaining difference is attributable to differences in level or scatter or ordering or some combination of these possibilities.

Moreover, there is a deeper conceptual problem in applying the psychometric distinctions among level, scatter, and ordering to the realm of personality profiles. It makes little psychological sense to employ level as a basis for evaluating subjects—does one individual have more or less "personality," on the average, than another? With a comprehensive and balanced set of personality variables, this question is meaningless. Differences in scatter also convey no uniquely useful information about the subject although these differences may be instructive about the nature of the measuring device or the raters employed. Such differences are likely to reflect only how easily the subject can be evaluated and this information can be conveyed as well and more readily via a directly relevant personality variable within the larger variable set. So, we are left with the ordering of variables as the remaining, simplified, and sufficient basis for defining the personality configuration of a subject. The reader will have anticipated that the Q-sort procedure, by its use of a forced distribution of item placements, eliminates unwanted level and scatter differences and provides the desired ordering information directly.

As an "indicator" of the resemblance of two orderings, it has been traditional to use the product-moment correlation coefficient and that tradition is continued here. Other indices might have been used but introduce no advantages that could dislodge the well established and well understood correlation coefficient. It should be kept in mind, however, that the correlation coefficient in this context is a purely descriptive index and may not be referred to its conventional sampling distribution.

The Discernment of Types

The method of transposed or Q-factor analysis was employed to group subjects into homogeneous clusters or types. More technically, the principal components procedure followed by varimax rotation was applied. Factor analysis, for those who do not know (or need to know) the method, is a mathematical procedure for determining the number of dimensions that can be said to underlie a large complex of interrelated data. It is a computational way of discerning an order or structure in a matrix of relationships that otherwise would be overwhelming and beyond the compass of the human eye and brain. When applied to the correlations among *variables,* factor analysis issues factor dimensions in terms of which the variables can be understood. When applied to the correlations among *people,* factor analysis issues factor types in terms of which the individuals can be viewed or categorized.

There are a number of problems associated with factor analysis in general and more particularly as applied in the present context. Various efforts were undertaken to evade these problems by using alternative grouping procedures such as Tryon's cluster analysis (Tryon & Bailey, 1966) and the non-metric factor analysis method of Lingoes and Guttman (1967). But these alternatives exchanged difficulties rather than removing them and did not provide illuminations heretofore unavailable from the more conventional factor approach.

The vagaries of factor analysis are largely known and the knowledgeable investigator need not be passive in using factor analysis as a schematizing tool. With more provisional and experimental multivariate procedures, perspective has not yet been formed and there is a danger of having an unknown method fortuitously determine, with hidden whimsicality, the structure of one's findings. For this reason, I opted to remain with the garden variety of factor analysis—it is a procedure of great power not so new as to be misunderstood and not so old as to be without interesting and useful application.

The problems of factor analysis primarily lie in (a) determining the "correct" number of factors or types that underlie the pattern of covariation being analyzed, and (b) positioning or rotating the factors or types so that they achieve a conceptually satisfactory psychological meaning. These problems are interrelated in that the rotational solution is often a fundamental function of the number of factors being rotated. And the decision as to the number of factors to be fixed upon is often influenced by the comparative clarity or comparative conceptual usefulness of one of the infinite number of rotational solutions possible. There are no hard and fast rules on these matters agreed to by the multifarious workers in multivariate analysis. Choice derives from temperament, esthetic inclination, or pragmatic response to the nature of the problem at hand.

For the present purposes, the method of factor analysis imposes an obvious dilemma. It was desired to establish homogeneous types of development so that the different characteristics and implications of these distinct personality configurations could be charted. In the pursuit of this interest, how best to partition the sample of subjects? The partitioning should "cleave Nature at its joints," of course, but the method of factor analysis proved quite ambiguous in deciding upon the natural anatomy of personality. Too few groupings would do an injustice to the variety of character types that exists in the personality domain; too many groupings would respect character diversity better but would reduce the number of individuals in each group thus depriving our subsequent statistical analysis of its power. The one emphasis—on a few types—would issue relatively gross but dependable results; the other emphasis—on many types—would offer a richer and more sensitive perspective but one that could well be unreliable or without generalization.

My decision, considered and advised, was to elect a firmly in-between position. After closely studying the psychometric consequences of various factor analyses of the data involving different numbers of factor types, I chose to employ a five-factor varimax solution for the male sample and a six-factor varimax solution for the female sample. This decision clusters the subject samples into groups that manifest homogeneity within each type, yet are interestingly heterogeneous between types. There are, by and large, enough representatives of each type so that statistical comparisons can be made since the great homogeneity of each type permits meaningful statistical comparisons even when sample sizes are, by ordinary standards, quite small.

Despite these procrustean inclinations, a number of subjects could not comfortably be fitted into one or another of the type categories. These are "residuals," of which there are two kinds. The one kind of residual consists of individuals who are representatives of relatively unusual character organizations not otherwise represented within the sample. Within the confines of this longitudinal study, there is little beyond individual case histories that can be attempted in order to understand these "pure residuals." These case histories could be useful from an idiographic standpoint but would not contribute to broader generalizations.

The second kind of residual includes individuals who show marked tendencies to belong to more than one of the defined types. Such subjects were left as residuals because their assignment to a particular type was anticipated to introduce more blur in later analyses than could be balanced by the increase in the sample size of each type.

The categorization of subjects into types thus represented a compromise structuring predicated upon a number of considerations no one of which could be paramount. Accordingly, these typologies cannot be viewed as polished and pure. But they arise with some clarity and persistence from the several prior and alternative analyses and they have integrating and heuristic possibilities. Tables 7–1 and 7–2 present, for the male and female samples respectively, some pertinent data regarding the homogeneity within each type and the relative separateness of the several personality configurations. This information is conveyed in the form of averaged factor loadings for the representatives of each type with respect to their own type and the other types. The number of representatives of each type is also indicated.

The clean quantitative partitioning of the samples is apparent upon inspection. Further, both the OGS and GS studies contribute to each type in more or less the proportions their relative sample sizes would suggest. This joint contribution to each typology is a small but required indicator of the tenability of merging the subjects from the two studies.

Beyond questions regarding the independence and sample-origin of the several character types, however, the fruitfulness and meaning of

Table 7–1
Averaged Factor Loadings for the Representatives of Each Type *Vis-à-vis* Their Own Type and the Other Types

	Number of Type representatives		Male Sample Homogeneity	Factors				
Types	From OGS	From GS	of type*	I	II	III	IV	V
A	11	8	.086	.711	.116	.045	.042	.017
B	5	6	.087	.149	.639	.067	.047	.040
C	7	5	.091	.052	.145	.632	.073	.019
D	8	3	.089	.120	.077	.113	.583	.015
E	4	6	.128	-.006	.107	.053	.129	.576
Residuals	14	7		.290	.225	.222	.144	.042

*The homogeneity of each type is conveyed here by the standard deviation of the set of factor loadings of the representatives of a type on its defining factor, e.g., Type A representatives with respect to Factor I, Type B representatives with respect to Factor II, and so on.

Table 7-2
Averaged Factor Loadings for the Representatives of Each Type
Vis-à-vis Their Own Type and the Other Types

Types	Number of Type representatives From OGS	From GS	Female Sample Homo-geneity of type*	I	II	III	IV	V	VI
U	12	7	.076	.708	.134	.020	.124	.056	.069
V	6	8	.074	.172	.632	.035	.004	.048	.039
W	7	3	.083	.096	.027	.605	.002	.112	.011
X	6	4	.094	.214	.012	.045	.594	.130	.137
Y	6	5	.093	.068	.084	.182	.166	.581	.042
Z	4	2	.083	.128	.144	.092	.129	.050	.593
Residuals	7	9		.395	.255	.177	.106	.149	.092

*The homogeneity of each type is conveyed here by the standard deviation of the set of factor loadings of the representatives of a type on its defining factor, e.g., Type U representatives with respect to Factor I, Type V representatives with respect to Factor II, and so on.

these pragmatically-evolved types becomes quite another matter. The incisiveness of the typology will best be seen when the personality constellations are described and related to data independent of the particular Q formulations from which they derive. It is only the usefulness and the psychological interest of the typology that ultimately can justify the categorization that has been imposed.

Factoring Courses of Personality Development

If only the Adult *CQ* formulations are factored, the result is a typology of adult character structure. If we factor only the JHS *CQ* formulations, a typology for the JHS years is developed. These two typologies have similarities but also important differences. Typologies developed in such separated ways will in part have discrepant emphases because of the error-fitting characteristics of factor analysis. In part, too, they will be different because different life stages are involved. The first of these sources of disparity is intrinsically unavoidable but its influence cannot be disentangled from the second source, to which meaning should be attributed. Consequently, the task of connecting typologies from different time intervals is made inordinately complicated without the possibility of achieving, at the end of the business of fitting and relating, a mapping of the two typologies into each other that satisfies.

A simple way of avoiding this problem and, more importantly, achieving a direct indication of the trend-lines of personality development involves factoring both JHS and Adult *Q* formulations conjointly. That is, for each individual the scores representing his Adult *CQ* formulation can be adjoined to the scores representing his JHS *CQ* formulations. For these analyses, only the 90 *Q* items *common* to the two time periods were used so that for each subject, a row of 180 scores (his particular item placements for 90 JHS *Q* items and his item placements for 90 Adult *Q* items) was developed. Correlations between subjects thus were calculated across 180 variables, half from each time period.

It is worthwhile dwelling, for a few paragraphs, on the implications of this data arrangement and the factors that will then derive from an inverse or *Q*-factor analysis. Each factor, because it is contributed to by both early and late data, expresses a reasonably homogeneous course or pattern of personality development. The early characteristics of the types arising in this analytical context can be quite different from the later characteristics so long as there is an essential uniformity in the trends or changes occurring over time. Thus, each factor type encompasses under one rubric the way the type members were, the way they are now, and parallelisms in the way the particular type members evolved. It will be seen that certain types manifest much change from JHS to Adulthood; others show little or no differences with the passage of time.

This analytical arrangement is, when the properties of the data permit, an especially useful way of applying factor analysis (e.g., to dyadic analysis). Ordinarily, when factor analysis is applied to merged sets of variables where each set stems from a different time or procedural domain, the factor approach is defeated or misled. There are two sources of this inadequacy of factor analysis. First, there is "method variance," the annoying tendency of conceptually unrelated variables within a particular method or procedure or test to cluster strongly with each other. This clustering often is so potent as to prevent or attenuate or confuse conceptual factors that otherwise would clearly intermix the variables of different methodological origins. Thus, a factor analysis of MMPI scale scores combined with psychophysiological measures would issue clear and strong factors integrating the several MMPI scales and equally clear factors grouping the psycho-physiological indices. But almost certainly, factor analysis would fail or be tenuous in relating the MMPI and the psychophysiological domains. With the *Q* variables being employed for our factor analysis, no "method variance" seems to arise. Although two widely separated and independently measured character formulations are under scrutiny, the measurement operations and resultant numbers are entirely equivalent. Since the variables being intermixed are methodologically commensurate, they may be conceptually intermixed.

The second confounder of the factor analysis of mixed bags of variables is the weighting problem. The results of a factor analysis are enormously susceptible to the usually implicit weightings underlying the sets of variables chosen for analysis. Redundancy of measurement breeds common factor variance which the factor analytic method over-respects. Important variables not redundantly measured may be swamped by a host of more easily measured variables and even defined as residuals and therefore cut off from further consideration. If we were to factor analyze a set of, say, 25 JHS variables intermixed with a set of 90 Adult variables, the resulting factors would be overdetermined and probably overweighted by the 90 Adult variables. In the analyses actually carried out, however, there is exact parallelism between the JHS and Adult Q variables so that the weighting problem is precluded from affecting the across-time typology. It is still true that within the 90-item Q set there are certain biases or weightings that will shape the content of our results. But these emphases have been previously discussed; they apply equally to the two time periods and can have no *differential* bearing on the courses of personality development factorially established. The same 90 variables indexed in JHS were also indexed in Adulthood—the two time periods have equivalent conceptual potential for determining the patternings found. It may also be added, as an empirical observation, that the JHS and Adult Q formulations show comparable and sufficient reliable item variance so that again, each time period makes an equivalent contribution to the typologies discerned.

Thus, neither "method variance" nor the weighting problem are bothersome in this analytical context. The typology, fixed by the states of the subjects during JHS and their states in their middle thirties, can proceed. Although a natural extension of this analytical logic might seem to call for including as well the 90 items of the SHS Q formulations, this addition is inadvisable at least within the factor analysis. It will be recalled that, by and large, the SHS Q formulations correlated highly with the JHS Q formulations. This correspondence obviously reflects the fact that only three or four years separated the two character formulations. To add the SHS data (thus constituting a vector of 270 scores for each subject) would have given excessive weighting in the factor analysis to the adolescent years and, by virtue of the strong relationships between the JHS and SHS data, would have made the *differences* between typologies less reliable. In addition, by omitting the SHS CQ formulations, these latter data remain entirely independent of the typology derived from the JHS–Adulthood Q sets and therefore can provide separate empirical support for the incisiveness of the personality structurings.

INDEPENDENT DATA SOURCES TO BE RELATED TO THE TYPOLOGY

Type membership will be related to a number of different sources and kinds of data that in no way contributed to the typing procedure. These measures or procedures have not previously been encountered by the reader. These additional data resources serve a number of purposes: They provide independent support and reinforcement of the validity of the character types that have been discerned; they extend the sense and significance of the typology to data realms that are far removed from the starting data, and they provide perspective on why and how the types differentially evolved. It may be noted too, before the reader does so, that the additional data being brought to bear relieves the exclusive, inbred, hothouse emphasis until now on the CQ-based character formulations.

But if supplemental data assets from the longitudinal store are to be employed, it is necessary first to describe their nature and their properties so that the reader can evaluate the relationships to be reported. Fortunately, this task can be accomplished relatively briefly since, with one exception, a full and complete description of these additional data developing procedures already exists in the literature.

Within the adolescent years of the subjects, three procedures were held out from the judges formulating the Q characterizations. These are the What I Like To Do Questionnaire, the Free Play Ratings (Newman, 1946), and the Frenkel-Brunswik Ratings (Frenkel-Brunswik, 1942). As part of the follow-up investigation during adulthood, the California Psychological Inventory (CPI) (Gough, 1957; 1964), a broad gauge personality inventory, was administered. Of course the responses of the adult subjects to the CPI were not made available to the Q-sorting judges. And, to gain understanding regarding the family origins of the subjects, the Early Family Ratings (Macfarlane, 1938), the Ratings of Mothers of Subjects (Macfarlane, 1938), and the Environmental Q set (Block, 1961) were employed. Again, all of these data resources were strictly independent of the typology to which they are to be related.

The What I Like To Do Questionnaire (WILTD)

The WILTD questionnaire consists of 50 interrogations regarding the subject's preferences and tendencies in a number of life situations. Subjects were provided a 5-point scale for their responses. The questionnaire was administered only to the OGS subjects who answered the questions on two occasions during their JHS period and once during SHS. The two JHS protocols for each subject were combined, the average response of the subject being taken as the best expression of his attitude during this time.

The WILTD questionnaires were factor analyzed, separately and combined, for the sexes and time periods, with the result that two primary overriding factors appeared to encompass the essential information in the questionnaire. The first factor derived was given the label, "Bland Socialization," connoting a stereotyped, excessively virtuous representation of self. It is unlikely that the banal qualities claimed by the highest scorers on this dimension are indeed owned by them. It is the fact that they are professed that is significant. Conversely, low scorers on the Bland Socialization continuum have acknowledged frailties that, by implication, suggest their lesser need for facade. The following WILTD items, keyed in the indicated direction, exemplify the Bland Socialization dimension:

1. Do you insist upon having things your own way? (Denied)
2. Do you usually give up soon if your work seems very hard? (Denied)
3. Do you dislike to play games when you know that you cannot play them well? (Denied)
4. Do you work better when people praise you? (Denied)
5. Are you likely to rush ahead and do things without thinking about them first? (Denied)
6. When you meet somebody whom you don't know very well, do you wait for him or her to speak first? (Denied)
7. Do you prefer to do the usual thing instead of something that is new and different? (Denied)
8. Do your feelings often change from being very happy to being very unhappy? (Denied)

The second WILTD factor was named "Over-control," indicating a tendency in those individuals loading high on this factor to be excessively constraining of their impulses and emotions and to be rigid and perseverating in ways and at times uncalled for by reality. Conversely, individuals scoring low on this continuum can be presumed to be impulsive, expressive, distractable, and unable to delay gratification. Some of the items indexing this dimension are as follows:

1. Do you always put things away where they belong? (Affirmed)
2. Can you stick to disagreeable work for a long time though no one makes you do it? (Affirmed)
3. Is it rather hard for you to make new friends? (Affirmed)
4. When you finish one thing, do you always know what you want to do next? (Affirmed)

5. Do you get excited over things that have happened or are going to happen? (Denied)
6. Do you prefer to keep changing the things that you do? (Denied)
7. Do you always let people know just how you feel? (Denied)
8. Do you get angry easily? (Denied)
9. Do you often get into trouble? (Denied)
10. Do people ever complain that you are careless in your work? (Denied)

Based upon the factor loadings of the WILTD items, two scales representing the Bland Socialization (10 items) and Over-control (17 items) dimensions were defined, scores then being developed for each subject. It is these factor-indexing scores that were then related to type membership.

The Free Play Ratings

During their adolescent years, the OGS subjects were observed by staff psychologists in a number of social situations. A clubhouse was set up by the Institute; there were group excursions and there were dances and athletic events, all of which provided the Institute staff with opportunities to observe the subjects in natural settings. Of special interest for our purposes is the series of observations deriving from what has been called "the Free Play Situation."

The Free Play Situation involved small groups of six or eight OGS subjects of the same sex brought together every six months. During a noon-hour recess from the battery of psychological and physical tests they were undergoing, the subjects would have an informal lunch or picnic on the Institute playground. These small gatherings were attended also by at least two Institute staff members, Dr. Mary Cover Jones and Dr. Caroline N. Tryon, and usually a third observer as well, Dr. Jeffrey Cameron or Dr. Howard Wells. These psychologists were familiar to the subjects, and their presence was expectable since they also lunched at this time. The available records suggest that the presence of these known adults did not constrain the subjects in any important ways in their social behaviors.

The small groups thus formed provided a useful context in which to observe the interpersonal style of the subjects, the pecking orders that evolved, and other personality-relevant social activities. The repetition of the basic situation every six months in a reasonably constant setting and with continuity of the participant observers enhances appreciably the value of the observations developed in the Free Play Situation.

The observers devised a rating schedule—known as the Institute Scales—to record their impressions of each subject. These ratings were independently contributed and subsequently averaged. The agreement between the independent raters was quite high, attesting to the reliability of the composite ratings. Almost all the OGS subjects participated in the Free Play Situation and were rated on numerous occasions. For our purposes, the Free Play ratings available for the JHS years of a subject were further averaged, as were the Free Play ratings from the SHS years, so as to develop for each subject the most representative ratings for each of these periods.

From the Free Play rating schedule, 33 ratings were selected for analysis, eliminating a number of variables that were simply the sum of other ratings. To organize these ratings into a simpler dimensional scheme, the method of factor analysis was applied to these data, separated by sex and by time period. The Free Play ratings for the SHS Boys, the JHS Girls, and the SHS Girls proved to have highly congruent three-factor solutions while the Free Play ratings for the JHS Boys manifested an understandably different three-factor structure.

For the SHS Boys, the JHS Girls, and the SHS Girls, the three factors emerging from the Free Play ratings are as follows:

1. Buoyant Self-Confidence—defined by such rated variables as Talkative, Active, Peppy, Busy, Animated, Eager, Sociable, Confident, and Assured.
2. Repose—defined by such rated variables as Matter-of-Fact, Unaffected, Relaxed, and Good-Natured.
3. Heterosexual Orientation—defined by such rated variables as Sex Appeal, Masculine (or Feminine) Behavior, Masculine (or Feminine) Physique, Attractive Coloring and Features, and Good Grooming.

For the JHS Boys, the Free Play ratings did not issue a Heterosexual Orientation factor, a result that is not surprising, given the appreciable maturity differences between boys and girls at this particular time. Girls begin to think of boys several years before boys begin to think of girls. By implication, the difference between the factor structures emerging from the JHS Boys Free Play ratings and the three other sets of Free Play ratings is testimony to the acuteness and validity of the recorded observations.

For the JHS Boys, the Free Play factors are as follows:

1. Masculine Self-Confidence—defined by such rated variables as Masculine Behavior, Masculine Physique, Leadership Qualities, Confidence, and Popularity.
2. Buoyancy—defined by such rated variables as Cheerfulness, Carefreeness, Animation, and Eagerness.

3. Repose—defined by such rated variables as Matter-of-Fact, Unaffected, Untalkative, and Inhibited.

In each of the several factor analyses, orthogonal factor scores were derived to represent the factors. It is these factor scores that have been related to type membership.

The California Psychological Inventory (CPI)

The CPI is a well-developed and well-established inventory seeking to assess a variety of personality attributes "with emphasis upon interpersonal behavior and dispositions relevant to social interaction" (Gough, 1968). It consists of 480 statements to which the respondent answers "yes" or "no." Eighteen CPI scales have been constructed by Gough measuring such dimensions as: Dominance (Do), Capacity for Status (Cs), Sociability (Sy), Social Presence (Sp), Self-acceptance (Sa), Sense of Well-being (Wb), Responsibility (Re), Socialization (So), Self-control (Sc), Tolerance (To), Good impression (Gi), Communality (Cm), Achievement via conformance (Ac), Achievement via independence (Ai), Intellectual efficiency (Ie), Psychological-mindedness (Py), Flexibility (Fx), and Femininity (Fe).

A feature of Gough's CPI approach is that the labels of the scales do, in large measure, mean what they say. That is, the lay person's interpretation of the meaning of a scale would be congruent with the interpretation of a professional psychologist because of the orientation of the CPI scales toward " 'folk concepts'—aspects and attributes of interpersonal behavior that are to be found in all cultures and societies, and that possess a direct and integral relationship to all forms of social interaction" (Gough, 1968).

The CPI scales have been extremely well validated by current psychological standards and will be related to type membership. The psychological interpretations that will be presented of the CPI scale differences characterizing each type derive from the various validation studies that surround the inventory, as reported in the inventory manual (Gough, 1964) or more recently in "an interpreter's syllabus" (Gough, 1968).

Four additional CPI scales developed by Block in the course of unpublished work were also scored. These measures indexed the variables Ego-Control (EC), Psychoneurosis (PN), Neurotic Over-Control (NOC), and Neurotic Under-Control (NUC). The first two of these scales reflect, respectively, the individual's relative placement on the over-control versus under-control dimension and on the dimension of neurotic instability. The last two of these scales identify, in a psychometrically unusual way, individuals with designated neurotic styles. A respondent earns a high score on NOC if and only if his neurosis is manifested in over-controlling ways—by rigidities, perseveration, a tightening up and a narrowing of focus when anxiety looms large. A high score is earned on NUC if and only if an individual is neurotic in under-controlling ways—by diffuse, transient falling apart and stimulus-bound behaviors when anxiety level increases.

In addition to the analyses of scale scores, analyses of CPI items will be reported because of the additional information and psychological color these more particular analyses can offer.

The CPI originally had been administered only to the OGS adult subjects. But, five years later, by which time the GS subjects had achieved the age when the OGS subjects had responded to the CPI, it proved possible to obtain cooperation of about sixty percent of the GS adults in responding to the inventory.

The Early Family Ratings (EFR)

When the GS children were between 21 and 36 months of age, the staff psychologist conducted interviews with both parents and a social worker observed the family situation *in vivo* by visiting the home of each subject.

The interviewers and observers independently rated the parents and the family constellation with respect to 64 characteristics, using a 5-point scale. The agreement between the several raters was reassuring despite the different informational contexts available to each judge. Accordingly, a consensus judgment was warranted. This consensus was formed by weighting each rater's evaluation by the confidence of the rater in his evaluation. The rationale for this weighting procedure was that one rater might have a better basis for his judgment than another and hence should be more determining of the final consensus.

As we have since learned (cf., e.g., Little, 1961), individual differences in the confidence of judges has little relation to individual differences in judge accuracy, and so this way of forming a composite, influenced as it was by differential assurance, probably is not so good an index as it might have been. But this retrospective complaint is more a niggle than a negation since the fully independent agreements prior to weighting were so impressive.

With 64 variables, many of them obviously related, the tactic of factor analysis as a means of organizing and reducing the number of dimensions in a data situation of course suggests itself. A factor analysis of the EFR variables was carried out for the sexes combined since, *a priori*, the sex of the subject should not affect importantly the characteristics of the subject's parents and their marital situation. Ten clearly interpretable factors emerged from this analysis. The ten EFR factors, together with some of the variables contributing toward their definition follow:

1. Marital Conflict versus Marital Adjustment—defined by such variables as Poor Adjustment of Mother and Father to Each Other, Hostility of Mother Toward Father, and Hostility of Father Toward Mother.

2. Maternal Dissatisfaction with Father's Competence—defined by such variables as Mother's Dissatisfaction with Father's Job, Low Family Income, and Mother's Unhappy Attitude Toward Her Home.

3. Parental Unconcern with Their Responsibilities—defined by such variables as Parental Indifference Toward Problems of Health, Parental Blame of Environment, Absence of Sex Instruction, and Inadequate Play Facilities.

4. Paternal Neuroticism versus Paternal Ego Integration—defined by such variables as Father's Nervous Instability, Father's Poor Health and Stamina, and Father's Lack of Confidence.

5. Paternal Introversion versus Paternal Extroversion—defined by such variables as Father's Worrisomeness, Father's Shyness, Father's Undemonstrativeness, and Father's Low Energy Level.

6. Maternal Neuroticism versus Maternal Ego Integration—defined by such variables as Mother's Nervous Instability, Mother's Poor Health and Stamina, and Mother's Lack of Confidence.

7. Maternal Introversion versus Maternal Extroversion—defined by such variables as Mother's Withdrawal and Shyness, Mother's Undemonstrativeness, Mother's Worrisomeness, and Mother's Low Energy Level.

8. Parental Rejection versus Parental Acceptance of the Child—defined by such variables as Uninterest of Father in the Child, Uninterest of Mother in the Child, Hostility of the Father to the Child, and Hostility of the Mother to the Child.

9. Maternal Rejection of a Submissive Role—defined by such variables as Mother's Avoidance of Housework, Mother's Preference for Outside Work, and Marital Conflict with Regard to Cultural Standards, Religion, and Relatives.

10. Maternal Somatic Self-concern—defined by such variables as Mother's Reluctance to Have More Children, Mother's Poor Health, and Mother's Uninterest in Father.

For technical reasons, EFR factor scores were not employed in evaluating the relevance of parental and family attributes for subsequent type membership. Rather, the entire set of Early Family Ratings was analyzed *vis-à-vis* the typology, the distinguishing EFR variables then being organized according to the factor rubric we have just described.

The Ratings of Mothers

In both the OGS and GdS studies, the mothers of the subjects, after interviewing by staff psychologists, were subsequently rated on the same set of 29 personality and intellectual characteristics. In the OGS study, the subjects' mothers usually were rated three times, when the child was about eleven years old, when the child was about fourteen, and when the child was about fifteen. Only one psychologist made the ratings each time and it was often the same psychologist who made all the ratings. Within the GdS study, the subjects' mothers were independently rated by a clinical psychologist and by a psychiatric social worker during the period when the children were from 21 months through three years of age. For each mother in each study, all the available ratings were averaged to provide the scores used for the present analyses.

Despite the different time periods during which the subjects' mothers were rated, it was decided for the purposes of the present inquiry to merge the data from the two samples since the identical variables had been evaluated in the two studies. The presumption underlying this decision was that the characteristics of the subjects' mothers would not have been appreciably changed by virtue of the different ages of their children or the slight differences in average maternal age at the time the ratings of the mothers were formulated. Comparison of the 29 variable covariance matrix based upon the OGS mothers with the covariance matrix derived from the GS mothers' ratings by means of a Monte Carlo empirical sampling procedure fully supported the propriety of merging the two data sets so as to bolster the sample size available for later statistical analysis of the several types.

The 29 ratings of the mothers were then factor analyzed, with seven reasonably clear factors emerging to structure the data. These factors, together with some of the variables defining them, follow:

1. Mother's Intellectual Competence—defined by such variables as Mother's Intelligence, Mother's Facility in Language Usage, and Mother's Thinking Accuracy.
2. Mother's Cooperative Openness—defined by such variables as Mother's Frankness, Mother's Cooperation in Discussing Her Child, and Mother's Trustfulness.
3. Mother's Neuroticism—defined by such variables as Mother's Dissatisfaction with Her Lot, Mother's Poor Self-esteem, and Mother's Melancholy.
4. Mother's Under-control—defined by such variables as Mother's Excitability, Mother's Restlessness, and Mother's Talkativeness.

5. Mother's Carpingness—defined by Mother's Tendency to Criticize Things in General, Mother's Tendency to Criticize Her Child, and Mother's Desire to Make an Impression.

6. Mother's Personal Attractiveness—defined by such variables as Mother's Pleasant Social Demeanor, Mother's Attractive Appearance, and Mother's Modulated Voice.

7. Mother's Interest in Her Child—defined by Mother's Preoccupation with Her Child, Mother's Desire to Make an Impression, and Mother's Satisfaction with Her Lot.

Factor scores were not derived to represent the factors issuing from the Ratings of Mothers. Instead, the entire set of Ratings of Mothers was analyzed *vis-à-vis* the typology. The statistically differentiating ratings are then reported but organized along the lines suggested by the factor structure just described.

The Environmental Q set (EQ set)

The Early Family Ratings and the Ratings of Mothers were the only sets of data available in the IHD files that bore upon questions regarding the early antecedents of personality in a usable way. Although these measures generated results of appreciable interest, their coverage in regard to many variables and issues of contemporary interest to personality psychologists clearly left a good deal to be desired. Moreover, the Early Family Ratings, although somewhat richer than the Ratings of Mothers in the kind and coverage of the dimensions it assessed, were available only for the GS subjects. The resulting tiny sample sizes thus greatly hampered the effort to find antecedent relationships. Yet, to read all the available material regarding a particular case was to develop usually a vivid sense of the family context in which the subject had grown up and the kinds of environmental influences to which he had been subjected. The not small technical problem was to codify these compelling impressions in a systematic way so that this domain of information could be related to subsequent personality development and life outcome.

This deficiency in the longitudinal archives early had been recognized in the course of the present integrative effort. Consequently, a proposal was made in 1962 to employ the then-named Developmental Q set (*DQ* set) constructed by Jack and Jeanne Block (cf. Block, 1961, pp. 120–122). The *DQ* set consisted of a number of *Q* items selected to permit a comprehensive, salience-conveying description of the circumstances and history of an individual out of which, presumably, his personality evolved. "The history-viewer (i.e., the judge) unifies and intertwines the multitudinous familial and cultural factors that contribute toward character" (Block, 1961, p. 121). The emphasis within the DQ set was exclusively historical, with no implications for personality outcome, whereas the emphasis in the CQ set was entirely contemporaneous with no indication within the item set as to how the particular individual may have evolved.

The DQ set as a procedure for codifying and systematizing the environmental histories of the longitudinally studied subjects could not gain the necessary support within the Institute at the time. The problem lingered, however, and in the subsequently separated and independent continuation of this study, this lack in possibility gnawed.

Well along in the writing of the last chapters of this book, because of the tantalizing yet insufficient results regarding family antecedents, it was decided to delay the proceedings in order to apply the historical Q set. This set of items, now named the Environmental Q set (Form IV), is a revised version of the DQ set earlier described. In the form in which it was used in this study, the EQ set is to be found in Appendix H. It consists of 92 items, to be sorted by the judge into nine piles. The judge is permitted to exclude from his consideration those EQ items which simply do not apply to the history of a subject (e.g., if the subject's father died before the subject was a year old and no substitute father figure became available for the subject, then those EQ items dealing with the characteristics of the father could properly be excluded from evaluation). The Q-sorting constraints on the judge required him to place as equal a number of considered items into each pile as is logically feasible. That is, if five items out of 92 are excluded by the judge, the remaining 87 items would be distributed into nine piles, three of which would contain nine EQ items and six of which would contain ten EQ items. The judge may decide where to place the small inequalities he is now permitted. The intent of this somewhat revised and more flexible sorting procedure is to avoid meaningless decisions by the judge and to increase the number of discriminations he provides while still maintaining judge comparability.

The circumstances within which the EQ set was applied were far less than optimal though still, as will be seen, worth the effort. The only source of extensive and comparable information regarding the family context of the subjects that was available in both the OGS and GS studies was the follow-up interviews conducted when the subjects were in their thirties. These interviews, earlier described, sought a good deal of memory regarding parental characteristics, the family, and the environmental situation. These retrospections are plagued by omissions, evaluations, projections, and self-justifications, and are certainly not to be accepted at face value. But also, these descriptions of the past are not to be set aside because they are not ideal. There are some genuine virtues in our necessary use of the adult follow-up interviews as the basis for the *EQ* formulations.

A number of previous studies have shown impressive correspondence between self-reports regarding childhood experience and independent assessments taken at the time of the situation more objectively specified. Bronson, Katten, & Livson (1959) report, for the GS sample, supporting correlations between adult memories and staff ratings of the parents made when the subjects were children. Rosenthal (1963) for the OGS sample, obtained similarly positive results. The present results, to be reported shortly, will be seen to confirm and extend these earlier findings. A study by Myers (1935) showed strikingly high relationships between what high school students said about various aspects of their parents and home life and what school social workers well acquainted with the homes and parents of these students said. Kohn et al. also found "a general consistency between the way that schizophrenics perceive their relations with their families and the way that other family members perceive these relationships" (1956, p. 310). Especially notable is the study by Brooks (1963) who related childhood experiences reported in life history interviews to independently assessed behaviors. Her approach is quite equivalent to the one to be reported and, because of the great psychological interest of the results she adduced, provides further support for the present effort.

So, the purist may achieve only sterility if he categorically excludes self-histories as invalid. Indeed, when the usual objectifying procedures for the assessment of parent-child relations and the family context are considered, it may well be that retrospective report by an adult subject committed to cooperation provides deeper and more valid information. The conventional procedures employ occasional, time-sampling, essentially distant observers who see primarily the non-salient and what the family chooses for public presentation. By contrast, the follow-up interviews were prolonged, probing, and reasonably systematic in their coverage of the way it was for the subject when he was growing up.

The psychologist judge need not accept everything said in the interview; some statements must be believed, others he places into a perspective different perhaps from what the respondent intended. The goal is a valid portrayal of the environment history of the individual and there is reason, from other research and from the nature of the interview situation, to think the retrospective approach has appreciable value.

To the extent that variables in the *EQ* set issue results corresponding to those discerned by like variables in the Early Family Ratings or the Ratings of Mothers, we have a further check on the usefulness of codifying self-histories. If the evidence is affirmative, then we are supported in the extrapolation that those *EQ* variables providing information on family matters *not* explicitly rated by observers a generation before likewise are valid.

Because of financial and temporal limitations, only one judge Q-sorted each case where before several judges had independently contributed toward a consensus. None of the three *EQ* judges had been involved earlier in the *CQ* descriptions of the adult subjects. To prevent the build-up of any judge-subject type interaction, each judge was assigned one-third of the members of each type. Thus, no confounding of judge idiosyncracy with type membership could occur.

In principle, it can be argued that another kind of confounding exists because of the inescapable intermixture in the adult follow-up interviews of material bearing on the childhood of the subject with material relating to his current status and personality. Presumably, a judge's impression of the subject as an adult could influence how the subject was characterized as a child. Brooks, in her own study, empirically found no tendency among judges to be so affected. The nature of the *EQ* set offers further protection against this possibility since the task of the *EQ* judge was *not* to describe the subject as a child but to describe the psychological environment of the child. The language possibilities built into the *EQ* set prevent any characterization of the child's personality; only events or relations impinging upon but not affected by the child are recorded by the *EQ* set. In other words, there is no way for impressions of a subject as an adult to affect the way his past environment is described short of using complex, highly articulated post-dictive formulas judges cannot be expected to possess or possess uniformly.

The environmental histories of residual subjects were not evaluated, again because of monetary and time pressures, so that the Complement group in our *EQ*-set analyses, although still large and heterogeneous, is somewhat different from our usual Complement group which does include the residual subjects.

The usual reliability estimates could not be developed, given the constraints, but for eleven cases—one from each type—all three judges formulated their *EQ* characterizations. The agreement among the judges in their use of the *EQ* set was comparable to the agreement earlier achieved with the *CQ* set. The average agreement for the *EQ* sortings was .53 and the reliability of the *EQ* composites, for the eleven cases where they could be derived, was .78, quite an adequate figure.

The Organization and Presentation of the Typological Findings

An unacknowledged reason for *not* employing a typological approach to personality data is that, having accepted the responsibility of a differentiated analysis, the subsequent job of elucidating relationships and reporting the findings becomes more complicated at an exponential rate. Inevitably, the task of communicating becomes burdensome, both for the reporter and the readers. The sense and significance of each type is contingent upon or is highlighted or given context by a variety of contrasts with other types. The characterization of one type cannot be conveyed fully unless first, or simultaneously, the characterizations of all other types is communicated. But such priorities or simultaneities are not possible—understanding can be developed only sequentially and by spiralling back over material earlier covered but not fully apprehended. The reader will simply have to spiral without becoming dizzy.

There will be many contrasts mentioned in subsequent pages. Each type can be paired with each other type and occasionally it is quite instructive to evaluate each of their pair comparisons. But usually, contrast of one type *vis-à-vis* simply the Complement of that type (*all* other subjects in the sample) provides substantially all (or enough) of the information that would be available from the more detailed pairwise comparison and of course it is more economical and statistically sounder to report only the one Complement comparison. Accordingly, in Chapters VIII and IX, all comparisons reported for a Type refer to contrasts against a Complement group consisting of all available subjects not defined as members of that Type. The task of assimilating the findings is difficult enough and the reader is likely to feel like a ping-pong ball soon even though he must attend only to Type versus Complement comparisons.

I shall be somewhat casual in regard to certain statistical properties, omitting details on the total number of significance tests calculated, overlap considerations, and the like. This tack is necessary if this book is to be written, for the reportorial task otherwise is oppressive and the results of such efforts would swamp the reader in a torrent of bath water in which it would be difficult to see the baby. I ask the indulgence and the trust of the reader on these matters and the willingness to live with an unknown but certainly not vitiating amount of Type II error. As will be observed, enough different and independent sources of information bear on each character type in reciprocally reinforcing ways so that, in the large, questions regarding the general validity of the findings do not arise.

For each type, the presentation of data follows the same plan, conveying the relationships found within the ongoing text rather than in the form of separate, unwieldy tables. The use of "textual tables" eases the reporting task and doubtless the burden of comprehension imposed upon the reader by eliminating the endless supply of means, standard deviations, *t* ratios, and other specific numbers usually included in works like this.

First, the statistically differentiating personality characteristics of the type as observed in the JHS period are reported. These characteristics are expressed in terms of both the *CQ* items and the Interpersonal *Q* items.

Moreover, because of concern with the absolute as well as relative description of personality, the differentiating character attributes are further grouped into those absolutely defining of the type and those only relatively defining. That is, some Q items are differentiating because they are absolutely salient in characterizing the type while other items are equally differentiating statistically but reflect the tendency of the Complement group to be extreme while type members are intermediate with respect to the attribute. In the latter instance, the type members would be said to be relatively high or relatively low on the personality characteristic. Operationally, this distinction was made by attending to standardized item factor scores (which arise in the obverse analytical context) above 60 and below 40 as signifying especially salient and therefore absolute properties of that type. Where factor scores were unavailable, the mean level of a statistically differentiating Q item was taken into account together with its associated dispersion.

Second, the statistically differentiating characterizations of the type during the SHS interval are presented through the same procedures organized in the same way.

Third, the statistically distinguishing character changes that the type has undergone from the JHS years to the SHS period are conveyed. These changes are discerned by the application of the correlated means t test to the CQ items and to the Interpersonal Q items. It will be recalled that both CQ and Interpersonal Q descriptions of the subjects were independently developed to characterize them during both the JHS era and the SHS years. The analyses identify the trends characterizing the personality changes within a given type over the three-year interval involved.

Fourth, additional statistical findings and relationships collected during or pertinent to the adolescent years are presented. These results draw upon a variety of procedures and data sources such as those just described.

Fifth, the statistically distinguishing personality characteristics of the type members as adults in their mid-thirties are indicated through the medium of the CQ variables. The statistically differentiating CQ items are again grouped into the absolute and the relative qualities of personality of the type.

Sixth, statistically significant character changes since the SHS years are presented, again using the correlated means t test, as derived from the comparison of CQ formulations developed during SHS with those developed to describe the subjects as adults.

Seventh, further statistical findings from a variety of sources that pertain to the adult years are detailed. The procedures and information sources employed have been described or will be explained where necessary.

Eighth, the adjustment and personality continuity shown by type representatives over the years is statistically assessed and tracked in relation to the group as a whole.

Ninth, having presented all the distinguishing characterological and outcome information available for the members of the type, we go back in time to their origins. Statistically differentiating features of the family context and environmental background differentially characterizing the type are reported, as conveyed by the procedures already described.

And tenth, having laid the available findings in straight-forward, unadorned form before the reader, an interpretive resumé of the constellation of relationships surrounding the type is offered. These resumés read like individual case histories but they should be understood as averaged, representative, statistically-based formulations characterizing groups of like personalities. A sense of the developmental course that has been followed, its shaping antecedents, and what may be anticipated in the future for representatives of the type is indicated. These interpretive remarks are not discursive since *res ipso loquitur*—the thing speaks for itself.

We are now ready to begin the accounting of the types.

Chapter VIII

COURSES OF PERSONALITY DEVELOPMENT —THE MALE SAMPLE

For a while, the several types will be designated by the neutral letters, A, B, C, D, and E. After the sense of a type is developed, a short-hand label or "tag" for the type will be suggested as a means of vivifying subsequent discussion in which that type figures.

Perhaps the best way to orient the reader to this tortuous and concatenating chapter is with some pertinent demographic and sociological data surrounding the several types that have been isolated. The reader will wish to know the implications for these types of such powerfully controlling variables as intelligence, education, socio-economic status, and the like. Accordingly, Table 8-1 contains information regarding each type with respect to IQ, years of education ultimately achieved, socioeconomic status during junior high school and later as adults, childhood family size, personal ordinal position, number of marriages, and the number of children issued. Although the reader may wish to scan these demographic characteristics now for his own purposes, our own usage of the many distinguishing and suggestive elements in this table will come later in the course of the systematic presentation of the relationships surrounding each type.

Another interesting set of relationships for the reader to consider before the particulars begin is the temporal change from JHS to SHS to adulthood in the similarities among the five types. To convey these shifting similarities, Table 8-2 presents the intercorrelations of *modal CQ* descriptions developed for each type for each time period. The modal Q description is simply an averaged Q description calculated from the individual Q descriptions of all the members of a type. Subsequent correlations among modal Q descriptions permit in a simple, content-free way the specification of the similarity among the types at each of our three time intervals.

Table 8–1
Demographic Characteristics of the Male Types

	Type A	Type B	Type C	Type D	Type E	Residuals
Number of Subjects in the Type	19	11	12	11	10	21
Mean Intelligence Quotient	128.3	106.7	120.0	114.4	128.2	121.5
Mean Years of Education	16.8	13.8	14.6	13.9	14.4	15.4
Socio-economic Status during Adolescence	2.58	3.64	3.25	3.36	2.10	3.24
Socio-economic Status during Adulthood	1.63	2.73	3.17	2.64	3.00	2.52
Childhood Family Size	2.32	2.54	2.73	3.09	2.50	2.28
Ordinal Position of Type Members	1.89	1.82	2.27	2.27	1.50	1.52
Number of Marriages	1.16	1.09	0.67	1.18	1.20	1.14
Number of Children	3.05	3.00	1.67	2.73	1.50	2.00

Table 8–2
Intercorrelations of Modal Type CQ Descriptions
for Each Time Period: Males

		A	B	C	D	E
	A	—				
	B	−.09	—			
JHS	C	.36	.57	—		
Intercorrelations	D	.51	.28	−.04	—	
	E	−.05	.58	.23	.25	—
	A	—				
	B	−.03	—			
SHS	C	.34	.36	—		
Intercorrelations	D	.25	.60	−.13	—	
	E	−.20	.57	.30	.36	—
	A	—				
	B	.74	—			
Adulthood	C	−.02	.11	—		
Intercorrelations	D	.01	.20	.70	—	
	E	.18	−.12	.04	.20	—

Inspection of the three small matrices in Table 8-2 reveals certain types (e.g., Types B and E) that were relatively similar in JHS are quite divergent by adulthood. Early dissimilarity (e.g., Types C and D) can presage appreciable later convergence. The clearly separable developmental trend-lines characterizing the several types points up in yet another way the vapidity of an undifferentiated approach in the personality realm.

As a third way of quickly characterizing the differences among the types, Figure 8-1 reports their mean CPI profiles, referenced to the standardization norms developed for the inventory. The particular CPI findings for each type will be discussed in the appropriate chapter sections; the profiles are presented here for the information of CPI-versed readers and as a further independent indication of the separations among the types.

And now to the nature and significance of the typology.

PERSONALITY TYPE A

Their Character During Junior High School

The CQ Set. Vis-à-vis the Complement group, boys falling within the A type may be well identified during JHS since 46% of the Q items are nominally significant at the .01 level.

Attributes *absolutely and relatively characteristic of Type A boys during JHS:* dependable, productive, ambitious, bright, values intellectual matters, likable, has a wide range of interests, verbally fluent, poised, straightforward, sympathetic, and interesting.

Attributes *relatively characteristic of Type A boys during JHS:* giving toward others, protective of those close to him, introspective, aware of his social stimulus value, warm, insightful, socially perceptive, esthetically reactive, reasonably satisfied with self, internally consistent, philosophically concerned, and comfortable with the decisions he makes.

Attributes *absolutely and relatively uncharacteristic of Type A boys during JHS:* changeable, testing of limits, negativistic, eroticizing, self-defeating, rebellious, brittle, gives up and withdraws, undercontrolled, self-indulgent, affected, lacks a sense of personal meaning, and distrustful.

Attributes *relatively uncharacteristic of the Type A boys during JHS:* uncomfortable with uncertainty, self-defensive, extrapunitive, hostile, touchy, self-pitying, fluctuating moods, group-conforming, and communicates non-verbally.

The Interpersonal Q Set. Thirty percent of the items differentiated the Type A boys from the Complement at the .01 level of significance.

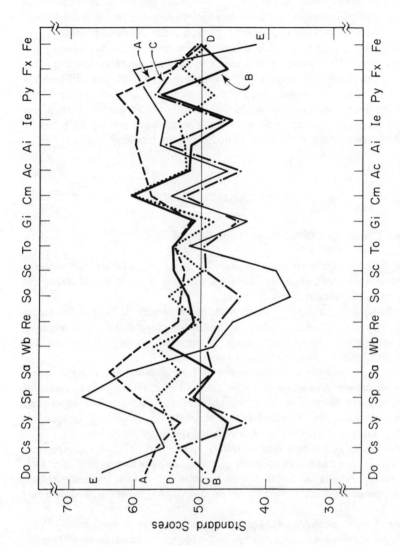

Figure 8–1 The Mean CPI Profiles of the Male Types

Items *absolutely and relatively characteristic of Type A boys during JHS:* respects his parents, liked by his peers, views his parents as consistent, straightforward with his peers, poised with his peers, and views parents as reasonable.

Items *relatively characteristic of Type A boys during JHS:* perceives his family as interesting, feels his mother is a respected woman as judged by societal standards, has genuine relationships with adults, achieves leadership roles with his peers, considerate with his peers, and protected by his peers.

Items *absolutely and relatively uncharacteristic of the Type A boys during JHS:* tends to be the butt of his group, rebellious with adults, and claims the privileges of adolescence.

Items *relatively uncharacteristic of Type A boys during JHS:* perceives his family situation as conflicted, covertly hostile to adults, employs attention-getting behaviors with his peers, and is changeable in his peer attachments.

Their Character During Senior High School

The CQ Set. *Vis-à-vis* the Complement group, 41 percent of the Q items distinguish the Type A individual at the .01 level of significance.

Attributes *absolutely and relatively characteristic of Type A boys during SHS:* dependable, bright, ambitious, productive, values intellectual matters, likable, protective of those close to him, and sympathetic.

Attributes *relatively characteristic of Type A boys during SHS:* has wide interests, giving, turned-to-for-advice, calm, socially perceptive, internally consistent, straightforward, cheerful, poised, verbally fluent, and comfortable with his decisions.

Attributes *absolutely and relatively uncharacteristic of Type A boys during SHS:* guileful, changeable, affected, testing of limits, under-controlled, rebellious, negativistic, self-pitying, brittle, self-defeating, irritable, and fluctuating moods.

Attributes *relatively uncharacteristic of Type A boys during SHS:* uncomfortable with uncertainty, self-defensive, thin-skinned, lacks a sense of personal meaning, extrapunitive, gives up and withdraws, hostile, self-indulgent, touchy, conforming to group pressures, and communicates through non-verbal behaviors.

The Interpersonal Q Set. Twenty-one percent of the Interpersonal Q items differentiated the Type A boys from the Complement at the .01 level of significance.

Items *absolutely and relatively characteristic of the Type A boys during SHS:* respects his parents, and is liked by his peers.

Items *relatively characteristic of Type A boys during SHS:* perceives his parents as interesting, views his parents as reasonable, is protective of his friends, is poised with his peers, sympathetic to his peers, and awarded leadership positions by his peers.

Items *absolutely and relatively uncharacteristic of Type A boys during SHS:* is the butt of his group, rebellious with adults, and claims the privileges of adolescence.

Items *relatively uncharacteristic of Type A boys during SHS:* covertly hostile to adults, and sensitive to anything that can be construed as a demand from his peers.

Character Changes from JHS to SHS

The CQ Set. During the interval from JHS to SHS, the Type A boys manifest certain personality changes as revealed by the correlated means *t* test. Thus, by SHS, Type A boys became significantly: more interested in the opposite sex, more calm, more eroticizing, more valuing of power, more concerned with philosophical problems, and more withdrawing when frustrated.

Compared with the way they were during JHS, the Type A boys during SHS have become significantly: less irritable, slower in tempo, less counter-active, less thin-skinned, less fluctuating in mood, less arousing of nurturance, and less likable.

The Interpersonal Q Set. As conveyed through the Interpersonal Q set, the Type A boys have, by SHS, become significantly: closer to their mothers, more oriented toward going steady, more spending of time with girls, and more involved at a fantasy level with girls.

Compared to the way they were during JHS, they are significantly: less likely to view their fathers as attractive men, less likable, and are less protected by their peers.

Further Findings from the Adolescent Years

The Type A boys manifest relatively high intelligence (their mean IQ is 128.3), significantly differing (.05) from the Complement. As a corollary, on the Terman Group Test taken when they were about eleven years old, they score very much higher than the Complement boys (133 versus 95, significant at the .01 level). Their familial socio-economic status is at a comfortable, though not the highest, level (.10 versus the Complement).

They had their spurt of adolescent growth relatively early and in general were physically grown earlier than their peers. In appearance, they were relatively tall and slender, without being unmuscular. Compared to the Complement group, Type A boys were less likely to wear glasses or to have acne. They experienced a normal amount of illness while growing up.

In their responses to the What I Like To Do questionnaire during SHS, the Type A boys reveal themselves as relatively higher than the Complement on the Over-control scale (.05). However, they are not high in an absolute sense on this scale but rather are less under-controlled than the Complement boys. During both the JHS and SHS intervals, the Free Play Ratings show the Type A boys to be more Reposed than the Complement (.01 and .01). The Frenkel-Brunswik Ratings indicate the Type A boys are relatively Intropunitive (.01) and are less oriented toward Interpersonal Power (.05).

In JHS, according to interviewers of Type A mothers, the boys appear to have led orderly existences: they tend to have harmonious sibling relationships (.05), they keep well-planned schedules (.05), they enjoy sound sleep (.10), and have no food problems (.10). Although "keen on writing" (.10), they are not interested in drama (.01).

In SHS, Type A boys attend church more often than Complement boys (.10) and, moreover, church is not simply a social interest (.05). Their fathers, however, were not especially religious (.05).

The Type A boys were spanked only through childhood and not thereafter, whereas the Complement subjects were spanked into the teen years (.05). The Type A parents emphasized high standards for their sons (.01).

Of especial interest and large significance is the finding that Type A boys consistently manifest appreciably higher skin conductance than Complement boys when asked to associate to stimulus words (.01). As a concomitant finding, Type A boys appear significantly more often (.02) in the small group of subjects defined by Harold E. Jones in the mid-1930s as Extreme Skin Conductance Reactors (Jones, 1950).

Their Character as Adults

The CQ Set. Forty-two percent of the Q items differentiated the Type A men from the Complement group at the .01 level.

Attributes *absolutely and relatively characteristic of the Type A men as adults:* ambitious, dependable, productive, bright, verbally fluent, values intellectual matters, poised, and straightforward.

Attributes *relatively characteristic of the Type A men as adults:* wide interests, giving, protective of those close to him, introspective, sympathetic, turned-to-for-advice and reassurance, aware of his social stimulus value, warm, interesting, insightful, socially perceptive, esthetically reactive, self-satisfied, internally consistent, philosophically concerned, skilled in social techniques of imaginative play and humor, and comfortable with the decisions he has made.

Attributes *absolutely and relatively uncharacteristic of the Type A men as adults:* gives up and withdraws, undercontrolled, brittle, self-defeating, feels a lack of personal meaning, negativistic, testing of limits, changeable, self-dramatizing, and eroticizing.

Attributes *relatively uncharacteristic of Type A men as adults:* uncomfortable with uncertainty, self-defensive, extrapunitive, hostile, distrustful, rebellious, self-indulgent, touchy, self-pitying, fluctuating of mood, group-conforming, and communicates through non-verbal behaviors.

Character Changes from Senior High School to Adulthood

The CQ Set. Relative to their characteristics during SHS, Type A individuals as adults are significantly: more insightful, more talkative, more changeable, more rapid in tempo, more turned-to-for-advice and reassurance, more likely to proffer advice, more condescending, more rebellious, more varying of roles, more verbally fluent, more concerned with philosophical problems, more cognizant of the motivations of others, and more assertive.

Since SHS, the Type A men have become significantly: less fantasizing, less responsive to humor, less withdrawing when frustrated, less submissive, less concerned with their own bodies, less somaticizing, less protective of close ones, less bright, less projective, and less uncomfortable with uncertainties.

Further Findings from the Adult Years

CPI Scale Scores. A large number of the scales from the California Psychological Inventory differentiate the Type A men from the Complement group. Thus, Type A men are significantly *higher* with respect to Self-Acceptance (*Sa*) (.01), Intellectual Efficiency (*Ie*) (.01), Psychological-Mindedness (*Py*) (.01), Achievement via Conformance (*Ac*) (.01), Achievement via Independence (*Ai*) (.05), Sense of Well-Being (*Wb*) (.05), Responsibility (*Re*) (.10), Socialization (*So*) (.10), and Good Impression (*Gi*) (.10). Type A men are *lower* than the Complement group on the Neurotic Undercontrol (*NUC*) scale (.05).

These many differences suggest that the Type A men are relatively confident, outgoing, efficient, capable, observant, independent, reliable, considerate, foresighted, relaxed, sincere, adaptable, tactful, and friendly. They are distinctly *un*neurotic and *un*chaotic in their orientation toward life.

CPI Item Analysis. In addition to the analysis of established inventory scales, the responses to individual CPI items were also analyzed by Fisher's Exact Method. Analyses of 2 by 2 tables with such small samples cannot be powerful—it is most difficult for an item to emerge as a statistically significant differentiator (cf. Block, 1960). Nevertheless, a number of items do distinguish Type A men from the Complement group and in ways that are psychologically congruent. The full set of differentiating items will not be reported; rather, only a sprinkling will be listed to convey their psychological flavor.

Thus, the Type A men more often than Complement men *affirm* the following inventory items:

CPI 72. I used to keep a diary.
CPI 166. In school I always looked far ahead in planning what courses to take.
CPI 215. I would like to write a technical book.
CPI 292. I used to like it very much when one of my papers was read to the class in school.
CPI 478. I would be uncomfortable in anything other than fairly conventional dress.

The Type A men more often than the Complement men *reject* the following inventory items:

CPI 36. When I was going to school I played hooky quite often.
CPI 57. I have sometimes stayed away from another person because I feared doing or saying something that I might regret afterwards.
CPI 109. I get pretty discouraged sometimes.
CPI 121. I was a slow learner in school.
CPI 153. If I am not feeling well I am somewhat cross and grouchy.
CPI 156. I hardly ever get excited or thrilled.

Current Status. Type A men in their fourth decade have achieved more education than the Complement group (.01), they have fathered more children (.05), they score appreciably higher on the Terman Group Test of Mental Ability (.01), and although somewhat favored in their own socio-economic origins, they have shown greater improvement in their adult socio-economic status than is typical of even this generally upward mobile sample (.01 versus the Complement regarding adult SES; .08 versus the Complement regarding temporal change in SES).

Type A men are in rather good health in their thirties, with fewer medical problems than beset their Complement peers (.05). They are moderate drinkers, by and large. Of the seventeen Type A men for whom alcohol usage is known, two are categorized as problem drinkers, two are abstainers, and the remaining thirteen are evaluated as social drinkers relaxed in their attitudes toward alcohol. There is a tendency for fewer of them to smoke than is typical of the Complement men. Their height and weight are typical of our adult males.

Type A men married at the conventional age for their group and time (age 23 to 24). None of them reports sexual intercourse before the age of 21, the Complement males experiencing sex a couple of years earlier on the average (.05). All of the Type A subjects married; three later were divorced and remarried, a frequency not at all unusual in our sample context. In the late 1950s, they were likely to define themselves politically as nominal Republicans, voting more for the man or the issue than for the party.

In adulthood, the Type A men do not see themselves as especially similar to their fathers, although the Complement men do tend toward perceived similarity (.05). They describe themselves more frequently as having been influenced in their development and life course by a person outside the immediate family such as a teacher or relative or someone else (.05). As parents, the Type A men do not see religion as especially important for the rearing of their children (.01) and, more generally, they say they are rearing their children rather differently from the way they themselves were reared (.10). The implication of this last observation is obscure since we cannot discern within this statement whether a deliberate change has been introduced or whether the societal changes have dictated the different childrearing context.

Type A men have higher vocational goals than Complement men (.05), they are reasonably well-satisfied with their educational training whereas the Complement men are not (.01), and they see themselves as having a good chance to achieve their occupational aspirations, whereas the Complement men are more likely to be defeatist or be unambitious (.05). Type A men plan more for the future (.10), and they have thought more about the problems of our society (.10).

The occupations of the Type A men include the following: an internist, two professors, three industrial scientists, a landscape architect, two consulting engineers, a government executive, a real estate developer, a commercial farmer, a hotel manager, a bank executive, a personnel director of a large firm, a store manager, two financial district employees, and a junior high school teacher.

It will be recalled that Type A individuals, in their adolescence, manifested greater skin conductance reactivity than did the Complement group. As adults, 25 years later, the Type A subjects again displayed greater skin conductance reactivity even though a quite different measurement situation was employed. Subjects observed a 20-minute sound film that was intended to arouse both empathy and sadness in the onlooker. The conductance measure employed was the number of non-specific GSRs. The measures employed and the experimental context are described in Block, 1962; a fuller report focussing upon the longitudinal continuity and the personality correlates of skin conductance measure will appear elsewhere. For the present, we note the significantly greater conductance reactivity of the Type A men to the sympathy-inducing film (.01).

Adjustment and Continuity over the Years

The Psychological Adjustment Index. The Type A individuals display consistent and impressive psychological adjustment at each of the three time periods. As objectified by the Psychological Adjustment Index, the Type A males are always markedly better off than the Complement males. For the Type A males, the mean *PA* Indices for the JHS, SHS, and Adult periods respectively are .39, .41, and .55. For the Complement males, by way of comparison, the parallel *PA* Index means are −.11, −.06, and .01. The differences are all highly significant (beyond the .01 level).

Personality Continuity. By and large, the Type A individuals show comparatively few indications of change over the years. They were well off early and remained well off. Their mean JHS–SHS correlation was .62 when the Complement correlation was .51. The Type A mean SHS–Adulthood correlation was .55 when the Complement average was .30. When these figures are adjusted for the attenuation introduced by the unreliability of the measures employed, an adjustment that is well justified conceptually, the JHS–SHS mean correlation becomes an impressive .90 for the Type A subjects and their SHS–Adulthood correlation becomes an astonishing .78. The respective Complement correlations, adjusted for attenuation, become .82 and .51. The SHS–Adulthood difference is highly significant, well beyond the .01 level. The JHS–SHS correlation difference between the Type A subjects and the Complement group falls slightly short of statistical significance.

Familial and Environmental Antecedents

The Early Family Ratings. The characteristics of the family setting within which the Type A subjects grew up is conveyed most readily by indicating the distinguishing characteristics of the Complement families. These qualities represent family properties relatively uncharacteristic of Type A families. Thus, Complement fathers appear to be introverted—they withdraw from conflict (.01), they are inactive and energyless (.05), they are placidly even-tempered and unreactive (.05). Complement mothers display dissatisfaction with the father's competence—they view as inadequate the income being brought into the family by the father and further, Complement mothers express little interest in their children (.10).

By implication, then, fathers of Type A subjects were relatively outgoing, active individuals, respected by their wives. The mothers of Type A children were relatively close to their offspring.

The Ratings of Mothers. Relative to Complement mothers, the mothers of the Type A males were evaluated as intellectually superior. They were judged as more accurate in their thinking (.01), more intelligent (.05), more facile in language usage (.05), more alert (.05), and so on. Type A mothers were also characterized as more cooperative and open (.05) but not quite as talkative—a sign of under-control—as the Complement mothers (.10).

The Environment Q Set. Vis-à-vis the familial contexts of the Complement subjects, the statistically distinguishing qualities of the family settings of the Type A males are as follows:

Environmental conditions *absolutely and relatively characteristic of the families of Type A subjects:* Subject's mother was available to the subject through adolescence (.05); subject's father dominated the fundamental family decisions (.05); subject's mother enjoyed her maternal role (.05).

Environmental conditions *relatively characteristic of the families of Type A subjects:* Subject's mother emphasized the life value of an intellectual orientation, of rationality in decision and outlook (.05); subject's mother emphasized the life value of tenderness, love, and related forms of interpersonal communion (.05); subject's father was restrictive about dating (.05).

Environmental conditions *absolutely and relatively uncharacteristic of the families of Type A subjects:* Subject was rejected by mother (.05); subject's father was manifestly a long-suffering, self-sacrificing, defeated person (.05); subject's home was a center for activities (.10).

Environmental conditions *relatively uncharacteristic of the families of Type A subjects:* Mother's interpersonal modes were conflict-inducing in children (.01); subject's mother was authoritarian (.10); subject's mother was neurotic, brittle, and anxiety-laden (.10); subject's mother was seductive with him (.10).

Interpretive Resume

The Type A person has been favored by circumstance from the beginning and he did not muff his opportunities. He was blessed with more than his share of native intelligence, good health, and physical endowment. His family situation was comfortable, of high status, secure, and long-lasting. His parents were themselves active, bright, and relaxedly assured individuals who shaped him toward competence more by modelling than by incantation. His family situation was culturally prototypical—a strong, outgoing, accomplishing father teamed with a loving mother who enjoyed mothering and was not personally neurotic or conflict-creating in her child. Both parents took seriously their responsibilities as value transmitters, as agents of a cultural heritage. They inculcated the values of love and reason and they set limits on the peer-determined desires of their adolescent children. They were able to do so without personal ambivalence and its consequence, ambiguity in communication.

By JHS, the Type A boy evidences an ego structure already well-formed but by no means foreclosed from new experiences and new values. He avoids the rashness of under-control without assuming the constriction of over-control, he has inner direction, an acceptance of responsibility, and both respect for and respect from his parents and his peers. His autonomic reactivity suggests that he has internalized the self as an object, one that is highly responsive to his impinging world. The flaws in his character at this time are few and must be searched for. Thus, there are some indications of over-socialization—the Type A boy can feel guilt more readily (too readily?), he views his parents as possibly too perfect, he is inhibited at the thought of public presentations of self.

By SHS, the Type A boy has changed in understandable ways but without losing his core qualities. He has become more interested in girls, his father is less idealized, he is more cognizant of the importance and usefulness of power in this world, and he is centered more on philosophical problems. He is more manly, more sure of himself now, and has less need to protect and advance his ego. He continues, as before, to be an essentially attractive person—dependable, bright, sympathetic, cheerful, poised, and perceptive. He is a leader among his peers but does not close himself off from the adult world and its values.

As an adult, the Type A individual shows further character changes since SHS but again the lines of continuity are strong. He is a man now and fits well into career and family. Compared to the way he was in SHS, the Type A man in his 30s enjoys a greater self-confidence and self-flexibility. He is more aware of his own psychology and the motivations that beset others, and he is looked to for advice and reassurance. His reflections on the nature of life have continued and have deepened. He is more persistent and even stubborn when frustrated.

Yet there appears to have been a lessening of cognitive spontaneity, perhaps because the Type A man is so caught up in the social fabric of his busy and full life, or perhaps because for all, with age, associative ramifying slows down (cf. Chapter V). For whatever the reason, the Type A man has become less responsive to humor, his fantasy life has attenuated, and he is less projective. The physical narcissism of his earlier years has abated also.

But the changes are less significant than the attributes that remain the same. From the time the Type A male was first assessed in JHS and through SHS and into adulthood, the cast of his character has been much the same and much to be respected. The productivity, scope, and zest of the Type A man continues together with the interpersonal qualities of empathy and social acuteness. As a man, he is alert, bright, well-educated, occupationally satisfied, economically successful, and supportive of and concerned with the society in which he prospers. He is in good health, maritally stable, child-producing, and at ease with his self.

In his surgent maturity, the Type A man accepts himself and has a sense of worth because he can see his personal value confirmed by his family and friends and society. Looking back over the years, this sense of personal value—of a clear, coherent, and effective identity—appears to have been achieved quite early and quite easily and naturally. Apparently, the personal crisis and self-confrontation that identity formation is often presumed to require is not always necessary.

Such untroubled, continuous, highly predictable development does not suggest that the Type A individual, by virtue of the absence of adolescent travail, has failed to become a truly differentiated or interestingly complex person. Beyond the unrelievedly virtuous Boy Scout traits of responsibility, productivity, ambition, and the like which certainly apply to him, there are deeper qualities as well which quicken our appreciation of the Type A man. He has inner life, he is compassionate, he is playful, he can sense the arts, and he is not unwise. If living is working and loving, then the Type A man has created for himself a good life's balance.

The course that the life of the Type A man has taken could have been foretold early and with great accuracy by the time he was twelve or thirteen years old. His personality changes over the years did not affect his personality core and, as time goes on, we may expect that the Type A man will continue to use life well.

It will be helpful, for later reference, to have a label for each type that is more informative than a simple letter designation. The Type A individuals I shall call *Ego Resilients*, a title that intends to suggest the long-standing characterological integrity and resourcefulness of these individuals.

PERSONALITY TYPE B

Their Character During Junior High School

The CQ Set. *Vis-à-vis* the Complement group, Type B boys are distinguished by 17 percent of the Q items at the .01 level of significance or, if the .05 level of significance is employed instead, by 34 percent of the items.*

Attributes *absolutely and relatively characteristic of Type B boys during JHS:* basically hostile, withdraws when frustrated, self-indulgent, self-defeating, bothered by demands, extrapunitive, brittle, projective, and negativistic.

Attributes *relatively characteristic of Type B boys during JHS:* seeks reassurance, lacks personal meaning in life, irritable, deceitful, reluctant to take action, ruminative, dependent, and communicates through non-verbal behavior.

Attributes *absolutely and relatively uncharacteristic of Type B boys during JHS:* values intellectual matters, philosophically concerned, turned-to-for-advice, verbally fluent, productive, has wide interests, poised, ambitious, interesting, esthetically reactive, socially perceptive, dependable, and aware of social stimulus value.

Attributes *relatively uncharacteristic of Type B boys during JHS:* giving, high degree of intellectual capacity, straightforward, skilled in techniques of imaginative play, and perceives self as causative of the occurrences in his life.

The Interpersonal Q Set. Fourteen percent of the items differentiated the Type B boys from the Complement at the .05 level of significance.

Items *absolutely and relatively characteristic of Type B boys during JHS:* covertly hostile to adults, and rebellious with adults.

Items *relatively characteristic of Type B boys during JHS:* employs attention-getting behavior with his peers, expresses hostile feelings directly to his peers, and manifests changeability of his peer attachments.

Items *absolutely and relatively uncharacteristic of Type B boys during*

---

*The reader should recall that the number of items significant is a most rough guide to the clarity of definition of a type unless the number of members of that group are taken into account. Rather, the mean factor loadings and standard deviations for each type should be inspected for information regarding comparative homogeneity of the several types.

JHS: able to have genuine relationships with adults, and evaluates self as superior to his peers.

Items *relatively uncharacteristic of Type B boys during JHS:* respects his parents, and knowledgeable of his peer culture.

Their Character During Senior High School

The CQ Set. Vis-à-vis the Complement group, 12 percent of the *Q* items distinguish the Type B individual at the .05 level of significance. Data were available for only seven subjects from Type B for this analysis.

Attributes *absolutely and relatively characteristic of Type B boys during SHS:* communicates through nonverbal behavior, gives up and withdraws when frustrated, negativistic, and testing of limits.

Attributes *relatively characteristic of Type B boys during SHS:* condescending to others.

Attributes *absolutely and relatively uncharacteristic of Type B boys during SHS:* turned-to-for-advice and reassurance, has a wide range of interests, evaluates the motivations of others, and productive.

Attributes *relatively uncharacteristic of the Type B boys during SHS:* has a high degree of intellectual capacity, interesting, and ambitious.

The Interpersonal Q Set. Only three items discriminated in this analysis wherein the Type B group contained only seven individuals.

Items *relatively characteristic of Type B boys during SHS:* claims the privileges and excuses afforded the adolescent in this culture.

Items *relatively uncharacteristic of the Type B boys during SHS:* selective in his choice of friends, and straightforward with his peers.

Character Changes from JHS to SHS

The CQ Set. During the period from JHS to SHS, the Type B boys change in certain ways. Thus, by SHS, Type B boys become significantly: more warm, more aware of the impression they make on others, more valuing of intellectual matters, and more internally consistent.

Compared to the way they were during JHS, the Type B boys during SHS have become significantly: less irritable, less extrapunitive, less hostile, less self-indulgent, less bothered by demands, and less ruminative.

The Interpersonal Q Set. As conveyed through the Interpersonal Q Set, the Type B boys have, by SHS, come to see their parents as significantly more old-fashioned.

Compared to the way they were during JHS, Type B boys during SHS have become significantly: less direct in their expressions of hostility to their peers, less fickle in their peer attachments, and less valuing of their fathers as attractive men.

Further Findings from the Adolescent Years

The Type B boys vis-à-vis the Complement are significantly lower (.01) in intelligence as measured in mid-adolescence. Their mean IQ is only 106.7, lowest by far of the types (cf. Table 8-1). The Terman Group Test taken at about the age of eleven also shows the Type B boys to be lower than the Complement (86.4 vs. 104.5). Their familial socio-economic status is also the lowest of the types (.10).

The Type B boys experienced their period of rapid physical growth comparatively late and in this skeletal sense of maturity were disadvantaged before their peers. In body build, they were furthest from the masculine ideal of muscularity and were relatively pudgy and broad-hipped (.05). By 1938, when they were in SHS, the Type B boys were appreciably heavier (.05) but not taller than the Complement boys (165 lbs. vs. 142 lbs.) and had significantly more subcutaneous fat (.10). They also tended to have lower diastolic blood pressure than the Complement boys. They were afflicted with the usual number of illnesses with the exception that they were troubled earlier and more frequently by acne (.01).

During JHS, the Type B boys appear more under-controlled as measured by the What I Like To Do Over-control Scale (.05). During SHS, they present themselves as "Blandly socialized" as measured by the WILTD scale (.01) and are evaluated via the Free Play Ratings as more reposed than the Complement group (.05).

In JHS, according to their mothers, the Type B boys are reported as indulging in immature, unconstructive play (.01), as not liking to read (.05), but as liking to dance (.10).

In SHS, the Type B boys have become more interested in their personal appearance than the Complement boys (.05), they more frequently go downtown alone (.10), they attend more undesirable movies (.10), and they do not appear to have creative interests (.10). But also, they are reported as attending Sunday School more frequently and as assuming responsibility for their own room and belongings.

There is a tendency for the Type B boys to be relatively unreactive as measured by their skin conductance responsivity to a series of verbal stimuli.

Their Character as Adults

The CQ Set. Sixteen percent of the Q items differentiate the Type B men from the Complement group at the .01 level (32 percent at the .05 level).

Attributes *absolutely and relatively characteristic of the Type B men as adults:* dependable, sympathetic, giving, protective, productive, likable, warm, calm, straightforward, cheerful, and internally consistent personality.

Attributes *relatively characteristic of Type B men as adults:* turned-to-for-advice and reassurance, socially perceptive, creates dependency in people, and ethically consistent.

Attributes *absolutely and relatively uncharacteristic of Type B men as adults:* rebellious, testing of limits, changeable, deceitful, expresses hostility directly, thinks unconventionally, under-controlled, distrustful, negativistic, complicating of simple situations, and condescending.

Attributes *relatively uncharacteristic of Type B men as adults:* bright, irritable, hostile, aloof, bothered by demands, ruminative, and fluctuating moods.

Character Changes from Senior High School to Adulthood

The CQ Set. Relative to the way the Type B individuals were during SHS, they are as adults significantly: more turned-to-for-advice and reassurance, more sympathetic, more dependable, more productive, more straightforward, more giving toward others, more fastidious, more likely to proffer advice, more compassionate, more calm, and more aware of impressions they make on others.

Since SHS, the Type B men have become significantly: less rebellious, less testing of limits, less negativistic, less bothered by demands, less deceitful, less irritable, less fantasizing, less overtly hostile, less changeable, less self-defensive, less withdrawing when frustrated, less brittle, and less self-defeating.

Further Findings from the Adult Years

CPI Scale Scores. A large number of CPI scales differentiate the Type B men from the Complement group. Type B men are significantly *higher* on the Communality (*Cm*) scale (.10). They are significantly *lower* on the Self-Acceptance (*Sa*) scale (.05), the Intellectual Efficiency (*Ie*) scale (.05), the Capacity for Status (*Cs*) scale (.05), the Flexibility (*Fx*) scale (.05), the Dominance (*Do*) scale (.10), the Sociability (*Sy*) scale (.10), and the Neurotic Over-control (*NOC*) scale (.10).

These scale differences indicate that the Type B men are dependable, moderate, cautious, stolid, shy individuals somewhat plagued by self-doubts. They have narrow interests, are unambitious and unassuming, and are staunch defenders of the status quo.

CPI Item Analysis. Some of the specific items which differentiate the Type B men from the Complement group are reported to "flesh out" the findings reported at the scale level of analysis.

Thus, the Type B men more often than the Complement men *affirm* the following inventory items:

CPI   83. I usually feel nervous and ill at ease at a formal dance or party.
CPI 165. I do not mind taking orders and being told what to do.
CPI 286. I have never done anything dangerous for the thrill of it.
CPI 340. Our thinking would be a lot better off if we would just forget about words like probably, approximately, and perhaps.
CPI 442. The trouble with many people is that they don't take things seriously enough.

The Type B men more than the Complement men *reject* the following CPI items:

CPI 152. I read at least 10 books a year.
CPI 154. I like tall women.
CPI 200. In a group of people I would not be embarrassed to be called upon to start a discussion or give an opinion about something I know well.
CPI 293. Every now and then I get into a bad mood, and no one can do anything to please me.
CPI 346. I must admit I am a pretty fair talker.

Current Status. Type B men in their middle thirties are less well educated than the Complement group (.05), a finding that is probably due both to the lower intelligence and lower socio-economic status of this subsample, as noted during the adolescent years. However, they have achieved a somewhat greater-than-average improvement in their social class and social comforts, and their scores on the Terman Group Test equal those attained by the Complement men (183 versus 183). All of the Type B men married and chose a wife a bit earlier than was usual; their divorce rate appears low; they have fathered more children than is typical for this sample (.10). They report having a very harmonious marriage (.05).

The health of the Type B men does not appear to be unusually good or unusually bad; they are light to moderate consumers of alcohol. They are a half inch shorter, on the average, than Complement men and are six pounds heavier. Politically, the Type B men describe themselves as middle-of-the-road Republicans and they belong to more clubs and fraternal organizations than the Complement men (.10).

Their occupations range widely—the Type B men include three well-unionized industrial craftsmen, an assistant hotel manager, an accountant for a city, an appliance salesman, the manager of a hardware store, a teacher, the vice-president of a small local bank, an office manager, and a supply agent for a large construction firm. Perhaps the common denominator of the occupational niches the Type B men have found is that their positions do not subject them to internal, self-set stresses. Thus, when questioned about their jobs, the Type B men indicate that they like their positions because of the absence of stress (.01), the convenience of the job for their families (.05), the amount of leisure time afforded by the job (.05), and the convenience of the hours worked (.10).

In their middle stage of life, they now view themselves as resembling their mothers more than they resemble their fathers (.01). They report having felt personally inadequate in the past (.10) but now, as parents, they view themselves comparatively as quite competent (.10).

There is continued evidence of skin conductance unreactivity in the Type B individuals as adults. When exposed to a sympathy-inducing film, they show significantly less shift in their general level of conductance than does the Complement group (.01) and their frequency of non-specific GSRs is lower, almost statistically so.

Adjustment and Continuity over the Years

The Psychological Adjustment Index. The Type B individuals evidence a striking discontinuity from adolescence to adulthood. During JHS, SHS, and Adult periods, the Type B group of men is significantly different from the Complement group with respect to our Psychological Adjustment Index. However, for the JHS and SHS periods, the Type B individuals are *lower* than the Complement while for the Adult period, the Type B subjects are appreciably *higher* than the Complement men. For the Type B males, the mean *PA* Indices for the JHS, SHS, and Adult periods respectively are $-.35$, $-.19$, and .39. For the Complement males, the parallel *PA* Index means are .05, .08, and .10. The differences are significant at the .01, .10, and .05 levels, respectively.

Personality Continuity. Comparatively, the Type B individuals show a marked number of changes over the years. They looked disturbed and sullen during adolescence but as adults, they appear reasonably self-comfortable and effective members of their society. Their mean JHS–SHS correlation was .55 (.80 corrected for attenuation) when the Complement mean for the JHS–SHS period was .54 (.84 corrected)—no difference in continuity for this interval. But the Type B subjects for the

SHS–Adulthood comparison have a mean continuity correlation of only .11 (.17 corrected) whereas the Complement group over this time span manifests a mean continuity of .39 (.56 corrected). The difference between the Type B subjects and the Complement individuals for this latter interval is significant beyond the .05 level.

Familial and Environmental Antecedents

The Early Family Ratings. As rated at the time, the parents of the Type B subjects are evaluated as compatible and mutually affectionate (or not hostile) to each other (.10). The mother was adjusted to not working and indeed enjoyed her homemaker role (.10) and there was significantly less conflict than was typical over the size and management of the income earned by the father (.10).

The Ratings of Mothers. Relative to the Complement mothers, none of the ratings reached statistical significance. There were marked trends, however, for the mothers of the Type B subjects to be evaluated as less intelligent and as less spontaneous than the Complement mothers.

The Environmental Q Set. Vis-à-vis the familial contexts of the Complement subjects, the statistically distinguishing qualities of the family settings of the Type B males are as follows:

Environmental conditions *absolutely and relatively characteristic of the families of Type B subjects:* Subject's father was available to the subject through adolescence (.01); subject's family emphasized the life value of fairness, equity, ethics, and responsibility to others (.05); subject was reared in a stable family setting (.10).

Environmental conditions *relatively characteristic of the families of Type B subjects:* Subject's father was manifestly a long-suffering, self-sacrificing, defeated person (.01); subject's home situation was warm and feeling-oriented (.10); subject's mother emphasized the life value of tenderness, love, and related forms of interpersonal communion (.10); subject's family was concerned with social and political problems and causes (.10).

Environmental conditions *absolutely and relatively uncharacteristic of the families of Type B subjects:* There was a family atmosphere of discord, conflict, and recrimination (.05).

Environmental conditions *relatively uncharacteristic of the families of Type B subjects:* Father pressured subject to achieve (.01); subject's father was authoritarian (.05); subject's father emphasized the life value of status, power, and material possessions (.05); subject's mother emphasized the life value of an intellectual orientation, of rationality in decision and outlook (.10).

Interpretive Resume

The Type B person, compared to our other types and the sample as a whole, has run his developmental course with several apparent disadvantages. Although of generally average intelligence, he was in this particular sample (and school) context always less bright than his peers. He came from lower, if not truly low, origins and his parents were less likely to have been within the dominant cultural majority. His family situation was stable, supportive, but non-intellectual, emphasizing the interpersonal values. His parents were in harmony with each other but there was little complexity and enrichment in the home. In particular, the fathers of the Type B subjects were humble, earnest, defeated individuals.

By JHS, the picture of the Type B boy can be clearly drawn—and it is a nasty adolescent that we see. He is narcissistic, sulky, fitful and fickle. He is sneakily hostile when prudence inhibits overtness and directly agressive when the consequences need not be feared. He does not know how to work and is not interested in the uses of the mind. There is an unrecognized and unaccepted passivity in the Type B boy at this time. He resents being controlled by others and yet confesses to personal inadequacy. He is not giving or productive or bright or interesting, and yet he expects the attention and respect of others.

By SHS, the Type B boy manifests various small signs of increasing maturity. He has become more of one piece and is more responsive to others. He shows greater recognition and acceptance of the social contract and does not hold grudges as intensely. There are indications of generational conflict, for his parents seem more archaic and his father explicitly is no longer so admired. Although slower to mature physically, and with a body configuration that is not popularly valued, the Type B teenager was not constrained in his dating behavior.

These changes, mostly for the better, must still be located in the context of the ongoing Type B character. Because in SHS, the Type B boy is still narrow in his interests, uncertain, readily frustrated, covertly antagonistic and now even defensively supercilious. His aspirations are not to shake the world but rather to get along on a day-to-day basis. Frank and insistent hedonism does not seem to characterize him; instead, there is a lack of a long-term and sustained time perspective.

As adults, the Type B men show marked change from their teenage years. Their adolescent oats have been sown and they are now what they were not before—contributing members of their society. They are cheerful, parental, and relaxed, and they are steady workers. They no longer explore to see what they can get away with and they are not wilfully contrary. They enjoy and even seek out the guiding beacon role that was once so inimical. They still cannot be judged especially bright, but they have found their place and within it do well.

Compared to the way they were during SHS, the Type B men are more socialized and less antagonistically evasive. Their world is well defined and they are inclined to resist and resent whatever will complicate its simplicity. The basis for the adult adaptation the Type B men manifest probably lies in their submission to circumscribed and easily predictable lives. Their limited talents are sufficient and even superior for the life situations they have found. The transitory, diffuse impulsivity of the past can be viewed as a manifestation and reaction to the sense of threat visited upon them by adolescence and a changing scene. But now, the known present and the extrapolatable future are comfortable and encompassable. The Type B man, within his niche, can be easy with his self, helpful, and effective. Residues of unconfidence and self-concern can still plague him, and the essential resourcefulness of the Type B man may be questioned if his world is made more chancy and demanding. He has changed a great deal and achieved much, but in many respects the plaintive concerns of adolescence are still to be seen beneath the comfortable adaptation of his adulthood.

I shall call the Type B individuals subsequently *Belated Adjusters* to signify the growth and competence they have achieved after a troublesome and unpromising adolescence.

PERSONALITY TYPE C

Their Character During Junior High School

The CQ Set. Vis-à-vis the Complement group, Type C boys are distinguished by 24 percent of the Q items at the .01 level of significance or, if the .05 level is applied, by 50 percent of the items.

Attributes *absolutely and relatively characteristic of the Type C boys during JHS:* over-controlled, aloof, thin-skinned, ruminative, uncomfortable with uncertainty, and distrustful.

Attributes *relatively characteristic of Type C boys during JHS:* submissive, lacks a sense of personal meaning, gives up and withdraws where possible, tends to delay action, brittle, feels victimized, does not vary roles, introspective, arouses nurturant feelings, self-defeating, has an internally consistent personality, and dependent.

Attributes *absolutely and relatively uncharacteristic of Type C boys during JHS:* assertive, testing of limits, under-controlled, deceitful, socially perceptive, expresses hostile feelings directly, rapid in tempo, turned-to-for-advice and reassurance, feels satisfied with self, self-indulgent, interested in the opposite sex, poised, unpredictable, proffering of advice, talkative, and cheerful.

Attributes *relatively uncharacteristic of the Type C boys during JHS:* likable, expressive, gregarious, responsive to humor, enjoys sensuous experiences, skilled in techniques of imaginative play, initiating of humor, interesting, and eroticizing.

The Interpersonal Q Set. Thirty-five percent of the items differentiated the Type C boys from the Complement at the .05 level.

Items *absolutely and relatively characteristic of Type C boys during JHS:* sensitive to slights from peers, keeps peers at a distance, feels the pattern of his life is laid down by his parents, worries about his parents, and predominately oriented toward adults rather than peers.

Items *relatively characteristic of Type C boys during JHS:* passive and nonreactive with adults, toadying with adults, tends to be butt of group, and has crushes on adults.

Items *absolutely and relatively uncharacteristic of Type C boys during JHS:* spends time with opposite sex, achieves leadership roles with peers, poised with peers, and assertive with peers.

Items *relatively uncharacteristic of Type C boys during JHS:* talkative with peers, emphasizes being with peers, initiates humor with peers, liked by peers, knowledgeable of peer culture, accepts sex-typing of self, competitive with peers, hostile directly with peers, and involved on a fantasy level with opposite sex.

Their Character During Senior High School

The CQ Set. *Vis-à-vis* the Complement group, 22 percent of the Q items distinguish the Type C individuals at the .01 significance and, at the .05 level, 32 percent.

Attributes *absolutely and relatively characteristic of Type C boys during SHS:* over-controlled, aloof, uncomfortable with uncertainty, critical, distrustful, feels guilty, emotionally bland, and tends to delay action.

Attributes *relatively characteristic of Type C boys during SHS:* fearful, lacks a sense of personal meaning, feels victimized, ruminative, complicates simple situations, submissive, brittle, and does not vary roles.

Attributes *absolutely and relatively uncharacteristic of the Type C boys during SHS:* emotionally involved with opposite sex, under-controlled, self-indulgent, talkative, skilled in social techniques of imaginative play, gregarious, poised, rapid in tempo, and assertive.

Attributes *relatively uncharacteristic of Type C boys during SHS:* responsive to humor, enjoys sensuous experiences, cheerful, initiating of humor, likable, expressive, group-conforming, and masculine.

The Interpersonal Q Set. Thirty-three percent of the items differentiate the Type C boys from the Complement at the .05 level of significance.

Items *absolutely and relatively characteristic of Type C boys during SHS:* keeps peers at a distance, worries about his parents, and perceives his family situation as conflicted.

Items *relatively characteristic of Type C boys during SHS:* passive with adults, toadying with adults, tends to be the butt of his group, perceives his father as an attractive man, perceives his parents as restraining, sees his parents as uninterested in him, and predominantly oriented toward adults.

Character Changes from JHS to SHS

The CQ Set. During the period from JHS to SHS, the Type C boys change in certain ways. Thus, by SHS, Type C boys become significantly: more turned-to-for-advice and reassurance, more rebellious, more condescending, more concerned with philosophical problems, and more prideful of self as objective and rational.

Compared to the way they were during JHS, the Type C boys during SHS have become significantly: less thin-skinned, less somaticizing, less fastidious, less concerned with own body, less giving, and less extrapunitive.

The Interpersonal Q Set. As conveyed through the Interpersonal Q set, the Type C boys have, by SHS, become significantly: more directly hostile to their peers, more likely to view their family situation as conflicted, more rebellious, and more spending of time with the opposite sex.

Compared to the way they were during JHS, the Type C boys during SHS have become significantly: less sensitive to slights from peers, less likely to evaluate their parents as happy people, less likely to be the butt of their group, less likely to view their family as affectionate, and less likely to view their mother as attractive.

Further Findings from the Adolescent Years

The Type C boys are of about average intelligence, given the context of our particular sample (their mean IQ is 120) and of typical socio-economic status compared to the Complement. Although of sample-typical height, the Type C boys were consistently and obviously skinnier than the Complement boys (.05) (e.g., at the age of 17, their average weight was 133 lbs. compared to the Complement average of 146 lbs.). If only as a consequence of their lesser weight, they were weaker in strength than their colleagues (.10). In their overall body appearance, they were judged as significantly less masculine (.05) and decidedly not muscular; more often, they wore glasses. Their skeletal age lagged appreciably behind their chronological age (with a reduced N of 6, the difference was significant at almost the .10 level), indicating the Type C boys were "late maturers."

The mothers of the Type C boys were significantly older at the birth of their sons than were Complement mothers (31.5 years versus 27.4 years) and there was a clearly related trend (almost significant at the .10 level) for the Type C boys to be later born within their families rather than being first born or only children.

In JHS, the mothers of the Type C boys describe them as not making friends easily (.01), as not playing organized games (.01), as not active with their peers (.01) and as having poor appetites (.10).

In SHS, the mothers of the Type C boys declare their sons get more than enough sleep (.05) but still lack energy and pep in the morning (.05). The Type C boys are further described as uninterested in their appearance or clothes (.01), as still not mature or constructive in their play activities (.01), and as playing infrequently (.05). Interestingly, the Type C mothers do not allow their sons to go downtown alone at night (.10) or to drive a car (.05), although the Type C boys are reported more frequently as earning money (.10). Their mothers further describe them as not goodnatured (.05) or energetic (.01) and as *not* fighting against the constraints imposed upon them by the parents (.10). The Type C boys did little (.05) or belated (.05) dating during adolescence.

In JHS, Type C boys are higher than Complement boys on the WILTD Banal Socialization scale (.05). The Free Play ratings developed during JHS reveal the Type C boys to be lower on Masculine Self-confidence (.01) and on Buoyancy (.01). During SHS, the Free Play ratings again identify the Type C boys as lower on Buoyant Self-confidence (.01) and now also as lower with respect to Heterosexual Orientation (.10).

The skin conductance data collected during JHS and SHS reveal no trends with respect to Type C boys, but it must be noted that only four Type C boys participated in this psychophysiological experiment.

Their Character as Adults

The CQ Set. Thirty-four percent of the *CQ* items differentiate the Type C men from the Complement group at the .01 level (49 percent at the .05 level).

Attributes *absolutely and relatively characteristic of Type C men as adults:* aloof, basically hostile, self-defensive, thin-skinned, ruminative, distrustful, uncomfortable with uncertainty, brittle, fearful, feels cheated and victimized by life, extrapunitive, bothered by demands from others, self-defeating, projective, compares self to others, and submissive.

Attributes *relatively characteristic of Type C men as adults:* lacks a sense of meaning in life, complicating of simple situations, basically anxious, self-pitying, negativistic, tends to delay action, and concerned with his adequacy as a person.

Attributes *absolutely and relatively uncharacteristic of Type C men as adults:* feels satisfied with self, insightful, poised, calm, socially perceptive, straightforward, gregarious, warm, likable, enjoys sensuous experiences, cheerful, and giving.

Attributes *relatively uncharacteristic of Type C men as adults:* satisfied with his physical appearance, assertive, responsive to humor, interesting, interested in opposite sex, masculine, initiating of humor, able to see to the heart of important problems, charming, wide interests, protective of those close to him, rapid in tempo, productive, verbally fluent, and skilled in techniques of imaginative play.

Character Changes from Senior High School to Adulthood

The CQ Set. Relative to the way the Type C individuals were during SHS, they are as adults significantly: more varying of their interpersonal roles, more thin-skinned, more talkative, more hostile, more self-indulgent, and more judging of self and others in conventional terms.

In addition, the Type C men are significantly: less bright, less emotionally bland, less interesting, less likely to give up and withdraw when frustrated, less responsive to humor, less masculine, less delaying of action than before, less straightforward, less over-controlled than before, and less fantasizing.

Further Findings from the Adult Years

CPI Scale Scores. A large number of CPI scales differentiate the Type C men from the Complement group, all of the differences disadvantaging the type. Thus, Type C men score significantly *higher* on the Psychoneurosis (*Pn*) scale (.01); they are significantly *lower* than the Complement group on the Sociability (*Sy*) scale (.01), the Self-acceptance (*Sa*) scale (.05), the Intellectual Efficiency (*Ie*) scale (.05), the Achievement via Conformance (*Ac*) scale (.05), the Sense of Well-being (*Wb*) scale (.05), and the Communality (*Cm*) scale (.05).

These scale differences suggest that the Type C men are relatively withdrawn, bitter, tense but passive, defensive individuals who are socially awkward and highly sensitive. Further, they are distrustful, complaining, apathetic, and are readily upset by novel situations.

CPI Item Analyses. Some of the specific items which differentiate the Type C men from the Complement are reported below.

Thus, the Type C men more often than the Complement men *affirm* the following inventory items:

CPI   38. It is hard for me to start a conversation with strangers.
CPI 156. I hardly ever get thrilled or excited.
CPI 186. I usually don't like to talk much unless I am with people I know very well.
CPI 390. I have not lived the right kind of life.
CPI 467. At times I think I am no good at all.

The Type C men more often than the Complement men *reject* the following items:

CPI 168. My home life was always happy.
CPI 197. Once in a while I laugh at a dirty joke.
CPI 292. I used to like it very much when one of my papers was read to the class in school.
CPI 316. My parents wanted me to "make good" in the world.
CPI 326. It is annoying to listen to a lecturer who cannot seem to make up his mind as to what he really believes.

Current Status. Type C men, as adults, have received about an average amount of education considering the sample context and they score at the sample mean on the Terman Group Test. However, their social class is about the same as it was during adolescence and currently, given the general upward mobility of the entire sample, the Type C men are significantly lowest (.05) with respect to our socio-economic index.

The adult height of the Type C men is exactly at the sample mean, but they still weigh a bit less than is typical (their mean weight is 162 lbs. compared to 168 lbs.). There are some slight indications that Type C men are in somewhat poorer health or at least express physical complaints more frequently. They are more likely to be abstainers from alcohol or no more than very moderate imbibers (.05).

Of the five bachelors in the sample of 84 men, four are to be found in Type C. The probability that four out of five bachelors would fall into the type by chance is less than one in a thousand, as computed by the hypergeometric distribution. Among the married Type C men, there are indications that the marriage is not viewed to be as gratifying as the marriages of Complement men.

The occupations of the Type C men are various—included are several mechanics, a civil engineer, a blueprint technician, a roof estimator, a construction integrator, a small businessman selling plumbing equipment, a partner in a commercial fishing boat, a clerk, a draftsman, a social worker, and a teacher in a denominational school. Compared to the

Complement men, the Type C men thoroughly dislike their vocations on all dimensions or facets. They find their jobs to be uninteresting (.05); they gain no sense of power or personal significance from their jobs (.05); and their jobs are not congenial or comfortable to them by reason of the positions' off-job advantages of leisure, convenience, or security (.05). They are dissatisfied with their present financial situation (.10), a complaint at least partially justified by their somewhat lower income *vis-à-vis* the Complement men (Type C men earned about $7000 yearly in 1957 compared to the Complement average of about $8300. The difference falls far short of significance, the *t* ratio being only .69). The aspiration for the future of the Type C men, as expressed in their mid-thirties, is to achieve retirement, whereas the Complement men in discussing their aspirations look forward to job advancement, a new and different job, or remaining in a position within which they already feel satisfied (.01).

Type C men describe themselves as politically independent and are not registered as members of any political party (.01). They describe themselves as attending church less frequently than do the Complement men (almost significant at the .10 level). They have fewer friends and see them less frequently (.05). They opine that their family and relatives are not too important to them (.05) and they contact their parents less frequently than do the Complement men (.10).

Adjustment and Continuity over the Years

The Psychological Adjustment Index. The Type C individuals manifest impoverishment of personality from adolescence to adulthood, as indexed by the Psychological Adjustment Index. During JHS, the mean *PA* Index for the Type C individuals was $-.26$. By SHS, an improvement was to be seen for the *PA* Index became less negative, the mean being $-.19$. But by adulthood an intensification of psychopathology is evidenced by the mean *PA* Index of $-.31$. By way of contrast, the Complement means for these three time periods were .04, .10, and .21, respectively; the differences between these pairs of means were significantly different at the .01, .05, and .01 levels.

Personality Continuity. With respect to our simple, overall index of personality continuity, the Type C individuals prove to be most typical. For the JHS–SHS interval, their mean continuity correlations was .54 (.81 corrected) when the Complement mean was also .54 (.83 corrected). Over the longer SHS–Adulthood period, the mean continuity of the Type C subjects was .39 (.57 corrected); during the same interval, the Complement mean was .36 (.55 corrected). These slight differences of course are not statistically significant. To the extent the Type C individu-

als can be distinguished from the Complement, it is not on the basis of
unusual personality continuity.

Familial and Environmental Antecedents

The Early Family Ratings. As evaluated at the time, the fathers of the
Type C boys were comparatively passive, uninvolved individuals (.10),
somewhat uncomfortable in the home and tending to withdraw when in
conflict situations as in the management of family finances (.05). The
mothers of the Type C boys were described as providing little or poor sex
information for their children.

The Ratings of Mothers. In the separate ratings of the mothers of subjects, the mothers of Type C boys were described as, in a relative sense,
personally unattractive. Compared to the Complement mothers, they
were less careful or concerned with their physical appearance (.01), they
appeared more worn or fatigued (.01), with less pleasant facial expression (.05), and they had disagreeable voices (.10). Further, the Type C
mothers manifested a lower level of energy and activity (.05), they were
less cheerful individuals (.10), and they were less trustful (.10) than were
the Complement mothers.

The Environmental Q Set. Vis-à-vis the familial contexts of the Complement subjects, the statistically distinguishing qualities of the family settings of the Type C males are as follows:
    Environmental conditions *absolutely and relatively characteristic of the
families of Type C subjects:* Subjects' mothers' interpersonal modes were
conflict-inducing in children (.01); subject's family context was politically
and philosophically conservative (.05); subject's parents were inhibited
about sex (.05); subject's mother was neurotic, brittle, and anxiety-laden
(.05); subject's mother emphasized the life value of status, power, and
material possessions (.05); the atmosphere of the subject's home was
constricted, suppressive, and cheerless (.10).
    Environmental conditions *relatively characteristic of the families of
Type C subjects:* Subject's mother discouraged and constrained the subject's steps toward personal independence and maturity (.01); subject
was physically disadvantaged *vis-à-vis* his childhood and adolescent
peers (.01); subject was subjected to some form of discrimination due to
race, religion, nationality, or social class (.10); subject's mother was
authoritarian (.10).
    Environmental conditions *absolutely and relatively uncharacteristic of
the families of Type C subjects:* Subject's mother emphasized the life
value of tenderness, love, and related forms of interpersonal communion
(.05); subject's family emphasized "togetherness" and did things as a

unit (.10); father's limitations, needs, and vulnerabilities were apparent (.10).

Environmental conditions *relatively uncharacteristic of the families of Type C subjects:* Subject's mother enjoyed her maternal role (.01); subject's mother was available to the subject through adolescence (.01); subject was physically healthy through adolescence (.05); subject was naturally physically competent (.05); subject had contact with many other children when young (.05); subject was reared in a stable family setting (.10).

Interpretive Resume

The Type C individuals were endowed with good intelligence—about average for our sample but well above the typical population mean—and they are of sample-typical socio-economic status. The psychological properties of their family contexts, however, distinguish the Type C subjects. Their mothers were tense, rigid, gloomy, neurotically-fatigued, sexually-inhibited women; their fathers were energyless, diffident, withdrawn men; and their siblings were older and therefore advantaged and dominant over them. The family atmosphere was a cheerless one, dominated by the mother who was authoritarian, suppressive, and without tenderness. These mothers appear to have goaded their sons toward the values of social prestige and possession, simultaneously restricting them in their efforts to achieve personal competence and autonomy.

Given this family origin, it is not surprising that by JHS the Type C boys are highly constricted, tense, and uneasy persons. They are introverted more because of their discomfort with other people than because of a positive attraction or tendency toward inner life. They are passive and brittle, awaiting experience fearfully rather than with optimism and curiosity. They are followers of what has been laid down for them to do and to be.

In SHS, the Type C boy is much the same. He is still predominantly characterized by over-control, an over-control which has been invoked to insulate his consciousness from the anxieties which assail him. He is discomforted by the amorphous and so he avoids decisions of which he cannot be sure. He is suspicious of others, and so he is emotionally unrevealing. His lack of self-confidence is deep and dispiriting. He is scapegoated by his peers for sufficient and insufficient reasons since he is skinny, weak, bespectacled, and immature in appearance.

Yet, during his later period of adolescence, there has been a leavening of the Type C boy's essential personality. Although still tight and passive, he has loosened somewhat and become more outgoing. Relative to his JHS days, he is more valuing of self, less compliant, less sensitive to slights, and more direct, more outward, and more selfish in venting his feelings and preferences.

In his adulthood, the personality of the Type C man is clearly recognizable from his character during adolescence, but there is a clearly recognizable difference as well. The essential difference appears to be that the over-controlling capacity so pervasively employed in youth to keep the difficulties and anxieties of life within bounds has in adulthood been used up or is otherwise insufficient to permit the Type C man to be tolerable to himself and sufficiently comfortable with others. The compartmentalization, denial, delaying, and simplifying techniques that provided some small margin for getting along in adolescence have worn thin and now, in manhood, the Type C individual is exposed to his despairs, confronted with his failures, and is resourceless before them.

The list of inadequacies is long. In adulthood the Type C man is anxious, insistently detached, hostile, explosive, procrastinating, resentful, whiny, and distorting. More simply, he is unhappy, at a loss as to how to live, and knows it.

Type C men have not found vocations that satisfy nor have they found women with whom to share a modus vivendi. They are out of touch with their familial past—their parents—and they have little familial future. They are disengaged and perhaps were never really caught up by life. If one readies oneself for old age by building earlier a diverse array of satisfactions and accomplishments and interests that continue, then the Type C man is ill-prepared for his later years. It seems likely that the Type C man, having approached the end of his tether, may go on to snap it.

Hereafter, the Type C individuals shall be labelled *Vulnerable Overcontrollers,* to indicate the excessive constriction characterizing their personalities, conjoined now in adulthood with the developing failure of ego defenses.

PERSONALITY TYPE D

Their Character during Junior High School

The CQ Set. Vis-à-vis the Complement group, Type D boys are distinguished by 20 percent of the *CQ* items at the .01 level of significance or, at the .05 level, by 34 percent of the items.

Attributes *absolutely and relatively characteristic of the Type D boys during JHS:* gregarious, masculine, assertive, likable, cheerful, poised, and conventional.

Attributes *relatively characteristic of the Type D boys during JHS:* turned-to-for-advice and reassurance, becomes involved with members of the opposite sex, eroticizing, expresses hostile feelings directly, tends to proffer advice, warm, rebellious, testing of limits, skilled in social techniques of imaginative play, becomes emotionally involved with members of the same sex, and initiating of humor.

Attributes *absolutely and relatively uncharacteristic of Type D boys during JHS:* fearful, has unconventional thought processes, complicates simple situations, aloof, ruminative, values intellectual matters, distrustful, over-controlled, emotionally bland, submissive, and self-defeating.

Attributes *relatively uncharacteristic of Type D boys during JHS:* fantasizing, questing for self-definition and meaning, thin-skinned, feels guilty, bothered by demands, and identifying with causes.

The Interpersonal Q Set. Twenty-nine percent of the Interpersonal Q items differentiated the Type D boys from the Complement at the .01 level of significance, with a total of 46 percent of the items being significant at the .05 level.

Items *absolutely and relatively characteristic of Type D boys during JHS:* gregarious with peers, accepts and appreciates sex-typing as it affects self, likable by peers, assertive with peers, knowledgeable of peer culture, achieves leadership roles with peers, spends time with opposite sex, talkative with peers, poised with peers, initiates humor with peers, and values self in terms set by peer group.

Items *relatively characteristic of Type D boys during JHS:* claims the privileges of adolescence, employs attention-getting behaviors with peers, involved on a fantasy level with opposite sex, and oriented toward going steady.

Items *absolutely and relatively uncharacteristic of Type D boys during JHS:* toadying with adults, tends to be butt of group, aloof with peers, oriented toward adults, perceives parents as restraining of activities, and tends to have crushes on adults.

Their Character during Senior High School

The CQ Set. Vis-à-vis the Complement group, 29 percent of the Q items differentiated the Type D individuals at the .05 level of significance.

Attributes *absolutely and relatively characteristic of Type D boys during SHS:* gregarious, becomes emotionally involved with members of the same sex, assertive, has a rapid personal tempo, cheerful, testing of limits, and under-controlled.

Attributes *relatively characteristic of Type D boys during SHS:* self-indulgent, expressive, enjoys sensuous experiences, rebellious, values self and others in terms set by his cultural group, self-dramatizing, skilled in social techniques of imaginative play, and initiates humor.

Attributes *absolutely and relatively uncharacteristic of Type D boys during SHS:* concerned with philosophical problems, complicating of simple situations, fearful, values intellectual matters, questing for self-definition, feels a lack of personal meaning, and aloof.

The Interpersonal Q Set. Thirty percent of the Interpersonal Q items discriminated at the .05 level of significance.

Items *absolutely and relatively characteristic of Type D boys during SHS:* gregarious with peers, accepts and appreciates sex-typing as it affects self, initiates humor with peers, knowledgeable of peer culture, spends time with members of the opposite sex, and claims the privileges afforded the adolescent in this culture.

Items *relatively characteristic of Type D boys during SHS:* assertive with peers, values self and others in terms set by peer group, and achieves leadership roles with peers.

Items *absolutely and relatively uncharacteristic of Type D boys during SHS:* perceives his family situation as conflicted, perceives his parents as restraining of his activities, feels the pattern of his life is laid down by his parents, has crushes on adults, sees his parents as singling him out as special, and tends to be the butt of his peer group.

Character Changes from JHS to SHS

The CQ Set. During the period from JHS to SHS, the Type D boys change in certain ways. Thus, by SHS, Type D boys become significantly: more self-defeating, more self-dramatizing, more (apparently) bright, more under-controlled, and more personally ambitious.

Compared to the way they were during JHS, the Type D boys during SHS have become significantly: less dependable, less masculine, and less productive.

The Interpersonal Q Set. As conveyed through the Interpersonal Q set, the Type D boys have, by SHS, become significantly: less likely to be leaders with their peers, less likely to view their lives as laid down by their parents, and less likely to view their parents as singling them out for special treatment.

Further Findings from the Adolescent Years

The Type D adolescents have a mean IQ (114.4), somewhat but not significantly lower than the full sample mean. The Terman Group Test of Mental Ability, taken in JHS, also indicates a lower intellectual level for the Type D boys (their mean was 86.5 versus the Complement mean of 106.0, a difference significant at the .10 level). The socio-economic status of their families was slightly but not importantly below the mean social position characterizing the sample. However, the Type D individuals come from significantly larger families (.10) and, as a corollary finding, they tend therefore to have later ordinal positions than the Complement subjects.

According to their mothers' reports, the Type D subjects were significantly heavier at birth than the Complement infants (9.1 lbs. versus 8.1 lbs., significant at the .10 level). In JHS, the Type D boys, although a bit shorter and lighter than the Complement boys, were nevertheless appreciably stronger (.01) than their peers and were judged to be significantly more mesomorphic in build (.01). In SHS the Type D subjects were significantly shorter (.10) than Complement boys (68.5 inches versus 70.3 inches) and they are no longer stronger than the average. Indeed, the Type D boys now manifest a slight tendency towards fat. Throughout adolescence, as objectified by various skeletal indices, the Type D boys may be regarded as "early maturers." In addition, during their first two decades, the Type D boys experienced significantly fewer illnesses than the Complement subjects (.01).

In JHS, the Type D boys were evaluated in the Free Play situation as higher than Complement boys with respect to Masculine Self-confidence (.01). They were also higher (.05) on the Interpersonal Power factor derived from the Frenkel-Brunswik Need Ratings.

In JHS, the mothers of the Type D boys report their sons as sleeping less (.05), as having fewer home duties (.05), as interested in clothes (.10), and as free to dress as they please (.05). The Type D boys, according to their mothers, were rarely alone (.10) and played significantly more often with younger children (.05). Their mothers viewed them as excessively interested in movies (.05) and as attracted to dramatics (.10).

In SHS, as conveyed by their mothers, the Type D boys still do not sleep sufficiently (.01) and their sleep is irregular (.05) and under poor conditions (.05). At this time, the parents express concern about the dress and appearance of the Type D teenagers (.10) and how they eat (.05) and sleep (.10). The complaint is registered that the Type D adolescents do not help with work chores (.10) although they do care for their own possessions (.10), suggesting a selfishness. The Type D boys more frequently know how to dance (.05), they go more frequently to unchaperoned parties (.01), they more frequently earn money outside the home (.10), and, more than the Complement subjects, they approve of smoking (.10) and of drinking (.05). Continuing the description of the Type D boys by their mothers, they are said to have easily bruised feelings (.05), to anger easily (.10), to cry easily (.05), and to worry more (.10) and lack calmness (.10). They criticize their families (.10) on the grounds the family is old-fashioned (.05). They go to see bad movies (.05), call up girls more frequently (.10), like popular music (.01) and social dancing (.05).

As may be divined from the foregoing constellation of characteristics, the Type D adolescents engaged in very frequent dating during high school (.01) and experienced sexual intercourse significantly earlier (.01) than their peers (during high school or by the age of 18 years, where the Complement adolescents did not experience intercourse until about age 20 or 21).

According to the Type D boys, their parents favored them over their siblings (.05). In particular, the Type D adolescents indicate they thought their fathers understood them during those years (.10) and the boys suggest that they reciprocated by positively valuing their fathers (.10). The Type D adolescents were significantly less often influenced by individuals beyond the immediate family (.01). At the end of high school, the vocational goals of the Type D boys were lower (.05) than those of the Complement subjects. The Type D boys aspired toward small businesses or minor professional or technical status, whereas the Complement boys aimed toward professional or executive positions.

Despite the small number of Type D subjects (N of 4) for whom skin conductance data during adolescence was available, there is a decided tendency (.10) for the Type D boys to manifest lower reactivity.

Their Character as Adults

The CQ Set. Thirty-four percent of the *CQ* items differentiate the Type D men from the Complement group at the .05 level of significance (14 percent at the .01 level).

Attributes *absolutely and relatively characteristic of Type D men as adults:* uncomfortable with uncertainty, basically hostile, self-defensive, repressive, brittle, irritable, conventional, and moody.

Attributes *relatively characteristic of Type D men as adults:* anxiety and tension find outlet in bodily symptons, deceitful, bothered by demands, feels cheated by life, emotionally bland, does not vary roles, is basically anxious, over-concerned with own adequacy.

Attributes *absolutely and relatively uncharacteristic of Type D men as adults:* introspective, insightful, philosophically concerned, socially perceptive, calm, valuing of intellectual matters, evaluates situations in motivational terms, verbally fluent, has wide interests, esthetically reactive, and aware of social stimulus value.

Attributes *relatively uncharacteristic of Type D men as adults:* able to see to the heart of important problems, high degree of intellectual capacity, sympathetic, prides self on objectivity, straightforward, socially poised, and personally charming.

Character Changes from Senior High School to Adulthood

The CQ Set. Relative to the way the Type D individuals were during SHS, they are as adults significantly: more hostile, more fearful, more complicating of simple situations, more aloof, more ruminative, more distrustful, more brittle, more over-controlled, more likely to feel cheated by life, more emotionally bland, and more likely to feel a lack of personal meaning.

In addition, the Type D men have become, since SHS, significantly: less testing of limits, less responsive to humor, less socially perceptive, less gregarious, less interesting, less aware of their social stimulus value, less evaluating of the motivations of others, less straightforward, less insightful, less expressive, less compassionate, and less poised.

Further Findings from the Adult Years

CPI Scale Scores. Only a few of the CPI scales differentiate the Type D men from the Complement group. Thus, Type D men score *higher* on the Communality (*Cm*) scale (.10) and higher on the Socialization (*So*) scale (.10); they score *lower* on the Psychological-mindedness (*Py*) scale (.01).

These scale differences do not provide a personality picture as rich or as compelling as is provided by the CPI for the other types. Nevertheless, the Type D men are describable as relatively cautious, dependable, honest, inhibited, obliging individuals who are overly conforming and conventional.

CPI Item Analyses. Some of the specific items which differentiate the Type D men from the Complement are reported below.

Thus, the Type D men more often than the Complement men *affirm* the following inventory items:

CPI   3. I looked up to my father as an ideal man.
CPI   88. I do not like to see people carelessly dressed.
CPI 297. At times I have a strong urge to do something harmful or shocking.
CPI 389. I get pretty discouraged with the law when a smart lawyer gets a criminal free.
CPI 439. The members of my family were always very close to each other.

The Type D men more often than the Complement men *reject* the following items.:

CPI   83. I usually feel nervous and ill at ease at a formal dance or party.
CPI 203. When things go wrong, I sometimes blame the other fellow.
CPI 258. In school I found it very hard to talk before the class.
CPI 331. I often start things I never finish.
CPI 335. There are times when I act like a coward.

Current Status. Type D men, as adults, have received significantly less education (.10) than Complement men and they score significantly lower on the Terman Group Test of Mental Ability (159.4 versus 187.2, the difference being significant at the .01 level). However, the Type D men show an upward social mobility about average for the total sample. Considering the mean IQ of this group during adolescence and the somewhat below average socio-economic status of the families of the Type D men, it would appear that the educational levels they have achieved and their contemporaneous social situations are reasonably expectable outcomes.

The Type D men married somewhat earlier than was typical for the Complement men 22.7 years versus 23.8 years, the difference being almost significant at the .10 level), and they have fathered a currently typical number of children. They continue to be somewhat shorter than Complement men, as in adolescence, and continue their late adolescent tendency to weigh a bit more than Complement subjects.

Of the eight Type D men for whom alcohol consumption data are available, four are problem drinkers, two are moderate drinkers, and two are light drinkers. Compared to the Complement men, the Type D men are much heavier drinkers (.01) and not infrequently embark upon alcoholic binges. Type D men also manifest a tendency to smoke a bit more than is usual.

Four of the Type D men have had, by their mid-thirties, unquestionable psychiatric disturbances as evidenced by hospitalization and the acknowledgment of "nervous breakdowns." When contrasted with the Complement subjects, the Type D men manifest more psychosomatic symptoms (.05) and have impairment of their functions because of poor health (.10).

The Type D men list the following kinds of occupations: several salesmen, the owner of an upholstery shop, the assistant manager of a furniture store, two civil engineers, a linoleum installer, a part-time nightclub waiter, and a self-employed commercial musician. By and large, they do not feel positively toward their jobs when compared to the Complement men. Their jobs do not interest them (.10) nor do their jobs enhance their self conception by virtue of the power of their positions (.10). Their jobs do not give them freedom to develop their ideas (.01) nor is there opportunity for advancement as they see it (.05), nor compensating security of employment (.05). They earn a bit less than Complement men.

Type D men report now that their parents encouraged them to enjoy themselves while young rather than instilling high, future-oriented standards (.10). Presently, they are in contact with their parents relatively often (.05).

Type D men favor spectator sports more than Complement men (.05) and they view themselves significantly more often as liberal Democrats (.05) although they also indicate that they are uninterested in politics.

In the follow-up interview situation, the Type D men were evaluated as having only a vague picture of themselves (.01).

Adjustment and Continuity over the Years

The Psychological Adjustment Index. There is an interesting and suggestive trend in the psychological adjustment manifested by the Type D individuals over the years. During JHS, they appear to be reasonably well adjusted, as indicated by the *PA* Index. Their mean *PA* Index was .21, significantly *higher* (.05) than the Complement boys at the time (mean of −.03). By SHS, the Type D boys drop somewhat in their *PA* Indices (mean of .10) while the Complement boys have improved their personal situation, climbing to a mean *PA* Index of .05, the difference no longer being significant. Then, by adulthood, the Type D men have plummeted in their overall adjustment (their mean *PA* Index is −.27) while the Complement men have matured toward a mean *PA* Index of .20. This last difference is significant at the .01 level.

Personality Continuity. The Type D individuals show typical stability over the JHS–SHS time period. Their mean continuity correlation is .54 (.82 corrected), while the mean of the Complement group is also .54 (.83 corrected). Over the longer SHS–Adulthood interval, however, the Type D subjects show appreciably less consistency. Their mean continuity correlation over these years is .21 (.28 corrected), while the mean for the Complement group is .39 (.56 corrected). The continuity difference for the SHS–Adulthood period is significant beyond the .01 level.

Familial and Environmental Antecedents

The Early Family Ratings. The mothers of the Type D boys were rated as comparatively uninterested in their husbands (.05) and also as comparatively uninterested in their children (.10), when contrasted with the Complement mothers. Trends in the data suggest that the mothers of Type D boys are somewhat undemonstrative and not overtly affectionate with their children. The father reciprocates the uninterest of the mother and there is apparent sexual conflict between the parents. Despite these indications of less than fulfillment, the family unit is a stable and continuing one.

The Ratings of Mothers. Compared to the Complement mothers, the mothers of Type D boys are lower in intellectual competence. They think more slowly (.05) and with less accuracy (.10). Temperamentally, they appear to be relatively over-controlled or, perhaps more simply, energyless. They are rated as relatively placid (.05), unemotional (.05), and hypoactive (.05).

The Environmental Q Set. *Vis-à-vis* the familial contexts of the Complement subjects, the statistically differentiating qualities of the Type D males are as follows:

Environmental conditions *absolutely and relatively characteristic of Type D subjects:* Subject was naturally physically competent (.05); subject had contact with many other children while young (.05); subject's father was authoritarian (.10); subject was rivalled by one or more siblings for the attention of his parents (.10).

Environmental conditions *absolutely and relatively uncharacteristic of Type D subjects:* Subject's mother discouraged and constrained the subject's steps toward personal independence and maturity (.05); subject's mother was manifestly a long-suffering, self-sacrificing, defeated person (.10).

Interpretive Resume

The Type D individuals are sufficiently intelligent to get along in their world and their familial social class seems ordinary enough in our sample context. It is in the psychological qualities of their families that some clues to their character become evident. Thus, the mothers of the Type D subjects were undemonstrative individuals lacking in spirit, spontaneity, or intellectual dash. The fathers of the Type D subjects, like their wives, were also not overtly affectionate and were domineering males as well. As a marital pair, father and mother were adapted to but uninvolved with each other. Often, they were so busy responding to the overall needs and responsibilities of their large families that they could not give any one child the particular attention and focus he might wish. It might well be said that the Type D individuals were socialized more by their siblings than by the parents. Certainly, great moral and achievement expectations were not visited upon them by their parents, and they were left to be shaped by their own desires and the accidental influences of their personal experiences and cultural time.

In JHS, the Type D boys appear as prototypical male adolescents—they are gregarious, vigorous, cheerful, unintraceptive, conventional, self-confident teenage boys. They enjoy practical jokes, they are interested in and tease girls, they know but like to circumvent the limits that have been placed on them. The picture they present is, on the whole, the pleasant normative one of the All-American boy. Perhaps these are not the most interesting adolescents—they think in truly tried and tiresome ways, they have little happiness in life, and they seek no deeper view of themselves or of their world—but they are likable, predictable, and not fundamentally disruptive.

In SHS, they appear much but not entirely the same. They are, as before, peer-oriented, assertive, evasive of rules but essentially conventional. The difference is that they have intensified their usage of the culturally-given adolescent role—they are more rebellious, more histrionic, less dutiful and relatively less competent. They are immersed in the immediacy of their adolescence, with little thought of the future or of the reasons for their being. Their early athleticism and competence is forsaking them, or diminishing in relevance, and no substantial adaptive substitute is being generated.

In adulthood, the Type D men display a repressive character structure and, at the level of their awareness, an anomie. The swinging, somewhat voracious confidence of their SHS days is gone and they are now tense, touchy, defensive individuals, moodily hostile. Although they are anxious and self-deceiving regarding their personal adequacy, this concern does not motivate them toward introspection, valid self-evaluation, or consideration of their life goals.

They perseverate in their behaviors, they are emotionally unreactive, they are envious, and they are threatened by anticipations of disruption of the rigid ways of living they have evolved. Yet, these rigidities at best leave them gnawing for qualities in their lives they vaguely miss but cannot define for themselves. They now reject the pleasure-seeking spontaneities of adolescence, they now do not seek to stretch or evade societal rules. In ironic recompense for these steps toward maturity, they are afflicted now by a lack of personal meaning and an integrity-consuming deceitfulness, an incessant suspiciousness, and a prevailing bitterness. The rather joyous days of adolescence are gone and replaced now by the tensely empty time that characterizes their adulthood. Their future cannot be one of promise and fulfillment.

In referring to this type subsequently, I shall call the Type D individuals *Anomic Extraverts* to convey the valuelessness and the absence of inner life that has so essentially characterized them.

PERSONALITY TYPE E

Their Character during Junior High School

The CQ Set. Vis-à-vis the Complement group, Type E boys are distinguished by 29 percent of the CQ items at the .01 level of significance or, if the .05 level is employed instead, by 48 percent of the items.

Attributes *absolutely and relatively characteristic of Type E boys during JHS:* rebellious, talkative, basically hostile, has unconventional thought processes, testing of limits, verbally fluent, extrapunitive, irritable, self-dramatizing, under-controlled, and negativistic.

Attributes *relatively characteristic of Type E boys during JHS:* brittle, changeable, self-indulgent, expresses hostile feelings directly, affected, condescending, expressive, self-defeating, projective, and self-pitying.

Attributes *absolutely and relatively uncharacteristic of Type E boys during JHS:* sympathetic, submissive, calm, feels satisfied with self, turned-to-for-advice and reassurance, arouses nurturance, protective, likable, giving, insightful, dependable, emotionally bland, internally consistent, fastidious, over-controlled, and warm.

Attributes *relatively uncharacteristic of Type E boys during JHS:* productive, straightforward, favors status quo, comfortable with the decisions he has made, dependent, prides self on objectivity, aware of his social stimulus value, poised, masculine, does not vary his roles, and becomes emotionally involved with members of the same sex.

The Interpersonal Q Set. Twenty-seven percent of the Interpersonal Q items differentiated the Type E boys from the Complement group at the .01 level of significance, with a total of 44 percent of the items being significant at the .05 level.

Items *absolutely and relatively characteristic of Type E boys during JHS:* talkative with peers, rebellious with adults, perceives his parents as restraining his activities, views his family situation as conflicted, employs attention-getting behavior with his peers, covertly hostile with adults, initiating of humor with peers, and assertive with peers.

Items *relatively characteristic of Type E boys during JHS:* expresses hostile feelings directly with peers, claims the privileges of adolescence, condescending with peers, tends to be the butt of his group, and shows changeability of peer attachments.

Items *absolutely and relatively uncharacteristic of Type E boys during JHS:* perceives his family as affectionate, perceives parents as consistent, protective of friends, liked by peers, protected by peers, accepts and appreciates sex-typing as it affects self, views his mother as an attractive woman, perceives his parents as accepting his steps toward maturity, and straightforward.

Their Character during Senior High School

The CQ Set. *Vis-à-vis* the Complement group, 26 percent of the *Q* items are differentiating at the .01 level of significance and 41 percent at the .05 level.

Attributes *absolutely and relatively characteristic of Type E boys during SHS:* rebellious, hostile toward others, thin-skinned, self-defeating, under-controlled, irritable, bothered by demands, fluctuating of mood, negativistic, and lacks a sense of meaning in life.

Attributes *relatively characteristic of Type E boys during SHS:* changeable, testing of limits, self-pitying, self-dramatizing, questing for self-definition, extrapunitive, has unconventional thought processes, distrustful, expresses hostile feelings directly, and is affected.

Attributes *absolutely and relatively uncharacteristic of Type E boys during SHS:* feels satisfied with self, calm, turned-to-for-advice and reassurance, submissive, productive, dependable, over-controlled, comfortable with his physical appearance, accepting of dependency in self, favors status quo, poised, and is cheerful.

Attributes *relatively uncharacteristic of Type E boys during SHS:* sympathetic, likable, straightforward, comfortable with the decisions he has made, giving, fastidious, protective, warm, internally consistent, and physically attractive.

The Interpersonal Q Set. Twenty-nine percent of the Interpersonal *Q* items discriminated at the .05 level of significance.

Items *absolutely and relatively characteristic of Type E boys during SHS:* rebellious with adults, bothered by demands from peers, perceives his family situation as conflicted, sensitive to slights from peers, and covertly hostile to adults.

Items *relatively characteristic of Type E boys during SHS:* expresses hostile feelings directly to peers, and tends to be the butt of his peer group.

Items *absolutely and relatively uncharacteristic of Type E boys during SHS:* perceives his family as affectionate, perceives his parents as reasonable, perceives his parents as happy, and is poised with peers.

Items *relatively uncharacteristic of Type E boys during SHS:* respects his parents, perceives his parents as consistent, liked by peers, able to have genuine relationships with adults, perceives parents as accepting his steps toward maturity, straightforward with peers, and sympathetic with peers.

Character Changes from JHS to SHS

The CQ Set. During the period from JHS to SHS, the Type E boys change in certain ways. Thus, by SHS, Type E boys become significantly: more lacking in a sense of meaning, more considerate, more concerned with philosophical problems, more protective of close ones, more masculine, more self-defeating, more insightful, more interested in the opposite sex, and more introspective.

Compared to the way they were during JHS, the Type E boys during SHS have become significantly: less fantasizing, less talkative, less conventional, less cheerful, less enjoying of sensuous experience, less productive, and less expressive.

The Interpersonal Q Set. As conveyed through the Interpersonal Q set, the Type E boys have, by SHS, become significantly: more protective of friends, more dependent on peers, more associated with formal or informal groups, more sensitive to demands from peers, and more considerate with peers.

Compared to the way they were during JHS, the Type E boys have, by SHS, become significantly: less talkative with peers, less worried about their parents, less changeable in their peer attachments, and less aloof from peers.

Further Findings from the Adolescent Years

The Type E adolescents are significantly higher (.10) than the Complement adolescents with respect to intellectual level (their mean IQ is 128.2 versus the Complement mean IQ of 119.7), and they experienced the most comfortable and advantageous socio-economic situation (.05).

According to their mothers, the Type E individuals were significantly lighter at birth than Complement individuals (.01), weighing an average of 6.3 lbs. versus the Complement mean of 8.4 lbs. The appreciably smaller weight probably betokens a prematurity of birth.

Throughout JHS and SHS, the Type E boys were shorter than their peers (.10). Although in JHS they were somewhat heavier than Complement boys (and were somewhat pudgy), in SHS the Type E boys were a bit lighter than the sample average as would follow from their lesser height. They were rated as significantly less ectomorphic (or lean) than Complement teenagers (.10) and as having both mesomorphic (muscular) and endomorphic (beefy) tendencies. They manifested physical maturity at an average rate; they wore glasses earlier than was usual (.01), and they were significantly weaker than their peers (.10).

In JHS, the Free Play Ratings reveal the Type E boys to be more Buoyant (.10) and less Reposed (.01). In SHS, the same trends continue, the Free Play Ratings showing the Type E boys to be almost significantly higher with respect to Buoyant Self-confidence and again lower on the Reposed dimension (.05).

In JHS, the Type E boys are reported as having disturbing dreams (.01), as uninterested in clothes, as playing more often with other children but in an unconstructive way, as having friendships that are not enduring or strong (.05), and as interested in dramatics.

In SHS, the Type E boy needs to be reminded to help around the home, he is permitted downtown at night (.10), he argues more often with his mother (.10), he does not get along well with adults (.05), and he is negative toward his father (.01) and rebellious (.10).

The Type E adolescent shows a decided tendency to be unreactive as measured by his skin conductance under mild stress. The subsample sizes are too small to warrant statistical tests, but as an indication of the trend toward unreactivity, note that our sample contained six of Harold Jones' Low Reactors. Of the four Type E boys who were psycho-physiological subjects as well, two were Low Reactors and two were not categorized (but were *not* High Reactors). No other type had more than one representative in the Low Reactor groups.

Their Character as Adults

The CQ Set. Twenty-nine percent of the Q items differentiate the Type E men from the Complement group at the .01 level of significance and, at the .05 level, 40 percent of the items are discriminating.

Attributes *absolutely and relatively characteristic of Type E men as adults:* talkative, interesting, rebellious, rapid in tempo, moody, undercontrolled, and bright.

Attributes *relatively characteristic of Type E men as adults:* expressive, changeable, responsive to humor, testing of limits, self-indulgent, eroticizing, expresses hostile feelings directly, self-dramatizing, initiating of humor, irritable, and skilled in techniques of imaginative play.

Attributes *absolutely and relatively uncharacteristic of Type E men as adults:* emotionally bland, calm, feels satisfied with self, conventional, over-controlled, does not vary roles, internally consistent, fastidious, satisfied with his physical appearance, repressive, and sympathetic.

Attributes *relatively uncharacteristic of Type E men as adults:* dependable, prides self on being objective, productive, moralistic, conservative, ethically consistent, giving, protective of close ones, turned-to-for-advice and reassurance, ambitious, physically attractive, and tends to proffer advice.

Character Changes from Senior High School to Adulthood

The CQ Set. Relative to the way the Type E men were during SHS, they are as adults significantly: more poised, more productive, more interested in the opposite sex, more turned-to-for-advice and reassurance, more eroticizing, more straightforward, more dependable, more likable, more aware of their social stimulus value, more cheerful, more socially perceptive, and more varying of roles.

In addition, the Type E men have become, since SHS, significantly: less fantasizing, less comparing of self with others, less moralistic, less bothered by demands, less emotionally bland, less likely to feel cheated by life, less self-defeating, less extrapunitive, and less distrustful.

Further Findings from the Adult Years

CPI Scale Scores. Many of the CPI scales discriminate the Type E men from the Complement group. Thus, Type E men score *higher* on the Dominance (*Do*) scale (.01), the Sociability (*Sy*) scale (.05), the Neurotic Under-control (*NUC*) scale (.05), and the Self-Acceptance (*Sa*) scale (.10). They score *lower* than the Complement men with respect to the Socialization (*So*) scale (.01), the Self-control (*Sc*) scale (.01), the Femininity (*Fe*) scale (.01), the Ego-Control (*EC*) scale (.01), the Neurotic Over-control (*NOC*) scale (.01), the Sense of Well-being (*Wb*) scale (.05), and the Responsibility (*Re*) scale (.10).

Type E men, as assessed by the CPI, appear to be relatively rebellious, hasty, forceful, clever, temperamental individuals who have wide interests and are self-confident. They are enterprising persons, opportunistic as well as imaginative. Although socially oriented, they are demanding, undependable, quarrelsome, spiteful, and ostentatious when with others. Their impulsivity leads them to unconventionality, hedonism, restless adventure, and carelessness.

CPI Item Analyses. Some of the specific items which differentiate the Type E men from the Complement are reported below.

Thus, the Type E men more often than the Complement men *affirm* the following inventory items:

CPI   29. I am often said to be hotheaded.
CPI 107. I can be friendly with people who do things which I consider wrong.
CPI 208. I like to go to parties and other affairs where there is lots of loud fun.
CPI 288. As a youngster, I was suspended from school one or more times for cutting up.

CPI 320. I would be willing to describe myself as a pretty "strong" personality.

The Type E men more often than the Complement men *reject* the following items:

CPI 186. I usually don't like to talk much unless I am with people I know very well.

CPI 276. I have very few quarrels with members of my family.

CPI 323. I have never done any heavy drinking.

CPI 389. I get pretty discouraged with the law when a smart lawyer gets a criminal free.

CPI 408. I always see to it that my work is carefully planned and organized.

Current Status. Type E men, as adults, have proceeded less far educationally than their adolescent intelligence level would have indicated. Moreover, their scores on the Terman Group Test of Mental Ability taken in adulthood reveal that their earlier intellectual superiority is no longer evidenced (their mean score on the Terman Test is 185.8 versus the Complement mean of 182.6). A particularly striking finding is the observation that although the Type E men initially were from families with the most advantageous socio-economic level (.05), the socio-economic status the Type E men themselves have achieved as adults shows significant *decline* (.01) in a sample context where upward mobility is the strong and very general rule.

The Type E married a bit later than Complement men (24.9 years versus 23.5 years) and they have fathered fewer children (.05). There is a decided trend for Type E men to be divorced more often.

As adults, they continue to be a bit shorter than Complement males (almost significant at the .10 level) and slightly lighter (164 lbs. versus 168 lbs.). Five of the six Type E men for whom data on alcohol consumption are available are problem drinkers, the sixth Type E man being a moderate drinker. This trend toward heavy alcohol usage is highly significant (.01).

The occupational histories of the Type E men indicate a marked tendency to have had many different jobs. Presently, their occupations are phenotypically diverse but with several threads of consistency. Two Type E men are salesmen in family-owned plants, two other are in police or investigative work, another owns a cabaret, a sixth is a part-time entertainer and part-time bill collector, a seventh is a used-car salesman, an eighth owns a small awning business, a ninth is an engineering test analyst, and the tenth is still a student, working in a university research project in physical chemistry. The Type E men express greater liking for their jobs than do the Complement men (.05) because they find their positions to be interesting, entertaining, and diverse (.05). They picked (or fell into) their current vocation at an average age greater than thirty years where the Complement men decided on their vocations no later than during their early twenties (.10).

The Type E men express an unconcern regarding the necessity of saving for their old age (.05). They deny the validity of religion and instead opt for atheism. They are politically unaffiliated (.05), with no tie to any party.

Only three Type E men participated in the follow-up psycho-physiological experiment and no trends regarding their skin conductivity while experiencing the film are apparent.

One Type E man has been jailed three times—once for an assaultive outburst, another time for black-marketing overseas, and on the last occasion for armed robbery, again while overseas. No Type E men appear to have experienced psychiatric treatment.

Adjustment and Continuity over the Years

The Psychological Adjustment Index. The psychological adjustment of the Type E individuals shows a consistent and somewhat surprising trend. During JHS, as conveyed by the *PA* Index, the Type E boys are significantly more maladjusted (their mean Index is −.27 where the Complement mean is .04, a difference significant at the .05 level). By SHS, there is not much relative change though both the Type E and the Complement boys show slight progress toward maturity (the Type E mean *PA* Index is −.24 where the Complement mean is .10, a difference significant at the .01 level). But by adulthood, the Type E men have moved an appreciable distance from their adolescent psychopathology. They are not as adults well adjusted, but they are not especially poorly off when compared to the Complement men (the Type E men as adults have a mean *PA* Index of .07 whereas the Complement men have a mean Index of .14; the difference is not close to being significant).

Personality Continuity. The Type E subjects are not especially deviant with respect to the general durability of their personalities. For the JHS–SHS period, their mean continuity correlation is .57 (.82 corrected) and the comparable mean for the Complement group is .53 (.83 corrected). Over the SHS–Adulthood interval, the Type E continuity mean was .40 (.63 corrected) and the Complement mean was .36 (.54 corrected). These differences do not begin to approach significance.

Familial and Environmental Antecedents

The Early Family Ratings. A host of the ratings made during the child-hood of the Type E boys distinguish their parents. The mothers of the Type E boys are described as tense (.05), unstable individuals (.10), with great privacy needs (.05). They appear unhappy as homemakers (.10) and do little housework (.10). They are unconcerned about their children's education (.05).

The fathers of the Type E boys have different preoccupations. Their health is bad (.05) and they are much concerned about it (.10). Perhaps because of their health problems, they appear to be uninterested in their child (.10) and they tend to withdraw when they find themselves in a conflict situation (.05).

Mother and father fight with each other. There is conflict over religion between them (.05) and they argue about how they will spend their recreational time and money (.10). The fathers of the Type E boys have been married significantly more often than Complement fathers (.05).

The Ratings of Mothers. The separately formulated ratings of the mothers of the subjects reveal the mothers of the Type E boys to be comparatively quite bright. Thus, they are judged to be unusually intelligent (.05), verbally facile (.05), mentally quick (.01), and accurate (.10). They impressed the raters as more fashionably dressed than were the Complement mothers (.10). Characterologically, the Type E mothers appeared to be relatively under-controlled. They were restless individuals (.10), over-active (.10), talkative (.10), and curious (.10).

The Environmental Q Set. Vis-à-vis the familial contexts of the Complement subjects, the statistically differentiating qualities of the family settings of the Type E males are as follows:

Environmental conditions *absolutely and relatively characteristic of the families of Type E subjects:* Subject's mother was neurotic, brittle, and anxiety-laden (.01); mother's interpersonal modes were conflict-inducing in children (.05); mother's limitations, needs, and vulnerabilities were apparent (.05); father's limitations, needs, and vulnerabilities were apparent (.05).

Environmental conditions *relatively characteristic of the families of Type E subjects:* Subject's mother was seductive with him (.05); subject experienced a complex, sophisticated home environment (.05); subject was rejected by his father (.05); the sexuality and sexual interests of the parents were apparent to the subject (.05); father teased subject and was playfully contradictory (.10); the financial condition of the family was comfortable when subject was a child (.10).

Environmental conditions *absolutely and relatively uncharacteristic of the families of Type E subjects:* Subject's mother emphasized the life value of tenderness, love, and related forms of interpersonal communion (.05); subject's mother emphasized the life value of physical activity, the outdoors, and nature (.10); subject's father was available to the subject through adolescence (.10).

Environmental conditions *relatively uncharacteristic of the families of Type E subjects:* Subject's father was knowledgeable and competent in masculine activities and skills (.05); subject's father emphasized the life value of physical activity, the outdoors, and nature (.05); subject's mother was knowledgeable and competent in feminine activities and skills (.05); subject's parents were inhibited about sex (.05); subject's family emphasized the life value of fairness, equity, ethics, and responsibility to others (.05); subject was naturally physically attractive (.05); subject's mother enjoyed her maternal role (.05); subject was given responsibilities and chores as a child and adolescent (.05); subject's family context was politically and philosophically conservative (.05); subject's home emphasized manners, propriety, and convention (.10); subject was reared in a stable family setting (.10); subject's home environment was well-structured, orderly, and predictable (.10); subject's family environment contained a significant and genuine religious element (.10).

Interpretive Resume

The Type E individual, on strictly actuarial grounds, would appear to be the most advantaged of all our male types. None of the other types was superior to him in intelligence (Type A individuals were tied with Type E with respect to mean IQ at 128), and the Type E subject was appreciably better off in regard to socio-economic status and all that is thereby entailed.

These rosy advantages of endowment and of circumstance are tempered, however, by a trying and tense parental situation. The father of the Type E boy typically had been married before, a finding that can come about a number of ways, most of which intimate a character flaw in the father. The Type E father was uninterested in his son, neurotically self-preoccupied, and often away from home. He did not communicate the usual, perhaps stereotyped masculine values and masculine skills, and interacted with his son—if at all—in volatile, teasing, contradictory ways. When tired or bored or conflicted, the Type E father would simply withdraw from his family role.

The mother of the Type E boy was also an unstable, restless, driven individual centered more on self than on her marital and parental responsibilities. A bright, sophisticated, curious woman, the mother of the Type

E boy was manifestly sexy as well, and her son early and repeatedly encountered this aspect of his mother's character. Because of her extreme and indulgent focus on self, the mother of the Type E boy was unmaternal, fashionable with respect to clothes, politics, and other contemporary happenings, and arbitrary and impulsive in her dealings with others.

With this parental pair, there inevitably was conflict—sexual, financial, value—between husband and wife, with the Type E boy present as a bystander. The parental requirement of imparting a sense of heritage and of continuity to each new generation was not taken up by either mother or father. The family context was unstructured, given direction by the affective vagaries of the parents, primarily the mother.

Already by JHS, the Type E boy is clearly marked as an under-controller. He is rebellious, desire-fulfilling, and gaily spontaneous. His moods fluctuate because his impulses do. He is outgoing, intense, dominant, and has a sense of the ridiculous. He cannot be likable at this time because of his brash independence and fortuitous inconsiderateness. Relations with his parents are strained.

In SHS, the impulsivity and gloriously wild thinking continue, but they are colored somewhat by a greater despair and edginess coupled with and perhaps a function of increased reflection on the nature of life. More, if not yet much, compassion is evidenced. The Type E boy is moving away from his parents into a greater dependence on friends. Some of his exuberance is gone but composure has not been attained.

In adulthood, the Type E individuals are still quick, moody, under-controllers. They are playful, involved, directly hostile when angry, somewhat selfish, highly self-critical, and freely emotional. They drink too much.

Since SHS, they have become more at ease with their personal style and have moved toward maturity. They are more responsible than they were and they may become more so since there is still much room for them to progress on this dimension. They are more perceptive of themselves and of others now and are not so aggressively suspicious as before. In other ways too, there are indications of progress toward mature relationships. Further, if under-control is viewed as in part due to a deficient or insufficient socialization, then it may be that the passage of time now is contributing the education for compassion these individuals have required. If so, then additional personality movement along the directions indicated can be expected in the next years.

And yet, perhaps because their styles were set and in evidence so early and the current changes are late, the Type E men appear to have fallen short of what might have been expected of them. Their innate brightness and their culturally advantaged environments have not helped them especially. Their vocations tend to be family-dependent or socially marginal, noncontributory, or dilettantish. Some have sought out jobs that approve their exhibitionism (e.g., entertainment) or approve their aggressivity (e.g., police and investigative work). Compared to their origins, Type E men have been *downwardly* mobile in a cultural context in which all the other types have advanced their socio-economic position. Thus, it would appear that the Type E men, although still bright and interesting and not in an overall sense particularly maladjusted, have failed to realize from their lives the potential that resided in them.

I shall label the Type E subjects hereafter as *Unsettled Under-controllers* to indicate the pervasive impulsivity within these individuals and our recognition that although their personal qualities probably will not change much subsequently, the Type E men have not yet fixed upon their niche in life.

Chapter IX

COURSES OF PERSONALITY DEVELOPMENT
—THE FEMALE SAMPLE

In the female sample, the six female types will be designated initially by the letters U, V, W, X, Y, and Z. Labels for each type will be forthcoming after the nature and correlates of each personality syndrome have been elucidated.

As with the presentation of the data for the male types, first some demographic data surrounding the several types are reported so that the reader can develop a quick sense of the actuarial characteristics of the groupings.

To further parallel the previous chapter, the temporal change from JHS to SHS to adulthood in the similarities among the six female types is also presented, as manifested by the intercorrelations of the modal *CQ* descriptions developed for each type for each time period.

The shifting pattern of similarities and of differences is intriguing. Thus, Types X and Y were similar during adolescence but characterologically different in adulthood; Type U and Type V subjects appear different during adolescence but manifest appreciable similarities by adulthood.

And as a final preliminary, CPI profiles for the several female types are reported in Figure 9–1.

Now the task is simply to describe the types.

PERSONALITY TYPE U

Their Character During Junior High School

The CQ Set. Vis-à-vis the Complement group, girls falling within Type U are very well identified during JHS with 41% of the *Q* items being nominally significant at the .01 level (55% at the .05 level).

189

Table 9–1
Demographic Characteristics of the Female Types

	Type U	Type V	Type W	Type X	Type Y	Type Z	Residuals
Number of Subjects in the Type	19	14	10	10	11	6	16
Mean Intelligence Quotient	116.5	121.4	111.4	117.2	110.8	120.5	118.3
Mean Years of Education	13.0	15.1	13.5	13.3	12.3	14.8	13.1
Socio-economic Status during Adolescence	3.16	3.36	3.10	3.20	3.64	2.67	3.25
Socio-economic Status during Adulthood	2.32	1.50	3.40	2.50	3.45	1.67	2.44
Childhood Family Size	2.37	2.93	2.70	1.60	2.45	3.17	2.69
Ordinal Position of Type Members	1.68	2.00	2.40	1.50	2.27	2.67	2.06
Number of Marriages	1.16	1.14	1.60	1.40	1.82	0.67	1.19
Number of Children	3.26	2.43	2.20	2.10	2.54	2.33	2.62

Attributes *absolutely and relatively characteristic of the Type U girl during JHS:* likable, poised, cheerful, gregarious, dependable, warm, productive, giving, sympathetic, straightforward, fastidious, physically attractive, socially perceptive, turned-to-for-advice and reassurance, protective, and aware of her social stimulus value.

Attributes *relatively characteristic of the Type U girl during JHS:* comfortable with her physical appearance, calm, evaluates the motivations of others, insightful, feels reasonably satisfied with self, internally consistent, skilled in social techniques of imaginative play, comfortable with the decisions she makes, responsive to humor, interesting, becomes emotionally involved with opposite sex, fluent, becomes emotionally involved with same sex, and initiating of humor.

Attributes *absolutely and relatively uncharacteristic of the Type U girl during JHS:* feels victimized, aloof, negativistic, self-defeating, distrustful, lacks personal meaning, changeable, deceitful, rebellious, brittle, complicates simple situations, pushes limits, fearful, basically hostile, bothered by demands, extrapunitive, reluctant to act, and withdraws when frustrated.

Table 9–2
Intercorrelations of Modal Type CQ Descriptions
For Each Time Period: Females

		U	V	W	X	Y	Z
	U	—					
	V	.11	—				
JHS	W	.54	.63	—			
Intercorrelations	X	.45	−.01	.44	—		
	Y	.07	.15	.36	.74	—	
	Z	.58	.10	.25	.52	.47	—
	U	—					
	V	.24	—				
SHS	W	.64	.59	—			
Intercorrelations	X	.46	.25	.44	—		
	Y	.46	.26	.36	.75	—	
	Z	.03	.45	−.07	.34	.39	—
	U	—					
	V	.75	—				
Adulthood	W	−.21	−.32	—			
Intercorrelations	X	.52	.29	−.17	—		
	Y	.45	.30	.46	.01	—	
	Z	.10	.48	.07	.31	.03	—

Attributes *relatively uncharacteristic of the Type U girl during JHS:*
self-defensive, thin-skinned, irritable, projective, ruminative, has fluctuating moods, uncomfortable with uncertainty, somaticizing, and affected.

The Interpersonal Q Set. Thirty-seven percent of the items differentiated the Type U girls from the Complement at the .01 level (44% at the .05 level).

Items *absolutely and relatively characteristic of the Type U girl during JHS:* poised with peers, able to have genuine relationships with adults, liked by peers, achieves leadership roles with peers, straightforward with peers, perceives parents as reasonable, knowledgeable of peer culture, sympathetic with peers, and emphasizes being with peers.

Items *relatively characteristic of the Type U girl during JHS:* perceives parents as being happy, perceives her family as affectionate, perceives her parents as accepting of her steps toward maturity, and perceives parents as consistent.

Items *absolutely and relatively uncharacteristic of the Type U girl during JHS:* covertly hostile to adults, tends to be the butt of her peer group,

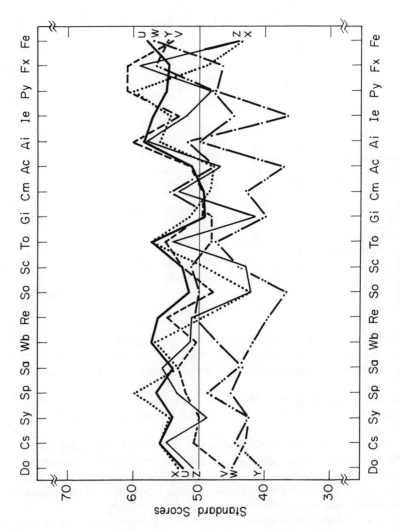

Figure 9–1 The Mean CPI Profiles of the Female Types

rebellious with adults, keeps peers at a distance, sees her parents as uninterested in her, has the social stimulus value of a younger person, toadying toward adults, and passive with adults.

Items *relatively uncharacteristic of the Type U girl during JHS:* perceives her family situation as conflicted, perceives parents as restraining of her activities, feels her parents are old-fashioned, sees her parents as singling her out for special treatment, sensitive to slights from peers, sensitive to demands from peers, and expresses hostile feelings directly to peers.

Their Character During Senior High School

The CQ Set. Vis-à-vis the Complement group, 28% of the Q items distinguish the Type U individuals at the .01 level of significance and, at the .05 level, 39% are significant.

Attributes *absolutely and relatively characteristic of the Type U girl during SHS:* poised, cheerful, likeable, responsive to humor, physically attractive, talkative, gesturally expressive, feminine, and gregarious.

Attributes *relatively characteristic of the Type U girl during SHS:* has wide interests, turned to for advice and reassurance, comfortable with her own physical appearance, feels satisfied with herself, skilled in techniques of imaginative play, initiating of humor, and verbally fluent.

Attributes *absolutely and relatively uncharacteristic of the Type U girl during SHS:* distrustful, fearful, self-pitying, compares herself to others, complicates simple situations, reluctant to take action, ruminative, self-defeating, aloof, critical, overcontrolled, and negativistic.

Attributes *relatively uncharacteristic of the Type U girl during SHS:* uncomfortable with uncertainty, thin-skinned, feels a lack of personal meaning in life, irritable, hostile toward others, brittle, guilty, bothered by demands, self-defensive, extrapunitive, judgmental, projective, and has fluctuating moods.

The Interpersonal Q Set. Twenty-one percent of the items differentiate the Type U girls from the Complement at the .01 level of significance (and 36% are significant at the .05 level).

Items *absolutely and relatively characteristic of the Type U girl during SHS:* poised with peers, liked by peers, talkative with peers, accepts and appreciates sex-typing as it affects self, and spends time with members of the opposite sex.

Items *relatively characteristic of the Type U girl during SHS:* achieves leadership roles with peers, perceives parents as being happy, perceives her family as affectionate, able to have genuine relationships with adults, initiates humor with peers, and knowledgeable of the peer culture.

Items *absolutely and relatively uncharacteristic of the Type U girl dur-

ing SHS: tends to be the butt of her peer group, keeps her peers at a distance, passive with adults, sees her parents as uninterested in her, worries about her parents, perceives her family situation as conflicted, perceives her parents as restraining of her activities, and has the social stimulus value of the young person.

Items *relatively uncharacteristic of the Type U girl during SHS:* covertly hostile to adults, sees her parents as singling her out for special treatment, is judgmental in regard to peer conduct, feels her parents are old-fashioned, and is sensitive to anything that can be construed as a slight from peers.

Character Changes from JHS to SHS

The CQ Set. During the period from JHS to SHS, the Type U girls change in certain ways. Thus, by SHS, Type U girls become significantly: more unpredictable, more self-dramatizing, more rebellious, more pushing against limits, more self-indulgent, more hostile, more deceitful, more talkative, more negativistic, more eroticizing, more distrustful, more self-defeating, and more brittle.

Compared to the way they were during JHS, the Type U girls during SHS have become significantly: less dependable, less productive, less straightforward, less warm, less turned-to-for-advice, less giving, less aware of the impression they create, less fastidious, less poised, less internally consistent, less guilty, less overcontrolled, less likable, less sympathetic, and less arousing of nurturance.

The Interpersonal Q Set. As conveyed through the Interpersonal Q set, the Type U girls have, by SHS, become significantly: more talkative with their peers, more rebellious with adults, more using of the privileges of the adolescent in this culture, more attention-getting with their peers, more covertly hostile to adults, more likely to see their family as egalitarian, more emphasizing of the exclusiveness of their peer group, more likely to spend time with members of the opposite sex, more oriented toward going steady, and more condescending in their relations with peers.

Compared to the way they were during JHS, the Type U girls have, by SHS, become significantly: less able to have genuine relationships with adults, less liked by their peers, less judgmental in regard to peer conduct, less likely to achieve leadership roles with the peers, less likely to feel their lives are determined by their parents, less poised with peers, less straightforward with peers, less respectful of their parents, less considerate with their parents, less passive with adults, and less gregarious with their peers.

Further Findings from the Adolescent Years

The Type U adolescent girls are of rather typical intelligence, considering the sample from which they have been drawn, although their mean IQ of 116 is appreciably higher than the national norm. Their socio-economic position is also unexceptional for our sample and is solidly middle-class.

According to their mothers' reports, the birth and labor pains surrounding the delivery of the Type U infants were less severe (.05) than for the Complement group. But this finding may reflect the somewhat younger age of the mothers of the Type U subjects at this time (25.9 years versus 28.6 years, the difference being barely short of significance) or a lesser neuroticism and hypochondriasis on the part of the mothers in recollecting their somatic concerns. There is a trend for the Type U subjects to be somewhat earlier in ordinal position, a finding necessarily related to the younger age of their mothers.

In JHS, the Type U girls were of typical height but weighed significantly less than Complement girls (.10) and were significantly weaker as well (.10). By SHS, the Type U girls continued being lighter (.05) and weaker (.10) than the Complement girls and were judged as skinnier (.10). Their diastolic blood pressure was lower as well (.10) (67.6 versus 72.3).

During JHS, as reflected by the Free Play Ratings, the Type U girls were significantly more Buoyantly Self-confident (.01) and Reposed (.05). During SHS, they continue to be relatively Buoyantly Self-confident (.10) and now manifest a greater Heterosexual Orientation (.10) than the Complement girls. They also were rated as lower (.05) on Achievement Need within the set of Frenkel-Brunswik Need Ratings.

The Type U girls were significantly prettier (.05) than the Complement girls. Prettiness was objectified by having 14 raters—7 males and 7 females—each rate facial photographs of the OGS women. The composite of these 14 highly inter-related ratings provides the *Prettiness Index* used. In keeping with their greater attractiveness, the Type U girls dated more in high school (barely short of significance at the .10 level). It appears, however, that they learned about and experienced sex a bit later than the Complement average.

According to their mothers' reports. during JHS the Type U girls were comparatively highly interested in dramatics (.01) and were not so much interested in attending movies (.10), a finding suggesting participation rather than observation suited the Type U girls. In SHS, the Type U girls are reported as seeing boyfriends in the evening more frequently (.05), as talking more frequently and at greater length to their girlfriends on the telephone (.05), and as being vivacious (.01), poised (.10), unirritable (.05) individuals.

Their fathers are said to have understood the Type U girls relatively well during their adolescence (.10) and, in addition, the Type U girls report having been importantly influenced during adolescence by a priest or minister (.10).

During both JHS and SHS, the Type U girls manifested significantly less skin conductance reactivity than the Complement girls (.05). Further, they tend to appear more frequently in the group of Low Reactors, as defined by Harold Jones.

Their Character as Adults

The CQ Set. Twenty-four percent of the Q items differentiate the Type U women from the Complement group at the .01 level of significance, and 41% of the items distinguish at the .05 level.

Attributes *absolutely and relatively characteristic of the Type U women as adults:* dependable, giving, likable, poised, cheerful, sympathetic, gregarious, productive, warm, feminine, fastidious, overcontrolled, and protective.

Attributes *relatively characteristic of the Type U women as adults:* turned to for advice and reassurance, calm, responsive to humor, feels reasonably satisfied with self, skilled in techniques of imaginative play, charming, satisfied with her physical appearance, and internally consistent.

Attributes *absolutely and relatively uncharacteristic of the Type U women as adults:* rebellious, pushes limits, thinks in unusual ways, feels a lack of personal meaning in life, distrustful, feels victimized, bothered by demands, complicates simple situations, and changeable.

Attributes *relatively uncharacteristic of the Type U women as adults:* thin-skinned, irritable, basically hostile, brittle, self-defeating, self-defensive, gives up and withdraws where possible, ruminative, basically anxious, overconcerned with her own adequacy as a person, and self-pitying.

Character Changes from Senior High School to Adulthood

The CQ Set. Relative to the way the Type U women were during SHS, they are as adults significantly: more overcontrolled, more fearful, more dependable, more philosophically concerned, more productive, more guilty, more giving, more turned to for advice and reassurance, more protective, more submissive, more sympathetic, warmer, more moralistic, more cheerful, more priding of self on objectivity, and more ambitious.

In addition, the Type U women have become, since SHS, significantly: less fantasizing, less self-indulgent, less rebellious, less withdrawing when frustrated, less under-controlled, less bothered by demands, less physically attractive, less pushing of limits, less interested in the opposite sex, less bothered by a lack of personal meaning, and less unpredictable.

Further Findings from the Adult Years

CPI Scale Scores. A large number of CPI scales discriminate the Type U women from the Complement group. Thus, Type U women score *higher* on the Sense of Well-Being (*Wb*) scale (.05), the Capacity for Status (*Cs*) scale (.10), the Sociability (*Sy*) scale (.10), the Intellectual Efficiency (*Ie*) scale (.10), and the Responsibility (*Re*) scale (.10). They score *lower* than the Complement women on the Psychoneurosis (*Pn*) scale (*.10*) and the Neurotic Overcontrol (*NOC*) scale (*.10*).

This is an impressive array of differences and suggests that the Type U women are relatively poised, calmly capable individuals. They enjoy life but not in selfish ways, being conscientious, trustworthy, tactful persons.

CPI Item Analysis. Some of the specific items which differentiate the Type U women from the Complement are reported below:

Thus, the Type U women more often than the Complement women *affirm* the following inventory items:

CPI   84. I have at one time or another in my life tried my hand at writing poetry.
CPI 280. I enjoy many different kinds of play and recreation.
CPI 357. For most questions there is just one right answer, once a person is able to get all the facts.
CPI 361. I like to have a place for everything and everything in its place.
CPI 480. I must admit it would bother me to put a worm on a fish hook.

The Type U women more often than the Complement women *reject* the following items:

CPI   81. I must admit I often try to get my own way regardless of what others may want.
CPI 177. I am certainly lacking in self-confidence.
CPI 316. My parents wanted me to "make good" in the world.

CPI 469. I must admit that it makes me angry when other people interfere with my daily activity.

CPI 471. I sometimes feel that I do not deserve as good a life as I have.

Current Status. Type U women went somewhat less far educationally than the Complement women, but their adult scores on the Terman Group Test of Mental Ability show them to be slightly above the Complement mean (167.1 versus 159.2). They married at a mean age of about 21, a bit earlier than the Complement women and they have tended to stay married, now having significantly more children, on the average, than the Complement group (.05). The Type U women have shown the upward social mobility characteristic of our time and of our sample.

Most list their occupations as housewife, but several are employed part- or full-time as receptionists or secretaries or bookkeepers. Their positions are all jobs requiring reasonably little training or long-term commitment. The men the Type U women married occupy themselves as follows: a small hardware merchant, an optometrist, a contractor, a real estate executive, a high school gymnastics instructor, a government supervisor, an army major, several accountants, a steel worker, several sales executives, and a school administrator.

The height and weight of the Type U women is at the Complement average. Their health is good. They are frequent social drinkers (.10) but have no problem in regard to alcohol usage. They like wine relatively more (.05) and explicitly reject beer.

The Type U women appear to be genuinely religious more often than Complement women (.10). They are essentially unpolitical, although identifying themselves as Democratic. Their family income was a bit above the Complement mean and they are regular savers (.10). They feel relatively close to their families of origin (.10) and find comparatively little in their past lives that they would wish to change (.10). They belong now to more clubs and are involved in more organizations than Complement women (.05) and they have more friends and more contact with friends (.10). Only one of the nineteen Type U women has been under psychiatric care at any time, none within the ten years before the follow-up study.

Adjustment and Continuity over the Years

The Psychological Adjustment Index. The Type U females manifest superior adjustment, in both an absolute and comparative sense, throughout our period of study. During JHS, the mean Psychological Adjustment Index for the Type U girls is .49 when the *PA* Index mean for the Complement girls is −.03 (significant well beyond the .01 level). During SHS, the Type U girls are evaluated as psychologically less well off than before, but they are still considered to be healthier than the Complement girls. At this time, the mean PA Index for the Type U girls is .28 and the Complement mean is − .05 (significant beyond the .01 level). By adulthood, the Type U women have moved more toward psychological maturity, as have the Complement women. In their mid-thirties, the Type U women have a PA Index average of .38 and the Complement women have a mean of .09 (significant beyond the .01 level).

Personality Continuity. The Type U subjects show average character stability during high school and moderately high personality consistency beyond the high school years. Their mean JHS–SHS CQ correlation was .58 (.79 corrected for attenuation) when the Complement mean for the JHS–SHS period was .52 (.84 corrected). But for the SHS–Adulthood comparison, the Type U mean continuity correlation was .46 (.67 corrected) when the Complement mean was .34 (.53 corrected). The difference for this latter interval is significant beyond the .10 level. Thus, the Type U subjects manifested greater personality consistency than was typical from adolescence to adulthood.

Familial and Environmental Antecedents

The Early Family Ratings. As evaluated at the time, the parents of the Type U girls were comparatively integrated, resilient individuals. The fathers of the Complement girls were, comparatively, of poor stamina (.05) and in poor physical health (.05), and they did not wish more children. The Complement mothers were relatively shy (.10), undemonstrative (.10), privacy-emphasizing (.05) individuals also plagued by poor health (.05) and poor stamina (.05). Complement parents, as a pair, were further viewed as nervously unstable (.10) and as sexually conflicted (.10). The Implication of this pattern of findings is that the parents of the Type U girls were psychologically well off and active individuals.

The Ratings of Mothers. In the separate ratings of the mothers of our subjects, the mothers of the Type U girls were described as bright, personable, self-assured individuals. When compared with Complement mothers, they were evaluated as relatively alert (.01) and rapid thinkers (.05), highly poised (.10), and presenting an attractive personal appearance and manner (.01).

The Environmental Q Set. Vis-à-vis the familial contexts of the Complement women, the distinguishing qualities of the family settings of the Type U females are as follows:

Environmental conditions *absolutely and relatively characteristic of the families of Type U subjects:* Subject's mother was available to the subject through adolescence (.05); subject's father was available to the subject through adolescence (.05); subject's mother was knowledgeable and competent in feminine activities (.10); subject's family emphasized the life value of conformity, acceptance by peers, popularity, and the like (.10).

Environmental conditions *relatively characteristic of the families of Type U subjects:* Subject's family emphasized the life value of fairness, equity, ethics, and responsibility to others (.01); subject's mother emphasized the life value of tenderness, love, and related forms of interpersonal communion (.01); subject's parents encouraged subject to discuss problems (.01); subject's home situation was warm and feeling-oriented (.01); subject's mother enjoyed the maternal role (.05); subject had contact with many other children when young (.05); subject was naturally physically attractive (.10); subject's father emphasized the life value of tenderness, love, and related forms of interpersonal communion (.10); subject's home was a centripetal center for activities (.10); subject's father enjoyed his paternal role (.10).

Environmental conditions *absolutely and relatively uncharacteristic of the families of Type U subjects:* Subject's mother was career-oriented for herself (.01); subject's mother was constructively active outside the home (.05); subject's family was beset by many tragedies and misfortunes (.10).

Environmental conditions *relatively uncharacteristic of the families of Type U subjects:* Father's interpersonal modes were conflict-inducing in children (.01); mother's interpersonal modes were conflict-inducing in children (.05); subject's father discouraged and constrained subject's steps toward personal independence and maturity (.05); there was a family atmosphere of discord, conflict, and recrimination (.05); subject's mother was manifestly a long-suffering, self-sacrificing, defeated person (.05); the atmosphere of the subject's home was constricted, suppressive, and cheerless (.05); subject was physically mature early (.05); subject's parents were inhibited about sex (.10); subject was rejected by her mother (.10); subject's father emphasized the life value of status, power, and material possessions (.10); father's limitations, needs, and vulnerabilities were apparent (.10).

Interpretive Resume

The Type U female has led a smoothly progressive and essentially satisfying life to date. Her life has not been uneventful; rather, she was well constituted and well prepared for each of the stages of development she encountered and was enabled to enjoy each phase at the time and then go on. Society's demands and values regarding the woman's role have meshed almost prototypically with her own needs and capacities, a state of congruence and *un*alienation that is unusual to find.

The family origins of the Type U subject were in the middle-class mainstream. Her mother was maternal and feminine (the two qualities need not overlap!) while her father was paternal and characterologically strong. Together, they exemplified the traditional American values of fairness, of family warmth, of sex-role differentiation, and the desirability of being liked. The highly compatible and harmonious, yet well differentiated family situation of the Type U girl appears to have socialized her early and instilled in her quite naturally the essential attitudes and personal ease of her parents. The family unit was an enduring one, providing a stable base for reassurance and recovery as the Type U girl tried out and developed her means of adaptation and expression in the world beyond home.

By JHS the Type U girl was already a vivacious, dependable, socially attuned person, with warmth and without guile. She was relaxed but still energetic, direct but not rude, peer-oriented but not devaluing of her parents. She was bright, if not intellectually distinguished, and she employed her intelligence in the service of interpersonal goals rather than book-learning *per se.* In a culture that places great value on the skin-deep qualities of females, the Type U girl was deemed to be pretty and consequently she escaped the oppressive burden girls carry around when they are not personally attractive. With all her social skills and outgoingness, the Type U girl was not overpowering. She was slender and weak (even skinny for a while) and not competitive, and so would not be viewed as threatening.

In SHS much the same picture continues. The Type U girl was still at this time a rather poised, pretty, gregarious and likable teenager. As befits the additional several years of adolescence, she is now more expressively feminine and is especially oriented toward boys, the dating whirl, and the peer culture. Her immersion in the adolescent experience has changed her in less obvious ways as well—the Type U girl in SHS compared to her personal qualities in JHS, has become more talkative, less candid, more histrionic, less compassionate, more negativistic; less ready to feel guilty. The two common denominators of these characterological changes are the self-centeredness and under-control earlier described (cf. Chapter V) as normative trends during these years.

By the time in adulthood we next encounter the Type U subject, she is a well-established wife and mother long-escaped from adolescence. Now she appears to be pretty much as her mother was: at ease with herself and with others, optimistic, nurturant, attractive, and now in her turn a communicator of the received social values. She is feminine, but in the particularly American style of the *Good Housekeeping* or *McCall's* woman—fastidious, poised, somewhat over-controlled, somewhat clichéd in her thinking and attitudes.

The character changes since SHS of the Type U woman have been primarily recoveries from that earlier "letting go" period. She has returned toward responsibility and guidance by conscience, she as an adult is again an extroverted, friendly, relatively unruffable individual. But to some extent, the Type U woman has over-corrected for her adolescent period of under-control by becoming in adulthood an over-controller and by propagating the virtues of self-control as a way of life.

How shall we sum up and evaluate the Type U woman? She is leading and has led a good life, giving as well as receiving from her family and community. The stability and continuity of our society must depend, in large part, on women like her weaving families together, providing models for daughters and for the wives their sons would seek, enjoying their lives while fulfilling their roles.

But the Type U woman is a transmitter of social values rather than a transmuter. She is temperamentally best suited for a time of cultural stability rather than for the cultural flux that typifies America in this last half of the century. Little that is innovative can be expected of her, but what she contributes is indispensable.

For subsequent reference, I shall label the Type U subjects as *Female Prototypes,* a phrase intended to convey the exemplary way in which these individuals, throughout our study, have manifested the qualities our culture prescribes as appropriate for its females.

PERSONALITY TYPE V

Their Character During Junior High School

The CQ Set. Vis-à-vis the Complement group, Type V girls are distinguished by 37% of the Q items at the .01 level of significance and by 54% of the items at the .05 level.

Attributes *absolutely and relatively characteristic of the Type V girl during JHS:* over-controlled, thin-skinned, aloof, distrustful, basically hostile, feels guilty, fearful, bothered by demands, fantasizing, uncomfortable with uncertainty, ruminative, self-defensive, and feels victimized.

Attributes *relatively characteristic of the Type V girl during JHS:* introspective, lacks personal meaning, prides self on objectivity, thinks in unusual ways, reluctant to take action, self-defeating, complicates simple situations, emotionally bland, does not vary roles, questing for self-meaning, submissive, judgmental, values intellectual matters, esthetically reactive, and philosophically concerned.

Attributes *absolutely and relatively uncharacteristic of the Type V girl during JHS:* feels satisfied with self, pushes limits, interested in opposite sex, under-controlled, cheerful, talkative, rapid in tempo, warm, poised, assertive, expressive, and socially perceptive.

Attributes *relatively uncharacteristic of the Type V girl during JHS:* likable, gregarious, responsive to humor, values self in terms of cultural norms, proffers advice, self-dramatizing, skilled in social techniques of imaginative play, becomes emotionally involved with members of same sex, initiating of humor, seeks reassurance, straightforward, feminine, concerned with her physical appearance, has shifting standards, perceives self as causative of her life directions, and comfortable with the decisions she makes.

The Interpersonal Q Set. Thirty-seven percent of the Interpersonal Q items differentiated the Type V girls from the Complement at the .01 level of significance, with a total of 51% of the items being significant at the .05 level.

Items *absolutely and relatively characteristic of the Type V girl during JHS:* keeps peers at a distance, sees her parents as singling her out for special treatment, feels her mother is a respected woman, sensitive to slights from peers, covertly hostile to adults, feels the pattern of her life is laid down by her parents, sensitive to demands from peers, judgmental, and selective in her choice of friends.

Items *relatively characteristic of the Type V girl during JHS:* perceives her family situation as conflicted, tends to have crushes on adults, passive with adults, cool and detached with adults, oriented and interested in adults rather than peers, has the social stimulus value of a younger person, tends to be the butt of her peer group, and sees her parents as uninterested in her.

Items *absolutely and relatively uncharacteristic of the Type V girl during JHS:* talkative with peers, initiating of humor with peers, employs attention-getting behavior with peers, spends time with members of the opposite sex, achieves leadership roles with peers, and claims the privileges afforded the adolescent in this culture.

Items *relatively uncharacteristic of the Type V girl during JHS:* poised with peers, emphasizes being with peers, assertive with peers, knowledgeable of peer culture, straightforward with peers, values self and others in terms set by her peer group, dependent on peers, liked by peers, and accepts and appreciates sex-typing as it affects self.

Their Character During Senior High School

The CQ Set. Vis-à-vis the Complement group, 14% of the Q items differentiated the Type V individuals at the .01 level of significance, while 30% of the items were significant at the .05 level.

Attributes *absolutely and relatively characteristic of the Type V girl during SHS:* over-controlled, has a high degree of intellectual capacity, dependable, productive, hostile toward others, and judgmental in regard to human conduct.

Attributes *relatively characteristic of the Type V girl during SHS:* critical, prides self on being objective, avoids close interpersonal relationships, values intellectual matters, ruminative, complicates simple situations, philosophically concerned, introspective, fearful, has a readiness to feel guilty, ambitious, and questing for self-meaning.

Attributes *absolutely and relatively uncharacteristic of the Type V girl during SHS:* under-controlled, rapid in tempo, initiating of humor, self-dramatizing, has shifting standards, and affected.

Attributes *relatively uncharacteristic of the Type V girl during SHS:* gesturally expressive, gregarious, cheerful, talkative, warm, assertive, values self and others in terms set by her cultural group, feminine, concerned with her physical appearance, and becomes emotionally involved with members of the same sex.

The Interpersonal Q Set. Twenty-seven percent of the Interpersonal Q items discriminated at the .05 level of significance.

Items *absolutely and relatively characteristic of the Type V girl during SHS:* feels her mother is a respected woman by societal standards, respects her parents, and judgmental of her peers.

Items *relatively characteristic of the Type V girl during SHS:* keeps peers at a distance, views mother as an attractive woman, is cool and detached with adults, sees her parents as singling her out for special treatment, and adult-oriented.

Items *absolutely and relatively uncharacteristic of the Type V girl during SHS:* claims the privileges afforded adolescents in this culture, employs attention-getting behavior with her peers, and initiates humor with her peers.

Items *relatively uncharacteristic of the Type V girl during SHS:* talkative with her peers, emphasizes being with peers, dependent on peers, expresses hostile feelings directly with peers, knowledgeable of peer culture, and accepts and appreciates sex-typing as it affects her.

Character Changes from JHS to SHS

The CQ Set. During the period from JHS to SHS, the Type V girls change in certain ways. Thus, by SHS, Type V girls become significantly: more interested in the opposite sex, apparently brighter, more responsive to humor, more insightful, and more proffering of advice.

Compared to the way they were during JHS, the Type V girls during SHS have become significantly: less likely to think in unusual ways, less distrustful, less unvarying in their roles, less cheerful, less over-controlled, less fantasizing, less aloof, less thin-skinned, less likely to feel victimized, less extrapunitive, and less esthetically reactive.

The Interpersonal Q Set. As conveyed through the Interpersonal Q set, the Type V girls have by SHS, become significantly: more spending of time with members of the opposite sex, more likely to achieve leadership roles with their peers, more oriented toward going steady, and more knowledgeable of the peer culture.

Compared to the way they were during JHS, the Type V girls have, by SHS, become significantly: less likely to see their parents as uninterested in her, less passive with adults, less likely to feel the pattern of her life is laid down by her parents, less likely to have crushes on adults, less likely to perceive the family situation as conflicted, less likely to see her parents as singling her out for special treatment, and less likely to have the social stimulus value of someone younger than her actual age.

Further Findings from the Adolescent Years

The Type V girls were somewhat higher in IQ than the Complement girls (121.3 versus 116.1). Their socio-economic position was not statistically unusual for our environmental context, the Type V girls coming from homes slightly less advantaged than is sample-typical. Further, their families were larger than Complement families, the difference falling a bit short of significance.

During JHS, the Type V girls were somewhat weaker physically than the Complement girls. Menarche came earlier for them, however (11.97 years versus 12.84 years, the difference being significant at the .10 level). By SHS, they were a bit taller, heavier, stronger, and more breasty than the Complement girls, although none of these trends were significant statistically. As evaluated via the Prettiness Index, the Type V girls were of only average attractiveness, and none of the available data distinguishes these girls with respect to dating or sexual behavior.

During JHS, their mothers describe them as uninterested in clothes (.01) and as responsibly doing home chores (.05). Later, in SHS, they are described as not needing reminding (.10), as not cooking (.10), as going downtown alone during the daytime (.10), as using the car (.10), as having feelings that are easily hurt (.10), and as listening to the radio too much (.05).

During JHS, the Free Play Ratings indicate the Type V girls are comparatively *not* Buoyantly Self-confident (.01). The Frenkel-Brunswik Need Ratings reveal them to have been higher with respect to their need for Autonomy (.05).

Their Character as Adults

The CQ Set. Twenty-two percent of the Q items differentiate the Type V women from the Complement group at the .01 level (35% at the .05 level).

Attributes *absolutely and relatively characteristic of the Type V women as adults:* dependable, introspective, values intellectual matters, verbally fluent, ambitious, has high intellectual capacity, values her independence, and esthetically reactive.

Attributes *relatively characteristic of the Type V women as adults:* has a wide range of interests, evaluates the motivation of others in interpreting situations, fantasizing, insightful, socially perceptive, philosophically concerned, able to see the heart of important problems, aware of her social stimulus value, calm, thinks in unusual ways, interesting, and ethically consistent.

Attributes *absolutely and relatively uncharacteristic of the Type V women as adults:* deceitful, pushes limits, negativistic, self-indulgent, under-controlled, unpredictable, and self-defeating.

Attributes *relatively uncharacteristic of the Type V women as adults:* uncomfortable with uncertainty, projective, extrapunitive, has fluctuating moods, power-oriented, and self-dramatizing.

Character Changes from Senior High School to Adulthood

The CQ Set. Relative to the way the Type V women were during SHS, they are as adults significantly: warmer, more rapid in tempo, more talkative, more aware of their social stimulus value, more socially perceptive, more giving, more introspective, more insightful, more verbally fluent, more sympathetic, more evaluating of situations in motivational terms, more straightforward, more esthetically reactive, more valuing of intellectual matters, more cheerful, more turned to for advice and reassurance, more expressive, more protective, more ambitious, and more philosophically concerned.

In addition, the Type V women have become, since SHS, significantly: less uncomfortable with uncertainty, less irritable, less self-indulgent, less distrustful, less rebellious, less hostile, less complicating of simple situations, less thin-skinned, less projective, less bothered by demands, less power-oriented, less emotionally bland, less pushing of limits, less self-defeating, less extrapunitive, less brittle, and less withdrawing when frustrated.

Further Findings from the Adult Years

CPI Scale Scores. On the CPI, the Type V women score significantly *higher* than the Complement women on the Psychological-Mindedness (*Py*) scale (.05) and the Flexibility (*Fx*) scale (.05). These differences suggest the Type V women are relatively capable, cool, sharp-witted persons of some originality and appreciable individualism.

CPI Item Analyses. Some of the specific items which differentiate the Type V women from the Complement are reported below.

Thus, the Type V women more often than the Complement women *affirm* the following inventory items:

CPI   83. I usually feel nervous and ill at ease at a formal dance or party.
CPI 181. I always tried to make the best school grades that I could.
CPI 215. I would like to write a technical book.
CPI 247. When a man is with a woman, he is usually thinking about things related to her sex.
CPI 471. Sometimes I feel that I do not deserve as good a life as I have.

The Type V women more often than the Complement women *reject* the following items:

CPI   18. A person who doesn't vote is not a good citizen.
CPI   85. I don't like to undertake any project unless I have a pretty good idea as to how it will turn out.
CPI 267. I am a better talker than a listener.
CPI 357. For most questions there is just one right answer, once a person is able to get all the facts.
CPI 463. It is hard for me just to sit still and relax.

Current Status. The Type V women have achieved significantly more education than the Complement women (.01), although they score no higher than Complement women on the Terman Group Test of Mental Ability (158.8 vs 161.8). They have manifested the greatest degree of socio-economic progress (.05) of all the types. They married somewhat later than the other women (.05) (22.38 years vs 20.78 years), but by no means late in life; they have stayed married; and they have a typical number of children.

The Type V women are slightly taller than the Complement women and are in comparatively better health (.10). They smoke little or not at all

(.10) and they use alcohol lightly. When they do drink, they prefer wine and positively reject hard liquor (.05).

Although several Type V women are career-oriented (a public health planner and a lawyer) and several others have been sustainedly employed (as an accounting clerk and as a teacher), most are housewives and are family-oriented. They assert their husband's attitude is not important in their personal decisions to work or not. They tend to dislike housekeeping more strongly or more overtly than the Complement women.

The men they have married by and large are doing well and hold significant positions: a government administrator, a scientific engineer, a lawyer, a clergyman, an architect, an executive of a large firm, several industrial engineers, a school teacher, a businessman, a plant owner, and a radio engineer.

The Type V woman feels that her parents were disappointed in her choice of her spouse (.10) and she sees herself as rather different from her mother (.10). She is in contact with her parents relatively more often than the Complement. She has thought and planned regarding the future more than has the Complement woman (.01) and she thinks seriously about national problems (.10). Politically, she is a Democrat.

One of the fourteen Type V women was under psychiatric treatment for a time.

Adjustment and Continuity Over the Years

The Psychological Adjustment Index. The Type V individuals show a remarkable progression toward psychological optimality from adolescence to adulthood. During JHS, their mean Psychological Adjustment Index was quite low, $-.16$, when the Complement mean was .13. The difference is significant beyond the .01 level. During SHS, the Type V girls achieve *PA* Index scores equivalent to the Complement girls, the two means being .00 and .02, respectively. By adulthood, however, the Type V women score higher than any other type on the *PA* Index, their mean being .43 when the Complement mean is .10. The Adulthood difference is significant well beyond the .01 level.

Personality Continuity. With respect to overall characterological consistency over the years, there is little to distinguish the Type V females from the Complement group. Their mean JHS–SHS *CQ* correlation was .52 (.87 corrected for attenuation) where the Complement JHS–SHS mean was .54 (.83 corrected). Over the SHS–Adulthood time span, the average Type V continuity coefficient was .36 (.56 corrected) when the Complement mean was .36 (.55 corrected).

Familial and Environmental Antecedents

The Early Family Ratings. The fathers of the Type V girls were rated as relatively dissatisfied with their jobs (.10) and as more affectionate with their wives (.05) when compared with Complement fathers. Trends within the data suggest the Type V parents are relatively placid, even-tempered individuals who are affectionate to each other and to their child and who are concordant in their values. The father's job leaves him relatively inadequate leisure time.

The Ratings of Mothers. In the separately developed ratings of mothers, the mothers of the Type V girls were evaluated as relatively bright (.05), verbally facile (.05) persons who were frank (.05) and cooperative (.10).

The Environmental Q Set. Vis-à-vis the familial contexts of the Complement subjects, the statistically distinguishing qualities of the family settings of the Type V females are as follows:

Environmental conditions *absolutely and relatively characteristic of the families of Type V subjects:* Subject's mother was knowledgeable and competent in feminine activities and skills (.10).

Environmental conditions *relatively characteristic of the families of Type V subjects:* Subject's mother emphasized the life value of an intellectual orientation and of rationality in decision and outlook (.01); subject's mother was a respected and admired woman by community standards (.10); subject's mother was over-controlled (.10); as a child, subject was socialized by verbally conveyed rational, explanatory means (.10); subject's parents were restrictive of subject's activities (.10).

Environmental conditions *relatively uncharacteristic of the families of Type V subjects:* Mother's limitations, needs, and vulnerabilities were apparent (.01); subject was naturally physically competent (.05).

Interpretive Resume

The Type V woman has blossomed with the years, going from inadequacy in adolescence to an admirable competence as an adult. She was bright as a youngster but not unusually so, given our sample context, and her socio-economic origin likewise was not exceptional. Yet she has gone on to more education than any other of our types and has accomplished the greatest leap upward in her socio-economic status. Characterologically, she has moved from appreciable maladjustment in high school to a degree of maturity in adulthood unmatched in our sample. How can we account for this clearly separable course of development?

The qualities of her family may provide some clues to understanding. There are indications that the mother of the Type V girl was the dominant figure in the home, overshadowing a pleasant but passive-dependent husband. The Type V girl's mother was herself relatively bright and valuing of the mind and this orientation was passed on to her daughter. To the Type V girl, her mother must have appeared to be a strong, sternly capable, and self-controlled person who could not be opposed or evaded.

Gawky and physically undistinguished as she was in JHS, it is not surprising to find the Type V girl to be an over-controlled but still at this time easily fearful person overwhelmed, guilt-ridden, latently angry, and overtly submissive. And, conjointly, concerned with intellectual matters, esthetically interested, and using her mind in unusual ways. This combination of qualities is not calculated to make one popular with one's peers and the Type V girl was not, having few friends rather than many, and generally being on the periphery of her peer groups. Her orientation instead was to the adult world which, hopefully, would see her true worth and lavish attention upon her.

In SHS, the Type V girl continues along the same characterological path but has greater self-confidence and special expertise with her peers. Her over-controlled behaviors are still present but camouflage an aggressivity now in addition to her earlier vulnerability. She is intellectualized, well organized, and effective; also, she is ambitious, supercilious, and afraid to become affectively close to other people. She is not yet her own master since she is overly introspective and conscience-goaded, and she searches for an identity that is both tolerable and her own. By this time, the Type V girl has become an independent person, for over-determined reasons, and she is bigger and stronger than her peers. Of average attractiveness, she moved toward heterosexuality in ordinary ways and at an average pace, and was less the social isolate than before.

As an adult, the Type V woman displays unusual personal maturity and social accomplishment. The external and unquestionable validations of her sense of competence have permitted her to outgrow the rigidities and tenuously maintained superciliousness of her adolescent past. Now, in mid-passage, the Type V woman is intellectually effective: she is receptive to and active upon her social environment; she is subtle, cognitively interesting, and guided by both principle and goals.

Over the years the Type V subject has become a warmer, more relating and trusting person, relaxed with and accepting of the motivational complications in self and in others. People look to her for help, for reassurance, and for wisdom.

When one looks at the available information surrounding the Type V subject, it is by no means clear or even compellingly suggestive why she developed into so impressive a woman, given her tense and constricted earlier qualities. In part, it appears she has modelled herself and sought to outdo an accomplished mother who pushed her and somewhat overwhelmed her in adolescence. But also, and not less important, the Type V subject, by virtue of the earnestness of her intellectuality, appears to have been continually open to experience and to the significance of experience. She has reworked herself, assimilating when she could and accommodating otherwise, and now she is a worthy product of her own cognitive efforts.

We need a label for the Type V females. None is especially felicitious, but I shall call them *Cognitive Copers* to signify the essentially intellectual way they have applied throughout life as a means of processing encounters with the world.

PERSONALITY TYPE W

Their Character During Junior High School

The CQ Set. Vis-à-vis the Complement group, Type W girls are identified by 9% of the *Q* items at the .01 level of significance and by 23% of the items at the .05 level.

Attributes *absolutely and relatively characteristic of the Type W girl during JHS:* feminine, repressive, dependable, uncomfortable with uncertainty, and compares self to others.

Attributes *relatively characteristic of the Type W girl during JHS:* submissive, gives up and withdraws, emotionally bland, favors status quo, dependent, accepting of dependency, fearful, reluctant to take action, and concerned with her physical appearance.

Attributes *absolutely and relatively uncharacteristic of the Type W girl during JHS:* thinks in unusual ways, interesting, ambitious, and verbally fluent.

Attributes *relatively uncharacteristic of the Type W girl during JHS:* skilled in techniques of imaginative play, talkative, rapid in tempo, expressive, assertive, responsive to humor, initiating of humor, and identifying with causes.

The Interpersonal Q Set. Thirteen percent of the Interpersonal *Q* items differentiated the Type W girls from the Complement group at the .05 level of significance.

Items *absolutely and relatively characteristic of the Type W girl during JHS:* dependent on her peers, values self and others in terms set by peer group, and perceives her parents as consistent.

Items *absolutely and relatively uncharacteristic of the Type W girl during JHS:* assertive with peers, initiating of humor with her peers, and achieves leadership roles with her peers.

Items *relatively uncharacteristic of the Type W girl during JHS:* competitive with her peers, and talkative with peers.

Their Character During Senior High School

The CQ Set. *Vis-à-vis* the Complement group, 13% of the Q items differentiate the Type W girls at the .05 level of significance.

Attributes *absolutely and relatively characteristic of the Type W girl during SHS:* calm and relaxed in manner, favors the status quo, feminine, sympathetic, accepting of dependency in self, and handles anxiety and conflicts by attempting to exclude them from awareness.

Attributes *relatively characteristic of the Type W girl during SHS:* emotionally bland, comfortable with her physical appearance, does not vary her roles, and comfortable with the decisions she makes.

Attributes *absolutely and relatively uncharacteristic of the Type W girl during SHS:* interesting, questing for self-meaning, has a wide range of interests, pushing at limits, introspective, valuing of intellectual matters, thinks in unusual ways, and rebellious.

Attributes *relatively uncharacteristic of the Type W girl during SHS:* irritable.

The Interpersonal Q Set. Only three percent of the Interpersonal items are significant at the .05 level in discriminating the Type W girls from the Complement group. For the sake of systematics, they are reported.

Items *absolutely and relatively characteristic of the Type W girl during SHS:* oriented toward going steady, and accepts and appreciates sex-typing as it affects self.

Character Changes from JHS to SHS

The CQ Set. During the period from JHS to SHS, the Type W girls change in certain ways. Thus, by SHS, Type W girls have become significantly: more turned to for advice, more satisfied with their physical appearance, more ambitious, more calm, more physically attractive, more valuing of personal independence, and more assertive.

Compared to the way they were during JHS, the Type W girls during SHS have become significantly: less esthetically reactive, less irritable, less somaticizing, less submissive, less moody, and less complicating of simple situations.

The Interpersonal Q Set. As conveyed through the Interpersonal Q set, the Type W girls have, by SHS, become significantly: more oriented toward going steady, more assertive with their peers, more considerate with their peers, more protected by their peers, more detached in their interactions with adults, more spending of time with members of the opposite sex, and more poised with peers.

Compared to the way they were during JHS, the Type W girls have, by SHS, become significantly: less likely to be the butt of their peer group, less dependent on their peers, less likely to feel the pattern of their lives is laid down by their parents.

Further Findings from the Adolescent Years

The intelligence of the Type W girls (mean IQ of 111) Is lower than is typical of our sample, but it is still appreciably higher than national norms. The socio-economic status of their families is comfortably middle-class and typical for the present study.

Their birth weight, as reported by their mothers, was significantly greater than the weight of Complement babies (8.75 pounds versus 7.38 pounds). Their ordinal position is somewhat later than that of Complement girls (2.5 versus 1.95). Fewer illnesses are reported for the Type W girls (.10) during childhood and adolescence. By JHS, the Type W girls are taller (.10), heavier (.10), and stronger (.10) than their peers and manifest greater breast development (.05). Their skeletal age is relatively advanced (.05) and their menarche came earlier (.10) (12.45 years versus 13.45 years). All of these are signs of early maturity in a physical or physiological sense.

In SHS, the Type W girls were of only average attractiveness, as reflected by the Prettiness Index, although their forms were evaluated as more feminine than the physiques of the Complement girls (.10). They report more menstrual pain, and the longest menstrual durations.

In JHS, the Free Play Ratings indicate the Type W girls are lower than the Complement girls with respect to Buoyant Self-confidence (.05). In SHS, the Type W girls score higher on the WILTD Over-control scale (.10).

In JHS, the Type W girls are described as having sleeping problems of various kinds (.05), as neat with their clothes (.10), as leading a scheduled life (.10), as not active in play (.10) or mature in play (.05), and as uninterested in music, writing, drama, and the arts (.01).

In SHS, the Type W girls still manifest high standards of cleanliness (.05), but they also are described as having friends of whom their families do not approve (.10), of having bad taste in movies (.05) and other undesirable interests (.10). They indicated that they planned to go on to college (.05).

Type W girls dated less while in high school (.10), but experienced intercourse somewhat earlier than was the average of the Complement girls (about 19 years versus about 20 years).

Their Character as Adults

The CQ Set. Forty-eight percent of the Q items are significant at the nominal .01 level (66% at the .05 level).

Attributes *absolutely and relatively characteristic of the Type W women as adults:* basically hostile, brittle, self-defensive, uncomfortable with uncertainty, distrustful, thin-skinned, aloof, feels cheated and victimized by life, irritable, has bodily concern, bothered by demands, projective, self-defeating, extrapunitive, moody, and negativistic.

Attributes *relatively characteristic of the Type W women as adults:* feels a lack of personal meaning in life, gives up and withdraws where possible, deceitful, fearful, changeable, eroticizing, complicates simple situations, basically anxious, self-pitying, reluctant to take action, undercontrolled, pushes limits, self-indulgent, ruminative, and emotionally bland.

Attributes *absolutely and relatively uncharacteristic of the Type W women as adults:* insightful, calm, socially perceptive, straightforward, verbally fluent, warm, has wide interests, turned to for advice and reassurance, interesting, socially poised, cheerful, philosophically concerned, values intellectual matters, evaluates situations in motivational terms, likable, giving, and aware of her social stimulus value.

Attributes *relatively uncharacteristic of the Type W women as adults:* dependable, bright, protective of close ones, sympathetic, rapid in tempo, productive, ambitious, ethically consistent, able to see to the heart of important problems, personally charming, talkative, prides self on objectivity, assertive, gregarious, responsive to humor, esthetically reactive, internally consistent, and values her independence.

Character Changes from Senior High School to Adulthood

The CQ Set. Relative to the way the Type W women were during SHS, they are as adults significantly: more hostile, more brittle, more self deceiving, more lacking a sense of personal meaning, more complicating of simple situations, more likely to feel cheated and victimized by life, more negativistic, more fearful, more irritable, more moody, more deceitful, more somaticizing, more unpredictable, more withdrawing when frustrated, more ruminative, more pushing of limits, and more distrustful.

In addition, the Type W women have become, since SHS, significantly: less gregarious, less calm, less dependable, less productive, less turned to for advice and reassurance, less feminine, less poised, less sympathetic, less protective, less likable, less assertive, less socially perceptive, less internally consistent, less giving, less conventional, less bright, and less proffering of advice.

Further Findings from the Adult Years

CPI Scale Scores. As adults, the Type W women score *higher* than Complement women on the Communality (*Cm*) scale (.10). They score *lower* than Complement women on the Intellectual Efficiency (*Ie*) scale (.01), the Capacity for Status (*Cs*) scale (.05), the Sociability (*Sy*) scale (.05), the Social Presence (*Sp*) scale (.05), the Self-Acceptance (*Sa*) scale (.05), the Tolerance (*To*) scale (.05), the Sense of Well-Being (*Wb*) scale (.10), the Psychological-Mindedness (*Py*) scale (.10) and the Flexibility (*Fx*) scale (.10).

This constellation of CPI findings suggests that the Type W women are relatively conventional and even sterotypic in their value orientation. They are weak, submissive, fearful, unorganized individuals who are also bitter, distrustful, infantile, and defensively rigid when confronted with innovation.

CPI Item Analysis. Some of the specific items which differentiate the Type W women from the complement are reported below.

Thus, the Type W women more often than the Complement women *affirm* the following inventory items:

CPI 136. Most people make friends because friends are likely to be useful to them.

CPI 149. I consider a matter from every standpoint before I make a decision.

CPI 188. I am quite often not in on the gossip and talk on the group I belong to.

CPI 254. I have never deliberately told a lie.

CPI 305. I often wish people would be more definite about things.

CPI 405. People often talk about me behind my back.

CPI 460. A strong person doesn't show his emotions and feelings.

CPI 462. Even though I am sure I am in the right, I usually give in because it is foolish to cause trouble.

The Type W women more often than the Complement women *reject* the following items:

CPI 152. I read at least ten books a year.

CPI 428. My home as a child was less peaceful and quiet than those of most other people.

Current Status. The Type W women went to school a typical number of years and their intelligence, as reflected by the Terman Group Test of Mental Abilities, continues to be somewhat lower than the Complement

mean (149.4 versus 163.1). Their socio-economic status now is significantly lower (.05) and, alone among the female types, they show a
downward mobility (.05) during a social epoch when almost everyone
was moving up the ladder of advantage. Type W women married a year
or so later than Complement women, and their marriages were relatively
unstable, ending in divorce more often. Type W women are rearing families smaller than the ones in which they themselves grew up; Complement women have families typically larger than those of their origins. It is
likely that this comparative difference in current family size derives from
the increased marital turnover and socio-economic regression just noted.

Type W women are of average height and weight for our sample. There
are indications among them of greater medical problems than afflict
Complement women, with further clues that these medical concerns have
an emotional basis. Of three problem drinkers within the sample of 87
women, two are to be found among the ten Type W women. Although
the Type W women are the heaviest users of alcohol, they are significantly more negative or ambivalent toward drinking than are the Complement women (.10). They smoke a bit less than is usual.

About half of the Type W women are employed, in undemanding positions, e.g., as clerks, switchboard operator, salesgirl. Their husbands list
the following occupations: carpenter, order clerk, automobile parts salesman, remodelling estimator and salesman, farmer, building goods salesman, real estate salesman, business manager, hardware store salesman,
and highway construction superintendent.

The Type W women perceive themselves as similar to their mothers
(.10), although they appear to have a very vague and unarticulated picture of themselves and who they are (.01). They are not pleased with their
immediate life situation (.05) and express dissatisfaction and disrespect
of their husbands (.05). They do not believe religious training has value
for children (.01); they have not thought about national problems (.10),
nor have they made plans for the future (.01) or laid away savings (.01).
Although their income is at the Complement mean, they are dissatisfied
with their current financial situation (.01), worry about it (.10), and are
pessimistic regarding its betterment (.05). They belong to fewer clubs
than do Complement women (.05), to fewer service or civic organizations, and are generally less involved in community life. They are essentially apolitical.

Four of the ten Type W women have been psychiatrically treated, one
having received the diagnosis of dementia praecox.

Adjustment and Continuity Over the Years

The Psychological Adjustment Index. The Type W females, when first
evaluated with respect to psychological adjustment during JHS,

appeared fairly neurotic. Thus, their mean Psychological Adjustment Index was −.05 when the Complement mean was .11. During SHS, the Type W girls appear to have psychologically improved, a trend that takes on a possible larger meaning when it is observed that the Complement girls during this time period move *away* from adjustment. For the SHS interval, the *PA* Index mean for the Type W girls is .05 and the Complement *PA* Index mean is .01. But the most striking finding is to be observed for the Adulthood period when the Type W women appear seriously disturbed and in need of psychiatric help. As objectified by the *PA* Index, the Type W women have a mean score of −.49, lower by far than any other female type. By contrast, the Complement women at this time have a mean *PA* Index of .23. The difference is significant well beyond the .01 level.

Personality Continuity. During the JHS–SHS interval, as we have seen, there can be little difference between a type and its complement because of the generally high character stability observed during this time. Thus, the JHS–SHS mean continuity coefficient for the Type W girls was .59 (.82 corrected for attenuation) when the Complement mean for this interval was .53 (.83 corrected). Over the longer and psychologically less continuous SHS–Adulthood interval, however, the Type W women evidence less personality consistency than the Complement women. The Type W women for this period have a mean consistency coefficient of .22 (.31 corrected); the Complement women have a mean personality consistency of .38 (.56 corrected). The difference is significant beyond the .10 level.

Familial and Environmental Antecedents

The Early Family Ratings. The fathers of the Type W girls were evaluated as relatively enervated individuals (.10), but despite their stamina problems, they were also evaluated as more interested (.10) and affectionate (.10) with their children and as interacting frequently with them (.10). Trends within the data further suggest a parental closeness and mutuality of affection.

The Ratings of Mothers. In the separate ratings of the mothers of the subjects, the mothers of the Type W girls were described, comparatively, as lacking in verbal facility (.05) and as mentally slow (.05) and lacking in curiosity (.10).

The Environmental Q Set. Vis-a-vis the familial contexts of the Complement women, the distinguishing qualities of the family settings of the Type W female are as follows:

Environmental conditions *absolutely and relatively characteristic of the families of Type W subjects:* Subject's parents were inhibited about sex (.10).

Environmental conditions *relatively characteristic of the families of Type W subjects:* Subject's mother was career-oriented for herself (.05); subject's father discouraged and constrained the subject's steps toward personal independence and maturity (.05); subject's father was seductive with her (.05); subject's mother was constructively active outside the home (.10); subject experienced much interaction with her father (.10).

Environmental conditions *absolutely and relatively uncharacteristic of the families of Type W subjects:* Father pressured subject to achieve (.05); subject's parents encouraged the subject to discuss problems (.05); subject was rejected by her father (.10).

Environmental conditions *relatively uncharacteristic of the families of Type W subjects:* Subject's father emphasized the value of an intellectual orientation, of rationality in decision and outlook (.01); subject experienced a sophisticated, complex home environment (.05); subject's father was an educated man (.10).

Interpretive Resume

The pattern of development of the Type W subject shows a moderate, not unique personal inadequacy in her early years. In adulthood, during which time the other female types by and large grew toward or maintained psychological health, the Type W woman has become a characterological shambles, unhappy, self-pitying, explosively but ineffectively reactive to frustrations, downward mobile. She is by far worse off than any of the other types. How is she to be understood?

It appears that the father of the Type W girl was crucially important in influencing the direction of her development. The mother of the Type W girl held a job and liked the idea of working outside the home. As a consequence, the father of the Type W girl picked up much of the slack in interacting with and socializing his daughter. Himself not an active or accomplished figure in the outside world, he could assume easy power and guaranteed adulation with a daughter necessarily dependent upon him. The Type W girl was not urged on toward accomplishment nor was she encouraged or instructed in the uses of the mind. The interactions with her father had a special quality: they were frequent but superficial, freighted with emotions (including sexuality) which Daddy failed to acknowledge. Apparently, he did not look forward to the growing up of his little girl and discouraged her efforts toward maturity.

By JHS, the Type W girl was an innocuous, fearful person, hyperfeminine, repressive of her feelings, and excessively dependent on her family and her peers. Although physically more mature than the other girls her age, she had little confidence in herself and sought to avoid personal distress by the tactics of unresponsiveness, blandness, and hyperconventionality.

In SHS, the Type W girl appears better off because her adaptive mechanisms are especially suited to the presses and values of later adolescence. She is still hysterically bland, repressive, and hyperfeminine. But she accepts and enjoys her unvaryingly dependent roles and, perhaps in unaware ways, even teases with her voluptuous body. Many adolescents are interesting persons, striving for self-definition or to know the world. Not so the Type W girl. She is trying to lead what she hopes will be the safe and predictable life. She is not seeking new rules or new fields to conquer or new access to her self. But even by the end of her adolescence, there are indications that a passively feminine orientation in a rather aggressive society will not for long go unexploited.

By adulthood, the Type W woman presents a beautifully complete picture of the hysteric personality. She is aloof but eroticizing, complicating of the simple and simplifying of the complex, moody but emotionally bland, rigid but impulsive also. She is preoccupied with her body and its functioning; she is whiny, guileful, and projectively accusatory. Her self concept is surprisingly undifferentiated and there is little in her life about which she does not grouse. She has become since the flush of adolescence a more brittle and edgy person, and consequently has found it difficult to maintain long-term interpersonal relationships. Presently, she is apathetic about friends and the larger community.

With the passage of time, she has vaguely come to recognize and ruminate over the lack of an inner core to her character and has sought to blot out this recognition. Beyond the ambivalent but often excessive usage of alcohol, there is little to help her escape her primitive sense of alienation because her affective ties to husband or to children or to parents or to community are all tinged with bitterness and anomie. The extrapolation into later years for the Type W woman cannot be optimistic. As her children leave the home, as her parents die, as her marriage further routinizes, as the world passes her by, as her energies and health fail, the Type W woman will be compelled more and more to confront herself and her own capacities and wastages. This will be an even less happy time for her, with even greater incentive then to evade the recognitions forced upon her. Further alcoholism could well be her route of escape from depression. That it will be a sufficient alleviator of her sense of emptiness and of missed opportunity we cannot know now.

We shall refer to the Type W subjects as *Hyper-feminine Repressives*. The psychiatrically-oriented reader might have preferred the label, hysterical character, because the developmental pattern and adult personality characteristics of these women fit impressively well the classical notion of hysteria. Currently, however, there is confusion and misuse of the concept of hysteria and so I have opted for a different name for the Type W women. However called, the essence of their personality is a repressive but unarticulated character structure, fitful emotionality alternating with blandness, and sexuality that is both unwitting and deliberate.

PERSONALITY TYPE X

Their Character During Junior High School

The CQ Set. Vis-à-vis the Complement group, 18% of the Q items are significant at the nominal .01 level of significance and 33% of the items reach the .05 level.

Attributes *absolutely and relatively characteristic of the Type X girl during JHS:* self-indulgent, self-defensive, rebellious, extrapunitive, under-controlled, interested in the opposite sex, conventional, expresses hostile feeling directly, eroticizes, and assertive.

Attributes *relatively characteristic of the Type X girl during JHS:* negativistic, deceitful, pushes limits, affected, projective, self-dramatizing, and has shifting standards.

Attributes *absolutely and relatively uncharacteristic of the Type X girl during JHS:* philosophically concerned, insightful, values intellectual matters, submissive, introspective, giving, overcontrolled, sympathetic, ruminative, fearful, arouses nurturance, dependable, evaluates situations in motivational terms, and prides self on objectivity.

Attributes *relatively uncharacteristic of the Type X girl during JHS:* feels guilty, thin-skinned, aware of her social stimulus value, and esthetically reactive.

The Interpersonal Q Set. Thirty-eight percent of the Interpersonal Q items differentiate the Type X girls from the Complement group at the .05 level of significance.

Items *absolutely and relatively characteristic of the Type X girl during JHS:* rebellious with adults, employs attention-getting behaviors with her peers, claims the privileges afforded the adolescent in this culture, spends time with the opposite sex, and cool and detached in her interactions with adults.

Items *relatively characteristic of the Type X girl during JHS:* covertly hostile to adults, expresses hostile feelings directly to her peers, and accepts and appreciates sex-typing as it affects self.

Items *absolutely and relatively uncharacteristic of the Type X girl during JHS:* able to have genuine relationships with adults, tends to have crushes on adults, and adult-oriented.

Items *relatively uncharacteristic of the Type X girl during JHS:* feels the pattern of her life is laid down by her parents, respects her parents, perceives her parents as reasonable, perceives her father as an attractive man, considerate with her peers, evaluates her family as affectionate, evaluates her family as an interesting one, perceives her parents as accepting her steps toward maturity, perceives her parents as consistent, protective of her friends, judgmental of her peers, selective in her choice of friends, and protected by her peers.

Their Character During Senior High Schoool

The CQ Set. Twenty-three percent of the Q items differentiate the Type X girls from the Complement group at the .05 level of significance.

Attributes *absolutely and relatively characteristic of the Type X girl during SHS:* extrapunitive, irritable, self-indulgent, distrustful, bothered by demands, eroticizing, and self-defensive.

Attributes *relatively characteristic of the Type X girl during SHS:* condescending, negativistic, deceitful, rebellious, pushing against limits, and undercontrolled.

Attributes *absolutely and relatively uncharacteristic of the Type X girl during SHS:* identifying with causes, sympathetic, accepting of dependency in herself, questing for self-meaning, warm, has a wide range of interest, valuing of intellectual matters, philosophically concerned, straightforward, insightful, and introspective.

Attributes *relatively uncharacteristic of the Type X girl during SHS:* dependable, and has a readiness to feel guilty.

The Interpersonal Q Set. Twenty-four percent of the Interpersonal Q items significantly discriminate the Type X girls from the Complement group at the .05 level.

Items *absolutely and relatively characteristic of the Type X girl during SHS:* rebellious with adults, claims the privileges afforded adolescents in this culture, perceives her family situation as conflicted, and covertly hostile with adults.

Items *relatively characteristic of the Type X girl during SHS:* condescending with her peers, and changeable in her peer attachments.

Items *absolutely and relatively uncharacteristic of the Type X girl during SHS:* protective of her friends, considerate with her peers, straightforward with her peers, and able to have genuine relationships with adults.

Items *relatively uncharacteristic of the Type X girl during SHS:* perceives her family as an interesting one, respects her parents, feels her father is a respected man by societal standards, liked by her peers, and is protected by her peers.

Character Changes from JHS to SHS

The CQ Set. During the period from JHS to SHS, the Type X girls change in certain ways. Thus, by SHS, Type X girls become significantly: more somaticizing, more distrustful, more bothered by demands, more bodily concerned, more irritable, more thin-skinned, more extrapunitive, more likely to feel victimized, more power-oriented, and more complicating of simple situations.

Compared to the way they were during JHS, the Type X girls during SHS have become significantly: less physically attractive, less satisfied with self, less straightforward, less cheerful, less satisfied with their physical appearance, less undercontrolled, narrower in interests, less responsive to humor, less productive, and less fastidious.

The Interpersonal Q Set. As conveyed through the Interpersonal Q Set, the Type X girls have, by SHS, become significantly: more oriented toward going steady, and more dependent on their peers.

Compared to the way they were during JHS, the Type X girls have, by SHS, become significantly: less condescending with their peers, less claiming of the privileges of the adolescent, and less talkative with their peers.

Further Findings from the Adolescent Years

The Type X girls are of good intelligence (their mean IQ is 117) although not untypical of our sample. Their socio-economic position is usual for our context and is best understood as middle-class. The Type X girls come from families significantly smaller (.01) than the families of Complement girls, and both their fathers and their mothers tended to have been married more than once (.10 and .01, respectively).

Their mothers report that the births of the Type X girls were especially difficult (.10). In JHS, there are no distinguishing physical characteristics of the Type X girls, although there are some indications of slower physical development. Menarche was later than average for the Type X girls (13.76 years versus 13.03 years) and their menstrual periods proved to be of shorter duration.

In SHS, the Type X girls were taller than Complement girls (.10) and tended also to be somewhat heavier. They were of average attractiveness, as measured by the Prettiness Index, and were involved in considerable high school dating (.10). Although their social development was relatively precocious (.10), the indications are that the Type X girls learned about sex later than did the Complement girls (.05) and experienced intercourse a bit later than was typical.

In JHS, the Free Play Ratings show the Type X girls to be higher than Complement girls with respect to the Heterosexual Orientation dimension (.05). In SHS, they continue to be higher on the Heterosexual Orientation variable (.10) and are significantly lower as well on the WILTD Overcontrol scale (.10). The Frenkel-Brunswik Need Ratings reveal the Type X girls to be lower with respect to Abasement (.05) and higher with respect to Interpersonal Power (.10).

In JHS, the mothers of the Type X girls describe them as having sleep problems (.10), as being interested in clothes (.10), and as uninterested in music (.10). By SHS, the differential descriptions become more elaborated and informative; now the Type X girls are characterized as interested in clothes (.05), as having parties at home (.10), as going to public dances and swims (.05), as asserting their independence (.05), as criticizing their families (.01), as questioning the judgment of their parents (.01), as feeling their family is old-fashioned (.01), as fond of social dancing (.10), as not liking reading (.10), and as going out more with friends than with family (.05).

Their Character as Adults

The CQ Set. Twenty percent of the Q items were significant at the nominal .01 level and 33% were significant if the .05 level is employed.

Attributes *absolutely and relatively characteristic of the Type X women as adults:* assertive, power-oriented, feels satisfied with self, socially poised, condescending, straightforward, proffers advice, and expresses hostile feelings directly.

Attributes *relatively characteristic of the Type X women as adults:* deceitful, undercontrolled, pushes limits, self-indulgent, values her own independence, prides self on her objectivity, expressive, and rebellious.

Attributes *absolutely and relatively uncharacteristic of the Type X women as adults:* introspective, ruminative, arouses nurturance, reluctant to act, submissive, fearful, feels guilty, fantasizing, warm, philosophically concerned, and seeks reassurance.

Attributes *relatively uncharacteristic of the Type X women as adults:* sympathetic, overcontrolled, protective of close ones, moralistic, and evaluates the motivations of others in interpreting a situation.

Character Changes from Senior High School to Adulthood

The CQ Set. Relative to the way the Type X women were during SHS, they are as adults significantly: more straightforward, more turned to for advice, more giving, wider in interests, more assertive, more productive, more philosophically concerned, more proffering of advice, more cheer-

ful, more poised, more verbally fluent, more valuing of intellectual matters, more protective, more ambitious, more dependable, more valuing of
independence, and more power-oriented.

In addition, the Type X women have become, since SHS, significantly:
less reluctant to act, less bothered by demands, less fantasizing, less
withdrawing when frustrated, less distrustful, less thin-skinned, less
rebellious, less feminine, less comparing of self to others, less projective,
less negativistic, less uncomfortable with uncertainty, less irritable, less
eroticizing, and less extrapunitive.

Further Findings from the Adult Years

CPI Scale Scores. The Type X women score higher than the Complement women on the CPI Sociability (*Sy*) scale (.05) and the Psychological-Mindedness (*Py*) scale (.10). They score lower than Complement
women on the Femininity (*Fe*) scale (.01), the Neurotic Overcontrol
(*NOC*) scale (.01), the Psychoneurosis (*Pn*) scale (.05), and the Socialization (*So*) scale (.10).

This set of CPI findings suggests that the Type X women are relatively
poised, outspoken, self-confident, capable individuals of verve and spontaneity. They are sharp-witted, somewhat undependable, pleasure-seeking, and a bit reckless.

CPI Item Analyses. Some of the specific items which differentiate the
Type X women from the Complement are reported below:

Thus, the Type X women more often than Complement women *affirm*
the following inventory items:

CPI   53. I think I would enjoy having authority over other people.
CPI 210. I very much like hunting.
CPI 267. I am a better talker than a listener.
CPI 315. People should not have to pay taxes for the schools if they
          do not have children.
CPI 397. Once I have my mind made up I seldom change it.

The Type X women more often than the Complement women *reject*
the following items:

CPI   40. I get very nervous if I think that someone is watching me.
CPI   69. I would disapprove of anyone's drinking to the point of
           intoxication at a party.
CPI 110. The thought of being in an automobile accident is very
          frightening to me.
CPI 165. I do not mind taking orders and being told what to do.
CPI 279. I often get disgusted with myself.

Current Status. The Type X women went through school for an average number of years and their adult intelligence, as reflected by the Terman Group Test, continues at the group mean. They have improved their lot in life by an average amount, given our sample context. It will be recalled that the Type X women grew up in small families and now, in turn, the average number of children they have had is the lowest of all the types. The Type X women married at a typical age and have not themselves divorced unusually often.

The Type X women often are employed outside the home, usually in a secretarial or office administrative capacity. For them, the security of a job is not a relevant consideration in evaluating its desirability. Their husbands are all in the business or industrial world and list the following occupations: contractor, superintendent for contractor, chief of a public utility maintenance crew, machinist, supervisor in a large industrial plant, salesman, career officer, engineer, owner of a small construction firm, and an automobile repair shop manager.

The adult height and weight of the Type X women is at the sample norm. Their health is positively good, with no psychosomatic ailments (.10). They smoke significantly more than Complement women (.10) and drink a bit more than is typical, but are still moderate in their alcohol usage.

They have a well-differentiated sense of self (.10); they are well satisfied with their husbands in the rearing of their children (.10); they feel somewhat inadequate on occasion as parents; they do not enjoy the drudgery of home care (.05); they like cultural activities such as music and drama more than Complement women do (.01). The Type X women describe themselves as politically conservative and as optimistic regarding their financial future. Their family incomes at the time of study were about twelve percent greater than the Complement mean. None of the ten Type X women, according to the available records, has been under psychiatric care at any time.

Adjustment and Continuity over the Years

The Psychological Adjustment Index. The Type X females during adolescence were consistently less adjusted, as indicated by the *PA* Index, than the Complement girls. During JHS, their mean *PA* Index was .00 when the Complement mean was .10. During SHS, the Type X girls regressed until their mean *PA* Index was −.23 while the Complement girls pretty much maintained their level of adjustment, with an average *PA* Index of .05. At this time, during SHS, the difference between the Type X girls and the Complement girls is significant at the .05 level. By the time of adulthood, however, the Type X women have shown appreciable progress toward maturity and their mean *PA* Index is somewhat higher than the Complement group's Index (means of .18 and .15, respectively).

Personality Continuity. With respect to character consistency over the years, little distinction can be made between the Type X subjects and the Complement group. For the JHS–SHS interval, the mean continuity coefficient for the Type X girls was .56 (.89 corrected for attenuation) when the mean for the Complement group was .53 (.83 corrected). Over the SHS–Adulthood period, the mean consistency coefficient was .35 (.49 corrected) for the Type X women and .37 (.55 corrected) for the Complement group. None of these differences is of course significant.

Familial and Environmental Antecedents

The Early Family Ratings. The fathers of the Type X girls were evaluated at the time as unhappy with their home life (.10) and as not wanting more children (.10). They are described as healthy, vigorous individuals (.05). The mothers of the Type X girls are described as undemonstrative (.10) but worrying (.10) women, much concerned about the health of their children (.10). They too were evaluated as being unhappy in their family situation (.05).

The Ratings of Mothers. In the separately developed ratings of mothers, the only differentiating quality identifies the mothers of Type X girls as relatively gloomy individuals (.05).

The Environmental Q Set. Vis-à-vis the familial contexts of the Complement women, the distinguishing qualities of the family settings of the Type X females are as follows:

Environmental conditions *absolutely and relatively characteristic of the families of Type X subjects:* Subject's father dominated the fundamental family decisions (.05); mother's limitations, needs, and vulnerabilities were apparent (.10).

Environmental conditions *absolutely and relatively uncharacteristic of the families of Type X subjects:* Subject's mother emphasized the life value of physical activity, the outdoors, and nature (.10).

Environmental conditions *relatively uncharacteristic of the families of Type X subjects:* Subject was rivalled by one or more siblings for the attention of her parents (.05); subject was reared in a stable family setting (.10); subject's father was introverted and internalizing (.10).

Interpretive Resume

The developmental pattern of the Type X subject has been a continuous one, the present being largely ordained by the past. But where her earlier undercontrolling and assertive characteristics in adolescence caused her to be looked upon as maladjusted and obstreperous, the same personal qualities only slightly moderated cause the Type X subject in adulthood to be evaluated as no less than typical in her overall psychological adjustment. What has changed is not so much the character of the Type X subject as the nature of the environmental circumstances within which she now functions.

The familial origins of the Type X girl contain some clues to her subsequent character. After earlier unsuccessful marriages, her parents had found each other. Now again, they were involved in an unhappy relationship. The father of the Type X girl was a dominant, self-indulgent, and extroverted individual; the mother was a retiring, somewhat dysphoric, neurotic, and clearly vulnerable person. At the insistence of the father, who wished to avoid further restraints on his freedom, the size of the Type X girl's family was deliberately kept small. In this family context, with a weak and unenviable mother on the one hand and an aggressively flamboyant but somewhat removed father on the other, it is not surprising that the Type X girl opted to emulate the parent with the greater interpersonal impact—her father.

In JHS, the Type X girl is a pushy, spoiled, impulsive, nasty, histrionic person. Further, she is undependable, projective, cool, and disrespectful toward adults, especially her parents. Despite her physical immaturity, she is socially precocious, affecting heterosexual interests. Withal, she is hyperconventional in her attitudes and values. Certainly, she is not a likable person during this period, for she gives very little of herself while taking much.

By SHS, the Type X girl has become even more objectionable. With greater self-confidence she has grown capable of condescension. She continues as a narcissistic impulsive, oriented toward maximizing pleasure and minimizing constraints. She over-reacts in her hostility to frustrations and criticisms, she is guileful and guiltless, she is suspicious, she is pseudo-sophisticated, she is fickle, she is more concerned with the functioning of her body. She could not care less for the kinds of great causes in which adolescents often immerse themselves, though she has become more power-oriented. She has little inner life and few intellectual interests. She dislikes her parents, in particular her father, to whom she is so similar.

In adulthood, the Type X woman is a highly poised individual, still extremely aggressive and direct in her interactions, and strongly valuing her independence. She continues to be undercontrolled and self-indulgent and condescending, and is quite comfortable with the image she has of self. She is a manipulative person, frankly and deliberately so as she seeks her ends. She is unconcerned with issues or values, consistency, or motivations—instead she is a compleat pragmatist, guided by expedience and aspiring toward materialism. Decisions come easy for the Type X woman since so many of the doubts and complexities besetting more ordinary mortals fail to loom large for her. Her deliberately smaller number of children further reflects her direct focus on self rather than seeking, as do many, the reflection of self through the children one produces.

The Type X woman has changed since adolescence—she feels less imposed upon by demands, she is less abrasive in the way she asserts herself, and is less distrustful. She is more relaxed and more dependable—all qualities coming with age and experience and practice. She is less the female now as the pulse of sexuality takes its downward turn. But essentially, she is as she was—an egotistically dominating, exploitative individual with only a thin veneer of socialization and considerateness. I shall call the Type X subjects hereafter *Dominating Narcissists* to indicate the self-absorption of these women and the aggressive interactions they employ to advance their desires.

PERSONALITY TYPE Y

Their Character During Junior High School

The CQ Set. Vis-à-vis the Complement group, Type Y girls can be identified by 29% of the Q items at the .01 level of significance and by 41% of the items if the .05 level is employed instead.

Attributes *absolutely and relatively characteristic of the Type Y girl during JHS:* talkative, self-dramatizing, under-controlled, pushes limits, self-indulgent, and changeable.

Attributes *relatively characteristic of the Type Y girl during JHS:* extrapunitive, irritable, negativistic, deceitful, brittle, rebellious, self-pitying, has fluctuating moods, has shifting standards, affected, basically hostile, self-defeating, projective, and expresses hostile feelings directly.

Attributes *absolutely and relatively uncharacteristic of the Type Y girl during JHS:* overcontrolled, calm, dependable, satisfied with her physical appearance, feels satisfied with self, prides self on objectivity, insightful, productive, poised, internally consistent, and turned to for advice and reassurance.

Attributes *relatively uncharacteristic of the Type Y girl during JHS:* fastidious, sympathetic, likable, aware of her social stimulus value, socially perceptive, physically attractive, favors status quo, has wide interests, protective of those close to her, submissive, arouses nurturant feelings, and accepting of dependency in self.

The Interpersonal Q Set. Twenty-seven percent of the Interpersonal Q items differentiated the Type Y girls from the Complement at the .05 level of significance.

Items *absolutely and relatively characteristic of the Type Y girl during JHS:* talkative with her peers, claims the privileges afforded the adolescent in this culture, and employs attention-getting behavior with her peers.

Items *relatively characteristic of the Type Y girl during JHS:* changeable in her peer attachments, covertly hostile to adults, rebellious with adults, expresses hostile feelings directly with her peers, and tends to be the butt of her group.

Items *absolutely and relatively uncharacteristic of the Type Y girl during JHS:* perceives her parents as happy.

Items *relatively uncharacteristic of the Type Y girl during JHS:* respects her parents, liked by her peers, selective in her choice of friends, perceives her family as an affectionate one, perceives her parents as reasonable, evaluates her parents as consistent, poised with her peers, and considerate with her peers.

Their Character During Senior High School

The CQ Set. Twenty-three percent of the Q items distinguish the Type Y girls from the Complement group at the .05 level of significance.

Attributes *absolutely and relatively characteristic of the Type Y girl during SHS:* identifying and romanticizing of individuals and causes, brittle, fantasizing, has fluctuating moods, enjoys sensuous experiences, undercontrolled, facially and gesturally expressive, and seeks reassurance from others.

Attributes *relatively characteristic of the Type Y girl during SHS:* has shifting standards depending on group and situation pressures, unpredictable, self-defeating, and self-pitying.

Attributes *absolutely and relatively uncharacteristic of the Type Y girl during SHS:* fastidious, comfortable with her physical appearance, physically attractive, feels satisfied with herself, aware of her social stimulus value, over-controlled, calm, internally consistent, and emotionally bland.

Attributes *relatively uncharacteristic of the Type Y girl during SHS:* productive, likable, socially poised, and comfortable with the decisions she makes.

     Lives Through Time

The Interpersonal Q Set. Ten percent of the Interpersonal Q items are significant at the .05 level in differentiating the Type Y girls from the Complement girls.

Items *absolutely and relatively characteristic of the Type Y girl during SHS:* involved on a fantasy level with the opposite sex.

Items *relatively characteristic of the Type Y girl during SHS:* expresses her hostile feelings directly to her peers.

Items *absolutely and relatively uncharacteristic of the Type Y girl during SHS:* achieves leadership roles with her peers, and evaluates herself as superior to her peers.

Items *relatively uncharacteristic of the Type Y girl during SHS:* selective in her choice of friends, poised with her peers, and liked by her peers.

Character Changes from JHS to SHS

The CQ Set. During the period from JHS to SHS, the Type Y girls change in certain ways. Thus, by SHS, Type Y girls have become significantly: more socially perceptive and more interesting.

Compared to the way they were during JHS, the Type Y girls during SHS have become significantly: less negativistic, less talkative, less pushing of limits, less assertive, and less irritable.

The Interpersonal Q Set. As conveyed through the Interpersonal Q Set, the Type Y girls have, by SHS, become significantly: more likely to evaluate their family situation as conflicted, more toadying toward adults, more worrying about their parents, and more condescending with their peers.

Compared to the way they were during JHS, the Type Y girls have, by SHS, become significantly: less straightforward with their peers, more gregarious with their peers, more poised with their peers, and more valuing of self and of others in the terms set by their peer groups.

Further Findings from the Adolescent Years

The Type Y girls are significantly lower in intelligence than the Complement girls (.10) (their mean IQ is 111), although they still score higher than the national norms. They come from homes somewhat less comfortable and advantaged than was typical for the Complement girls. The fathers of the Type Y girls have been married significantly more often than the Complement fathers (.01) and so have the Type Y mothers (.10). In six of the eleven Type Y families, the parents divorced or separated subsequent to the birth of their daughter; in a seventh instance, both parents died during the adolescence of the Type Y girl.

The mothers of the Type Y girls report relatively difficult deliveries (.10) and the birth weights of the Type Y girls were less than the weights of the Complement infants (6.7 pounds versus 7.7 pounds). The Type Y girls experienced more illnesses than the Complement girls (.10). In JHS, they were somewhat shorter and somewhat heavier than their peers. During SHS, they continued to be somewhat shorter and somewhat heavier, a combination that caused them to be evaluated as pudgy by an index of the amount of subcutaneous fat (.10). Throughout adolescence, the Type Y girls were a bit stronger than Complement girls, although as measured by various physical and physiological indices, they consistently appeared to be "late maturers." The Prettiness Index reveals the Type Y girl to have been significantly less attractive than the other girls in the study (.05).

In JHS, the Free Play Ratings indicate the Type Y girls were less Reposed than the Complement girls (.01) and were lower with respect to Heterosexual Orientation (.10). In SHS, the Free Play Ratings again show the Type Y girls to be less Heterosexually Oriented (.05).

In JHS, the mothers of the Type Y girls report almost nothing that distinguishes their daughters. By SHS, a clear picture is presented of Type Y daughters who do not help with home chores (.01) and who fight with their parents regarding their assigned responsibilities (.01). They go out with boyfriends and with girlfriends in the evening (.10), they use the family car more frequently (.10), they do not spend money wisely (.05), they are moody (.01), uncalm (.10), worrying (.10), and lacking in energy (.05).

At the end of high school, the Type Y girls had lower or no occupational goals as compared to the aspirations of the Complement group (.10). Moreover, they appeared to have no specific concern regarding this absence of direction (.10).

There appears to have been no difference between the Type Y girls and the Complement girls with respect to dating frequency. The Type Y girls experienced sexual intercourse significantly earlier than did the Complement group (.05), while in high school or by age 18.

Their Character as Adults

The CQ Set. Eighteen percent of the Q items differentiate the Type Y women from the Complement group at the .01 level (27% at the .05 level).

Attributes *absolutely and relatively characteristic of the Type Y women as adults:* arouses nurturance, submissive, seeks reassurance, has bodily concern, moody, self-defeating, and feels a lack of personal meaning in life.

Attributes *relatively characteristic of the Type Y women as adults:*

gives up and withdraws where possible in the face of frustration, changeable, undercontrolled, uncomfortable with uncertainty, thin-skinned, brittle, and basically anxious.

Attributes *absolutely and relatively uncharacteristic of the Type Y women as adults:* feels satisfied with self, condescending, values her own independence, skeptical, satisfied with her physical appearance, ambitious, prides self on her objectivity, and fastidious.

Attributes *relatively uncharacteristic of the Type Y women as adults:* dependable, has a wide range of interests, productive, values intellectual matters, and overcontrolled.

Character Changes from Senior High School to Adulthood

The CQ Set. Relative to the way the Type Y women were during SHS, they are as adults significantly: more submissive, more arousing of nurturance, more insightful, more turned to for advice, more internally consistent, more fearful, more philosophically concerned, more protective, more giving, more sympathetic, more likable, and warmer.

In addition, the Type Y women have become, since SHS, significantly: less projective, less self-dramatizing, less skeptical, less fantasizing, less valuing of personal independence, less rebellious, less distrustful, less interesting, less eroticizing, less self-defensive, less gregarious, and less sensuous.

Further Findings from the Adult Years

CPI Scale Scores. On the CPI, the Type Y women score significantly *higher* than the Complement women on the Neurotic Over-control (*NOC*) scale (.05), and the Psychoneurosis (*Pn*) scale (.10). They score significantly *lower* than the Complement women on the Well-Being (*Wb*) scale (.01), the Responsibility (*Re*) scale (.01), the Socialization (*So*) scale (.01), the Achievement via Conformance (*Ac*) scale (.01), the Good Impression (*Gi*) scale (.05), the Communality (*Cm*) scale (.05), the Dominance (*Do*) scale (.10), the Sociability (*Sy*) scale (.10), the Self-Control (*Sc*) scale (.10), the Tolerance (*To*) scale (.10), and the Intellectual Efficiency (*Ie*) scale (.10).

This set of CPI findings suggests that the Type Y women are relatively brittle, impulsive, self-pitying, improvident individuals who are unconventional, awkward, careless, and lazy as well. They are changeable yet stubborn, pessimistic, undependable, and generally unstable.

CPI Item Analyses. Some of the specific items which differentiate the Type Y women from the Complement women are reported below.

CPI   13. I am very slow in making up my mind.

CPI   36. When I was going to school, I played hooky quite often.

CPI 101. I must admit that I often do as little work as I can get by with.

CPI 170. I often act on the spur of the moment without stopping to think.

CPI 297. At times I have a strong urge to do something harmful or shocking.

CPI 337. Much of the time my head seems to hurt all over.

CPI 430. The things some of my family have done have frightened me.

The Type Y women more often than the Complement women *reject* the following items:

CPI 181. I always tried to make the best school grades that I could.

CPI 213. It makes me angry when I hear of someone who has been wrongly prevented from voting.

CPI 280. I enjoy many different kinds of play and recreation.

CPI 290. I have never been in trouble because of my sex behavior.

Current Status. Type Y women terminated their educations significantly earlier, on the average, than Complement women (.05) as was foretold by the absence of educational plans and goals observed during their adolescence. As measured by the Terman Group Test of Mental Ability, the intelligence of the Type Y women continues to be somewhat lower than is typical of our sample but not appreciably so (155.8 versus 162.2). The socio-economic situation of the Type Y women has remained essentially static over the years and they are now appreciably lower than the Complement women (.01). This socio-economic stability in the context of a general upward mobility suggests the Type Y women have not shared proportionately in the material benefits accruing to their generation. Perhaps this comparative failure to better their socio-economic status is best understood by recalling the earlier-charted intellectual ability and familial origins of the Type Y girls. These were both comparatively low and, in conjunction, may not have augured more than has been achieved.

The Type Y women married quite early, at an average age of 19.6 years, as compared to the Complement average marriage age of 21.3 years (.10). Since then, the Type Y women have contracted more than their share of marriages (1.82 versus 1.21) (.05). Of the six Type Y women who have been married only once, four show clear evidence of profoundly inadequate marriages, e.g., multiple separations and reconciliations, the bearing of a child not sired by the husband, and explicitly acknowledged continuing sexual problems. They have produced an average number of children despite their marital instabilities.

As adults, the Type Y women average a half inch taller than the Complement women and weigh on the average eleven pounds more (the weight difference is significant at the .10 level). There are indications in their recent histories of somewhat more frequent medical problems, which appear to be emotionally linked (.05). They are very heavy smokers (.01), smoking more than two packs daily. Although moderately frequent social drinkers, with no apparent excesses in alcohol intake, the Type Y women are significantly more ambivalent or negative in their attitudes toward alcohol (.05).

Most of the Type Y women declare themselves as housewives but a couple are salesgirls, two more are secretaries, one is a practical nurse, and another is an occasional waitress. Their husbands are listed as: a carpenter, a distillery worker, a bartender in the bar of the subject's father, an automobile mechanic, a part-time delivery man and fish store clerk, two salesmen, two office managers, and a maintenance engineer. In earlier marriages, one of the Type Y women was married to a man she discovered was a part-time pimp; another was at one time married to a bigamist. The family income at the time of study was about fifteen percent less than that of the Complement group.

Type Y women do not express many opinions and those they do manifest are related closely to their personal situation and desires. Thus, they express more dislike for housekeeping than Complement women (.05); they value the positions of their husbands primarily for the convenience, security, and leisure provided (.05); and they are not desirous of making new acquaintances (.10). Further, they presently find their family of origin to be of little or no importance to them (.05); they have negative feelings toward their mothers (.10); and they do not perceive themselves as similar to their mothers (.10).

Finally, the Type Y women are comparatively unsatisfied with their life situations at the time of study (.05). Were they able to do so, the Type Y women would change many of the experiences that have happened to them in their lifetimes (.01). Of the eleven Type Y women, the available records indicate one experienced a schizophrenic episode and two others suffered nervous breakdowns requiring psychiatric care.

Adjustment and Continuity over the Years

The Psychological Adjustment Index. At each interval studied, the Type Y females appear psychologically less comfortable than the Complement subjects. During JHS, the mean Psychological Adjustment Index of the Type Y girls is $-.22$ and the mean *PA* Index of the Complement girls is

.13. This JHS difference is significant beyond the .01 level. During SHS, the Type Y girls and the Complement girls converge somewhat in their overall level of adjustment, but the Type Y girl is still less well off, with a mean *PA* Index of −.13 while the Complement girls have a *PA* Index average of .04. This SHS difference falls short of significance. During adulthood, the Type Y women have a mean *PA* Index of −.03 when the Complement women have an average *PA* Index of .18. This last difference is significant at the .10 level. It is of further interest to note that the Type Y subjects have shown a steady and appreciable progress over the years. If they are not yet well adjusted, they are certainly less neurotically strained than they were in their earlier years. Perphas an extrapolation of this trend into the future years of the Type Y women is warranted.

Personality Continuity. Our indices of character consistency over the years are unrevealing in connection with the Type Y subjects. For the JHS–SHS period, the average across-time correlation of the Type Y girls was .50 (.89 corrected for attenuation) compared to the average of .54 (.83 corrected) for the Complement girls. During the SHS–Adulthood interval, the average continuity correlation for the Type Y subjects was .38 (.54 corrected) compared with the mean of .36 (.55 corrected) for the Complement subjects.

Familial and Environmental Antecedents

The Early Family Ratings. There are numerous indications of parental discordance between the parents of the Type Y girls. Thus, the fathers of the Type Y girls were rated as nervously unstable (.05) and as providing poor sex instruction to their children (.01). The mothers of the Type Y girls were, compared to Complement mothers, also nervously unstable (.05), distant from their children (.10), indifferent toward the health of their children (.05) and their sex instruction (.05), and unadjusted to the housewife role (.10). As husband and wife units, the Type Y parents are sexually conflicted (.05), had discrepant intellectual interests (.10), and argued about the size and management of the family income (.05) which was lower than was typical of the sample (.05).

The Ratings of Mothers. In the separate ratings of mothers, the mothers of the Type Y girls were evaluated as relatively restless (.05) and talkative (.05) individuals, anxious to make a good impression (.10) but soured with their lot in life (.05).

The Environmental Q Set. Vis-à-vis the familial contexts of the Complement women, the distinguishing qualities of the family settings of the Type Y females are as follows:

Environmental conditions *absolutely and relatively characteristic of the families of Type Y subjects:* Subject's mother emphasized the life value of status, power, and material possessions (.05); there was a family atmosphere of discord, conflict, and recrimination (.10); mother's interpersonal modes were conflict-inducing in children (.10).

Environmental conditions *relatively characteristic of the families of Type Y subjects:* The sexuality and sexual interests of the parents were apparent to the subject (.01); subject was subjected to some form of discrimination due to race, religion, nationality, or social class (.05); as a child, subject was socialized, controlled, and directed by physical punishment or by threats of physical punishment (.10); subject's father was seductive with her (.10); subject's family was beset by many tragedies and misfortunes (.10); subject's father was manifestly a long-suffering, self-sacrificing, defeated person (.10); subject's mother teased and was playfully contradictory (.10).

Environmental conditions *absolutely and relatively uncharacteristic of the families of Type Y subjects:* Subject's family emphasized "togetherness" and did things as a unit (.10).

Environmental conditions *relatively uncharacteristic of the families of Type Y subjects:* Subject's mother was over-controlled (.01); subject was reared in a stable family setting (.01); subject's mother was knowledgeable and competent in feminine activities and skills (.01); subject's home environment was well structured, orderly, and predictable (.05); subject's mother was available to the subject through adolescence (.05); subject's mother enjoyed her maternal role (.05); subject's mother was a respected and admired woman by community standards (.10); subject's parents were inhibited about sex (.10).

Interpretive Resume

The developmental progression of the Type Y subject has seen her begin relatively disadvantaged in intelligence and socio-economic origins vis-à-vis her peers in the larger sample, move toward a personal unpleasantness and undercontrol in adolescence and on to a pathetic self-unsureness in adulthood. The sequence is not to be explained in actuarial sociological terms for her home, though less advantaged than some, was still middle-class; her intelligence, though lowest of the types, was still appreciably higher than average. Rather it was the context for learning provided by her parents that begins our understanding of the Type Y subject.

Both her father and her mother were neurotically brittle individuals, incompatible in a multitude of ways. Their marriage was almost frankly temporary, not entered into with the usual commitment toward a family and its responsibilities. The mother of the Type Y girl tended to be a crude, grasping, restless, shortsightedly hedonistic person; the father of the Type Y girl was a more passive and beaten person but still able to fitfully react and over-react to his frustrations and to his desires. In their interactions with their daughter, the mother would be, perhaps unwittingly, contradictory in her demands and instructions; the father would be seductive. The home situation of the Type Y girl was ever chaotic, with little functioning of the family as a unit. Instead, each parent would seek his own gratifications with overt disregard of the needs of the young. As an additional impingement on the Type Y girl, she experienced in the course of her development various kinds of discrimination by virtue of her religion or ethnicity or the socially disapproved behaviors of her parents.

By JHS, the Type Y girl shows clearly the results of her thoughtless upbringing and her absence of models. She is a largely unsocialized being, unmodulated in her impulsivity by internalized precepts or concern for others. She is volatile, self-indulgent, casually hostile, irresponsible, and histrionic. Although agitatedly unhappy, her orientation and level of differentiation direct her against the world as a frustrating agent rather than toward examination of the self. The Type Y girl is not well received by her peers in JHS despite her efforts to be liked, because she is hostile and inconsiderate and domineering, while also being pudgy, unattractive, and from a devalued family.

In SHS, the Type Y girl evidences greater inner life but in the form of immature and romantic adolescent fantasies. Overtly, she is uncertain and diffident with males. And vulnerable to them. She is still moody and inconsistent, impulsive and hostile, unpoised and unattractive. With the impact of more years of peer rejection, she has come to devalue herself and to seek acceptance and affection in unselective ways. Pervading the Type Y girl is a sense of already recognized defeat, even at this time of late adolescence when life tends to be confronted with zest and confidence. She has no special plans or anticipations regarding her future. It will happen and she will be unable to control it.

As an adult, the Type Y woman is a disorganized, dependent, brittle person, and still impulsive. She is credulous, unkempt, uninformed, and anxious. If only because of her inability to influence or control her environment, strange and dire happenings beset her, whereupon she is then at the mercy of these environmental onslaughts. She is a patently exploitable female. Those who would do so have exploited her; in more moral individuals, the Type Y woman elicits nurturance and support. There are indications that the unhappy life led by the Type Y woman has deepened her somewhat and made her more insightful than before and consequently a more pitiable human being. But her situation is still pitiful, especially comparatively (and comparison is still the way lives tend to be evaluated). The Type Y woman has moved past personal and interpersonal turmoil to a state of apathetic dismay. She is eking things out, knows she has missed much she would have wanted, and experienced much she should have avoided. She does not know how she might have been different or how to change what will be.

I shall call the Type Y subject *Vulnerable Under-controllers*, a label conveying their unmodulated impulsivity of action and reaction together with the poignant and plaintive submissiveness that prepares the way for their exploitation by others.

PERSONALITY TYPE Z

Their Character During Junior High School

The CQ Set. Vis-à-vis the Complement group, 5% of the items are significant at the .01 level and 18% are significant at the .05 level.

Attributes *absolutely and relatively characteristic of the Type Z girl during JHS:* assertive, values independence, interesting, expressive, and ambitious.

Attributes *relatively characteristic of the Type Z girl during JHS:* proffers advice, critical, turned to for advice and reassurance, values intellectual matters, straightforward, expresses hostile feelings directly, and perceives self as causative in her life.

Attributes *absolutely and relatively uncharacteristic of the Type Z girl during JHS:* submissive.

Attributes *relatively uncharacteristic of the Type Z girl during JHS:* submissive, feminine, fastidious, fantasizing, dependent, concerned with her physical appearance, and accepting of dependency in herself.

The Interpersonal Q Set. Thirteen percent of the Interpersonal Q items significantly distinguished the Type Z girls from the Complement group at the .05 level.

Items *absolutely and relatively characteristic of the Type Z girl during JHS:* expresses her hostile feelings directly to her peers, assertive with her peers, achieves leadership roles with her peers, and straightforward with her peers.

Items *absolutely and relatively uncharacteristic of the Type Z girl during JHS:* toadying with adults, and oriented toward going steady.

Items *relatively uncharacteristic of the Type Z girl during JHS:* accepts and appreciates sex typing as it affects self, feels the pattern of her life is laid down by her parents, and involved on a fantasy level with the opposite sex.

Their Character During Senior High School

The CQ Set. Twenty-five percent of the Q items significantly character-ize the Type Z girls vis-à-vis the Complement group at the .05 level.

Attributes *absolutely and relatively characteristic of the Type Z girl during SHS:* values her own independence and autonomy, values intel-lectual matters, ambitious, critical, interesting, rebellious, introspective, irritable, bothered by demands, and has a high degree of intellectual capacity.

Attributes *relatively characteristic of the Type Z girl during SHS:* thinks in unusual ways, philosophically concerned, prides self on her objectivity, negativistic, expresses her hostile feelings directly, and quest-ing for self-meaning.

Attributes *absolutely and relatively uncharacteristic of the Type Z girl during SHS:* feminine, favors status quo, comfortable with her physical appearance, accepting of dependency in herself, feels satisfied with her-self, and enjoys sensuous experiences.

Attributes *relatively uncharacteristic of the Type Z girl during SHS:* repressive, fastidious, values self and others in terms set by cultural group, becomes emotionally involved with members of the opposite sex, and physically attractive.

Interpersonal Q Set. Sixteen percent of the Interpersonal Q items distin-guish the Type Z girls from the Complement group at the .05 level of sig-nificance.

Items *absolutely and relatively characteristic of the Type Z girl during SHS:* expresses her hostile feelings directly to her peers, and straightfor-ward with her peers.

Items *relatively characteristic of the Type Z girl during SHS:* tends to have crushes on adults, predominantly adult-oriented, and rebellious with adults.

Items *absolutely and relatively uncharacteristic of the Type Z girl dur-ing SHS:* accepts and appreciates sex typing as it affects self, and ori-ented toward going steady.

Items *relatively uncharacteristic of the Type Z girl during SHS:* socially poised with her peers, involved on a fantasy level with the opposite sex, and spends time with members of the opposite sex.

Character Changes from JHS to SHS

The CQ Set. During the period from JHS to SHS, the Type Z girls change in certain ways. Thus, by SHS, Type Z girls have become significantly: more reluctant to act, more philosophically concerned, more introspec-tive, more bothered by demands, more ambitious, more likely to think in unusual ways, more comparative of self to others, more moralistic, more prideful of self on objectivity, more overcontrolled, and more evaluating of situations in motivational terms.

Compared to the way they were during JHS, the Type Z girls during SHS have become significantly: less sensuous, less dependable, less turned to for advice and reassurance, less talkative, less likable, less satisfied with self, less giving, less expressive, less satisfied with their physical appearance, less bodily concerned, less productive, less cheerful, less straightforward, less proffering of advice, and less sympathetic.

The Interpersonal Q Set. As conveyed through the Interpersonal Q set, the Type Z girls have, by SHS, become significantly: more likely to be the butt of their peer group, more likely to have crushes on adults, more involved on a fantasy level with the opposite sex, more oriented toward going steady, and more aloof with their peers.

Compared to the way they were during JHS, the Type Z girls have, by SHS, become significantly: less liked by their peers, less talkative with their peers, and less likely to achieve leadership roles with their peers.

Further Findings from the Adolescent Years

The Type Z girls are among the most intelligent girls of the sample (their mean IQ was 121). They come from somewhat higher status and more privileged homes than do the Complement subjects. The size of their families was comparatively large for the times (3.17 children versus 2.48 children), although the difference falls short of significance. If only as a corollary of the larger family size, the Type Z girls tend to be later-born than the Complement girls (.10).

Their mothers report that the Type Z girls at birth weighed less than Complement infants (.05) (5.8 pounds versus 7.8 pounds). In JHS, the Type Z girls were somewhat shorter and lighter than their peers and were significantly weaker as well (.10). They lagged behind the Complement girls in breast development at the time (.05) and were later to achieve menarche (13.6 years versus 13.1 years). By SHS, the Type Z girls continued to be slightly shorter and lighter and weaker than the Complement group. At the age of 17 their body forms were evaluated as less feminine in appearance than the physiques of Complement girls, the difference barely falling short of significance. The Type Z girls were also evaluated as less pretty via the Prettiness Index, the difference again falling a bit short of significance because of the unusually large variation within the Type Z group with respect to attractiveness.

In JHS, the Free Play Ratings indicate the Type Z girls were lower than Complement girls with reference to the Heterosexual Orientation dimension (.05). During SHS, the Free Play Ratings again evidence a lower degree of Heterosexual Orientation on the part of the Type Z girls (.05). The Frenkel-Brunswik Need Ratings record the Type Z girls as lower than Complement girls with respect to Abasement (.05).

In JHS, their mothers report the Type Z girls to be uninterested in clothes (.10), as following a well-planned schedule (.10), active in play (.05), a leader in her group (.10), liking drama (.05), and interested in things mechanical (.01). In SHS, the Type Z girls are described as earning money (.05), as being paid for home chores (.01), as approving of smoking (.05) and drinking (.05), as angering relatively easily (.10), and as seeing bad movies (.10).

Type Z girls less frequently fell in love during adolescence (.10); they dated somewhat less often, and they experienced intercourse, on the average, later than the Complement subjects and sometime after the age of 21 (the difference falls a bit short of statistical significance).

The Type Z girls during adolescence expressed high vocational goals, aspiring toward executive or professional positions (.05).

There was a decided trend for the Type Z girls to manifest high reactivity within the skin conductance situation of Harold Jones.

Their Character as Adults

The CQ Set. Sixteen percent of the Q items were significant at the .01 level and 34% were significant at the .05 level.

Attributes *absolutely and relatively characteristic of the Type Z women as adults:* values her independence, assertive, basically hostile, skeptical, aloof, has high intellectual capacity, feels cheated and victimized by life, distrustful, bothered by demands, and feels a lack of personal meaning in life.

Attributes *relatively characteristic of the Type Z women as adults:* prides self on her objectivity, complicates simple situations, negativistic, evaluates the motivation of others in interpreting situations, rebellious, proffers advice, and basically anxious.

Attributes *absolutely and relatively uncharacteristic of the Type Z women as adults:* feels satisfied with self, conventional, calm, submissive, gregarious, arouses nurturance, cheerful, feminine, self-indulgent, socially poised, eroticizing, and interested in opposite sex.

Attributes *relatively uncharacteristic of the Type Z women as adults:* seeks reassurance from others, enjoys sensuous experiences, creates and exploits dependency in people, likable, and internally consistent.

Character Changes from Senior High School to Adulthood

The CQ Set. Relative to the way the Type Z women were during SHS, they are as adults significantly: more turned to for advice and reassurance, more evaluating of situations in motivational terms, more satisfied with their physical appearance, more giving, more complicating of simple situations, more productive, more dependable, and more skeptical.

In addition, the Type Z women have become, since SHS, significantly: less self-indulgent, less gregarious, less withdrawing when frustrated, less interesting, less rebellious, less pushing of limits, less eroticizing, and less fantasizing.

Further Findings from the Adult Years

CPI Scale Scores. As adults, the Type Z women score *lower* than the Complement women on the Femininity (*Fe*) scale (.05), the Self-control (*Sc*) scale (.05), and the Good Impression (*Gi*) scale (.05). Thus, these scales suggest the Type Z woman is relatively dissatisfied, restless, touchy, untactful, lacking in generosity, aggressive, lacking in self-control, and cynically individualistic.

CPI Item Analysis. Some of the specific items which differentiate the Type Z women from the Complement are reported below.

Thus, the Type Z women more often than the Complement women *affirm* the following inventory items:

    CPI   6. I have a very strong desire to be a success in the world.
    CPI 105. I am fascinated by fire.
    CPI 156. I hardly ever get thrilled or excited.
    CPI 250. I must admit I find it very hard to work under strict rules and regulations.
    CPI 268. At times I have been very anxious to get away from my family.
    CPI 375. There are certain people whom I dislike so much that I am inwardly pleased when they are catching it for something they have done.

The Type Z women more often than the Complement women *reject* the following items:

    CPI 165. I do not mind taking orders and being told what to do.
    CPI 245. Most of the time I feel happy.
    CPI 286. I have never done anything dangerous for the thrill of it.
    CPI 367. My home life was always very pleasant.

Current Status. The Type Z women went further through school than was typical of the sample (.10) but recall that they were bright to begin with and they came from families relatively well favored socio-economically so the longer period of education is expectable rather than noteworthy. They have shown appreciable improvement in their socio-economic status, even considering their initial advantages (.10). Their adult intelligence, as reflected by the Terman Group Test, is higher than the average recorded by the Complement women (.10) (183.3 versus 159.8).

Of the four spinsters in the total sample of women, two are to be found among the six Type Z women. By the hypergeometric distribution, the likelihood of this connection of spinsterhood with the Z Type is significant well beyond the .05 level. There have been no divorces among the four Type Z women who did marry and from these marriages have come somewhat more children than is typical (3.5 children versus 2.6 children). It will be recalled that the original families of the Type Z women also were large.

Five of the six Type Z women occupy positions, the one housewife being married to a physician. The other three married Type Z women are, respectively, an accountant for her husband, a manager of a store partly owned by a relative, and a part-time bookkeeper. The two unmarried Type Z women are, respectively, a real estate agent and a middle-level employee of a health insurance organization. The Type Z women like autonomy and freedom from supervision in their jobs (.01); they like the usefulness of their work (.01), and they themselves do not like to supervise others (.01).

The husbands of the Type Z women list the following occupations: physician, school administrator (and part-time businessman), repair shop owner, and a designer.

In adulthood, the Type Z women continue to be somewhat shorter and lighter than the Complement women. They have minor health problems (.10), are light alcohol users, and are light smokers.

The Type Z women describe their marriages as being comparatively less happy (.05) and they express explicit dissatisfaction with their husbands to a greater extent than do the Complement women (.10). They describe themselves as rearing their own children in a way similar to the way they were brought up by their own parents (.05). They and their husbands are less likely to belong to any religious grouping (.10) and they manifest at the time of study comparatively less prejudice against Negroes than was average for the Complement women (.10). Finally, the Type Z women indicate they have fewer friends than the Complement women and infrequent contact with those few friends that they do have (.01).

The one Type Z woman who does not hold a job was under psychiatric care for several years and was for a brief period adjudged to be psychotic.

Adjustment and Continuity over the Years

The Psychological Adjustment Index. The Type Z females appeared moderately more adjusted than the Complement subjects during JHS (*PA* Index means, respectively, of .24 versus .07. The difference is not significant). By SHS, the Type Z girls had fallen to the Complement mean (*PA* Index means, respectively, of .00 versus .02). And in adulthood, the Type Z women evidence no particular improvement over their SHS psychological status while the Complement women manifest an appreciable growth toward maturity. The Type Z women have a mean *PA* Index in adulthood of .04 versus the Complement mean of .16; the difference is not statistically significant.

Personality Continuity. The Type Z subjects are not distinguishable from Complement subjects with respect to character consistency. During the JHS–SHS period, the average continuity correlation of the Type Z girls was .50 (.93 corrected for attenuation) versus the Complement JHS–SHS average of .54 (.83 corrected). For the SHS–Adulthood interval, the average continuity correlation of the Type Z women was .37 (.52 corrected) versus the Complement SHS–Adulthood average of .36 (.55 corrected).

Familial and Environmental Antecedents

The Early Family Ratings. The fathers of the Type Z girls were described as hyperactive (.05), tense (.05), hot-tempered (.10) individuals with little or no interest in their children (.01). The mothers are described, perhaps by way of contrast, as lacking in energy (.10). As a marital pair, the parents were described as sexually conflicted (.10), with different intellectual values (.05) and as generally incompatible.

The Ratings of Mothers. The ratings of the mothers revealed no significant qualities characterizing the mothers of the Type Z girls.

The Environmental Q Set. Vis-à-vis the familial contexts of the Complement women, the distinguishing qualities of the family settings of the Type Z females are as follows:

Environmental conditions *absolutely and relatively characteristic of the Type Z subjects:* Subject's family had strongly-held principles, opinions, prejudices, and moral convictions (.10).

Environmental conditions *relatively characteristic of the families of Type Z subjects:* Father pressured subject to achieve (.01); subject's father emphasized the life value of an intellectual orientation and rationality in decision and outlook (.05); subject experienced a sophisticated, complex home environment (.10).

Environmental conditions *relatively uncharacteristic of the families of Type Z subjects:* Subject was naturally physically attractive (.05); subject's family emphasized the life value of conformity, acceptance by peers, popularity, and the like (.10).

Interpretive Resume

The Type Z subject appeared to be bright and driving and relatively mature early in adolescence but by adulthood, her intelligence and independence seemed to be exacerbating a sense of separateness that dominates her existence. The Type Z woman has many personal resources but they are increasingly insufficient to cope with the alienation that agitates her. What were the factors antecedent to her adult circumstances?

Her father was a tense, hot-tempered, self-justifying person; the mother of the Type Z girl was a subdued, somewhat submissive individual. As a marital pair, the parents of the Type Z girl were at odds with each other. Yet, these parents produced a large family and surrounded their young with an interesting, differentiated home environment. The father was an achiever and instilled the value of achieving in his children. The necessity of departing, in intelligent ways, from established expectations was also an inculcated value. These parental urgings toward accomplishment and shrewdness were coincident with the pressures the Type Z girl was experiencing growing up among (and sometimes submerged by) many, mostly older, siblings. Moreover, as an ugly and weak duckling, she tended not to receive the compensating favoritism often accorded the youngest in families.

By JHS, the Type Z girl appears remarkably assertive, autonomous, and self-respecting. But looked at more closely, there are indications that her independence is excessive, her ambitiousness cloaks appreciable hostility, and her seeming sense of identity is predicated upon an exclusion from her awareness of the softer (hence, weaker) aspects of herself. The Type Z girl is physiologically less advanced than her JHS peers, she is vehemently uninterested in boys, and she is disturbed by the increasingly salient fact that she is female.

In SHS, the Type Z girl manifests but in accentuated form the characteristics observed in JHS. She is insistently independent, intellectualized in her orientation, extraordinarily ambitious, resentful of the demands or controls placed upon her. She is intensely ambivalent toward adults, being attracted to grownups, yet rebellious with them. She is uncomfortable with her femininity and, in her awkwardness and self-hatred, she makes the worst of her possibilities of attraction. As a consequence, she is unpoised and blatantly hostile with her peers.

During the adolescent period, the Type Z girl moved toward a deeper introspectiveness conjoined with prideful control of self. She increased her level of aspiration regarding career and moved further away from affect and from relationships with others. She became colder and less likable as she emphasized her total objectivity in approaching self and world.

In adulthood, the personality core of the Type Z woman continues much as before—she is intellectually active, rigidly independent, pushy, and suspicious regarding the motivations of others. She is, as before, uneasy with affect and consequently is avoidant of interpersonal relationships. She is hard on herself and on others in raw, unfeminine, dislike-engendering ways. She is unhappy, fearing she has missed out on much in life—as in fact she has. She continues to be trapped in her emptiness and she is unable to participate relaxedly and fully in the interpersonal contacts and connections that can lead to deeply felt and deeply supporting relationships. The porcupine, no matter how wanting of affection it might be, finds it difficult to be approached and therefore loved. So, with the Type Z woman.

Looking forward, it appears that the Type Z woman will be increasingly depressed by the separateness of her existence. Further activities, broadened or engaged in more frenetically, may anesthetize her ache of aloneness, but she will be bothered in her transitional or unoccupied moments by the disparity between the way she is and the way she would like to be.

I shall call the Type Z subjects *Lonely Independents,* to indicate the highly motivated assertiveness and desire for autonomy of these individuals together with the interpersonal unconnectedness that characterizes them.

Chapter X

TAKING STOCK

The proper task of the concluding chapter is not so much to summarize what has gone before as to develop perspective on the entire effort. The burdensome details of the findings have been spelled out, listed, and organized; precious little summarization is feasible beyond what the reader already has encountered. Now the job is to look less closely at the study so that the forest can be seen as well as the trees, so that a range of principles—not just peaks of empiricism—may be discerned. It is a further duty to evaluate the research past so that a more productive research future can be projected.

In addition, the final pages provide at last an opportunity for an author to write in an explicitly personal way, to convey how he evaluates his work and wants it to be understood and to have consequence. Accordingly, it would be misleading to avoid the egocentric "I" in much of what follows. It is easier, more politic, and certainly traditional to simulate total objectivity in one's approach; it is tempting to convey an inexorability to one's conclusions. But it would be misleading to do so.

Science in general and psychology in the very particular is a passionate game, a special way of manifesting ego and of realizing self. We have been foolish in trying for so long to keep this recognition from becoming public, because science is not thereby subverted. The scientific approach is protected against solipsism or venality by the rules it insists upon for inference and for proof; science does not require uncommitment. Indeed, such neutrality of value dulls an inquiry and even may guarantee its triviality. So, in what follows, I will be asserting my sense of what this ten-year-long involvement in a 30-year-old study has contributed to the scientific understanding of personality development. I do not mean to suggest by this prior notice of the first-person orientation that my conclusions will abandon connection with the data or that my more general remarks on the problems and possibilities residing in the longitudinal

247

enterprise are casually or whimsically offered. I shall be trying to speak truth and wisdom and I shall try to be persuasive. But *caveat lector!* The reader has the responsibility of accepting exactly what he should of what I have to say—not too much and not too little.

The chapter is loosely organized and is divided into two main sections. The first section deals with some implications I have drawn from the typological analyses reported in Chapters VII, VIII, and IX. (The findings reported in Chapters V and VI received their discussion within those chapters.) Having reported the several types in separate, closely detailed presentations, it now becomes possible and useful to stand back and view these personality constellations with the intention of achieving a broader and consequential perspective. Some generalizations are in order; some surprises and some confirmations must be remarked upon. Some old saws seem to me to have been reaffirmed, while other folk or professional cliches must at least be particularized when they are not altogether misleading.

I should note in regard to this psychologically substantive section that my remarks will tend to be brief, little elaborated, and will not be fully related to the previous writings and research findings of other investigators. This book is already too complicated and delayed, and my concern therefore is to deliver the sense and substance of *this* study into the literature. There will be time enough later for an integrative and scholarly literature review and more considered essays on some of the conceptual issues I shall be mentioning. But for now the reader requires only a statement of the implications of this particular investigation. So be it.

The second main section of this chapter focuses upon issues related to research effectiveness rather than issues of psychological substance. Looking backward, the methodological and organizational problems surrounding longitudinal studies are assessed. Looking forward, suggestions are offered regarding what should be done to improve these studies to enhance their scientific possibilities. Strategies and procedures that have worked well must be separated from those that have not; the organizational obstacles to implementation of the longitudinal approach must be frankly recognized so that they can better be hurdled; the areas wherein information is deficient must be identified if the continuation studies that are perhaps inevitable are to be strengthened and made worthwhile.

SOME IMPLICATIONS OF THE TYPOLOGICAL ANALYSES

Loevinger's Stages of Ego Development as an Organizing Continuum for the Personality Types

In a study such as this one, it would be the greatest of good fortunes to find the analytical possibilities highly attuned to the needs of theory-testing and theory-development. We were not so blessed. Nevertheless, I am impressed by how neatly the various types from both the male and female samples fit within the stages of ego development recently articulated by Loevinger (1966a).

Loevinger's stages of ego development do not represent a theory in the formal sense of an interpreted deductive system. Rather, her formulation is pre-theoretical and ostensive: she points to correlated and developmental phenomena that inductively might provide a basis for the positing of constructs and rules of relationship that would encompass and predict personality-related behaviors. The particular succession of ego stages, as presented by Loevinger, has large theoretical implications but she reports this ordering only descriptively or normatively and does not hazard a "reconstruction of the inner logic of the sequence."

Within its proclaimed intentions, Loevinger's stages of ego development seem to me both incisive and challenging—various aspects of behavior may be seen as integrated facets signifying the achievement of a given ego stage and also, she poses arguments and paradoxes that serious theorizing about the development of ego structure will have to consider. For our present purposes, the contribution of the Loevinger formulation lies in the way it brings order into our otherwise seemingly unconnected personality types. To convey this connection, it is necessary first to characterize briefly the stages she has proposed.

The first differentiated ego level is the *impulse-ridden stage*. At this time, the individual views his social world as a more or less illogical jungle. Impulse control generally is lacking. However, one's actions for pleasure may also, without rationale, receive harsh punishments. The teachable child at this ego level may, as a matter of repeated contiguities and the simple pragmatism of reinforcement, learn to contain certain of his desires, not because they are bad—indeed, the idea of badness does not exist—but in order to avoid the anticipated retribution. "Better control myself, otherwise someone will *hurt* me" is the control paradigm at this stage.

In the following *opportunistic stage*, the individual apprehends an orderly social world, but seeks to bend it to his desires. Personal pleasure and personal advantage are the aims; expedience is the way. Alas, manipulation cannot always be successful—instead of controlling his environment, the individual at this stage may find his environment threatening to control him. The exploiter of others is, in a fundamental way, also dependent upon those he exploits. In many interactions, it is a matter of interpretation, doubt, or taste as to which party dominates; certainly, the dominance relations often shift in an on-going relationship. Confronted with the possibility that his actions for advantage may have adverse consequences, the opportunistic individual may choose to prevent the chance of loss by forgoing the chance of gain. He will not pick up on an opportunistic opportunity, and will thus appear self-controlled, not because of high considerations of morality, but rather for reasons of situational expedience. "Better control myself, otherwise someone will *dominate* me" is the control paradigm of this stage.

In the *conformist stage*, the individual is oriented around a social world that is well-structured, finite, and predictable. Rules are followed for the same reason mountains are climbed—because they are there. There is a routinization of life and a preoccupation with externals. Unexpected or unsanctioned behaviors do not fit well into the social context and are frowned upon. Inner life presents complexities for which the grooves of response have not been prepared. Accordingly, spontaneous impulses are troublesome to the individual because he can recognize within himself that these desires will, if expressed, elicit condemnation from the environment upon which he depends for affirmation. "Better control myself, otherwise someone will *shame* me" is the control paradigm of this stage.

In the *conscientious stage*, the individual approaches his social world through a set of principles he has evolved for himself over time. "Inner moral imperatives take precedence over group-sanctioned rules. The sanction for transgression is guilt . . . Conscious preoccupation is with obligations, ideals, traits, and achievement, as measured by inner standards rather than by recognition alone" (Loevinger, 1966a, p. 199). The conscientious individual, as one in the common humanity, is also beset by desires whose fulfillment would be personally satisfying. And he, too, will manifest the ability to delay gratification. His behavioral constraint, however, is a function of a criterion radically different from that employed at the earlier stages of ego development. In the earlier ego stages, the manifestation of ego control always directly served the interest of the acting individual. In the conscientious ego stage, the ego control that is displayed is motivated by a concern for others than the actor, or a concern for principle. The actor is only indirectly served, by the avoidance of guilt. "Better control myself, otherwise someone *else* will be hurt, or dominated, or shamed, or made guilty, and then I will feel guilty" is the control paradigm of this stage.

In the *autonomous stage*, the individual has the problem of striking a better balance among his evolved principles, his continuing needs, and the social world in which he lives. The developmental task at this stage is to reconcile and cope with "conflicting duties, conflicting needs, conflict between needs and duties, and so on" (Loevinger, 1966a, p. 199). Having achieved the characterological components required for ego maturity, the autonomous individual has the problem of arranging the emphases or connections of these ego capacities and ego values so as to serve self as well as others. Although developmentally, impulse-control and con-

science emerge and progress more or less concomitantly, the achievement of true maturity requires that conscience and compassion as determinants of behavior become separated from impulse-control as a behavioral influence. The problems of choice and of expression are most complex, and in a fundamental sense are often irreconcilable. A manifestation
of this stage that can be misconstrued by the uncognizant observer is the
increased expression of impulse (an apparent trend toward under-control)
shown by the autonomous individual who in the earlier stage had been
conscientious to the point of self-abnegation. This reversal, however,
toward greater "selfishness" is highly differentiated and principled; it is
not gross and unqualified as in the impulse-ridden or opportunistic
stages. "Better control my excessive conscientiousness, otherwise I will
be held back from my achievable competencies" is the control paradigm
of this stage.

This sequence of ego stages is prefaced by a stage of un-differentia-
tion, when the task of the individual is to separate himself from what is
not himself. All non-psychotic individuals pass from this stage and it is
not especially pertinent to the present discussion. The final stage, coming
after autonomy, is the *integrated stage*. This is a time of self-actualiza-
tion, of the "reconciliation of conflicting demands, . . . renunciation of the
unattainable, . . . the achievement of a sense of integrated identity"
(Loevinger, 1966a, p. 200). Few people attain this level, and then usually
late in life, so that at least for now and here this stage does not require
the full consideration it may require later on for theoretical purposes.

With these stages of ego development in mind, consider now the
typologies. In the male sample, the *Ego Resilients* appear to be characterized early by the conscientious stage of development. In adulthood, there
are intimations they are moving into the autonomous stage.

The *Belated Adjusters,* after an adolescence indicative of the opportunistic stage, have in adulthood certainly attained the conformist stage and
perhaps many of the achievements of the conscientious level as well.

The *Vulnerable Overcontrollers* were brought early and abruptly to the
conformist stage—they had no opportunity to develop the shewd
resourcefulness that can be available from dwelling within the opportunistic stage and they seem unable to go onward to a more satisfying ego
level.

The *Anomic Extraverts* in a fundamental sense have never gone
beyond the opportunistic stage. A veneer of conformism is to be seen in
them, but this manifestation comes about more because of their failure to
live the opportunistic life successfully than because of a true move into
the next stage of conformism.

The *Unsettled Undercontrollers* do not seem to have ever left the impulse-ridden stage that was identified so early in them. Had they moved into opportunism, it would seem likely that given their intelligence and social origins, they would have been far better situated in life as adults than they are. There are some indications that these men are showing a long-delayed personality development in their adult years, but for the present they still must be viewed as at the impulse-ridden level of ego development.

Within the female sample, the *Female Prototypes* appear to be readily assignable to the conscientious stage of ego development. As yet, there do not seem to be the indications in these women, as there are in their male analogues, the *Ego Resilients,* of further growth toward the autonomous phase of maturity.

The *Cognitive Copers* were in adolescence characterized by the conformist and somewhat later by the conscientious stages of ego development. In adulthood, they seem to have moved on and are well into the autonomous stage.

The *Hyperfeminine Repressives* have not been able to move beyond the impulse-ridden stage of ego development by adulthood. The repressive controls that they manifest are extraordinarily brittle and undifferentiated; they do not imply conformism. The sorry situation of these women also precludes assigning them to the opportunistic stage.

The *Dominating Narcissists* magnificently exemplify Loevinger's opportunistic stage of ego development. They achieved this level of personality development by junior high school; they display it in adulthood; and because it works so well for them, they are likely to continue with this mode of ego structure.

The *Vulnerable Undercontrollers,* like the *Hyperfeminine Repressives,* fall within the impulse-ridden stage of ego development. There is no basis in their lives or in their character structure to assign them to one of the later phases.

The *Lonely Independents* are perhaps a bit anomalous with respect to Loevinger's stages. During early adolescence these women appear to have been in the opportunistic stage, moving somewhat later during adolescence toward a conscientiousness that was not first visible as conformism. In adulthood, these women do not appear to be at any one level of ego development or even between two adjacent levels. Rather, they seem to be locatable at no less than three different levels of ego development—the opportunistic, the conscientious, and the autonomous. Perhaps in the very irregularity of their ego development is to be seen the locus of their personal problems.

In the main, then, Loevinger's stages subsume the types reasonably well. A continuum of maturation and of maturity may be seen to be involved, with different individuals achieving different places along it. For some, the positionings now seem fixed; for others, further growth toward integration may be expected although it is never easy.*

The Recognizability of Parents in Their Offspring

Although the character evaluations of the parents of the subjects are far from adequate, nevertheless the several sources of information regarding the parents usually convey a sense of the parental personalities with respect to at least a couple of powerful dimensions. And, as I evaluate the parental temperaments associated with each of the character types, there are striking congruences between the essential personality of the subject as an adult and the personality characteristics of his parents. The parallels are discernible, without exception, for each of the five male character types; certain exceptions are apparent within the female typology, but even these are instructive.

Consider the male types first. The fathers of the *Ego Resilients* were active, bright, productive, respected individuals, and the mothers also are impressive as intelligent, warm, and psychologically healthy persons. Their sons present a fitting fusion of these admirable qualities, and there is no impressing indication that the personality qualities of the *Ego Resilients* are more aligned with one parent than the other.

The fathers and the mothers of the *Belated Adjusters* were quite similar, both being warm, responsible, unambitious, personally compatible and affectionate individuals. And, after a troublesome adolescence, so are their sons. Again, there is no suggestion in the data that the sons, in the personality qualities not dictated by sex and by sex-role, are more similar to one parent than the other.

The fathers of the *Vulnerable Overcontrollers* were passive, withdrawn, timid men; the mothers were neurotic, rigid, sexually-uncomfortable women. Their sons, sadly, have coalesced the unfortunate qualities of both parents. There is no basis for suggesting the sons take more after their fathers than their mothers.

The fathers of the *Anomic Extraverts* are not really clearly characterizable; nor are the mothers. But the fathers appear to be domineering, undemonstrative, and uninvolved individuals; the mothers seem apathetic and intellectually mediocre. During adolescence, the *Anomic Extraverts* appeared different from their parents. But in adulthood, they have a constellation of unhappy qualities—of insistent pretensions to self-adequacy, affective blandness, detachment from others—that relates

---

*Loevinger has been developing a sentence completion test to measure level of ego development. It would be most worthwhile, as a reciprocal validation of both the present interpretation and the Loevinger test, to administer the test to the IHD sample to see whether the ego levels of the various types, as measured by the test, conform to the interpretations advanced here.

well to the impressions gained of their parents. There is insufficient information to suggest a differential similarity of the son *vis-à-vis* his father and his mother.

The fathers of the *Unsettled Undercontrollers* were transparently selfish and remote individuals, preoccupied with personal pleasure and the avoidance of the unpleasant. So were the mothers. And so, in adult life, were the sons—they, too, are impulsive, intensely reactive but transient in their commitments. And again, there is no clear indication that the son takes more after one parent than the other in his basic personality attributes.

Now consider the female types. The mothers of the *Female Prototypes* were themselves personable, resourceful, affectionate women; the fathers were firm, competent, warm men. Throughout adolescence, and now in adulthood, their daughters have consistently evidenced the parental templates by which they have been shaped. Excepting the obvious and appropriate sex-linked personality attributes, there is no obvious basis for viewing the *Female Prototype* as particularly more like one parent than the other.

The mothers of the *Cognitive Copers* were apparently bright, active, ambitious, impressively capable, and self-disciplined women; there is little information distinguishing the fathers, but this absence of definition of his role and characteristics perhaps is itself informative. In adulthood, the *Cognitive Coper* is very much the kind of person her mother appears to have been—accomplishing, socially engaged, and well integrated, although not conveying the sternness that characterized her mother. It is clear that, for the *Cognitive Copers,* the mother was more influential than the father in determining later character.

The mothers of *Hyperfeminine Repressives* were mentally mediocre, uncurious, conforming individuals; the fathers were inadequate, sexually ambivalent, unintellectual men—also conformists. Their daughters manifest a character structure that merges qualities from both parents. Both in adolescence and in adulthood, the *Hyperfeminine Repressives* are not bright or interested persons; they are inadequate in almost everything they attempt, they are inconsistent and disjunctive in their sexuality. The picture of their parents is not sufficiently clear, but the daughter appears less adaptive than her parents. Yet, qualities that were salient in them are discernible also in the daughter; in particular, the daughter's personality in adulthood seems reminiscent somewhat more of the character of her father than of her mother.

The mothers of the *Dominating Narcissists* were despairing, neurotic women; the fathers were dominant, outgoing, self-centered men. In adolescence and in adulthood, the *Dominating Narcissist* appears in central ways to be as her father was—aggressive, independent, and egotistical. The characterological qualities of her mother are not evident in the *Dominating Narcissist* as an adult.

The mothers of the *Vulnerable Undercontrollers* were neurotically impulsive, restless women, bitter about life and looked down upon by others; the fathers were neurotic, vanquished, but still contrary men. In adolescence as well as in adulthood, the *Vulnerable Undercontroller* is clearly in the image of her parents—she is readily swayed and readily crushed, and she is always despairing. The impetuousness of the *Vulnerable Undercontroller* perhaps derives mainly from her mother, but her father as well conveys indications of impulsivity; the antecedents of her suffered discontent are most obviously to be seen in her father, but her mother also was soured on life. The tenuousness of her adaptation has its lineage in both parents.

The mothers of the *Lonely Independents* are not richly-enough distinguishable to warrant much confidence in formulations of their essential character, but the indications are clearly that she is *not* the kind of person her daughter proved to be. The mothers, to the slight extent they are characterizable, were meek and easily overwhelmed women. The fathers of the *Lonely Independents* are more confidently describable—they were vital, arrogantly self-assured, opinionated, striving, and pressuring men. The *Lonely Independent,* both in adolescence and in adulthood, has adopted the assertiveness and drive for achievement manifested by her father. In adolescence, it appeared that the *Lonely Independent* girl also had or was on the way to developing the self-assuredness characteristic of her father. But by adulthood, this quality is clearly absent. As was already noted, the characterological mark of the mother is not apparent.

Now, just what does this set of recognizabilities signify? Of course, there are cautions to be observed before drawing a generalization—the typological analysis has neglected a large number of "residual" individuals who might importantly have affected the trends that emerged, and I have already noted that the characterizations of the parents are far from ideal. Nevertheless, the observed personality similarities are impressive. There is indeed wisdom in the folk recommendation that a look at the parents of one's fiancé can be extremely enlightening.

To begin understanding, note that these personality similarities across the generations do not necessarily augur well for the psychological adjustment of the reminiscent individuals. Some of the subjects were personally well off, and others were not. Personality recurrence is simply not linked *per se* to the level of psychological functioning of the individual.

Within the male sample, perhaps because of the psychological similarities of the fathers and mothers and perhaps because the discriminations are insufficiently fine, there is no indication that the boys resemble fathers more than mothers with respect to dimensions of temperament that are not sex- or sex-role-related. The subjects appear masculine enough, if only because of the influence of these sex-related dimensions. But this achievement of masculinity cannot be credited in detectable ways to a particular influence of the father (or the mother).

Among the female types, it is apparent that in one instance (for the *Cognitive Copers*) the mother is clearly the decisive characterological model for her daughter. For two other female types (the *Dominating Narcissists* and the *Lonely Independents*), and perhaps for another type also (the *Hyperfeminine Repressives*), the daughter resembles her father more than her mother. With the exception of the *Lonely Independents,* in all these types, a tolerable manifestation of the female sex-role evolved over the years.

No special importance is attributed here to our particular observation that instances of differential parental influence are found within the female sample and not within the male sample. Possibly, this finding is reliable and implicative. More likely, it is a chancy thing, predicated upon our inability to consider the many residual subjects and other fortuitous sample characteristics. None of our male types, for example, appears to have derived from family constellations elsewhere observed wherein the mother is a domineering figure and the father a milquetoast figure. So it does not appear wise, as yet, to respect this difference between the male and female samples.

Reflection on the origins of differential parental impact should not leave one perplexed. It is not surprising, after all, that an unformed personality seeking to find ways of reacting that will be satisfying and viable should be susceptible to structure from his parental surround, whereupon "what one does becomes what one is" (Loevinger, 1966b, p. 437).

In particular, the parent who is seen as having most consequence upon the world is most likely to be taken up as the model for the character-forming child. Note well that in each instance where differential influence of the parents was discernible, it was the active and consequential parent who provided the character template that molded the child. The later outcome of adopting a powerful figure as a model may not be a happy one, as appears to be the case with the *Lonely Independents*. But the large principle that the developing character adopts structuring orientations (and the character structure) that are emphatically visible to him in his parents seems supported. The forming person may learn only later, or not at all, that his adopted ways of behavior are not intrinsically or sufficiently satisfying. The parents serving as behavioral models may not be intending or be aware of their consequence. But where structuring of behavioral alternatives is sought by the child because of the reassurance it so immediately provides, structure will be found. And simple principles of perceptual learning and response reinforcement will dictate the behaviors the child learns now and will shape what he will be later.

Usually, both parents will have identities of their own and be reasonably clear and demarcated figures. And so the child has the opportunity to be influenced by each parent and even to merge his behavioral models selectively and interactively, achieving thereby a personal style that is unique but has a discernible heritage. Where the parents, or a parent, provide an indistinct or contrary mold, the child will be shaped by that parent (or the environmental happenstance) that insistently and persistently registers upon him. By and large (but witness the *Cognitive Copers!*), it appears that differential parental impactfulness eventuates in a personality product that is incomplete or imbalanced. One can learn to be a man by following a man and one can learn to be a man by observing the reactions of a woman. It is better if these two ways to a sense of sexual self come as complementary instead of alternative experiences.

It is important to note before going on that these intergenerational personality similarities do not relate to "identification," at least as I wish to see the term employed. I prefer to use the term "identification" in its original psychoanalytic sense as referring to the striving by a child or adolescent or adult to take on the attributes of a person he has adopted as an ego ideal. If the ego ideal of a formational person is a parent, then that person is "identified" with his parent (Freud, 1933, p. 92).

This conception as originally formulated has often been misused or distorted. Thus, the implication often has been drawn that the existence of characterological similarity between child and parent is automatic evidence for identification. Obviously, such similarity may exist behaviorally despite the deepest rejection by the child of his parent as an ego ideal. A wastrel can still hate his wastrel father (if only because he hates himself). The term "identification" is not well used for such instances.

Conversely, an offspring may not achieve characterological similarity with the parent who is viewed as an ego ideal. The child may be intrinsically less adequate or may be subjected to additional pushes and pulls so that although the respect and the aspiration remain, the achievement of similarity is lacking. To conclude that identification is not present in such individuals would be misleading.

Within these definitions and recognitions concerning the concept of identification, the findings regarding "recognizability" do not provide evidence that identification has been the motivating basis for the intergenerational personality similarities observed. Although, for example, it can be argued that the *Ego Resilient* males or the *Female Prototypes* truly identified with their parents in that they desired as well as achieved similarity in fundamental ways to the parents from whom they derived, other types such as the *Unsettled Undercontrolling* males or the *Vulnerable Undercontrolling* females appear to be characterologically similar to their parents, but certainly never viewed their parents as ego ideals. More (or less) than personality similarity is involved in the idea of identification; i.e., value equivalences and intentions toward modeling are the essential core of an identification rather than the fact of characterological similarity or the existence of imitative behaviors. So, the findings of parent-off-spring personality similarity cannot be understood in identification terms. The next section of this chapter will take up the theme of identification again and more positively, indicating its basis and the role it appears to play in behavior.

The Importance of a Benign Family Environment

What comes through, for both sexes and without exception, in viewing the various types is an unequivocal relationship between the family atmosphere in which a child grew up and his later character structure. Subjects reared in family situations that the common culture generally would regard as healthy or positive or "good" proved in later life to be more adjusted and generally more admirable individuals. Subjects reared in family contexts that would be called sick or negative or otherwise "bad" tended to be, as adults, disturbed or unenviable persons. This finding of course confirms conclusions reached in other ways in other studies, various observations recorded in the psychiatric literature, and the implications of certain sociological indices of family disorganization. The finding, although expectable, is nevertheless nice to have.

This strong relationship between the family situation and later character is to be seen despite the particular and sizable differences between the family situations of the several types. Where different family equations result in generally equivalent products, it is usual that some common factors are involved. What do they appear to be? Abstracting across the types and the sexes, several family components emerge as significant influences upon the general psychological health and resourcefulness of our subjects as adults.

First, however, it is worthwhile noting that the "good" family situation seems to be more readily characterizable than is the "bad" family situation, suggesting a greater uniformity or homogeneity within the "good" families. The implication of these homogeneity differences is that there are many ways to leave a person incomplete; fewer ways to render him a whole and sufficient being.

The psychologically constructive family situation appears to have been one where the father was a father and the mother was a mother. The male and female sex roles were each well exemplified by the parents. The father was effective in his work, forthright in his interactions, respected in his world. The mother was comfortable and competent in the maternal role. She was bright, and she was warm. As a marital pair, the parents harmonized well. As instructors of the young, they emphasized and illustrated the values of responsibility and fairness; they were clear and consistent in conveying the principles of the social contract; they encouraged child participation in family discussions and their child's moves toward selfhood; they were affectionate and available to their young. After apprenticeship to such parents, it is not surprising that their children were well-prepared for life-journeys on their own and of their own.

The psychologically pathogenic family situation was one characterized by great family discord. The parents were intensely at odds with each other with respect to almost all marital matters—sex, money, time allocations, child-rearing, and so on. With regard to their child, some were rejecting; some were over-involved; some were unaffectionate; some were conflict-inducing, some were neurotic; some were away from home much of the time; some were diluted in their impact and relevance for the child because of the presence of too many other siblings; some were suppressive. In these various alternative but psychologically equivalent ways, the parents were neither suitable models for emulation nor sufficient providers of the instruction and reassurance required for the identification process that leads to identity. Social guidelines were not available to the developing child or else he was ruled by fiat; the place of the child within the family structure was not respected; his efforts toward growing up were treated with antagonism or indifference or parental superciliousness. The individual forced to develop without the provision of parental structures and structuring had to seek elsewhere for secure auspices under which he could grow. Many did not find what they needed and remained, as adults, alienated from their origins and yet trapped by them. Others, over-provided with parental instruction and constraints, were impoverished in their growth because they could not develop within these confines the adaptive resourcefulness required in order to realize their personal possibilities.

The massively evidenced findings that "good breeds good" are of course of great social significance in regard to matters of mental health and preventive psychiatry. Yet, these converging observations require a theoretical context if their full ramifications are to be understood. For theoretical perspective, I believe it useful to view the role of parents in achieving successful socialization and the concept of identification in terms somewhat different from the customary ones.

The importance of proper parental models and proper child-rearing techniques is not that the child is provided with a behavior to emulate or that the child is taught a response and the contingency for its emission. Imitative behavior or rote-learned behavior tends to be automatically invoked, highly specific, perseverative, and is often maladaptive when the conditions are changed from the context of initial learning. Rather, parents, both as models and in their teachings, provide illustrations from

which the child, motivated by love for his mother and father (call it positive reinforcement from potent instrumental interpersonal agents, if you
wish), can induce the principles needed for conscience and ego maturity.
Concept formation is involved, where the conceptual instances being
evaluated are not mundane, helpfully abstracted figures of varying shapes
and sizes and colors, but are instead fuzzy and complex instances of interpersonal behavior. The fully socialized individual has not "internalized"
values, i.e., taken something over from someone else and made it his
own. Instead, he has *evolved* the values himself, as a concept formed
from instances of interpersonal transactions.

As Loevinger (1959) has noted, the interpersonal concepts educed by
the child sometimes seem almost willfully different from those the parents were hoping to instill. Yet, the parents have no choice but to attempt
to deliver their precepts.

In this framework, identification may be distinguished from imitation in
that the individual who has only imitation as his guide to behavior is
nonplussed by situations or a world different from the one in which he
has learned; the individual who has truly identified has evolved a set of
behavioral premises or values that can guide him even in a changing
society. For identification but not for imitation, the child must attain certain interpersonal concepts. The necessary contribution of parents is to
provide the environment and examples of behavior so that the desired
concepts arise in their young.

As a final observation within this section, it is worth noting that psychologically maladjusted subjects in the present study experienced *opposite*-sexed parents who apparently were especially neurotic, tense, and
brittle persons. That is, the maladjusted men derive from mothers who
were manifestly anxious and tight individuals; the maladjusted women
had fathers who appear to have been particularly anxiety-laden and marginal in their own adjustment. The like-sexed parents of the maladjusted
subjects appeared to be usual enough *vis-à-vis* the like-sexed parents of
the healthy subjects, insofar as extent of neuroticism is concerned. This
finding requires replication, of course, but it does suggest that the primary
locus of the family discordances resides with the opposite-sexed parent.
A good father married to a neurotically ineffective woman cannot produce a good son; a good mother married to a neurotically ineffectual man
cannot produce a good daughter.

Ego-Control Capacity as a Function of Parental Efforts at Parenthood

Within the immediately preceding large picture of what leads to psychological health and what leads to psychological pathology, it proves

possible to focus upon a personality dimension of particular conceptual and social significance in order to assess the developmental antecedents of the different positions individuals achieve on this continuum.

The construct of ego control, developed some years ago (Block, 1950; Block, 1951), relates to the individual's characteristic mode of monitoring impulse. When dimensionalized, the underlying continuum is conceived as representing excessive containment of impulse and delay of gratification at one end (over-control) versus insufficient modulation of impulse and inability to delay gratification at the other end (under-control). Behaviorally, an overcontroller appears to be constrained and distant, with minimal expression of his personal emotions; he is highly organized and categorical in his thinking, tending to adhere rigidly to previous understandings; he can continue to work on uninteresting tasks for long periods of time; he is over-conforming, indecisive, and with narrow and relatively unchanging interests; he delays gratification even when pleasure is a sensible course of action, not threatening of long-range intents.

Behaviorally, an undercontroller is unduly spontaneous, with enthusiasms neither held in check or long sustained; his decisions are made (and unmade) rapidly and his emotional fluctuations are readily visible; he disregards, if he does not disdain, social customs and mores; he tends toward immediate gratification of his desires even when such gratification is inconsistent with the reality of his situation or his own ultimate goals; his grooves for behavior are not deeply ingrained and, accordingly, his actions can frequently cut across conventional categories of response in ways that are (for better or for worse) original.

The construct has proved useful both predictively and as an organizing rubric for a heterogeneous set of perceptual, cognitive, and motoric behaviors (cf., e.g., Block, J., 1950; Block, Jeanne H., 1951; Block & Block, 1951; Block & Block, 1952; Block & Thomas, 1955; Block & Martin, 1955). In some form or another, under a variety of labels, most personality theorists have proposed as a central determinant or mediator of behavior a variable akin to what is subsumed by the concept of ego control. How the characterological ability to delay gratification and modulate impulse is developed is obviously a question of great theoretical and applied importance.

Although analysis solely of the dimension of ego control might have been preferable, conceptually and analytically, the typological analyses also respond to this question and with suggestive, even confirmatory answers. The implications that can be drawn are clearer with respect to undercontrol than to overcontrol, and clearer too with respect to males than to females.

What leads to undercontrol? Several of the types, both male and female, manifest marked undercontrol as a dominating feature of their character structure. The antecedents of undercontrol for both sexes appear to involve essentially the same family factors but are most directly obvious when we compare the male *Unsettled Undercontrollers* with the male *Ego Resilients*.

The comparison of the *Unsettled Undercontrollers* with the *Ego Resilients* is usually interesting for another reason as well. As sampling luck would have it, the *Unsettled Undercontrollers* and the *Ego Resilients* proved to be almost perfectly matched with respect to adolescent IQ (means of 128) and initial socio-economic status (comparatively high). Earlier studies related to the antecedents of undercontrol often have been confounded in their interpretation by the concomitant variables of intelligence and social class.

The most elegant empirical analysis regarding the origins of undercontrol is the study by McCord, McCord, & Howard (1961), who investigated the familial antecedents of aggression in nondelinquent children. The definitions of aggressiveness, assertiveness, and non-aggressiveness employed by McCord, McCord, & Howard impress me as assimilable to various levels of ego control. The particular nicety of their design was the matching of groups of aggressive, assertive, and non-aggressive boys with respect to the absence of delinquency, social class (which was low), and ethnicity. Intellectual measures apparently were not available for their subjects, but it seems fair to presume the general level of intelligence of their sample was somewhat lower than average.

The opportunity of studying the origins of undercontrol by comparing matched groups of subjects at the upper ends of the intellectual and SES continua thus can be especially clarifying. It is one of those rare instances when preferred principles of experimental design and inference can be applied reasonably well to samples fortuitously come by. In a sense, the comparisons made between these male types can be viewed as a completion of the analytical design begun by McCord, McCord, & Howard.

Direct comparison of the *Ego Resilients* who achieved an appropriateness of impulse expression with the *Unsettled Undercontrollers* who displayed excessive and fitful expression of impulse results in a set of relationships that need to be only briefly described here since they are almost identical to those earlier reported in Chapter VIII, where each type separately was contrasted with its respective Complement group.

Thus, to recapitulate our own findings, the adult under-controlling male as a child was neglected by both his mother and his father. His mother was a neurotic, self-indulging woman who was narcissistically seductive with her son, rather than selflessly maternal. His father was a detached, indifferent, self-absorbed man. The home situation was frantic, complicated, unpredictable, ever-changing. Because of the essential selfishness of the parents in pursuing their own lives, little effort was expended on socializing the boy via verbal, rational means, or on showing him skills, or on encouraging his interests, or in simply being present. Not least, the parents were manifest in their egocentricity and in the casualness of their concern for their son. In contrast, the appropriately-controlled man had experienced parents who took seriously the responsibilities of parenthood. The characteristics of these latter parents were generally the converse of those just listed as descriptive of the parents of undercontrollers.

For the females, the relevant comparisons would appear to be between the *Dominating Narcissists* and the *Female Prototypes* and also between the *Vulnerable Undercontrollers vis-à-vis* the *Female Prototypes*. The matchings with respect to intelligence and social class are quite good for the first of these comparisons, somewhat inadequate for the second but certainly not flagrantly so. And again, essentially the same pattern of psychological relationships observed within the male sample is found.

In the general welter of psychological findings that do not replicate or have convergent implications, it is heartening to encounter the present findings, largely similar for the two sexes, and to note the impressive correspondence of these results with those earlier and differently generated by McCord, McCord, & Howard (1961), and by Bandura & Walters (1959) in a related context. As I evaluate these several studies, appreciable overlap appears to exist and the convergence of conclusions is extraordinary.

What are the implications of these generally-obtained parental differences for understanding the different developmental learning contexts that eventuate in appropriately-controlling and under-controlling adults? In order for a child to become appropriately controlled, someone has to invest time and trouble. The responsibilities of parenthood take much effort, and, perhaps most crucial, the proper *timing* of the effort. It is often the case that when the child requires some parental response, the parent would much rather be doing something other than being parental. The test of the good parent is that she (or he) functions parentally even when she (or he) could gain more immediate pleasures otherwise. Responding in the middle of the night to a crying infant is not something one looks forward to; nor is helping a child with his geography assignment in the evening after your own hard day's work intrinsically satisfying. The parent warms the 3:00 a.m. bottle or relearns the whereabouts of the Straits of Marmora because of a sense of parental obligation and empathy.

In order for a child to learn ego control, he must know what to learn and be drawn to do so. The contribution of parents is to provide both illustration and motivation, guiding the child toward certain forms and timing of behavior and away from the "natural" state of unmodulated and immediate response. As Loevinger and Fisher (1966) have remarked, "Interpersonal schemas serve as model and as impetus for intrapersonal schemas."

In the early stages of personality development, the child will be able to learn prudence through punishment if his parents control his world, ensuring its structure and seeing to it that there is a consistency of rein-forcement. But sustained parental attention is required to maintain a predictively consequential environment. It is troublesome, interrupting, and onerous to have to discipline a child; it is far easier—immediately —to ignore the occasion for instruction or punishment. The parents of the undercontrollers, by virtue of their own impulsivity and self-absorption, simply did not invest the time nor exhibit the constancy needed to deliv-er the precepts of self-regulation to their child. Controlling the world of their child for the good of their child was not felt or acted on as a re-sponsibility. A conversely related aspect of the self-indulgence of these parents was their tendency to invoke discipline only when they them-selves were extremely angered. Stark discipline administered under fury to a young child will be perceived as a fearsome aggression and will not register cognitively as, given socialization goals, it should. The over-whelmed child will simply be panicked by parental rage into a fearful and rigid passivity; the shrewder child will learn when to be discrete or def-erent and when he can be franker in his expressions.

It is often the case that children make adults out of parents. It is easy enough to conceive a child, but rearing one is a sobering and instructive responsibility. The parents of children who never grow away from under-control are parents who did not accept the day-to-day and moment-to-moment necessary impositions of their children upon their own plea-sures. They were oriented toward self-gratifications—out of narcissism, indolence, limitations of intellectual vision, the value context of their subculture, or even desperateness—and so they did not provide to their children motivating illustrations of the general interpersonal principle that at times one must not do what one really wants to do, simply for the sake of another person. As a consequence, their children grew up without the tutelage required for full participation in and contribution to an on-going social system.

What leads to overcontrol? For the male sample, the type comparisons of interest are between the *Vulnerable Over-controllers* on the one hand and either the *Ego Resilients* or *Belated Adjusters* on the other, since both of these latter groups may be considered to be relatively appropri-ately controlled. The *Ego Resilients* are of somewhat higher intelligence and socioeconomic origins than the *Vulnerable Over-controllers;* the *Belated Adjusters* are somewhat lower. The psychological gist of what we seek lies in the relationships shining through *both* comparisons, since the intellectual and socioeconomic differences between the groups would appear to balance out. When direct comparisons are made of the *Vulner-able Overcontrollers* with both of the appropriately-controlled groups, the results are almost identical with those early reported in Chapter VIII when the familiar origins of the *Vulnerable Over-controllers* were described.

Thus, the adult overcontrolling male as a child experienced a highly authoritarian, joyless, and constraining family situation. Objects rather than people, proprieties rather than affects were emphasized. The parents were generally conservative and inhibited, particularly in regard to sexual matters. The mother was dominant in the family constellation, the father deferring to his tightly controlling but essentially brittle wife and finding his own pleasures in prosaic masculine hobbies and competencies. Chores were a regular responsibility for the boy; expectations of compliance were strongly put to him; guilt induction by invoking the mother-martyr role was the method of imposing punishment. In the course of growing up, these parents—primarily the mother but abetted also by the father—so overcontrolled their son that in adulthood, he is still naive or fearful before the pleasures and even requiredness of impulse-expression.

For the female sample, typological comparisons that are clearly relevant to the understanding of overcontrol do not exist. Perhaps this absence of possibility is an accident of sample; my own surmise is that a deeper reason underlies the absence of an overcontrolling group within our women that begins to approximate the degree of overcontrol manifested in the male sample by the *Vulnerable Overcontrollers*. The cultural setting within which the female subjects developed set great store on female decorum and control and provided in great detail the rules and conventions by which a girl should live (or at least disguise her spontaneities). Intelligent girls or reminded girls were reluctant to hazard their futures by dangerous forms of impulse expression. It may not be unfair to suggest that overcontrol for our girls and women was appropriate control, given the environmental structuring and values around them.

The *Female Prototypes,* who as adults are somewhat over-controlled but also effective and attractive individuals, illustrate this argument. Their familial origins were described in Chapter IX, but in brief summary, the parents of the *Female Prototype* typically were a mutually complementary and stable pair, providing affection conjoined with conservative and required values for their children. As with the boys who went on to a characterological overcontrol, the parents of the *Female Prototypes* overcontrolled the lives of their daughters. But where such parental restrictiveness eventuated in men who were not what they wanted to be, the women who endured these shaping constraints pretty much like the selves they see.

In this study, there is a difference between the origins of overcontrol in males and females that is worthy of note and perhaps of interpretation. The male overcontroller typically derived from a parental constellation wherein the mother was dominant and guilt inducing, the father uninvolved and tacitly capitulating in family decisions. The female overcontrollers (admittedly less extreme or vulnerable than the male over-controllers) experienced parental pairs whose harmony reflected a complementariness of relationship rather than a one-sided deference.

For boys becoming men, the impetus toward achieving identity is almost inevitably seen as requiring confrontation or escape from parents, if only for an interval; for girls becoming women, the achievement of identity has not as a rule been viewed as requiring such discontinuities in relationship.* The boy experiencing a controlling father can fight him or can, as a situational or temporary tactic, submit. There is abundant empirical evidence that domination *per se* (in the form of a dominating, punishing father) does not diminish the ability of sons to assert themselves (cf., e.g., Bandura & Walters, 1959; McCord, McCord, & Zola, 1959).

But such dominating fathers in these studies dominated by means of a thinly veiled or actually displayed physical superiority over their sons. The boy who grows into strength himself or who otherwise escapes such paternal power can afford to express the desires he previously prudentially contained. Mothers, however, cannot control their sons and even their daughters into adolescence on the basis of an implied physical domination; other means are necessary and the maternal gambit evolved over the years has been threat of love loss (also used by fathers, but to a lesser extent). This threat, once it has been registered upon the child, is portable; it continues to constrain him, even though the inducer of the threat is no longer present. It is perhaps by this construction of events that the tendency of overcontrolling males to be related to a certain kind of maternal dominance may be understood.

The Co-significance of the Father in Shaping Character Development

Inspection of the set of typological findings indicates that the role of the father in guiding the course of personality development is far more potent and decisive than generally has been assumed. Perhaps because mothers have been more accessible to study than fathers, psychologists in the past have tended to emphasize the influence of the mother in determining the personality of the child. Perhaps, too, the greater frequency of contact of the child with the mother in earlier years has been presumed to imply the greater significance of the mother. Nash (1965) in his review has further remarked upon the relative underemphasis on the role of the father in child rearing and in studies of child rearing. But the evidence of the present study agrees well with the conclusion of Becker: "where both mothers and fathers have been studied, . . . the father's influence on the child's behavior (is) at least equal to that of the mother" (Becker, 1964, p. 204). We should not now forget the role of the mother,

---

* A corollary of this difference in expectation is that a man can know more clearly whether or not he is his own person; the continuity of progression prescribed for a woman can introduce in her a troubling uncertainty regarding the attainment of selfhood.

but we can no longer omit study of the nonbiological contribution of the father to his children. Happily, trends in the literature suggest this correction in emphasis is underway.

The reasons for the psychological impact of the father upon his child are embarrassingly obvious, once the psychologist thinks to look. The irreducible requirements for preparing a child to be a mature adult involve more than a mother alone can (or should be asked to) provide. In particular, the father has been a neglected structuring influence upon the developing child.

If the father's contact frequency with his child is perhaps lower than the contact frequency of the mother, these contacts also gain in effect by their timing and the emphasis they are accorded by mother and child. Further, certain socialization tasks are largely the province of the father—discipline, joking, techniques of camaraderie, and the teaching of masuculine prowess and skills to boys and of masculine reactions to girls. The father can provide a bulwark from which the developing youngster can venture when he wishes and toward which he can return when the foreign world is threatening. The child who knows he has such a protector will be different from one who knows he does not.

In adolescence, the need for a father who is a father-figure becomes even more poignant. The ramifying adolescent requires confirmation that his personal extrapolations about motley matters such as Thursday night's math homework and the nature of life are reasonable ones; he wishes authoritative support of certain directions of inquiry and he seeks discouragement of other inclinations or temptations that manifestly pull him. Fatherly presence, fatherly values, and fatherly structuring provide great and enduring support for the adolescent seeking to find his own way. There is a danger that such fatherly authority may be or may be viewed as stultifying or as opposed to the full and free individuation of the youth. Famous inter-generational battles have been and will be fought on such grounds. But such warfare only testifies further to the significance of the father as a characterological influence upon his offspring.

The Striking Evidence for Personality Coherence

The typological analyses, by identifying and then focussing upon homogeneous subgroups, permit relationships to emerge that often would have been missed or canceled out in analyses based upon the entire sample. With so many different kinds or times of longitudinal data, the use of subgroup analyses has adduced numerous relationships surrounding each type. The reader will find it difficult to scan through the materials specifying the types without becoming aware of strong patterning in the network of empirical relationships each type has elicited.

The unity or consistency of personality is compellingly apparent in these data and is manifest in so many and so diverse ways as perhaps to establish the unity principle empirically once and for all. Personality coherency has always been assumed by personologists because it *must* be assumed. But the empirical support for this proposition has appeared to be weak or contrary. Although much of the empiricism relating to personality consistency is of extraordinarily poor quality or is otherwise irrelevent, vigorous arguments against the very *idea* of personality consistency have been mounted.

I view the sets of empirical relationships surrounding the several types over time and across diverse measures as sufficient proof for the principle of personality consistency. The congruences that have emerged can be assailed and denied existence only by a highly "original" oppositionist weaving a convoluted and fragile web of counter-explanation. I suggest that psychologists stop concerning themselves with the issue of personality consistency—yes or no? Our field will profit more by examination of the conditions and the measurement approaches under which such indications of integrality may be observed or do not appear. We should move on to this more productive phase.

The Inadequacy of Distal Organizing Variables and the Importance of Type Belongingness as a Complex Moderator

There are endless ways in which to apprehend experience and there are endless ways in which to look at data. Investigators will organize their analyses differently, but there are some general scientific criteria in terms of which the relative fruitfulness of analytical rubrics can be evaluated. To be useful, an approach to data should develop many rather than few relationships; it should permit integration of the obtained relationships rather than simply their enumeration; it should suggest implications of what has been found rather than be nonconsequential.

Within this frame of reference, it seems fair to say that the typological approach has fared well. The typological emphasis has generated many findings amidst the longitudinal data, the findings harmonize, and some interesting extrapolations flow from what has been observed. Given knowledge of an individual's type, that type category serves as a "moderator" predicting quite well that individual's placement on a number of rather diverse variables.

The types, while certainly not falling within a satisfactorily tight theoretical scheme, are nevertheless best understood in terms that involve the *configuration of psychological variables*. For convenience in communication, we may be forced to use labels of various kinds and varying degrees of aptness in identifying the types. But each type must be viewed more or less as a complex system of personality variables, as a characterological syndrome, as a psychologically concordant entity. Within this configurational approach, the relationships are abundant and they fit together well.

The personality data developed for the present study have sometimes been approached in more simple ways. Investigators already have analyzed portions of these Q data, seeking the personality Q correlates of such convenient and distal indices as: smoking frequency, early or late skeletal maturity, social adjustment, social mobility, childhood activities, and the like. A stream of equivalent analyses, each small and simple, can be expected in the future now that these data have been prepared and have become accessible to later investigators. This general approach, of studying the relationships accruing to singled-out variables without concern for the personality or situational context surrounding the focussed-upon variable, is a popular one. It is perceptually and professionally attractive because conclusions are readily visible and are readily delivered into the literature. Many of these analyses can be of interest, at least dramaturigically, e.g., the correlates of divorce, republicanism, bizarre sexual experience, and so on.

But this simple approach can be simplistic and downright misleading as well. To discern the difficulties residing in simple analyses, say, of the correlates of smoking or similar such fetching criteria, an analogy from medicine is useful.

The proper research physician does not single out an interesting symptom and establish its correlates. He does not seek the correlates of fever or of death or of headache or of rapid pulse or of fatigue, because fever and death and headache and rapid pulse and fatigue each eventuate for many quite different, often unrelated, and sometimes even opposed reasons. Very few symptoms are pathognomonic. One can die of thirst or from drinking too much water. The correlates of symptoms during a flu epidemic are quite different from the correlates of those same symptoms otherwise.

A good physician develops understanding and diagnostic knowledge by seeking the antecedent conditions and the sympton syndromes that form a coherent configuration. He uses particular symptoms as signs but not as criteria for diagnosis. The disease has a central systematic basis from which the symptoms derive more or less directly, but rarely unequivocally.

So with personality—it is a constellation of system-related core variables. It may be expected that smoking and adjustment and personality change and rate of maturity and other socially seized-upon indices will be "symptoms" or signs of a type. But simple or direct relationships are likely to be the exception rather than the rule because these distal, "outcome" indicators are so far from the prime variables of the personality system.

Thus, early skeletal maturity, when evaluated for the entire IHD sample, has been reported to have generally positive personality and social implications. This index, when evaluated *vis-à-vis* the types, shows thoroughly inconsistent results. Early skeletal maturity for some types seems associated with attractive or tenable styles of adaptation (e.g., the *Ego Resilient* males or the *Cognitive Coper* females), while for other types the relationship appears reversed (e.g., the *Anomic Extraverted* males or the *Hyperfeminine Repressives*). The conclusions previously reported with respect to skeletal maturity appear to have been inadvertent functions of the relative frequency of the several types. Certain personality types are to be found relatively frequently in the total samples and it seems likely that the slight positive (undifferentiated) relationship of skeletal maturity to personality in the full samples is attributable primarily to these differences in the type proportions.

The personality correlates of smoking frequency have also been assessed for the IHD sample and statistically significant relationships have been isolated. But again, viewed from a typological framework, the implications of the smoking symptom can be seen to be contingent upon the particular personality context within which it is imbedded.

As a final illustration, consider again the preoccupation by psychologists with the predictive correlates of adult adjustment. There are good social reasons for interest in this question, but the strategy of inquiry is all-important. There are many routes to the achieving of a comfortable and competent character. An undifferentiated approach, employing adjustment as a homogeneous criterion rather than as a highly derivative outcome (cf., e.g., Livson & Peskin, 1967), can deliver only accidental averages that are no better than weakly predictive. This averaging approach homogenizes man and often describes no one since averages are useful only insofar as variation about the average is small.

In Chapters VIII and IX, type partitioning permits great predictability of adjustment to be seen for certain kinds of character but little or no predictability is in evidence for other types. Moreover, the richness of the sets of relationships surrounding each type offers possibilities of understanding why adjustment predictability or unpredictability characterizes a type. This wealth of relationships does not empirically develop when the polymorphous, distal, and atheoretical "adjustment" variable is employed as a polarizing dimension around which to organize inquiry. We would do better empirically if we worked with concepts or continua that are dimensionally unequivocal in their implication, that refer to mediating processes within the individual rather than simply distal outcomes, and that can be related to a theoretical system. Hit-and-run analysis of topical-relevant indices is a noisy but not a sound way to advance a science.

The Necessity of Psychologizing the Notion of Social Class

It is well known that indices of socio-economic status relate in non-chance ways to a great variety of psychological variables. Thus socio-economic status correlates with IQ, with character structure, with child-rearing practices, and so on. For many sociologists, these relationships have been viewed as demonstrations of the central significance of the concept of social class.

If one accepts the importance of social class, it of course follows that social class must be controlled or partialed out or evaluated first before hunting for other systematic sources of relationship. And research designs and research interpretations routinely have done so, surrounding the parameter of social class with an ever-growing array of relationships.

The atheoretical and conceptually unwieldy nature of the notion of social class has not been deterring because pragmatically, the social class variable "works"—it laces together an extensive correlative network. It is true that these relationships have not been entirely consistent in their implications due to ethnic or subcultural or time period variations. Even today, for example, no firm and unqualified generalization can be offered regarding the relation of child-rearing practices to social class. Are middle-class parents more restrictive or more permissive than lower-class parents? It all depends on when the question is asked, now or thirty years ago. Or whether reference is to Mexican-American Catholics or Russian-American Jews. Or whether we sample New York City or Orange County.

Also, there has been on occasion an overvaluation of the predictive usefulness of the social class variable. Statistically significant but relationally weak associations based on large samples have been viewed as more consequential or diagnostic than in fact they are. Certainly, personality variations *within* social classes far exceed the variations *between* social classes (cf., e.g., Allinsmith, 1960; McCord, McCord, & Howard, 1961; Strauss, 1962; Robins, 1966).

My quarrel with the social-class variable, however, is not based upon the empiricism surrounding its usage. Rather, my argument is conceptual. The very employment of the idea of social class, although not altogether wrong, is also not altogether right. There are some large gaps or puzzles when psychological variables are organized under a social class rubric, and, by way of illustration, the typological analysis can be used to embarrass social class as an organizing variable.

Consider again, for example, the *Ego Resilient* males and the *Unsettled Undercontrolling* males. Both types are comparatively quite high with respect to their initial socioeconomic status (and are equal with respect to intelligence, as well). Yet, the *Ego Resilients* show upward social mobility and a generally admirable characterological course, while the *Unsettled Undercontrollers* are downward mobile and are far less attractive personalities from either a societal or a psychological viewpoint.

Similarly, the *Belated Adjusters* and the *Anomic Extraverts* also are reasonably well matched initially with respect to socioeconomic status and intelligence (the *Belated Adjusters* being a bit disadvantaged *vis-à-vis* both variables, in comparison with the *Anomic Extraverts*). Yet, the *Belated Adjusters* by adulthood are fundamentally different psychologically from the *Anomic Extraverts* and are, from an adjustment point of view, in far better personal situations. Other type comparisons demonstrating personality divergence despite socioeconomic equivalence can be located by the interested reader.

The point of these illustrations is not that the variable of social class is a necessary but clearly insufficient parameter for understanding personality. Rather, such findings demonstrate that the idea of social class is, in a more fundamental way, inappropriate. Holding the social class variable constant or partialing it out or introducing another variable in addition to the social class variable—none of these analytical tactics will get to the hub of the matter. Which is that *the social class concept, so easily objectified and invoked, is a rather poor and confounded indicator of several rather different determinants of behavior.*

Knowledge of the social class of an individual conveys in an ill-defined way information regarding the stimulus or learning context in which that individual was formed. Knowledge of social class also tells us something about the characteristics of the psychological environment in which an already formed individual must issue behaviors. And, knowledge of social class often implies some genetic selectivity that has behavioral consequences. Of these three components of the notion of social class, it is the first that is most important for the discussion here.

Various social classes, relatively homogeneous with respect to ethnicity and during certain historical periods, provide relatively uniform social learning contexts for the developing child. The values, reinforcement schedules, and other practices of a sociocultural tradition dictate socialization techniques and emphases that will have approximately equivalent character-shaping effects on all the children born into that particular social milieu. A lower-class child will have a different personality from the middle-class child because of different orientations *learned* with regard to time perspective, the experience of predictability of the world, the logical consistency of reinforcement, the strategies to invoke in situations of uncertainty, and the like. The problem of understanding why the child of one social class has personality attributes different from the child of another class is the psychological problem of identifying the stimulus variables and stimulus patterning that ingrain one character structure rather than another. The connection of social classes to different patterns of socializing stimuli is essentially epiphenomenal and fortuitous. We can use this connection as a way of evaluating the effects of certain experimentally-unmanipulable variables, or otherwise allow for it, as required. But we should not depend on the connection between social class and personality for psychological understanding. Indeed, in a society showing massive trends toward cultural homogenization because of the artificial dissemination of values and attitudes, the differentials formerly or even presently related to social class *per se* can be expected to shrivel away. The same psychological variables that underlie learning contexts presently differentially associated with social class will continue to be relevant; they simply will not be related to social class any longer. Which means the already obtained relationships between social class and character are historically descriptive but not intrinsic or ultimately dependable.

Besides reflecting a learning context shaping the developing child, social class alludes to—for the individual whose character already has been formed—the psychological parameters of the contemporaneous environment in which the person must function. A member of a social class is subject to various pushes and pulls, constraints and possibilities, specified as conditions of his class membership. He must operate within or at least respond in terms of his social class, even after his personality structure has been evolved. The conceptual distinction between the learning context implications of social class and the environmental press implications of social class is most clearly to be seen in an individual who has been reared in one social class or learning context and now functions in a different social class, with its different environmental parameters. Another example that separates these two aspects of the social class concept is the individual formed by middle-class values of a half-century ago who must get along and cope with very different middle-class values, dictates, and freedoms today. The distinction being made, then, is between the *rules of character formation* on the one hand and the *contemporaneous environmental conditions affecting character functioning* on the other. Social class is an environmental influence on both the formative and the functional components of personality. In societies which are structured, stable, and well-meshed, the distinction between character formation and character functioning loses importance because form follows function and function follows form. But in a culture such as our own, epitomized by flux and contradiction, the societally-prepared character of an individual may prove a poor fit for the later society in which he is plumped down.

Our final aspect of social class—genetic selectivity— is less important for our purposes, but is included for the sake of systematics. In a reasonably free and mobile society, it can be expected that individuals with certain qualities of intellect and temperament will gravitate toward certain

steps of the socioeconomic ladder. Whereupon the usual factor influencing marriage patterns—ecological propinquity (i.e., in general, you marry
someone you have met rather than someone you have not met)
—operates with the result that subsequent generations perpetuate to at
least some degree the different qualities that have earned different placements in the socio-economic hierarchy. These different qualities, related
to socioeconomic status, obviously would have important implications for
the environmental context genetically selected parents would construct
for their children and also the inherent qualities of the children placed
within these different milieus.

This digressive diatribe against the notion of social class as it so often
has been employed must now make its moral. The most that can be
expected of the social class variable is that it will serve as an indicator of
several sets of influences, measuring none of them well. Accordingly, it is
far better to be rid of the notion. For the sake of both predictability and
understanding—two scientific aspirations that only rarely coincide—the
gross measure of social class should be abandoned and be replaced by
separate, psychological measures, each of which would be finely tuned to
represent the concepts and influences now so imperfectly conveyed by
social class indices. By psychologizing the concept of social class and
partitioning it into its proper components, the possibility is developed of
achieving strong and invariant relationships between socialization experiences and subsequent personality. But so long as social class remains a
ding-an-sich rather than being separated into the host of psychological
influences it so imperfectly represents, the relation of one's social origins
to one's character will only dimly be seen.*

The Chancy Role Intrinsically High Intelligence Plays in Affecting the Course of Life

The various types often differ with respect to intelligence level, as
measured in adolescence. It seems clear that the intellectual differences
often had consequences in specifying and restricting the life happenings
and alternatives experienced by the people studied. But the influence of
intelligence in shaping the course of character development and the life
opportunities presented to an individual seems greatest for the types
characterized by a relatively *low* intellectual level. For the *Belated Adjusters,* the *Anomic Extraverts,* the *Hyperfeminine Repressives,* and the

---

*The argument just advanced, regarding the necessity of psychologizing the notion of social
class, can be applied as well to the concept of race. "The black experience" in American society
may be better understandable if we attempt to delineate the learning context in which a black
child grows up and the shaping constraints in the psychological environment in which a black
person must function. "Blackness" unanalyzed, can only be a correlate susceptible to political
rather than dispassionate interpretation.

Vulnerable Undercontrollers, the accommodations or niches that have been worked out reflect constraints imposed by their essential ordinariness of intellect. The intelligence level of the individuals in these groups could have predicted quite well various aspects of their later adjustment.

With types of appreciably greater intelligence, however, intellectual level does not appear to be especially predictive. The *Ego Resilients* employed their intellectual gifts well; the *Unsettled Undercontrollers* have remained at the mercy of the ramblings of their gifted minds; the *Cognitive Copers* were characterologically transformed by their centering upon the uses of the mind as a way of life, and the *Lonely Independents* were finally let down by an over-reliance on their intellectual capabilities.

For the lower ranges of ability, then, intelligence appears to be a shaping force on character and the consequences of life; for the upper ranges, character and life are more likely to determine the shape of one's intelligence.

The Influence of Cultural Change on the Generalizability of Longitudinally-Obtained Findings

In the thirty years or so since these studies started, America has experienced vast transformations and the very style of American life has undergone fundamental, still only partially understood change. Growing up now is very different from the way growing up used to be. Even the apparent logic of our environment, seen through a child's eyes and incorporated then as a basis for his own behavior, has been fundamentally affected. Sequentiality has been replaced by concomitance; events no longer are caused, they happen. Interpersonal values have shifted in importance, some up and some down, so that the emphases of the 1920s and 1930s can seem amusing today. It is entirely reasonable to suggest that new forms or new integrations of personality are appearing now, predicated on unprecedented premise systems and therefore not understandable in the terms of the past.

For example, in regard to the handling of impulse, it seems clear that radical changes have occurred in the way important segments of the population formulate their behaviors. My own impression is that many in the generation born in the 1940s and 1950s, at the time the longitudinally-followed subjects generally were having their children, have learned somehow to keep matters of conscience separate from matters of impulse control. In their parents (e.g., our subjects), conscience development generally went along with the development of ego control. At least in the white, reasonably affluent, middle-class members of this more recent generation, moral concerns and moral anguish appear unrelated to the level of ego control (cf., eg., Becker, 1964, p. 188). No longer is an undercontroller reasonably predicted to be unperturbed by pangs of guilt or issues regarding morality; by the same token, no longer may one presume the overcontroller is guided by moral precepts as well as by his rigidities. The reasons for this separation of qualities usually characterologically linked is obscure. My own surmise—quickly put—is that moral development and the development of ego control begin to have the opportunity of disengaging when the value of avoiding hurting others is given special and elaborate emphasis in a context generally favorable to pleasures and comforts. In a harsher world, which still exists for most, this disengagement cannot be registered upon children. The connection between ego control and conscience is one societies always have depended upon; the breaking of this connection has untold implications that may make our history.

Within the present volume, the importance of this illustration of cultural change is to call attention, with dismay, to the possibility that longitudinal studies, by the time they are brought to some point of completion, may provide dependable results valid only about a time or circumstance that will never recur.

LOOKING BACKWARD AND LOOKING FORWARD

In Retrospect

Evaluating the IHD studies from the perspective achieved after the prior years and pages, a number of strengths and weaknesses in the archives, the longitudinal design, and the analyses must be mentioned. Some of these were recognized at the outset of this analytical voyage; others could not be known before the trip was underway; still others could be perceived only at the end.

The Q-sort approach to personality description, together with the use of systematically permutated personality assessors, worked rather well as a means of integrating the diverse, otherwise non-comparable material available for the subjects. Clinical psychologists were able to employ the method to express their formulations of adolescents who had lived a generation earlier, and the data so provided proved both reliable and, in numerous ways, consequential. In addition, the properties of the scores provided by the Q method proved useful for charting character changes over time that could not be revealed by correlation coefficients alone. Conventional rating methods could not have conveyed this kind of information. And, not least, the fact that a methodology could generate data of appreciable interest and implication testifies to the essential quality of the material in the IHD archives.

The California Psychological Inventory contributed in important ways to the sense of incisiveness and validity of the types reported in Chapters VIII and IX. The scales of the CPI, developed and validated in other contexts, showed a pattern of relationships *vis-à-vis* the types that should be heartening to assessment psychologists. The CPI emerges from this application surrounded by a host of additional relationships supporting its usefulness and power.

Although I am not unhappy (and am even pleased) with the typology described in Chapters VIII and IX, it would have been most interesting and possibly of great alternative consequence to try one of the "natural" grouping procedures in addition to or instead of factor analysis. These "natural" schemes seek to partition a sample into subgroups so that within-subgroup variance is minimized and between-subgroup variance is maximized (cf., e.g., Friedman & Rubin, 1967). This approach to clustering has come to be recognized as entirely general and as escaping many of the assumptions or limitations of methods such as factor analysis. However, this more "natural" strategy of cluster identification involves large computational problems because the number of possible partitionings is usually enormous and beyond full calculation. Empirical computer sampling of partitioning possibilities coupled with heuristic procedures is required. The limited resources available for the typological analyses and the time pressure for completion of the study and the reluctant recognition that much thinking still was required to implement the "natural" method—these three reasons were more than enough to push this analytical ambition aside. It may be worthwhile, though, in some more leisurely, abundant and developed time to explore this alternative approach to grouping individuals.

In the personality realm, there was, unfortunately, little objective testing of the IHD samples, even when the subjects were adults. As Witkin, Goodenough, & Karp (1967) recently have shown, such tests have much to contribute to an understanding of developmental trends. This omission in IHD coverage is understandable historically because of the emphasis in these studies on tracking mental and physical development with the procedures or conventions established at the inception of the investigations.

The one non-interview, non-projective, non-paper and pencil personality measure available on a fair number of Institute subjects both as teenagers and as adults 25 years later was a measure of electrodermal reactivity, which proved to relate to certain of the personality types in ways fitting current theoretical formulations. In addition, measures of electrodermal reactivity correlated significantly for each sex over the 25-year period, a most substantial finding. These relationships make one wish the decision had been made to include a broad battery of perceptual, cognitive, and motor tasks and of psychophysiological measures in the longitudinal plan. The possibility was broached, at least during the later years of the study but concern was expressed regarding how the participants would react to such an "impersonal" approach. My own evaluation is that the morale and interest of the subjects was sufficiently high to have permitted properly explained experimental procedures to be employed successfully.

With all the archival information, there are still large gaps or insufficiencies that greatly limit the possibilities of understanding. The years from the end of high school until the time of the follow-up investigation, when the subjects were in their thirties, were almost unstudied. Occasionally, study participants would drop by informally to visit a staff member and a report of the meeting would be entered into the files. Or, a staff member would note in the newspaper a happening to a subject and file it away. The extensive interview held during the follow-up study delved for information regarding this period. Valuable though this retrospective information was, the fact remains there is little systematic contemporaneous knowledge of the subjects during their twenties, at the times most were making their choices of career and of mate. The factors operating at life's choice points are for some people or some times overdetermined; for others, or for other occasions, the fundamental cast of a life is chancy as can be. The archives, because of the long hiatus in data collection during young adulthood, tell us little regarding the drama or the inevitability of these decisions.

The sparseness of archival information regarding parent character and family environment already has been remarked upon. The reasons why are understandable in the context existing when the studies were started. But by the time of the follow-up evaluations, the emphasis within the longitudinal programs had shifted heavily toward an understanding of personality development. During the follow-up study, it would have been a good idea to study more explicitly and systematically the parents of the subjects. In addition, it would have been worthwhile to study, again systematically, the personality attributes of the children—almost all quite young then—of the subjects, preparing the way for current and later studies of parental influence upon children. Such studies would have been unprecedented in the kinds of information available and the kinds of analyses feasible.

The last few observations derive from and allude to what appears to be an endemic disease of longitudinal studies. Besides matters of research design and research organization, a longitudinal study must be concerned with the problem of maintaining a long-term research vitality. In the several longitudinal studies across the country of which I have knowledge, each of the investigations reached a time when the *raison d'être* for the ongoing organization became unclear. I of course do not know all the reasons why longitudinal studies characteristically enter a phase of busyness without purpose and staff demoralization. In part, this anomie develops because the longitudinal idea takes so long until payoff. Also, there inevitably are personnel replacements seeking a job rather than a purpose, who do not contribute to the necessary sense of meaning in the undertaking.

The catalog of organizational ills will vary from institution to institution and an exhaustive list is not required. What *is* required is the simple recognition that such problems can be expected to arise in the course of a longitudinal study. Only after this recognition can efforts be taken to fend off these troubles or, if they occur anyway, to resolve them. No longitudinal study can survive, usefully, unless it is sustained by an intelligent, resourceful, dedicated cadre of professional staff. Even so, there will be a need every now and then for a re-invigoration of the longitudinal enterprise by the introduction of new ideas and new people. What has gone before must continue to be known and respected. But also, there must be a responsivity in the organization or the longitudinal endeavour to the new possibilities coming onto stage.

In Prospect

It may be that once a longitudinal study reaches a critical mass or a critical time or a critical quality, it will endure forever because the past investment alone warrants continued support and interest. Despite the problems which have beset the IHD studies over the years, it seems likely that they will continue. As the IHD subjects approach their fifties, it makes sense, therefore, to consider some ways in which this longitudinal enterprise might become more efficient and more fruitful.

In essential *continuation of the present study,* it would appear that more objective and more contemporaneous measures should be employed to expand upon the past kinds of information gathered for each subject. The host of additional measures to be employed should include various measures and indices of the environmental context of the subject, so that personality can be viewed *in vivo* rather than *in vacuo.* Also, it may not be too late even now to initiate, in addition to characterological evaluations of the children of the IHD subjects and of their spouses, analyses of the interactions and communication styles of the family participants, so as to study better than before but in a new generation the ways in which parents have influence upon their children. The measures and procedures that have proved valuable in the past should of course be continued. And, as a feature of all these suggestions, it is necessary to renew the motivations of both subjects and investigators if the intentions of the perpetuated research are to be realized.

In *extension of the present study,* it may not be entirely fanciful to consider collaboration and even further merging with other longitudinal studies as a means of increasing the contributions to be gained from continued longitudinal study. For example, it seems likely that the material available in the Fels longitudinal archives could be approached using the methods and principles of the present study, resulting in data fairly mergeable with the data generated from the IHD archives. Perhaps other longitudinal archives also might be processed so as to make commensurate the personality information residing in each. The attraction of this grandiose and Procrustean proposal is that sample sizes would be greatly enlarged with consequent enlargement of the analytical possibilities. Particularly if differentiated analyses are to be undertaken, large samples are required. Additionally, the introduction of a common data framework for several longitudinal studies may invigorate diffident investigations and bring them needed support and dedication so that their latent worth may become manifest. Obviously, implementing this suggestion would require many kinds of negotiation and commitment among many kinds of parties. It is pertinent to raise the possibility within these pages, but elaborated discussion of the suggestion is best left for other circumstances.

In *initiating new longitudinal studies,* where the investigator need not be constrained by the research past, I believe that it is time now for the atheoretical emphases of longitudinal studies to be abandoned. The questions psychology wishes to ask regarding personality development and the role of environmental factors can be phrased much more pointedly now than was the case years ago. The research design that will respond efficiently to such focussed inquiries must, of necessity, scant the kinds of information theory does not deem pertinent. It was the strength, and the onerous burden, of the longitudinal studies that they tried to capture *all* the answers to *all* the questions. But this intention, ineluctably (and soon), is doomed to failure; in the strategy of science, this catholic approach makes its greatest contribution at the outset of inquiry into a domain, since it quickly provides orientation and hypotheses. As the field advances, however, the heuristic gift of theory must be employed so that deeper understanding may be gained.

The immediately preceding ponderous remarks are the rationale for the recognition that longitudinal studies do not need to begin with "representative" or unselected subject samples, and indeed, for theoretical inquiries, should not. In a longitudinal study getting underway today, I believe subjects should be selected so as to meet specified and systematically permutated conceptual criteria regarding their personal characteristics or environmental contexts. In the natural world, individuals meeting these various criteria will be found with differential frequency, a troublesome fact of life when subjects are being sought. But this complication would have to be endured because of the advantages for understanding offered by the unconfounding of otherwise intertwined variables and the inclusion of psychological configurations theoretically crucial but usually underrepresented or even omitted in a "representative" study.

The problem of locating subjects doubtless can be eased if, first, an easily invoked screening procedure is employed. For example, subsequent to this volume, it might be decided to devote further attention to certain of the types reported in Chapters VIII and IX, which might require increasing the numbers of representatives of these types. Toward this end, the California Psychological Inventory easily could be given to large samples of potential subjects. Since for each type, a set of four optimally-weighted CPI scales predicts type-membership with multiple correlations not lower than .44 and ranging up to .75 (with an average type-predictability of .58), it is clear that the inventory could serve as an impressively good initial selection device. Subsequent interviews and screening of the CPI-nominated subjects could serve to further exclude the "false positives" slipping by the CPI. This sequence would not be burdensome. More generally, the task of selecting subjects with designated characteristics has a greater chance of being surmounted if it is confronted than if it is shied away from. The truly significant problem is to conceptualize and define incisive, theory-advancing criteria for the selection of subjects.

Bell (1959), who for a long time has been almost alone in writing on such matters, has discussed in a most stimulating fashion the limitations for understanding personality development of the longitudinal approach using unselected samples. He too is concerned with the under-sampling of certain kinds of subjects, the perseveration of fact-gathering that is no longer germane, and the frequent absence of the information singularly required for understanding transitions. Although Bell notes the greater flexibility and easier focussing of retrospective research studies, he is bothered as are many others that "the very freedom of the retrospective orientation which is so productive of hypotheses also encourages considerable magical and omnipotent thinking" (1959, p. 140), and by the inadequacy of the *post-hoc* approach in discerning stages and transitions in earlier development.

Bell's suggestion, and he has already successfully applied it in a limited way (1953; 1954), is to employ numbers of relatively short-term longitudinal studies, phased and overlapping so that theoretically desired concentration can be achieved, no one study is too expensive, and so the effect of cultural change can be evaluated. Schaie (1965) more recently has presented a rather formal design model along some of these same lines.

The suggestions of Bell and of Schaie are valuable and, if applied, would improve almost any longitudinal investigation. But, despite the drawbacks, there remain many indisputable reasons for truly long-term longitudinal studies of lives. For such ventures, the kinds of control or contrast samples envisaged by Bell and Schaie simply are not feasibly employed by mortal men. In these latter kinds of investigation, I believe the selection of subjects according to theoretical criteria can respond to many of the criticisms otherwise leveled against the longitudinal method.

It may be argued that theories or perspectives regarding personality development still have not advanced to a stage where they should control what the investigator is enabled to observe. A non-selective approach to subject samples and to information-gathering, coupled with serendipitous data analysis, certainly could be productive scientifically and could well shame a theoretically-oriented research design based upon poor theory. But I think there are a number of generally-held, widely-supported personality dimensions whose antecedents and consequences, separately and in different configurations, it would be of fundamental importance to know. A longitudinal study designed to inquire powerfully regarding such questions has not been started. It would be well to do so.

EPILOGUE

There is an old joke about the optimist and the pessimist encountering a glass holding some water. The optimist, in his exuberance, views the glass as already half-*full;* the pessimist, corroborating his hopelessness, sees a glass that is already half-*empty.*

I myself oscillate in my evaluation of the significance of the longitudinal analyses that have been reported here. I am sometimes impressed by the findings and the relationships that have been developed and I am sometimes suspicious or disparaging of the value of the study and its results. My wavering between optimism and pessimism persists because certain of the findings I believe to be firm and generalizable and important, while other findings impress me as tenuous or without implication for other samples, or trivial otherwise. Also, I waver because a thirty-year-long study and a massive investment in analyzing and understanding what it all means must be judged in larger terms than are usual. Was it all worthwhile, considering the costs and the commitments?

In my own mind, I really do not know. From a study and a data basis characterized by great richness and great deficiencies, a number of interesting findings have emerged. But do these findings and their psychological significance warrant the time and treasure and tempers that have been consumed in winning these results? Perhaps, and perhaps not. Or could the same results have been sought more economically by other, more targeted investigatory designs? But would we have known to hunt more efficiently for these relationships if not for the costly, dilatory, but irreplaceable longitudinal results? Perhaps, and perhaps not. And so the argument can go, the claims and counter-claims for and against the usefulness of the longitudinal investment continuing without end.

Perhaps the primary contribution of this book will be that it permits a fair assessment to be made at last of the practical possibilities afforded by longitudinal studies. Although the reasons for longitudinal study are logically unassailable, all longitudinal studies are subject to inevitable, and human, vicissitudes so that what ultimately eventuates deviates greatly from what has been promised or from what might have been. It is the actual accomplishment and not the promissory proclamation of the longitudinal idea that must be judged. The present report describes a longitudinal study more prolonged than most, with a rather large sample, with reasonably rich data, and analyzed more closely than has been the practice. It is no immodesty to suggest that this book defines for the while the upper limits of what may be achieved by the longitudinal study of personality. If that achievement is unworthy of the effort, so be it. This conclusion would be an important one for it would suggest that the longi-. tudinal approach need not be further pursued until its limitations can be removed. If the judgment of the psychological sciences on the worth of longitudinal studies is favorable, then the venture is revitalized and in its renewal will find ways to betterment of its strategy and method. So, the "is it all worthwhile?" question is not just a moody concern; rather, the question has appreciable implications for the way psychological research resources will be directed subsequently.

BIBLIOGRAPHY

Allinsmith, B. B. Expressive styles: II. Directness with which anger is expressed. In D. R. Miller & G. E. Swanson, *Inner conflict and defense.* New York: Holt, 1960.

Bandura, A., & Walters, R. H. *Adolescent aggression.* New York: Ronald Press, 1959.

Becker, W. C. Consequences of different types of parental discipline. In M. L. Hoffman & L. W. Hoffman (Eds.), *Review of child development research.* Vol. 1. New York: Russell Sage Foundation, 1964.

Bell, R. Q. Convergence: An accelerated longitudinal approach. *Child Development,* 1953, *24,* 145–152.

Bell, R. Q. An experimental test of the accelerated longitudinal approach. *Child Development,* 1954, *25,* 281–286.

Bell, R. Q. Retrospective and prospective views of early personality development. *Merrill-Palmer Quarterly of Behavior and Development,* 1959, *6,* 131–144.

Block, Jack. An experimental investigation of the construct of ego control. Unpublished doctoral dissertation, Stanford University, California, 1950.

Block, Jack. The difference between Q and R. *Psychological Review,* 1955, *62,* 356–358.

Block, Jack. A comparison between ipsative and normative ratings of personality. *Journal of Abnormal and Social Psychology,* 1957, *54,* 50–54.

Block, Jack. On the number of significant findings to be expected by chance. *Psychometrika,* 1960, *25,* 369–380.

Block, Jack. *The Q-sort method in personality assessment and psychiatric research.* Springfield, Ill.: Charles C. Thomas, 1961.

Block, Jack. Measurement dimensions in a palmar resistance situation. *Psychological Reports,* 1962, *11,* 319–331.

Block, Jack. The equivalence of measures and the correction for attenuation. *Psychological Bulletin,* 1963, *60,* 152–156.

285

Block, Jack. Recognizing attenuation effects in the strategy of research. *Psychological Bulletin,* 1964, *62,* 214–216.

Block, Jack. *The challenge of response sets.* New York: Appleton-Century-Crofts, 1965.

Block, Jack, & Block, Jeanne H. An investigation of the relationship between intolerance of ambiguity and ethnocentrism. *Journal of Personality,* 1951, *19,* 303–311.

Block, Jack, & Thomas, H. Is satisfaction with self a measure of adjustment? *Journal of Abnormal and Social Psychology,* 1955, *51,* 254–259.

Block, Jeanne H. An experimental study of a topological representation of ego structure. Unpublished doctoral dissertation, Stanford University, California, 1951.

Block, Jeanne H., & Block, Jack. An interpersonal experiment on reactions to authority. *Human Relations,* 1952, *5,* 91–98.

Block, Jeanne H. & Martin, B. Predicting the behavior of children under frustration. *Journal of Abnormal and Social Psychology,* 1955, *51,* 281–285.

Blos, P. *On adolescence—A psychoanalytic interpretation.* New York: Free Press of Glencoe, 1962.

Brooks, J. B. The behavioral significance of childhood experiences that are reported in life history interviews. Unpublished doctoral dissertation, University of California at Berkeley, 1963.

Campbell, D. T., & Fiske, D. W. Convergent and discriminant validation by the multitrait-multimethod matrix. *Psychological Bulletin,* 1959, *56,* 81–105.

Cattell, R. B. The three basic factor-analytic research designs—their interrelations and derivatives. *Psychological Bulletin,* 1952, *49,* 499–520.

Cattell, R. B., Coulter, M. A., & Tsujioka, B. The taxonometric recognition of types and functional emergents. In R. B. Cattell (Ed.), *Handbook of multivariate experimental psychology.* Chicago: Rand-McNally & Co., 1966.

Cronbach, L. J. Correlations between persons as a research tool. In O. H. Mowrer (Ed.), *Psychotherapy theory and research.* New York: Ronald Press, 1953.

Cronbach, L. J., & Gleser, G. C. Assessing similarity between profiles. *Psychological Bulletin,* 1953, *50,* 456–473.

Edwards, A. A social and economic grouping of the gainful workers of the United States. *Journal of the American Statistical Association,* 1933, *28,* 377–387.

Erikson, E. H. The problem of ego identity. *Journal of the American Psychoanalytic Association,* 1956, *4,* 56–121.

Erikson, E. H. Identity and the life cycle: Selected papers. *Psychological Issues* 1, No. 1, 1959.

Erikson, E. H. *Childhood and society.* (2nd ed.) New York: W. W. Norton, 1963.

Frenkel-Brunswik, E. Motivation and behavior. *Genetic Psychology Monographs,* 1942, *26,* 121–265.

Freud, S. *New introductory lectures on psychoanalysis.* New York: Norton, 1933.

Friedman, H. P., & Rubin, J. On some invariant criteria for grouping data. *Journal of the American Statistical Association,* 1967, *62,* 1159–1178.

Gough, H. G. *Manual for the California Psychological Inventory.* Palo Alto, Calif.: Consulting Psychologists' Press, 1957. Revised edition, 1964.

Gough, H. G. An interpreter's syllabus for the California Psychological Inventory. In P. McReynolds (Ed.), *Advances in psychological assessment.* Palo Alto, Calif.: Science and Behavior Books, Inc., 1968.

Haan, N. Comparisons of various Oakland Growth Study subsamples. Unpublished manuscript. Institute of Human Development, University of California at Berkeley, 1962.

Haan, N. The relationship of ego functioning and intelligence to social status and social mobility. *Journal of Abnormal and Social Psychology,* 1964, *69,* 594–605.

Hartmann, H. *Ego psychology and the problem of adaptation.* New York: International Universities Press, 1958.

Honzik, M. Review of J. Kagan & H. A. Moss, *Birth to maturity. Merrill-Palmer Quarterly of Behavior and Development,* 1965, *11,* 77–88. (a)

Honzik, M. Personal communication, 1965. (b)

Honzik, M. Personal communication, 1966.

Jones, H. E. The California Adolescent Growth Study. *Journal of Education Research,* 1938, *31,* 561–567.

Jones, H. E. The Adolescent Growth Study. I. Principles and methods. *Journal of Consulting Psychology,* 1939, *3,* 157–159. (a)

Jones, H. E. The Adolescent Growth Study. II. Procedures. *Journal of Consulting Psychology,* 1939, *3,* 177–180. (b)

Jones, H. E. The study of patterns of emotional expression. In M. L. Reymert (Ed.), *Feelings and emotions: the Mooseheart Symposium.* New York: McGraw-Hill, 1950.

Kagan, J. American longitudinal research on psychological development. *Child Development,* 1964, *35,* 1–32.

Kagan, J., & Moss, H. A. *Birth to maturity.* New York: Wiley, 1962.

Kephart, W. H. *The family, society, and the individual.* Boston: Houghton Mifflin, 1961.

Klein, G. S., & Schlesinger, H. Where is the perceiver in perceptual theory? *Journal of Personality,* 1949, *18,* 32–47.

Kohn, M. L., & Clausen, J. A. Parental authority behavior and schizophrenia. *American Journal of Orthopsychiatry*, 1956, *26*, 297–313.

Lingoes, J. C., & Guttman, L. Nonmetric factor analysis: A rank reducing alternative to linear factor analysis. *Multivariate Behavioral Research*, 1967, *2*, 485–505.

Little, K. B. Confidence and reliability. *Educational and Psychological Measurement*, 1961, *21*, 95–100.

Livson, N., & Peskin, H. Prediction of adult psychological health in a longitudinal study. *Journal of Abnormal Psychology*, 1967, *72*, 509–518.

Loevinger, J. Patterns of parenthood as theories of learning. *Journal of Abnormal and Social Psychology*, 1959, *59*, 148–150.

Loevinger, J. The meaning and measurement of ego development. *American Psychologist*, 1966, *21*, 195–206. (a)

Loevinger, J. Three principles for a psychoanalytic psychology. *Journal of Abnormal Psychology*, 1966, *71*, 432–443. (b)

Loevinger, J., & Fisher, A. Cathexis: a logical and epistemological critique. Paper presented at the meeting of the American Psychological Association, New York, September 1966.

Macfarlane, J. W. Some findings from a ten-year guidance research program. *Progressive Education*, 1938, *7*, 529–535. (a)

Macfarlane, J. W. Studies in child guidance. I. Methodology of data collection and organization. *Monographs of the Society for Research in Child Development*, 1938, *3* (6, Whole No. 19). (b)

McCord, W., McCord, J., & Howard, A. Familial correlates of aggression in non-delinquent male children. *Journal of Abnormal and Social Psychology*, 1961, *62*, 79–93.

McCord, W., McCord, J., & Zola, I. K. *Origins of crime*. New York: Columbia University Press, 1959.

Myers, T. R. Intra-family relationships and pupil adjustment. *Teachers College Contributions to Education*, 1935, No. 651.

Nash, J. The father in contemporary culture and current psychological literature. *Child Development*, 1965, *36*, 261–297.

Neugarten, B. L. & Associates. *Personality in middle and late life*. New York: Atherton, 1964.

Newman F. B. The adolescent in social groups: Studies in the observation of behavior. *Applied Psychology Monographs*, 1946, No. 9.

Rapaport, D. On the psychoanalytic theory of motivation. In Jones, M. R. (Ed.), *Nebraska symposium on motivation, 1960*. Lincoln: University of Nebraska Press.

Robins, L. N. *Deviant children grown up*. Baltimore: Williams & Wilkins, 1966.

Rosenthal, I. Reliability of retrospective reports of adolescence. *Journal of Consulting Psychology*, 1963, *27*, 189–198.

Schaie, K. W. A general model for the study of developmental problems, *Psychological Bulletin*, 1965, *64*, 92–107.

Stephenson, W. *The study of behavior*. Chicago: University of Chicago, 1953.

Strauss, M. A. Deferred gratification, social class, and the achievement syndrome. *American Sociological Review*, 1762, *27*. 326–335.

Symonds, P. M., & Jensen, A. R. *From adolescent to adult*. New York: Columbia University Press, 1961.

Terman, L. M., & Oden, M. H. *The gifted group at mid-life*. Stanford, California: Stanford University Press, 1959.

Tryon, R. C., & Bailey, D. The BC TRY System of cluster and factor analysis. *Multivariate Behavioral Research*, 1966, *1*, 95–111.

Tuddenham, R. D. The constancy of personality ratings over two decades. *Genetic Psychology Monographs*, 1959, *60*, 3–29.

Witkin, H. A., Goodenough, D. R., & Kays, S. A. Stability of cognitive style from childhood to young adulthood. *Journal of Personality and Social Psychology*, 1967, *7*, 291–300.

APPENDIX A

The Items in the California Q Set (Form IHD)
Specified 9-point distribution (N = 100):
5, 8, 12, 16, 18, 16, 12, 8, 5

1. Is critical, skeptical, not easily impressed.
2. Is a genuinely dependable and responsible person.
3. Has a wide range of interests. (N.B. Superficiality or depth of interest is irrelevant here.)
4. Is a talkative individual.
5. Behaves in a giving way toward others. (N.B. regardless of the motivation involved.)
6. Is fastidious.
7. Favors conservative values in a variety of areas.
8. Appears to have a high degree of intellectual capacity. (N.B. whether actualized or not.) (N.B. Originality is not necessarily assumed.)
9. Is uncomfortable with uncertainty and complexities.
10. Anxiety and tension find outlet in bodily symptoms. (N.B. If placed high, implies bodily dysfunction; if placed low, implies absence of autonomic arousal.)
11. Is protective of those close to him. (N.B. Placement of this item expresses behavior ranging from over-protection through appropriate nurturance to a laissez-faire, under-protective manner.)
12. Tends to be self-defensive.
13. Is thin-skinned; vulnerable to anything that can be construed as criticism or an interpersonal slight.
14. Basically submissive.
15. The "light touch" as compared to the "heavy touch."
16. Is introspective. (N.B. Introspectiveness *per se* does not imply insight.)
17. Behaves in a sympathetic or considerate manner.
18. Initiates humor.
19. Seeks reassurance from others.
20. Has a rapid personal tempo.
21. Arouses nurturant feelings in others of both sexes.
22. Feels a lack of personal meaning in life. (Uncharacteristic end means zest.)
23. Extrapunitive; tends to transfer or project blame.
24. Prides self on being "objective," rational. (Regardless of whether person is really objective or rational.)
25. Tends toward overcontrol of needs and impulses; binds tensions excessively; delays gratification unnecessarily.

291

26. Is productive; gets things done. (Regardless of speed.)
27. Shows condescending behavior in relations with others.
28. Tends to arouse liking and acceptance in people.
29. Is turned to for advice and reassurance.
30. Gives up and withdraws where possible in the face of frustration and adversity.
31. Is satisfied with physical appearance.
32. Seems to be aware of the impression he makes on others.
33. Is calm, relaxed in manner.
34. Over-reactive to minor frustrations; irritable.
35. Has warmth; is compassionate.
36. Is negativistic; tends to undermine and obstruct or sabotage.
37. Is guileful and deceitful, manipulative, opportunistic.
38. Has hostility toward others. (N.B. Basic hostility is intended here; mode of expression is to be indicated by other items.)
39. Thinks and associates to ideas in unusual ways; has unconventional thought processes. (Either pathological or creative.)
40. Is vulnerable to real or fancied threat, generally fearful.
41. Is moralistic. (N.B. Regardless of the particular nature of the moral code.)
42. Reluctant to commit self to any definite course of action; tends to delay or avoid action. (Uncharacteristic end indicates quick to act.)
43. Is facially and/or gesturally expressive.
44. Evaluates the motivation of others in interpreting situations. (N.B. Accuracy of evaluation is not assumed.) (N.B. again. Extreme placement in one direction implies preoccupation with motivational interpretations; at the other extreme, the item implies a psychological obtuseness, S does not consider motivational factors.)
45. Has a brittle ego-defense system; has a small reserve of integration; would be disorganized and maladaptive when under stress or trauma.
46. Engages in personal fantasy and daydreams, fictional speculations.
47. Tends to feel guilty. (N.B. regardless of whether verbalized or not.)
48. Aloof, keeps people at a distance; avoids close interpersonal relationships.
49. Is basically distrustful of people in general; questions their motivations.
50. Is unpredictable and changeable in behavior and attitudes.
51. Genuinely values intellectual and cognitive matters. (N.B. Ability or achievement are not implied here.)
52. Behaves in an assertive fashion in interpersonal situations. (N.B. Item 14 reflects underlying submissiveness; this refers to overt behavior.)
53. Tends toward undercontrol of needs and impulses; unable to delay gratification.
54. Emphasizes being with others; gregarious.
55. Is self-defeating.
56. Responds to humor.
57. Is an interesting, arresting person.
58. Enjoys sensuous experiences (including touch, taste, smell, physical contact).
59. Is concerned with own body and the adequacy of its physiological functioning. (Body cathexis.)
60. Has insight into own motives and behavior.
61. Creates and exploits dependency in people. (N.B. Regardless of the techniques employed; e.g., punitiveness, over-indulgence.) (N.B. At the other end of scale, item implies respecting and encouraging the independence and individuality of others.)
62. Tends to be rebellious and non-conforming.
63. Judges self and others in conventional terms like "popularity," "the correct thing to do," social pressures, etc.

64. Is socially perceptive of a wide range of interpersonal cues.
65. Characteristically pushes and tries to stretch limits; sees what he can get away with.
66. Enjoys esthetic impressions; is esthetically reactive.
67. Is self-indulgent.
68. Is basically anxious.
69. Is bothered by anything that can be construed as a demand. (N.B. No implication of the kind of subsequent response is intended here.)
70. Behaves in an ethically consistent manner; is consistent with own personal standards.
71. Has high aspiration level for self.
72. Over-concerned with own adequacy as a person, either at conscious or unconscious levels. (N.B. A clinical judgment is required here; number 74 reflects subjective satisfaction with self.)
73. Tends to perceive many different contexts in sexual terms; eroticizes situations.
74. Is consciously unaware of self-concern; feels satisfied with self.
75. Has a clearcut, internally consistent personality. (N.B. *Amount* of information available before sorting is not intended here.)
76. Tends to project his own feelings and motivations onto others.
77. Appears straightforward, forthright, candid in dealings with others.
78. Feels cheated and victimized by life.
79. Tends to ruminate and have persistent, preoccupying thoughts (either pathological or creative.)
80. Interested in members of the opposite sex. (N.B. At opposite end, item implies *absence* of such interest.)
81. Is physically attractive; good-looking. (N.B. The cultural criterion is to be applied here.)
82. Has fluctuating moods.
83. Able to see to the heart of important problems.
84. Is cheerful. (N.B. Extreme placement toward uncharacteristic end of continuum implies gloominess.)
85. Is self-pitying (whiny).
86. Handles anxiety and conflicts by repressive or dissociative tendencies.
87. Interprets basically simple and clearcut situations in complicated and particularizing ways.
88. Is personally charming.
89. Compares self to others. Is alert to real or fancied differences between self and other people.
90. Is concerned with philosophical problems; e.g., religion, values, the meaning of life, etc.
91. Is power oriented; values power in self or others.
92. Has social poise and presence; appears socially at ease.
93a. *Behaves* in a masculine style and manner.
93b. *Behaves* in a feminine style and manner. (N.B. If subject is male, 93a. applies; if subject is female, 93b. is to be evaluated.) (N.B. again. The cultural or sub-cultural conception is to be applied as a criterion.)
94. Expresses hostile feelings directly.
95. Tends to proffer advice.
96. Values own independence and autonomy.
97. Is emotionally bland; has flattened affect.
98. Is verbally fluent; can express ideas well.
99. Is self-dramatizing; histrionic.
100. Does not vary roles; relates to everyone in the same way.

APPENDIX B

The Items in the Adolescent *CQ* Set
Specified 9-point distribution (N = 104):
6, 9, 13, 15, 18, 15, 13, 9, 6

1. Is critical, skeptical.
2. Behaves in a dependable and responsible way.
3. Has a wide range of interests. (N.B. Superficiality or depth of interest is irrelevant here.)
4. Is a talkative individual.
5. Behaves in a giving way toward others. (N.B. Regardless of the underlying motivation involved, be it genuine or not.)
6. Is fastidious in behavior and appearance. (N.B. As opposed to *sloppy*).
7. Favors status quo of the world as he perceives it.
8. Has a high degree of intellectual capacity (N.B. whether actualized or not).
9. Is uncomfortable with uncertainty and complexities.
10. Anxiety and tension find outlet in bodily symptoms. (N.B. If placed high, implies bodily dysfunction; if placed low, implies absence of autonomic arousal.)
11. Is protective of those close to him. (N.B. Placement of this item expresses behavior ranging from over-protection through appropriate nurturance to a laissez-faire, underprotective manner.)
12. Tends to be self-defensive, blame avoidant.
13. Is thin-skinned; sensitive to anything that can be construed as criticism or an interpersonal slight.
14. Genuinely submissive.
15. Is skilled in social techniques of imaginative play, pretending, and humor.
16. Is introspective; self-observing; concerned with self as an object. (N.B. Introspectiveness *per se* implies neither insight nor narcissism nor brooding.)
17. Behaves in a sympathetic or considerate manner (N.B. regardless of the motivation involved).
18. Behaves in a dependent fashion.
19. Seeks reassurance from others.
20. Has a rapid personal tempo; behaves and acts quickly.
21. Arouses nurturant feelings in others.
22. Feels a lack of personal meaning in life.
23. Extrapunitive; tends to transfer or project blame.
24. Prides self on being "objective," rational.

25. Tends toward overcontrol of needs and impulses; binds tensions excessively; delays gratification unnecessarily.
26. Is productive; gets things done.
27. Shows condescending behavior in relations with others. (N.B. Extreme placement toward uncharacteristic end implies simply an *absence* of condescension, not necessarily equalitarianism or inferiority.)
28. Tends to arouse liking and acceptance in others.
29. Is turned to for advice and reassurance.
30. Gives up and withdraws where possible in the face of frustration and adversity. (N.B. If placed high, implies generally defeatist; if placed low, implies *counteractive*.)
31. Is comfortable with own physical appearance.
32. Aware of the impression he makes on others; accurately perceives his social stimulus value.
33. Is calm, relaxed in manner.
34. Reactive to minor frustrations; irritable.
35. Has warmth.
36. Is negativistic; tends to undermine and obstruct or sabotage.
37. Is guileful and deceitful, manipulative, opportunistic.
38. Has hostility toward others. (N.B. Basic hostility is intended here; mode of expression is to be indicated by other items.)
39. Thinks and associates to ideas in unusual ways; has unconventional thought processes.
40. Behaves as if generally fearful in manner and approach, anticipating real or fancied threats.
41. Is judgmental in regard to human conduct. (N.B. Regardless of the ideological nature of the moral code.)
42. Reluctant to commit self to any definite course of action; tends to delay or avoid action.
43. Is facially and/or gesturally expressive.
44. Evaluates the motivation of others in interpreting situations. (N.B. Accuracy of evaluation is not assumed.) (N.B. Again, extreme placement in one direction implies pre-occupation with motivational interpretation; at the other extreme, the item implies a psychological obtuseness; S does not consider motivational factors.)
45. Disorganized and maladaptive when under stress or trauma; has a small reserve of integration.
46. Engages in personal fantasy and daydreams, fictional speculations.
47. Has a readiness to feel guilty. (N.B. Regardless of whether verbalized or not.)
48. Keeps others at a distance; avoids closer interpersonal relationships.
49. Is basically distrustful of people in general.
50. Is considered unpredictable and changeable in behavior and attitudes. (N.B. Behavioral lability is intended here, not long-range predictability.)
51. Genuinely values intellectual and cognitive matters. (N.B. Ability or achievement are not implied here.)
52. *Behaves* in an assertive fashion. (N.B. Item 14 reflects underlying submissiveness; this refers to overt behavior.)
53. Various needs tend toward relatively direct and uncontrolled expression; unable to delay gratification.
54. Emphasizes being with others; gregarious. (N.B. Genuineness of quality is not of concern here.)
55. Is self-defeating in regard to his own goals.

56. Responds to humor, wit, and jokes. (N.B. Item 15 refers to the quality and refinement of the humorous orientation.)
57. Is an interesting, arresting person; has individuality. (N.B. The *sorter's judgment is required here rather than judgment by peers.*)
58. Enjoys sensuous experiences (including touch, taste, smell, physical contact).
59. Is concerned with own body and the adequacy of its physiological functioning.
60. Has insight into own motives and behavior.
61. *Perceives* self as the crucial and causative agent in determining the occurrences in his life. (N.B. Opposite end implies life and consequences are seen as impersonally or fortuitously determined.)
62. Tends to be rebellious.
63. Values self and others in terms set by his cultural group, like "popularity," presumed adolescent norms, social pressures, etc.
64. Is socially perceptive of a wide range of interpersonal cues.
65. Characteristically pushes and tries to stretch limits; sees what he can get away with.
66. Enjoys esthetic impressions; is esthetically reactive.
67. Is explicitly self-indulgent; considers satisfaction of own desires as of paramount importance (N.B. as opposed to asceticism).
68. Is concerned with physical appearance.
69. Is touchy and sensitive to anything that can be construed as a demand from others. (N.B. No implication of the kind of subsequent response is intended here.)
70. Has shifting standards, depending on group and situation pressures.
71. Has high aspiration level for self as adult. (N.B. Goal is self-defined.)
72. Is affected.
73. Tends to construe or define many different contexts in sexual terms; eroticizes situations.
74. Feels satisfied with self.
75. Has a clearcut, internally consistent personality. (N.B. *Amount* of information available before sorting is not intended here.)
76. Tends to project his own feelings and motivations onto others.
77. Behaves in a straightforward, forthright fashion in dealings with others.
78. Self-pitying; feels cheated and victimized by life.
79. Tends to ruminate and have persistent, preoccupying thoughts.
80. Becomes emotionally involved with members of the opposite sex (N.B. At low end implies inability to relate to members of opposite sex.)
81. Is physically attractive; good-looking. (N.B. The cultural criterion is to be applied here.)
82. Has fluctuating moods.
83. Comfortable with the decisions he has made.
84. Is cheerful. (N.B. Extreme placement toward uncharacteristic end of continuum implies gloominess.)
85. Communicates through non-verbal behavior, expresses attitudes and feelings through the context of behaviors. (N.B. Item 43 refers to facial and gestural expressiveness *per se.*)
86. Handles anxiety and conflicts by attempting to exclude them from awareness.
87. Interprets basically simple and clearcut situations in complicated and particularizing ways.
88. Becomes emotionally involved with members of the same sex. (N.B. Placement at low end implies inability to relate to members of same sex.)

89. Compares self to others, whether favorably or unfavorably; is alert to real or fancied differences between self and other people. (N.B. Regardless of the reaction subsequent to the comparison.)

90. Is explicitly concerned with philosophical problems, e.g., religion, values, the meaning of life, death, etc.

91. Is power or status oriented; values power or status in self or others.

92. Has social poise and presence with others.

93a. *Behaves* in a masculine style and manner.

93b. *Behaves* in a feminine style and manner. (N.B. If subject is male, 93a applies; if subject is female, 93b is to be evaluated.) (N.B. again. The cultural or sub-cultural conception is to be applied as a criterion.)

94. Expresses hostile feelings directly.

95. Tends to proffer advice.

96. Values own independence and autonomy.

97. Is emotionally bland. (N.B. At high end, implies flattened affect; at low end, implies extreme and deep emotionality.)

98. Is verbally fluent, articulate. (N.B. Talkativeness *per se* is expressed by item 4)

99. Is self-dramatizing; histrionic.

100. Does not vary roles; relates to others in the same way.

101. Questing for meaning, self-definition or redefinition.

102. Initiates humor, wit, and jokes. (N.B. Item 15 refers to the quality and refinement of the humorous situation.)

103. Accepting of dependency in self; functions comfortably when dependent.

104. Is identifying and romanticizing of individuals and causes. (N.B. *Irrespective* of nature or values of the cause of the individuals.)

APPENDIX C

The Items in the Interpersonal Q Set
Specified 9-point distributions (N = 63)
3, 5, 8, 10, 11, 10, 8, 5, 3

1. S worries about his parents (e.g., their health, happiness, and general welfare).
2. S feels closer to M (High placement shows closeness to Mother and low end is closeness to Father).
3. S feels the pattern of his life is laid down by his parents.
4. S perceives parents as being happy people.
5. S perceives his family as an affectionate one.
6. S perceives his family as an interesting one.
7. S perceives his family situation as conflicted.
8. S sees his family as egalitarian, behaves toward parents as if they were peers.
9 S respects his parents.
10. S perceives parents as fair, equitable, and reasonable.
11. S feels Mother is a respected woman as judged by societal standards.
12. Tends to have crushes on adults.
13. S is able to have genuine and appropriate relationships with adults.
14. Claims the rights, privileges, and excuses afforded the adolescent in this culture. (N.B. High placement implies a "wallowing" in the adolescent experience; low placement implies S did not experience the adolescent role.)
15. S is covertly hostile to adults.
16. S perceives Father as an attractive man.
17. S feels his Father is a respected man as judged by societal standards.
18. S is rebellious with adults. (N.B. Extent of rebelliousness is to be judged in absolute terms rather than in terms of adolescent norms.)
19. S views Mother as an attractive woman
20. S is passive and non-reactive with adults.
21. S is cool, detached, and independent in his interactions with adults.
22. Adopts pseudo-compliant, toadying attitude toward adults.
23. S perceives parents as restraining of his activities.
24. S perceives parents as accepting of his growth and his steps toward maturity. (N.B. Low placement means S perceives his parents as prolonging his dependency.)
25. S perceives parents as consistent in their attitude and rules for him. (N.B. The quality of the consistency is expressed by other items.)
26. S feels his parents are old-fashioned.

27. S sees his parents as singling him out for special evaluation and treatment. (N.B. The character of the special treatment is irrelevant here.)
28. S sees his parents as detached, uninvolved, and uninterested in him.
29. Is protective of friends. (N.B. Placement of this item expresses behavior ranging from over-protection through appropriate nurturance to a laissez-faire, under-protective manner.)
30. Behaves in a straightforward, forthright fashion in dealings with peers.
31. Has social poise and presence with peers.
32. Is competitive with peers.
33. Attention-getting behavior with peers, e.g., clowning, unusual dress.
34. Is a talkative individual with peers.
35. Predominant orientation and interest is toward adults as opposed to peers; adult-oriented.
36. Emphasizes being with peers; gregarious. (N.B. Genuineness or quality of inter-action is not of concern here.)
37. Behaves in an assertive fashion with peers. (N.B. This item refers to overt behav-ior, not underlying submissiveness.)
38. Sensitive to anything that can be construed as criticism or an interpersonal slight from peers.
39. Sensitive to anything that can be construed as a demand from peers. (N.B. No implication of the kind of subsequent response is intended here.)
40. Values self and others in terms set by his peer group, like "popularity," pre-sumed adolescent norms, social pressures, etc.
41. Is judgmental in regard to peer conduct. (N.B. Regardless of the ideological nature of the moral code.)
42. Evaluates self as superior to his peers.
43. Seeks reassurance from peers.
44. Behaves in a sympathetic or considerate manner to peers. (N.B. Regardless of the motivation involved.)
45. Is dependent on peers.
46. Initiates humor; makes attempts to be funny with peers. (N.B. Regardless of quality.)
47. Keeps peers at a distance; avoids closer interpersonal relationships with peers. (N.B. A few close friends means this item cannot be placed as an extreme high.)
48. Tends to arouse liking and acceptance in peers.
49. S's social stimulus value is that of a younger person or child. (N.B. Low place-ment means S acts older than his age, and medium placement implies age-appropriate behavior.)
50. Expresses hostile feelings *directly* to peers.
51. Shows condescending behavior in relations with peers. (N.B. Extreme placement toward uncharacteristic end implies self-abasement.)
52. Is selective in choice of friends. (N.B. Low placement means indiscriminate in choice of friends.)
53. Extent to which S is butt of group, tends to be fall guy.
54. Emphasizes in-group's status to the detriment of out-group's status; emphasis on exclusiveness of own group.
55. Achieves leadership in roles with peers.
56. Knowledgeable of peer culture.
57. Needs to be associated with formal or informal groups or cliques. (N.B. Other items indicate the quality of the association.)
58. Is protected by peers.
59. Involved on fantasy level with opposite sex (actual behavior is irrelevant here).

60. Acceptance and appreciation of sex-typing as it affects self. (N.B. High placement indicates positive accentuation of sex role differences and low placement
implies disparagement or denial.)
61. Oriented toward going "steady," i.e., toward extended predictable, safe relations
with opposite sex.
62. Changeability of peer attachments.
63. Spends time with members of the opposite sex, e.g., dating, parties, boy-girl relationships.

APPENDIX D

Means and Standard Deviations of Reliabilities of the Q Composites for Different Adolescent Time Periods

		OGS Sample					
		JHS Period			SHS Period		
		Boys	Girls	Combined	Boys	Girls	Combined
CQ	Mean	.72	.73	.72	.74	.75	.75
Composite	S.D.	.12	.15	.13	.16	.16	.16
Interpersonal	Mean	.75	.75	.75	.75	.77	.76
Q Composite	S.D.	.16	.17	.16	.17	.16	.16

		GdS Sample					
		JHS Period			SHS Period		
		Boys	Girls	Combined	Boys	Girls	Combined
CQ	Mean	.73	.73	.73	.76	.74	.75
Composite	S.D.	.14	.16	.15	.15	.13	.14
Interpersonal	Mean	.75	.76	.75	.77	.78	.77
Q Composite	S.D.	.16	.15	.16	.19	.18	.18

Means and Standard Deviations of Reliabilities of the CQ Composite at Adulthood

	OGS Sample		
	Men	Women	Combined
Mean	.751	.734	.742
S.D.	.144	.118	.133

	GdS Sample		
Mean	.743	.740	.742
S.D.	.156	.141	.147

APPENDIX E

Across-Time Correlations of the *CQ* Items for the Male Sample

(Two item numbering systems are employed. The Original *CQ* item numbers are those indicated in Appendices A and B. The Aligned *CQ* item numbering system was necessary in order to bring into ordinal correspondence the 90 *CQ* items common to both the Adult and the Adolescent *CQ* sets. See the text for a fuller explanation. Uncorrected correlations reaching .212, .279, and .352 are significant at the .05, .01, and .001 levels, respectively.)

Original *CQ* Item No.	Aligned *CQ* Item No.	JHS – SHS		SHS – Adulthood	
		Uncorrected r	Corrected r	Uncorrected r	Corrected r
1	1	.229	.430	.259	.409
2	2	.584	.685	.532	.616
3	3	.485	.680	.529	.774
4	4	.452	.537	.376	.465
5	5	.472	.660	.090	.116
6	6	.566	.723	.303	.417
8	7	.701	.813	.605	.735
9	8	.319	.736	.358	.581
10	9	.443	.698	.222	.324
11	10	.444	.635	.234	.312
12	11	.283	.546	.062	.119
13	12	.426	.717	.079	.122
14	13	.268	.419	.106	.172
16	14	.249	.498	.279	.409
17	15	.524	.693	.120	.152
19	16	.345	.652	.000	.000
20	17	.498	.642	.196	.254
21	18	.329	.590	−.113	−.207
22	19	.435	.689	.292	.380
23	20	.384	.605	.085	.134
24	21	.299	.452	.409	.678
25	22	.562	.735	.426	.538
26	23	.566	.678	.422	.511
27	24	.362	.563	−.080	−.133
28	25	.610	.727	.170	.208

APPENDIX E (Continued)

Original CQ Item No.	Aligned CQ Item No.	JHS – SHS Uncorrected r	Corrected r	SHS – Adulthood Uncorrected r	Corrected r
29	26	.547	.760	.277	.396
30	27	.408	.541	.053	.066
31	28	.507	.786	.290	.407
32	29	.246	.486	.237	.385
33	30	.415	.537	.378	.454
34	31	.450	.782	.292	.403
35	32	.521	.803	.144	.194
36	33	.507	.670	.226	.312
37	34	.352	.508	.114	.163
38	35	.413	.588	.261	.370
39	36	.409	.673	.196	.306
40	37	.349	.501	.212	.320
41	38	.323	.549	.034	.053
42	39	.508	.831	.192	.260
43	40	.391	.665	.170	.319
44	41	.108	.424	.161	.303
45	42	.503	.696	.343	.450
46	43	.362	.777	.294	.611
47	44	.362	.648	.102	.164
48	45	.514	.666	.273	.355
49	46	.387	.587	.134	.182
50	47	.450	.666	.360	.505
51	48	.639	.784	.591	.751
52	49	.472	.567	.170	.218
53	50	.569	.738	.588	.705
54	51	.400	.530	.356	.458
55	52	.504	.689	.424	.531
56	53	.428	.694	.279	.492
57	54	.316	.506	.422	.582
58	55	.248	.599	.139	.318
59	56	.411	.917	.259	.513
60	57	.207	.369	.160	.215
62	58	.579	.717	.294	.374
63	59	.268	.447	.362	.494
64	60	.375	.785	−.031	−.048
65	61	.625	.744	.391	.499
66	62	.347	.535	.579	.830
67	63	.544	.775	.208	.316
69	64	.362	.845	.240	.435
71	65	.639	.822	.356	.473
73	66	.362	.531	.236	.400
74	67	.580	.900	.223	.312
75	68	.314	.550	.286	.396
76	69	.252	.453	−.009	−.015
77	70	.230	.393	.050	.083
78	71	.562	.826	.334	.422
79	72	.336	.555	.066	.109

APPENDIX E (Continued)

Original CQ Item No.	Aligned CQ Item No.	JHS – SHS Uncorrected r	JHS – SHS Corrected r	SHS – Adulthood Uncorrected r	SHS – Adulthood Corrected r
80	73	.457	.566	.094	.141
81	74	.616	.740	.428	.532
82	75	.367	.608	.391	.605
84	76	.566	.752	.264	.339
86	77	.257	.606	.264	.548
87	78	.301	.542	−.034	−.060
89	79	.268	1.024	−.063	−.175
90	80	.387	.610	.413	.529
91	81	.305	.630	−.048	−.082
92	82	.508	.620	.314	.393
93	83	.369	.564	.387	.543
94	84	.159	.260	.262	.415
95	85	.214	.396	.108	.187
96	86	.378	.605	.182	.268
97	87	.345	.551	.272	.386
98	88	.544	.717	.536	.706
99	89	.487	.778	.426	.610
100	90	.329	.757	.011	.021
7	91	.226	.433		
15	92	.536	.776		
18	93	.349	.501		
61	94	.419	.944		
68	95	.279	.651		
70	96	.389	.707		
72	97	.281	.416		
83	98	.382	.697		
85	99	.222	.438		
88	100	.316	.565		
101	101	.439	.855		
102	102	.455	.638		
103	103	.327	.507		
104	104	.051	.168		

APPENDIX F

Across-Time Correlations of the CQ Items for the Female Sample

(Two item numbering systems are employed. The Original CQ item numbers are those indicated in Appendices A and B. The Aligned CQ item numbering system was necessary in order to bring into ordinal correspondence the 90 CQ items common to both the Adult and the Adolescent CQ sets. See the text for a fuller explanation. Uncorrected correlations reaching .212, .279, and .352 are significant at the .05, .01, and .001 levels, respectively.)

Original CQ Item No.	Aligned CA Item No.	JHS – SHS Uncorrected r	Corrected r	SHS – Adulthood Uncorrected r	Corrected r
1	1	.137	.275	.409	.695
2	2	.555	.638	.310	.356
3	3	.430	.663	.422	.604
4	4	.599	.711	.369	.478
5	5	.395	.553	.308	.411
6	6	.566	.699	.351	.455
8	7	.599	.715	.609	.792
9	8	.334	.725	.327	.594
10	9	.288	.445	.227	.308
11	10	.389	.540	.034	.057
12	11	.424	.847	.213	.364
13	12	.272	.480	.096	.166
14	13	.498	.710	.455	.627
16	14	.222	.430	.411	.585
17	15	.376	.484	.272	.352
19	16	.196	.355	.330	.525
20	17	.507	.668	.318	.420
21	18	.314	.520	.235	.375
22	19	.204	.372	.398	.642
23	20	.450	.657	.131	.185
24	21	.409	.628	.223	.361
25	22	.543	.708	.247	.330
26	23	.540	.728	.207	.269
27	24	.426	.639	.250	.337
28	25	.500	.606	.375	.472

APPENDIX F (Continued)

Original CQ Item No.	Aligned CQ Item No.	JHS – SHS Uncorrected r	Corrected r	SHS – Adulthood Uncorrected r	Corrected r
29	26	.318	.447	.204	.298
30	27	.340	.616	.173	.291
31	28	.358	.500	.406	.528
32	29	.395	.823	.080	.204
33	30	.457	.592	.106	.145
34	31	.319	.478	.103	.158
35	32	.441	.651	.281	.364
36	33	.236	.343	.107	.146
37	34	.555	.730	.270	.371
38	35	.439	.657	.292	.470
39	36	.426	.735	.253	.394
40	37	.375	.514	.224	.310
41	38	.238	.463	−.031	−.057
42	39	.415	.657	.166	.282
43	40	.397	.587	.194	.272
44	41	.089	.343	.193	.762
45	42	.382	.639	.079	.129
46	43	.312	.556	.051	.089
47	44	.400	.730	.193	.308
48	45	.474	.611	.327	.453
49	46	.297	.523	.147	.240
50	47	.316	.485	.155	.251
51	48	.584	.785	.511	.668
52	49	.529	.674	.437	.558
53	50	.566	.799	.245	.308
54	51	.386	.489	.433	.574
55	52	.305	.481	.194	.297
56	53	.327	.530	.305	.583
57	54	.498	.967	.252	.383
58	55	.139	.311	.091	.161
59	56	.212	.474	.144	.310
60	57	.424	.664	.201	.282
62	58	.476	.613	.487	.637
63	59	.398	.669	.365	.533
64	60	.382	.748	.192	.312
65	61	.525	.658	.347	.442
66	62	.500	.952	.415	.668
67	63	.354	.480	.367	.493
69	64	.207	.427	.062	.100
71	65	.415	.601	.356	.588
73	66	.492	.707	.330	.564
74	67	.389	.609	.356	.495
75	68	.356	.829	.277	.764
76	69	.341	.632	.094	.169
77	70	.562	.817	.000	.000
78	71	.277	.378	.227	.304
79	72	.384	.568	.053	.081

APPENDIX F (Continued)

Original CQ Item No.	Aligned CQ Item No.	JHS – SHS Uncorrected r	Corrected r	SHS – Adulthood Uncorrected r	Corrected r
80	73	.319	.393	.188	.266
81	74	.511	.625	.450	.566
82	75	.241	.673	.090	.160
84	76	.503	.693	.360	.459
86	77	.303	.682	.146	.307
87	78	.508	.979	.100	.189
89	79	.189	.703	.096	.382
90	80	.446	.671	.415	.603
91	81	.288	.527	.096	.149
92	82	.466	.579	.387	.490
93	83	.518	.720	.382	.543
94	84	.343	.512	.290	.409
95	85	.245	.420	.237	.383
96	86	.389	.594	.483	.681
97	87	.419	.709	.207	.330
98	88	.404	.612	.371	.558
99	89	.606	.832	.461	.621
100	90	.314	.784	.227	.538
7	91	.452	.808		
15	92	.428	.642		
18	93	.264	.464		
61	94	.125	.317		
68	95	.250	.561		
70	96	.444	.832		
72	97	.310	.407		
83	98	.240	.455		
85	99	.090	.583		
88	100	.397	.602		
101	101	.367	.856		
102	102	.419	.559		
103	103	.483	.677		
104	104	.206	.418		

APPENDIX G

Reliability of *CQ* Items
(Calculated by Intraclass Correlation. Decimals Omitted.)

(Two item numbering systems are employed. The Original *CQ* item numbers are those indicated in Appendices A and B. The Aligned *CQ* item numbering system was necessary in order to bring into ordinal correspondence the 90 *CQ* items common to both the Adult and the Adolescent *CQ* sets. See the text for a fuller explanation.)

Original *CQ* Item No.	Aligned *CQ* Item No.	Male Sample			Female Sample		
		JHS	SHS	Adult	JHS	SHS	Adult
1	1	51	55	73	45	55	63
2	2	83	87	86	86	88	86
3	3	68	75	62	64	65	75
4	4	82	86	76	81	88	68
5	5	64	80	74	70	72	77
6	6	75	81	65	83	79	76
8	7	86	86	79	84	83	71
9	8	33	57	66	36	59	51
10	9	64	62	75	58	72	76
11	10	65	75	75	74	70	51
12	11	65	42	65	47	53	65
13	12	63	56	74	56	58	58
14	13	73	56	68	68	73	72
16	14	44	57	81	44	60	82
17	15	75	76	82	75	81	74
19	16	53	52	52	52	59	67
20	17	74	82	73	71	81	71
21	18	56	56	53	63	58	68
22	19	54	74	79	59	51	76
23	20	63	64	62	65	72	69
24	21	61	72	51	60	71	53
25	22	71	82	76	73	81	69
26	23	79	88	78	73	75	78
27	24	70	59	61	60	74	74
28	25	86	82	81	85	80	79

308

APPENDIX G (Continued)

Original CQ Item No.	Aligned CQ Item No.	Male Sample			Female Sample		
		JHS	SHS	Adult	JHS	SHS	Adult
29	26	72	72	68	78	65	72
30	27	75	76	83	60	51	69
31	28	60	69	73	69	74	80
32	29	51	50	75	57	40	38
33	30	72	83	83	72	82	65
34	31	49	68	77	66	67	63
35	32	62	67	81	63	72	82
36	33	74	77	68	67	71	75
37	34	69	70	69	70	82	65
38	35	73	67	74	71	63	61
39	36	63	59	69	64	52	79
40	37	72	67	65	72	74	71
41	38	56	62	65	52	50	58
42	39	67	72	75	66	60	57
43	40	61	57	50	59	78	65
44	41	16	40	70	54	12	51
45	42	71	73	79	64	56	67
46	43	54	40	58	53	60	55
47	44	54	57	68	51	59	66
48	45	79	75	78	76	79	66
49	46	62	69	78	58	55	68
50	47	65	70	72	59	72	53
51	48	79	84	73	73	76	77
52	49	82	84	72	78	78	78
53	50	72	83	84	62	81	78
54	51	72	79	76	78	79	72
55	52	67	79	80	65	62	69
56	53	64	60	54	60	63	43
57	54	57	68	77	42	64	68
58	55	30	57	33	34	59	54
59	56	44	45	56	54	37	58
60	57	46	68	82	60	68	74
62	58	82	80	78	79	76	76
63	59	51	70	77	63	56	83
64	60	38	59	69	46	57	66
65	61	86	82	75	78	81	76
66	62	58	72	67	51	54	72
67	63	66	75	58	71	77	72
69	64	29	62	49	37	64	60
71	65	73	83	68	75	64	58
73	66	66	70	50	72	67	51
74	67	61	68	75	62	66	78
75	68	48	68	77	35	52	25
76	69	47	66	52	52	55	55
77	70	58	59	62	63	75	56
78	71	60	77	81	71	75	74
79	72	59	62	59	67	68	62

APPENDIX G (Continued)

Original CQ Item No.	Aligned CQ Item No.	Male Sample			Female Sample		
		JHS	SHS	Adult	JHS	SHS	Adult
80	73	80	82	54	77	86	58
81	74	80	86	75	81	82	77
82	75	58	63	66	25	52	61
84	76	72	79	77	68	77	80
86	77	42	43	54	44	44	51
87	78	54	57	57	48	56	50
89	79	16	43	30	35	21	30
90	80	50	81	75	61	73	65
91	81	40	58	58	48	62	66
92	82	85	79	81	79	82	76
93	83	65	65	78	73	70	70
94	84	64	59	68	65	69	72
95	85	49	59	56	62	55	69
96	86	59	66	69	61	70	72
97	87	60	65	76	56	62	63
98	88	78	74	78	71	61	72
99	89	60	66	74	69	76	72
100	90	35	54	51	36	45	40
7	91	43	64	76	52	60	75
15	92	69	69	56	65	68	61
18	93	70	69	69	59	55	68
61	94	38	52	43	36	43	49
68	95	43	42	70	55	36	51
70	96	52	58	69	50	57	66
72	97	65	70	67	70	83	37
83	98	49	62	79	44	63	69
85	99	52	49	82	38	06	74
88	100	52	60	62	62	70	65
101	101	48	55		29	62	
102	102	72	70		73	77	
103	103	68	61		72	71	
104	104	21	44		48	50	

APPENDIX H

Items in the Environmental Q Set (Form IV)

N = 92; prescribed distribution is 9 equal piles after omission of all inapplicable items.

1. Father and mother generally shared similar values and orientations.
2. S's mother was career-oriented for herself.
3. S was physically healthy through adolescence.
4. S's mother was constructively active outside the home (e.g., employed, community activities, etc.).
5. S's father was knowledgeable and competent in masculine activities and skills (e.g., handy about the house, athletic, mechanical, outdoorsy, etc.).
6. S's father emphasized the life value of physical activity, the outdoors, and nature.
7. Mother was a respected and admired woman by community standards.
8. S was naturally physically competent.
9. S's home environment emphasized manners, propriety, and convention.
10. S's family was concerned with social and political problems and causes.
11. S's mother was overcontrolled.
12. S was reared in a stable family setting.
12. S's home environment was well structured, orderly, and predictable.
14. S's father was overcontrolled.
15. S's family environment contained a significant and genuine religious element. (N.B. not simply ritual or church attendance.)
16. S's mother was authoritarian.
17. S's mother was knowledgeable and competent in feminine activities and skills (e.g., a good homemaker, cook, decorator, gardener, dressmaker, etc.).
18. As a child, S was socialized, controlled and directed by physical punishment or by threats of physical punishment.
19. Father pressured S to achieve.
20. S's father was authoritarian.
21. Mother pressured S to achieve.
22. S's mother (or a genuine mother-surrogate) was available to the S through adolescence. (N.B. Placement at opposite end implies the absence of a motherly presence, for whatever reason.)
23. S's father dominated the fundamental family decisions. (N.B. Opposite placement implies mother dominated.)
24. S's mother was neurotic, brittle, and anxiety-laden.

311

25. S's mother emphasized the life value of an intellectual orientation, of rationality in decision and outlook.
26. S's mother emphasized the life value of status, power, and material possessions.
27. S's father emphasized the life value of an intellectual orientation, or rationality in decision and outlook.
28. S's parents were inhibited about sex (as opposed to a naturalistic attitude.).
29. S's father was career-oriented for himself.
30. S's mother was an educated woman.
31. S experienced much father-S interaction.
32. S's family emphasized the life value of fairness, equity, ethics, and responsibility to others.
33. S's mother emphasized the life value of tenderness, love, and related forms of interpersonal communion.
34. As a child, S was socialized, controlled, and directed by rewards and punishments offered in the form of conditional love.
35. S was naturally physically attractive.
36. S experienced much mother-S interaction.
37. S's father discouraged and constrained S's steps toward personal independence and maturity. (N.B. Opposite end implies encouragement and support).
38. There was a family atmosphere of discord, conflict, and recrimination.
39. S's mother discouraged and constrained S's steps toward personal independence and maturity. (N.B Opposite end implies encouragement and support.)
40. S's opposite-sexed parent was seductive with him (her).
41. Father was a respected and successful man by community standards.
42. S's family emphasized "togetherness," did things as a unit. (N.B. Regardless of the quality of the "togetherness.")
43. S's mother was introverted and internalizing.
44. S's father was introverted and internalizing.
45. S's father emphasized the life value of tenderness, love, and related forms of interpersonal communion.
46. S's family was beset by many tragedies and misfortunes (e.g., illness, death, accidents, radical dislocations. Consider cumulative effect.).
47. As a child, S was socialized by verbally conveyed rational explanatory means.
48. S's parents were restrictive of S's activities. (N.B. Placement at opposite end implies parental laissez-faire attitude.)
49. S's father was neurotic, brittle, and anxiety-laden.
50. S was rejected by mother. (N.B. Opposite placement implies excessive valuation or favoring by mother.)
51. S's parents encouraged S to discuss problems.
52. S's father emphasized the life value of status, power, and material possessions.
53. S's father was knowledgeable and competent in regard to culture, the arts, and senses (art, music, theatre, decoration, cooking, gardening, etc.).
54. S's father was an educated man.
55. S's mother emphasized the life value of culture and the arts.
56. S experienced a sophisticated, complex home environment.
57. S was physically disadvantaged *vis-a-vis* his childhood and adolescent peers.
58. S was rivalled by one or more siblings for the attention of parents.
59. S's mother was manifestly a long-suffering, self-sacrificing, defeated person. (N.B. The genuineness of the martyrdom is irrelevant here.)
60. S's father was manifestly a long-suffering, self-sacrificing, defeated person. (N.B. The genuineness of the martyrdom is irrelevant here.)

61. S's mother emphasized the life value of physical activity, the outdoors, and nature.
62. Relatives played a role in S's socialization.
63. S's home situation was warm and feeling-oriented. (N.B. Opposite end implies family cold and undemonstrative.)
64. S's father teased, was playfully contradictory.
65. S was rejected by father. (N.B. Opposite placement implies excessive valuation or favoring by father.)
66. S's mother teased, was playfully contradictory.
67. S's mother was knowledgeable and competent in regard to technology, science, construction, and mechanics (e.g., mechanically inclined, etc.).
68. S was subjected to some form of discrimination due to race, religion, nationality, or social class.
69. S experienced cultural discrepancies or cultural conflict before the end of adolescence.
70. Financial condition of family was comfortable when S was a child. (N.B. High placement implies wealth; low placement implies poverty).
71. S's home situation was child-oriented. (N.B. Placement at opposite end implies an adult-oriented home.)
72. S's home was a centripetal center for activities (e.g., play, parties, meetings, visitors, etc.).
73. Intra-family communication was direct and open.
74. The atmosphere of S's home was constricted, suppressive, and cheerless. (N.B. Opposite end implies family atmosphere was cheerful).
75. S's mother enjoyed her maternal role.
76. S's father enjoyed his paternal role.
77. S's family emphasized the life value of conformity, acceptance by peers, popularity, and the like.
78. S was given responsibilities and chores as a child and adolescent.
79. S had contact with many other children when young.
80. S's family context was politically and philosophically conservative.
81. S's father (or a genuine father surrogate) was available to S through adolescence. (N.B. Placement at opposite end implies the absence of a fatherly presence, for whatever reason.)
82. S's mother was indulgent of S.
83. S's father was indulgent of S.
84. Mother's interpersonal modes were conflict-inducing in children.
85. Father's interpersonal modes were conflict-inducing in children.
86. The sexuality and sexual interests of parents were apparent to S.
87. S's mother was restrictive about dating.
88. S's father was restrictivve about dating.
89. Mother's limitations, needs, and vulnerabilities were apparent.
90. Father's limitations, needs, and vulnerabilities were apparent.
91. S's family had strongly-held principles, opinions, prejudices, and moral convictions.
92. S was physically mature early.